FREE MOVEMENT OF GOODS IN THE E.E.C.

UNDER ARTICLES 30 to 36 OF
THE ROME TREATY

by
PETER OLIVER
Barrister-at-Law
Middle Temple.

LONDON
EUROPEAN LAW CENTRE LIMITED
1982

European Law Centre Limited,
4 Bloomsbury Square, London WC1A 2RL

© Peter Oliver 1982

Index compiled by
Wyn Brown

British Library Cataloguing in Publication Data:
Free Movement of Goods
  Oliver, Peter
  Free Movement of Goods in the E.E.C.
  1. European Economic Community Countries
  I. Title
  341.7.'54'026 HC241.2

ISBN 0 907451 05 5

Printed in Great Britain by
The Eastern Press Ltd. of London and Reading

FREE MOVEMENT
OF GOODS
IN THE E.E.C.

CONTENTS

CHAPTER VII

Measures of equivalent effect: II

CHAPTER VIII

The main exception: Article 36 EEC 126

CHAPTER IX

Other exception clauses   173

CHAPTER X

Agriculture   208

CHAPTER XI

State monopolies of a commercial character   219

CONTENTS

CHAPTER XII

Community legislation relating to the free movement of goods

CHAPTER XIII

Conclusion   242

Preface

A proper understanding of Articles 30 to 36 of the Treaty of Rome is essential to anyone wishing to come to grips with the concept of the free movement of goods, which is one of the fundamental objectives of the common market. Awareness of this fact has been growing in recent years among practitioners and academics alike, especially in the light of the landmark judgment of the European Court of Justice in the *Cassis de Dijon* case. This is the first book in a major Community language to be devoted to this subject.

The law is stated as at Easter 1982. Since the judgments in *Blesgen* v. *Belgian State* and *Holdijk* were delivered only a few days before then, the commentary on those judgments is to be found in Annexe I.

My thanks go first and foremost to Professors Heinrich Matthies and Rolf Wägenbaur, both of the Legal Service of the Commission of the European Communities, for their inspiration and encouragement. I am also particularly grateful to Julian Currall, who read the manuscript and made many helpful suggestions. Many others have read parts of the manuscript and made useful comments on it. These include Jonathan Faull, Hans Peder Hartvig, Pieter Jan Kuyper, Thomas van Rijn and my wife, Philippa Watson. Miss Andrée Godart typed the lion's share of the manuscript. To all of these I express my gratitude, as I do also to all the lawyers and secretaries in the Legal Service who gave me help with this book.

Peter Oliver

Brussels, April 1982

CHAPTER I

Introduction

At the very heart of the EEC lies the customs union. As testimony to this the fathers of the Treaty chose to set out the provisions relating to it in Title I of the Treaty, immediately after the eight introductory articles. Likewise, Article 3 which lists eleven 'activities' of the EEC, begins with 'the elimination, as between Member States, of customs duties and of quantitative restrictions on the import and export of goods, and of all other measures having equivalent effect', followed by 'the establishment of a common customs tariff and of a common commercial policy towards third countries'.

The purpose of this book is to examine only a part of Title I, namely Articles 30 to 36, which in principle prohibit quantitative restrictions and measures of equivalent effect on imports and exports between Member States. Briefly stated, quantitative restrictions are non-tariff quotas or total bans on trade, while the concept of measures of equivalent effect covers a multitude of other trade restrictions not falling under any other chapter of the Treaty of Rome. It cannot be sufficiently emphasised that this concept is not limited to technical customs matters but covers such questions as intellectual property, price controls and indications of origin. However, this prohibition on quantitative restrictions and measures of equivalent effect is subject to a number of exceptions, which will also be examined. In addition, this book will briefly consider the powers of the Community under Article 100 to pass directives to eliminate technical barriers to trade. On the other hand, trade between the EEC and third countries falls outside the scope of this work.

First, Articles 30 to 36 must be put in their context, both in historical terms and in terms of their place in the European Community as a whole. To understand the historical context of these provisions one must glance at two quite separate organisations, the GATT and the OEEC.

The General Agreement on Tariffs and Trade[1] was concluded by 23 countries in October 1947 and came into force 'provisionally' in January 1948. Its object was and is to guard against protectionism in international trade. It was conceived as part of a much grander plan, the establishment of an International Trade Organisation which

---

[1] See generally Jackson, *World Trade and the Law of GATT* (1969) and Dam, *The GATT, Law and International Economic Organisation* (1970).

1

never saw the light of day as it was blocked by the United States. Yet with the aid of a number of changes, the GATT has been able to operate on its own without its intended institutional base. While the GATT provides that tariffs are only to be reduced, it requires the outright abolition of quantitative restrictions: Article XI, entitled 'General Elimination of Quantitative Restrictions', provides in paragraph 1 that 'no prohibitions or restrictions other than duties, taxes or other charges, whether made effective through quotas, import or export licences or other measures, shall be instituted or maintained' between contracting parties.[2] The subsequent paragraphs and articles contain a number of exceptions to this rule, the most important of which is the balance of payments exception in Article XII. This permits a contracting party to adopt import restrictions necessary

'(i) to forestall the imminent threat of, or to stop a serious decline in its monetary reserves, or
(ii) in the case of a contracting party with very low monetary reserves, to achieve a reasonable rate of increase in its reserves'.

Without using the term 'measures of equivalent effect to quantitative restrictions', the GATT does in fact contain certain rules relating to such measures. These are to be found not only in Article XI already mentioned but also in Article III which states, *inter alia*, that measures on the sale, transportation, distribution or use of products 'should not be applied to imported or domestic products so as to afford protection to domestic production'.

In practice these provisions have not been notably successful in reducing non-tariff barriers in international trade, but that is perhaps not surprising given that the parties to the agreement are a large number of States from all corners of the globe and are at varying stages of economic development. These parties now number over 80. In any case, although all Member States of the European Community are parties to the GATT,[3] they are no longer bound by it as between themselves.[4] Naturally, though, the Community must still observe the GATT in its relations with third countries.[5]

---

[2] This is the provision of the GATT that was in point in the judgment of the European Court of Justice in the *International Fruit* case, see note 5 below.

[3] By the end of 1951 the only one of the Nine not to have joined was Ireland which became a member in 1967. Greece is also a party to the GATT.

[4] See *E.C. Commission* v. *Italy* and *Nederlandse Spoorwegen* cases and other sources cited in note 5 below.

[5] On the relationship between the GATT and the EEC see generally Case 10/61 *E.C. Commission* v. *Italy* [1962] E.C.R. 1, [1962] C.M.L.R. 187 ('in matters governed by the EEC Treaty, that Treaty takes precedence over agreements concluded between Member States before its entry into force, including agreements made within the framework of GATT'); Cases 21–24/72 *International Fruit Co.* v. *Produktschap voor Groenten en Fruit* [1972] E.C.R. 1219, [1975] 2 C.M.L.R. 1; Case 9/73 *Schlüter* v. *Hauptzollamt Lörrach* [1973] E.C.R. 1135 and Case 38/75 *Nederlandse Spoorwegen* v. *Inspecteur der Invoerrechten* [1975] E.C.R. 1439, [1976] 1 C.M.L.R. 167; casenotes by Ehlermann and Forman [1973] C.M.L.Rev. 336, Rideau [1973] C.D.E. 465 and Nicolaysen [1974] EuR 51; Bourgeois 'De GATT-Overeenkomst en het EEG-Verdrag' [1974] S.E.W. 408.

The Organisation for European Economic Co-operation (OEEC)[6] was set up by a Convention signed shortly after the GATT, in April 1948. It was primarily intended to administer the aid provided under the Marshall Plan for the post-war economic reconstruction of Western Europe. Accordingly it included all non-communist European States other than Finland, with the Federal Republic of Germany and Spain not becoming members until 1949 and 1959 respectively. In addition, the United States and Canada became associate members in 1959 and Yugoslavia took part in certain activities of the Organisation as from 1957. Since the abolition of barriers to trade was seen as being intimately linked to Europe's economic recovery, the Council of the OEEC called on its members as from 1949 to make a series of fixed reductions of their import quotas, subject to certain escape clauses. This culminated in a decision of January 1955 to raise the basic minimum level of liberalisation to 90 per cent. of the value of imports, which decision is referred to in Articles 31 and 33 (6) of the Treaty of Rome. By the end of 1956 overall liberalisation was over 85 per cent. so that much had been done to pave the way for the entry into force of the Treaty of Rome. Subsequently, in 1961, the Organisation was transformed into the Organisation for Economic Co-operation and Development (OECD) including the United States, Canada, Australia, New Zealand and Japan among its members.

The immediate forerunner of the EEC is the European Coal and Steel Community (ECSC), set up by the Treaty of Paris of 1951. On 1 January 1958 the ECSC was joined by the European Economic Community itself, established by the Treaty of Rome signed in March of the previous year, and by the European Atomic Energy Community (Euratom) set up by another Treaty of Rome of the same date. Each of these three Communities continues to exist as a separate legal entity functioning according to its own rules, but they are now run by the same institutions—the Commission, the Council of Ministers, the Parliament, the Court of Justice and, a more recent addition, the Court of Auditors. In reality the EEC is by far the most important of the three Communities. This book is therefore confined to the EEC. Thus throughout this book the term 'Treaty of Rome' will be used to designate the Treaty establishing the EEC, and not the Euratom Treaty.

Returning, then, to the Treaty of Rome itself, it is necessary to give a brief outline of its principal provisions[7] so that Articles 30 to 36 can be seen in the context of the Treaty as a whole. As was stated at the beginning, one of the fundamental aims of the Treaty was to establish a customs union between the parties to it. According to

---

[6] See generally Palmer and Lambert, *European Unity—A Survey of the European Organisations* (1968).

[7] General works on EEC law include Lipstein, *The Law of the European Economic Community* (1974); Wyatt and Dashwood, *The Substantive Law of the EEC* (1980).

a widely received definition, a customs union, in contrast to a free trade area, does not merely involve liberalisation of trade between the parties: it also entails the establishment of essentially uniform rules for goods coming from third countries. Acceptance of this definition is to be found both in an opinion of the Permanent Court of International Justice of 1931[8] and in Article XXIV of the GATT. The terms of the Treaty of Rome are in line with this definition. Accordingly, the Treaty contains provisions for the establishment of a common customs tariff (Articles 18 to 29) and further provides for a common commercial policy with respect to trade with third countries (Article 113). Likewise, Article 9 stipulates that the provisions on the free movement of goods apply not only to products originating in Member States but also to goods originating in third countries but in free circulation in the Community. This means, in essence, that goods from third countries are assimilated to Community goods for this purpose when they have undergone all the appropriate import formalities and any customs duties payable have been levied.[9]

The Treaty provisions on the free movement of goods fall into two distinct sections—and a bit. Articles 12 to 17 lay down total prohibitions on customs duties and charges of equivalent effect between Member States, which fall outside the scope of this book. As already stated, Articles 30 to 36 cover quantitative restrictions and measures of equivalent effect on imports and exports between Member States. In addition Article 37 relates to trade restrictions linked to or forming part of State monopolies. However, it is far from clear to what extent Article 37 is independent of the other provisions on the free movement of goods, a matter to which Chapter XI of this book is devoted.

Nevertheless, the free movement of goods is only one of the 'four freedoms' existing between Member States within the Community. The others are the free movement of persons, covering both employed workers on the one hand (Articles 48 to 51) and the establishment of self-employed persons and undertakings on the other (Articles 52 to 58); the free movement of services (Articles 59 to 66) and the free movement of capital (Articles 67 to 73), which is as yet the least advanced of the four.

Furthermore, Articles 92 to 94 of the Treaty govern aids granted by Member States. Article 92 (1) states in effect that such aids are 'incompatible with the common market' in so far as they affect trade between Member States. However, by way of exception to this, Article 92 (2) states that certain rather narrow categories of aid, such as compensation for natural disasters, 'shall be considered compatible

---

[8] On the 'customs system between Germany and Austria' Permanent Court of International Justice, Compendium of Consultative Decrees, Directives and Opinions, Series A–B, no. 41, p. 51.

[9] See paras. 2.11 *et seq.*

with the Common Market'. Also the subsequent provisions lay down the conditions and procedures according to which the Commission or the Council may exempt other aids from the rule in Article 92 (1). Next, Article 95 prohibits internal taxation which discriminates against identical or competing importing products in favour of domestic products.

The Treaty also provides for a common agricultural policy (Articles 38 to 47) and a common transport policy (Articles 74 to 84). In addition, Articles 85 and 86 prohibit certain types of restrictive agreements and practices and the Commission is empowered to take action against undertakings infringing these prohibitions, if necessary by means of fines. More important for the purposes of this book is Article 100 on harmonisation policy, which states that

> 'the Council shall, acting unanimously on a proposal from the Commission, issue directives for the approximation of such provisions laid down by law, regulation or administrative action in Member States as directly affect the establishment or functioning of the common market'.

This article is considered at length in Chapter XII of this book.

These provisions did not all take immediate effect when the Treaty came into force on 1 January 1958. Article 8 provides for a 12-year transitional period consisting of three four-year stages. Some articles of the Treaty are expressed to take effect during this transitional period; this is the case with Article 34 prohibiting quantitative restrictions and measures of equivalent effect on exports, which took effect at the end of the first stage of the transitional period. Other articles of the Treaty, such as Article 30 prohibiting the same measures on imports, were not expressed to take effect until the end of the transitional period. However, the Treaty also foresaw the possibility of accelerating certain measures and use was made of this. Furthermore, as the reader will be aware, Denmark, Ireland and the United Kingdom did not join the EEC until 1 January 1973. Their Act of Accession set out transitional measures, although certain provisions of the Treaty of Rome took effect before then. Finally, Greece acceded to the EEC on 1 January 1981 but also benefits from a similar system of transitional measures. The whole question of the dates at which Articles 30 to 36 have taken and will take effect under the Treaty of Rome and the Acts of Accession will be discussed in greater detail in Chapters V and VI below.

How are the provisions of Articles 30 to 36 enforced?[10] This can occur in three ways: under Article 169, Article 170 or under Article 177. By virtue of Article 169, the Commission, acting of its own-

---

[10] See generally Annex III to this book and L. Neville Brown and F. G. Jacobs, *The Court of Justice of the European Communities* (1977); G. Vandersanden and A. Barav, *Le contentieux communautaire* (1977); A. G. Toth, *Legal Protection of Individuals in the European Communities* (1978); H. G. Schermers, *Judicial Protection in the European Communities* (2nd ed. 1979).

motion or by a complaint from a Member State or private party,[11] may ask the Court for a declaration that a Member State has failed to fulfil its Treaty obligations in a certain matter. This is the culmination of a pre-trial procedure consisting of two stages: the Commission must first ask the Member State concerned to submit its observations, after which the Commission can deliver a reasoned opinion to the Member State requiring it to terminate its infringement. If the Member State does not comply with the reasoned opinion within the period specified by the Commission, the latter can then bring the matter before the Court of Justice. The purpose of the pre-trial procedure is primarily to inform the Member State concerned of the exact nature of its infringement. The procedure under Article 170 is broadly similar, the principal difference being that the action is brought by one Member State against another. This provision has been dormant until recently: the Court delivered its first judgment on the basis of it in October 1979.[12]

Article 177 provides for a quite different procedure. If a question of interpretation of Community law is raised before a court or tribunal of a Member State, that court or tribunal may refer the question to the Court of Justice for a preliminary ruling. If the question is raised before the court of final appeal for that particular case, then the court is bound to make such a reference. In contrast to the procedure under Article 169, the Court of Justice never rules on the compatibility of the national measure with Community law. This is left to the national court, whose role it is to apply the Court's ruling to the particular case. The importance of the procedure set out in Article 177 becomes apparent, when it is pointed out that the incompatibility of a national measure with the prohibition of quantitative restrictions and measures of equivalent effect may be raised by any party before a national court.

Since the prohibition on quantitative restrictions and measures of equivalent effect is directly applicable,[13] it may be invoked by any party to proceedings before national courts. As Community law takes precedence over the law of the Member States,[14] the national court may not apply a national measure which infringes this prohibition. If the point at issue is a matter of settled law, there is no need for the national court to make a reference. This means that many actions challenging the compatibility of a national measure with Articles 30 to 36 may never reach the Court of Justice.

---

[11] See generally Kuyper and Van Rijn 'Procedural Guarantees and Investigatory Methods in European Law' [1981] *Yearbook of European Law* (forthcoming).
[12] Case 141/78 *France* v. *UK* [1979] E.C.R. 2923, [1980] 1 C.M.L.R. 6.
[13] See paras. 5.05 and 6.01.
[14] Case 6/64 *Costa* v. *ENEL* [1964] E.C.R. 585, [1964] C.M.L.R. 425; Case 106/77 *Amministrazione delle Finanze* v. *Simmenthal SpA (No. 2)* [1978] E.C.R. 629, [1978] 3 C.M.L.R. 263; and the works at note 10 above.

It now remains only to explain the layout of this book, which is as follows: Chapters II, III and IV are all concerned with the scope of Articles 30 to 36, in terms of subject-matter, territory and the persons bound respectively. Chapters V, VI and VII are the focal point of the book; Chapter V deals with the meaning and effect of the prohibitions on quantitative restrictions, while Chapters VI and VII examine measures of equivalent effect. Chapter VIII deals with Article 36, the only exception clause in the Treaty relating exclusively to Articles 30 and 34. The other principal exception clauses which are of relevance are covered by Chapter IX. Next, Chapters X and XI deal with the applicability of Articles 30 to 36 to two special areas respectively: agricultural products, and measures linked to or forming part of State monopolies. Finally, Chapter XII is concerned with harmonisation and the conclusion is contained in Chapter XIII.

CHAPTER II

Scope: Subject matter

2.01   This is the first of three chapters dealing with the scope of the Treaty provisions on the free movement of goods between Member States, and more particularly Articles 30 to 36. It is the purpose of this chapter to examine first the concept of goods and then the transactions which benefit from these provisions. Consequently, the first part of this chapter is devoted to the definition of the term 'goods', while the second part is concerned with the concept of goods 'in free circulation' in the Member States. In the third section we shall see that the nationality of the owner of goods is irrelevant for the purposes of the rules on the free movement of goods. Lastly, in the fourth section we shall consider which transactions are governed by the Treaty provisions on the free movement of goods, and in particular the relationship between these rules and those relating to the other three freedoms enshrined in the Treaty—the free movement of workers, services and capital.

As already mentioned in Chapter I, the ECSC and Euratom Treaties fall outside the scope of this book. Article 232 EEC states that the provisions of the EEC Treaty shall not 'affect' the provisions of the ECSC, nor shall they 'derogate' from those of the Euratom Treaty. Therefore Articles 30 to 36 EEC do not apply to these Treaties. Consequently, 'coal' and 'steel' as defined by Annex I to the ECSC Treaty, and 'goods subject to the nuclear common market', as defined by Annex III to the Euratom Treaty, will not be considered here.[1]

It should also be pointed out that the structure of Title I of the Treaty requires that 'goods' have the same meaning for purposes of Articles 12 to 17 (customs duties and taxes of equivalent effect) as for Articles 30 to 36 (quantitative restrictions and measures of equivalent effect). This is why some cases on Articles 12 to 17 will be discussed in this chapter, although those provisions fall outside the scope of this book.

I. THE MEANING OF 'GOODS'

2.02   The first point to notice is that, whereas in certain cases such as Article 9 (1), the Treaty uses the term 'goods', in others such as

---

[1] Arts. 4 (a) ECSC and 93 Euratom prohibit quantitative restrictions on imports or exports of the products to which they apply respectively. Measures of equivalent effect are not expressly prohibited in those Treaties, although they are perhaps prohibited impliedly.

Articles 9 (2) and 10 (1) the expression 'products' has been preferred. However, although a similar distinction is to be found in the French, Italian and Dutch[2] texts, this appears to owe more to a desire to ring the changes than to convey any difference of meaning[3]—indeed the German text uses the word 'Waren' throughout.[4] Consequently, it is clear that the term 'goods' covers 'agricultural products' within the meaning of Article 38 of the Treaty, that is products listed in Annex II thereto.[5]

Furthermore, neither Article 30 nor Article 34—laying down the prohibition on quantitative restrictions respectively on imports and on exports—uses the terms 'goods' or 'products'. Instead they refer respectively to 'imports' and 'exports.' There can be little doubt that by this is meant imports and exports of 'goods'—an interpretation which is confirmed by the reference in Article 36 to 'restrictions on imports, exports or goods in transit.'

2.03 Nowhere in the Treaty is the concept of 'goods' defined. However, the Court of Justice has stated that

> 'by goods, within the meaning of [Article 9 of the Treaty], there must be understood products which can be valued in money and which are capable, as such, of forming the subject of commercial transactions'.

This definition was laid down in Case 7/68 *E.C. Commission* v. *Italy*[6] in which the Italian Government, brought before the Court for failing to lift its duty on exports of articles of artistic, historic, archaeological or ethnographic nature in accordance with Article 16, claimed that such articles did not constitute 'goods.' This submission was rejected by the Court, since art treasures fell within its definition of goods. Had the Court reached the opposite conclusion it would have deprived of all meaning the exception clause in Article 36 covering restrictions justified on the grounds of 'the protection of national treasures possessing artistic, historic or archaeological value'.[7] As already pointed out, 'goods' must have the same meaning under Articles 30 to 36 as under Articles 12 to 17.

2.04 Quite naturally, in *E.C. Commission* v. *Italy* the Court defined goods as products having commercial value. Yet refuse, if anything, has a negative value: people are paid to remove it. An interesting case on this point arose in the United States in the following circumstances: in 1973 New Jersey passed a law prohibiting, with a few narrow exceptions, the importation of solid or liquid waste which originated or was collected outside the territorial limits of the State. Large cities in other States, and in particular Philadelphia

---

[2] The French text uses 'marchandises' and 'produits', the Italian 'merci' and 'prodotti' and the Dutch 'goederen' and 'produkten'.
[3] Campbell, *Common Market Law* (1969), Vol. 2, para. 2014.
[4] Likewise Danish only uses 'varer.'
[5] See generally Chap. X.
[6] [1968] E.C.R 423, [1969] C.M.L.R. 1.
[7] See paras. 8.33 *et seq.* below.

and New York, had been disposing of much of their refuse in certain privately-owned sites in New Jersey. The United States Supreme Court held the law unconstitutional in that it discriminated against refuse from other States.[8] If a similar case arose in the Community, it is submitted that refuse must be treated as goods even though it only has 'negative' value.[9]

2.05 Some further light was shed on the meaning of 'goods' in the *Sacchi*[10] case. Criminal proceedings had been brought against the operator of a private television station for allegedly infringing the Italian State monopoly over television broadcasting. One question put to the court was whether the principle of the free movement of goods applied to this activity.[11] In this connection it should be pointed out that the first paragraph of Article 60 states that 'services shall be considered "services" within the meaning of this Treaty where they are normally provided for remuneration, *in so far as they are not governed by the provisions relating to the freedom of movement for goods,* capital and persons'.[12] Thus the rules on the free movement of services and those on the free movement of goods cannot apply to the same aspect of a given measure.

The Court replied in the following terms:

> 'In the absence of express provision to the contrary in the Treaty, a television signal must, by reason of its nature, be regarded as provision of services.
>
> Although it is not ruled out that services normally provided for remuneration may come under the provisions relating to goods, such is however the case, as appears from Article 60, only in so far as they are governed by such provisions.
>
> It follows that the transmission of television signals, including those in the nature of advertisements, comes, as such, within the rules of the Treaty relating to services.
>
> On the other hand, trade in material, sound recordings, films, apparatus and other products used for the diffusion of television signals are subject to the rules relating to freedom of movement for goods'.[13]

Confirmation of this ruling is to be found in the recent case of *Procureur du Roi* v. *Debauve*[14]. A number of individuals and undertakings engaged in the diffusion of cable television had been prosecuted before the Belgian courts for infringing the prohibition on television advertising in Belgium. Asked by the Liège Court to

---

[8] *Philadelphia* v. *New Jersey* 437 U.S. 617, 98 S.Ct. 2531 (1978). For a comparison between the rules on the free movement of goods under the Treaty of Rome and under the American Constitution see Slot, *Technical and administrative obstacles to trade in the EEC* (1975); Roth, *Freier Warenverkehr und staatliche Regelungsgewalt in einem Gemeinsamen Markt* (1976).

[9] This conclusion is supported by the reference to waste and scrap in Art. 4 (2) (i) of Reg. 802/68 on the definition of the origin of goods—see para. 2.10 below. However that regulation does not purport to define 'goods'.

[10] Case 155/73 [1974] E.C.R. 409, [1974] 2 C.M.L.R. 177. See March Hunnings [1975] Journal of Business Law 72.

[11] Other questions concerned the interpretation of various provisions including Arts. 37, 86 and 90. With respect to Art. 37 see para. 11.03 below.

[12] The italics are those of the author.

[13] Paras. 6 and 7 of the judgment.

[14] Case 52/79 [1980] E.C.R. 833, [1981] 2 C.M.L.R. 362; Bennett [1980] E.L.Rev. 224.

rule whether this prohibition contravened the Treaty provisions on the freedom to provide services, the Court began by stating that:

'Before examining those questions the Court recalls that it has already ruled in its judgment of 30 April 1974 (Case 155/73 *Sacchi* [1974] E.C.R. 490), that the broadcasting of television signals, including those in the nature of advertisements, comes, as such, within the rules of the Treaty relating to services. There is no reason to treat the transmission of such signals by cable television any differently.'[15]

March Hunnings[16] criticises the court's ruling on this point in both *Sacchi* and *Debauve*. In his view both types of broadcasting are movements of goods:

'We are faced in reality with two different forms of transportation, the difference being that between sending a photographic print or matrix from the *Financial Times* in London to its second printing plant in Frankfurt by post or special messenger and sending it by wireless or teleprinter or fax. The end result is exactly the same: the physical object in London has been transported into the hands of the recipient in Frankfurt'.

2.06 In *R. v. Thompson, Johnson and Woodiwiss*[17] the court was called upon to distinguish the concept of goods from those of capital and current payments. Articles 67 to 73 of the Treaty govern the free movement of capital between Member States 'to the extent necessary to ensure the proper functioning of the common market'[18] without defining what is meant by 'capital'. However, the Council has adopted two directives for the implementation of Article 67[19] and, although these directives do not purport to give a definition of 'capital' either, they incorporate a list of capital movements. Current payments on the other hand are governed by Article 106, which requires Member States to 'authorise, in the currency of the Member State in which the creditor or the beneficiary resides, any payments connected with the movement of goods, services or capital' to the extent that such movement has been liberalised pursuant to the Treaty.[20] Such payments are not further defined in the Treaty either.

In *Thompson* the three defendants were charged before the English courts with importing Krugerrands and exporting silver alloy coins

---

[15] Para. 8 of the judgment.

[16] [1980] C.M.L.Rev. 564.

[17] Case 7/78 [1978] E.C.R. 2247, [1979] 1 C.M.L.R. 47; Prout [1979] E.L.Rev. 187.

[18] By reason of this qualification the effect of the Treaty provisions on free movement of capital is more limited than that of the other three freedoms—goods, persons and services. Furthermore, the principle of the free movement of capital is subject to a wide variety of exceptions contained, for instance, in Arts. 68 (3), 70 (2) and 73. See generally van Ballegooijen, 'Free Movement of Capital in the European Economic Community' [1976] 2 *Legal Issues of European Integration* 1; Seidel, 'Escape Clauses in European Community Law' [1978] C.M.L.Rev. 283; Mègret and Sarmet in *Le droit de la Communauté économique européenne* (1971) Vol. 3; Waschk in Groeben, Boeckh, Thiesing, *Kommentar zum EWG-Vertrag* (1974) Vol. 1, 540; Campbell, *op. cit.* note 3 above, Vol. 3, 797.

[19] Dir. of 11 May 1960 ([1960] O.J. Spec. Ed. 921) amended by Dir. 63/21 of 18 December 1962 ([1963] O.J. Spec.Ed. 62).

[20] Börner, 'Rechtsfragen des Zahlungs- und Kapitalverkehrs in der EWG.' [1966] EuR 97; Ehlermann in Groeben, Boeckh, Thiesing, note 18 above, Vol. I at 1374; Mègret, 1976, note 18 above; see also paras. 6.22 and 7.24.

between April and June 1975 contrary to various provisions of English law. The coins fell into three categories:

(i) Krugerrands (which were legal tender only in South Africa),

(ii) British silver alloy coins minted before 1947 which were still legal tender,

(iii) British silver alloy half-crowns minted before 1947 which, although no longer legal tender, could be exchanged at the Bank of England and were protected from destruction other than by the State on the grounds that the State enjoyed a right akin to a property right in them.

In each case the commodity value of the coins far exceeded their face value. When this case came before it on appeal by the defendants, the Court of Appeal referred four questions under Article 177 to ascertain whether the import and export restrictions were compatible with Community law. It sought to do so essentially by asking whether the coins were 'capital' within the meaning of Articles 67 to 73, and in any case whether these restrictions were justified by Article 36.

The difficulty posed by these questions is underlined by the fact that the first directive implementing Article 67 [21] includes gold imports and exports in the list of capital movements, while the Common Customs Tariff[22] mentions coins which are not collectors' pieces (heading number 72–01), as well as coins which are collectors' pieces (heading number 99–05), and banknotes (heading number 49–07).

2.07 Many of the intervenors before the Court deduced from this that the decision as to which Treaty provisions to apply depended not on the nature of the items, but on the purpose for which they were imported—though as to the exact criterion to be applied there were distinct differences between those intervenors.

However, the Court appears to have concentrated rather on the nature of the articles, since it ruled as follows:

> 'The aim of Article 106 is to ensure that the necessary monetary transfers may be made for the liberalisation of movements of capital and for the free movement of goods, services and persons.
>
> It must be inferred from this that under the system of the Treaty means of payment are not to be regarded as goods falling within the purview of Articles 30 to 37 of the Treaty.
>
> Silver alloy coins which are legal tender in a Member State are, by their very nature, to be regarded as means of payment and it follows that their transfer does not fall within the provisions of Articles 30 to 37 of the Treaty.
>
> Although doubts may be entertained on the question whether Krugerrands are to be regarded as means of legal payment it can nevertheless be noted than on the money markets of those Member States which permit dealings in these coins they are treated as being equivalent to currency.

---

[21] Dir. of 11 May 1960, note 19 above.

[22] The Common Customs Tariff is brought up to date annually. For 1982 see Regs. 3300/81 and 3433/81.

Their transfer must consequently be designated as a monetary transfer which does not fall within the provisions of the said Articles 30 to 37.

Having regard to the above-mentioned considerations it is unnecessary to deal with the question under what circumstances the transfer of these two categories of coins might possibly be designated either as a movement of capital or as a current payment.

Question 1 (c) refers to silver alloy coins of a Member State, which have been legal tender in that State and which, although no longer legal tender, are protected as coinage from destruction.

Such coins cannot be regarded as means of payment within the meaning stated above, with the result that they can be designated as goods failing within the system of Articles 30 to 37 of the Treaty.'

Thus it held that the coins in categories (i) and (ii) were not goods, whereas those in category (iii) were goods.[23]

In an area that is already beset with conceptual difficulties, it is perhaps unfortunate that the court chose to introduce new concepts which it did not define. Presumably the notion of 'means of payment' is wider than that of legal tender, but how wide is it? Is ' means of legal payment' the same as 'means of payment'? And what is meant by being 'treated as being equivalent to currency'?

The only clear proposition that can be distilled from this judgment is that coins which are still legal tender in a Member State, are not 'goods'.[24]

2.08 We can summarise the Court's case law on the meaning of 'goods' as follows:

'Goods' means 'products which can be valued in money and which are capable, as such, of forming the subject of commercial transactions.' Neither television broadcasts nor 'means of payment' are 'goods'.

II. GOODS 'ORIGINATING IN THE MEMBER STATES' AND GOODS FROM THIRD COUNTRIES IN 'FREE CIRCULATION' IN THE COMMUNITY

2.09 Article 9 (2) of the Treaty stipulates that the provisions on the free movement of goods, including Articles 30 to 36, apply to

---

[23] As to the third category, see para. 8.23 below.

[24] The sequel is of some interest. Naturally, on the basis of the Court of Justice's ruling the Court of Appeal dismissed the defendants' appeal. However, events did not turn out very well either for a German company called AGOSI (Allgemeine Gold- und Silberscheideanstalt), which claimed to be the owner of the Krugerrands and to have been induced to part with them to Thompson and Johnson by fraud on the part of these two. AGOSI therefore brought an action before the English courts against the British Customs and Excise Commissioners seeking a declaration that they were entitled to the return of these Krugerrands, which the Commissioners had confiscated. AGOSI claimed, inter alia, that the Krugerrands were not 'goods' for the purposes of the Customs and Excise Act 1952, s. 44, which provides that: 'Where . . . (f) any imported goods are concealed or packed in any manner appearing to be intended to deceive an officer, those goods shall be liable to forfeiture'. On an analysis of customs legislation since 1833 the Court of Appeal found, however, that 'goods' must be construed as including gold and silver bullion and coin, and therefore Krugerrands. On this and other grounds AGOSI's action failed: *Allgemeine Gold- und Silberscheideanstalt* v.

'products originating in Member States and to products coming from third countries which are in free circulation in Member States.[25] Each of these two concepts will be examined in turn.

As to the territorial extent of the Member States for this purpose, the reader is referred to Chapter III of this book.

A. Goods originating in the Member States

2.10 This concept is nowhere defined in the Treaty. However, assistance is to be derived from Regulation 802/68[26] defining the concept of the origin of goods. Article 1 of this Regulation states that the definition it lays down shall apply for the purposes of

'(a) the uniform application of the Common Customs Tariff, of quantitative restrictions, and of all other measures adopted, in relation to the importation of goods, by the Community or by Member States;

(b) the uniform application of all measures adopted, in relation to the exportation of goods, by the Community or by Member States;

(c) the preparation and issue of certificates of origin'.

The concept of origin is defined principally in Articles 4 and 5 of the Regulation. Article 4 provides as follows:

'1. Goods wholly obtained or produced in one country shall be considered as originating in that country.

2. The expression 'goods wholly obtained or produced in one country' means:

(a) mineral products extracted within its territory;

(b) vegetable products harvested therein;

(c) live animals born and raised therein;

(d) products derived from live animals raised therein;

(e) products of hunting or fishing carried on therein;

(f) products of sea-fishing and other products taken from the sea by vessels registered or recorded in that country and flying its flag;

(g) goods obtained on board factory ships from the products referred to in (f) originating in that country, if such factory ships are registered or recorded in that country and flying its flag;

(h) products taken from the sea-bed or beneath the sea-bed outside territorial waters, if that country has, for the purposes of exploitation, exclusive rights to such soil or subsoil;

(i) waste and scrap products derived from manufacturing operations and used articles, if they were collected therein and are only fit for the recovery of raw materials;

(j) goods which are produced therein exclusively from goods referred to in subparagraphs (a) to (i) or from their derivatives, at any stage of production'.

Article 5 provides:

'A product in the production of which two or more countries were concerned shall be regarded as originating in the country in which the last substantial

---

Customs and Excise Commissioners [1980] 2 W.L.R. 555, [1980] 1 C.M.L.R. 488. Nevertheless it does not appear that the Court of Appeal's judgment conflicts in any way with that of the Court of Justice in *Thompson*.

[25] Matters relating to quantitative restrictions and measures of equivalent effect in direct trade between the Community and third countries fall outside this book, but see note 121 to Chap. VI below.

[26] [1968] J.O. L148/1.

process or operation that is economically justified was performed, having been carried out in an undertaking equipped for the purpose, and resulting in the manufacture of a new product or representing an important stage of manufacture.'

By virtue of Article 3 these provisions do not apply to the petroleum products listed in Annex I to the Regulation. Furthermore, special rules have been adopted in relation to particular products.[27] The picture is further complicated by the fact that a large number of agreements concluded by the Community both with developing and developed countries contain specific rules of origin.[28]

B. Goods from third countries in free circulation in the Community

2.11 As regards this second category of goods benefiting from free movement within the Community according to Article 9 (2), Article 10 (1) of the Treaty stipulates that:

'Products coming from a third country shall be considered to be in free circulation in a Member State if the import formalities have been complied with and any customs duties or charges having equivalent effect which are payable have been levied in that Member State, and if they have not benefited from a total or partial drawback of such duties or charges.'

Various commentators have suggested that these conditions are fulfilled if the customs duties payable have merely been determined, whether or not they have been paid.[29] This is in fact to be permitted by Directive 79/695[30] which harmonises procedures for the release of goods into free circulation. Article 13 (1) of that Directive provides that

'the customs authority may release the goods for free circulation only when import duties have been paid or guaranteed or payment of them has been deferred under the conditions laid down in Directive 78/453'.[31]

Article 2 (1) of that Directive provides:

---

[27] For instance, eggs Reg. 641/69 ([1969] J.O. L83/15); essential spare parts for motor cars Reg. 37/70 ([1970] J.O. L7/6); certain textile products Reg. 1039/71 ([1971] J.O. L113/13, as amended); slide fasteners (zips) Reg. 2067/77 ([1977] O.J. L242/5) declared invalid by the Court in cases 34/78 *Yoshida Nederland* v. *Kamer van Koophandel* [1979] E.C.R. 115, [1979] 2 C.M.L.R. 747, and 114/78 *Yoshida* v. *Industrie- und Handelskammer Kassel* [1979] E.C.R. 151, [1979] 2 C.M.L.R. 747, noted by Usher [1979] E.L.Rev. 184 and repealed by Reg. 1628/79 ([1979] O.J. L190/35). On rules of origin see generally Forrester, 'EEC Customs Law: Rules of Origin and Preferential Duty Treatment' [1980] E.L.Rev. 167 and 257.
[28] For instance, the agreements with the EFTA countries, *e.g.* Austria ([1972] J.O. L300/3, 38), with certain non-EFTA Mediterranean countries (*e.g.* Cyprus [1977] O.J. L339/19), and with the African, Caribbean and Pacific countries (Lomé I [1976] O.J. L25/41 and Lomé II [1980] O.J. L347).
[29] Waelbroeck in *Le droit de la Communauté économique européenne* (1970) Vol. I, 43; Laubereau in Groeben, Boeckh, Thiesing, note 18 above, Vol. I at 154.
[30] [1979] O.J. L205/19. The directive is based on Art. 100. The Member States are not bound to implement it until 1 July 1982 (Art. 27 as amended by Dir. 81/853 ([1981] O.J. L319/1)). The same applies to the Commission's implementing directive, Dir. 82/57 ([1982] O.J. L28/38).
[31] [1978] O.J. L146/19.

'Subject to the applicant giving appropriate security, the form of which shall be specified by the competent authorities of the Member States, they shall... grant him deferment of the import duties . . . for which he is liable . . .'

As required by Article 10 (2), first sub-paragraph, the Commission adopted a number of measures on the methods of administrative co-operation for applying this provision.[32] As required by the second sub-paragraph of Article 10 (2) the Commission also laid down provisions applicable, as regards trade between Member States, to goods originating in another Member State in whose manufacture products have been used on which the exporting Member State has not levied the appropriate customs duties or charges of equivalent effect, or which have benefited from a total or partial drawback of such duties or charges.[33]

2.12 The assimilation of goods from third countries put into free circulation in a Member State to goods originating in the Community was categorically underlined by the court in *Donckerwolcke* v. *Procureur de la République*[34] in the following terms:

'It appears from Article 9 that, as regards free circulation of goods within the Community, products entitled to "free circulation" are definitively and wholly assimilated to products originating in Member States.

The result of this assimilation is that the provisions of Article 30 concerning the elimination of quantitative restrictions and all measures having equivalent effect are applicable without distinction to products originating in the Community and to those which were put into free circulation in any one of the Member States, irrespective of the actual origin of the products.'[35]

2.13 However, this principle only applies to customs matters, as the Court emphasised in the *EMI Records* v. *CBS*[36] cases. There, the facts were as follows: until 1917 one undertaking had held the 'Columbia' trade mark for records both in the United States and in Europe. That year saw the first of a series of transactions which resulted in CBS holding the trade mark in the United States and EMI owning it in all the Member States of the Community. EMI brought proceedings against CBS in the United Kingdom, Denmark and West Germany, giving rise to three parallel references. The Court held that Article 30 had no bearing on this question, since

[32] See in particular the Decisions of 5 December 1960 ([1961] O.J.Spec.Ed. 29/61), 17 July 1962 ([1962] O.J.Spec.Ed. 2140/62), 64/503 ([1964] O.J.Spec.Ed. 2293/64), 70/41 ([1970] O.J.Spec.Ed. L13/13), 71/14 ([1971] O.J.Spec.Ed. L6/35). The Council has now adopted Dir. 79/695 on the harmonisation of procedures for the release of goods for free circulation; see note 30 above. See also generally Regs. 222/77 and 223/77 as amended ([1977] O.J. L38) on the Community transit procedure.
[33] See, in particular, decision of 16 December 1958 ([1958] J.O. 614), decision of 28 June 1960 ([1960] J.O. 933], Dec. 63/637 ([1963] J.O. 2782), Dec. 68/284 ([1968] J.O. L167/10). Also Reg. 222/77, note 32 above. Also Art. 45 Act of Accession and Regs. 385/73 ([1973] O.J. L42) and 3335/73 ([1973] O.J. L341/10), *inter alia.* The rules on inward processing are laid down by Council Dir. 69/73 ([1969] O.J.Spec.Ed. L58/1) as amended.
[34] Case 41/76 [1976] E.C.R. 1921 at 1933; [1977] 2 C.M.L.R. 535 at 550.
[35] For the application of that principle in the *Donckerwolcke* case see para. 9.33 below.
[36] Case 51/75 [1976] E.C.R. 811, [1976] 2 C.M.L.R. 235; Case 86/75 [1976] E.C.R. 871, [1976] 2 C.M.L.R. 235; Case 96/75 [1976] E.C.R. 913, [1976] 2 C.M.L.R. 235; see para. 8.85 below.

movement of goods between Member States was not involved. It rejected the defendants' reliance on the principle of the assimilation of third country goods in free circulation in the Member States, in the following terms:

> 'Since [Articles 9 (2) and 10 (1)] only refer to the effects of compliance with customs formalities and paying customs duties and charges having equivalent effect, they cannot be interpreted as meaning that it would be sufficient for products bearing a mark applied in a third country and imported into the Community to comply with the customs formalities in the first Member State where they were imported in order to enable them to be marketed in the Common Market as a whole in contravention of the rules relating to the protection of the mark.'[37]

It is submitted that Advocate General Warner's rather drier response to this particular argument of the defendants is more accurate:

> 'The argument of the defendants is, as I understand it, that once records made in America and bearing the mark Columbia have been cleared through customs in a Member State, they are, provided they have not benefited from a drawback, to be assimilated to records originating in a Member State. So they are. But I do not see how this assists the defendants. If they were to manufacture similar records in a Member State, they would not thereby render themselves entitled to market them in infringement of EMI Records Limited's registered marks, either in that Member State or in any other'.[38]

Nevertheless the Court's ruling on this point is of interest as it may eventually build on it, perhaps in the context of technical standards.[39]

2.14   Also, certain provisions create exceptions to the rule that goods originating in third countries are to be treated as Community goods once the appropriate customs formalities have been completed:

(i) The most important of these is Article 115 of the Treaty which applies where the execution of national commercial policy measures is threatened by 'deflection of trade' or where 'differences between such measures [of national commercial policy] lead to economic difficulties in one or more of the Member States'. In such circumstances, the Commission 'shall authorise Member States to take the necessary protective measures, the conditions and details of which it shall determine'.

This provision is considered at length in Chapter IX of this book.[40] Suffice it to say here that, although this provision is intended to become gradually redundant as purely national measures of com-

---

[37] Paras. 16, 16 and 9 of the respective judgments.
[38] At 860.
[39] See para. 6.50 below.
[40] Para. 9.21 et seq.

mercial policy are replaced by the common commercial policy based on uniform principles in accordance with Article 113 EEC, recourse to this exception has considerably increased in the last few years.

2.15   (ii) A further exception is contained in the Protocol on German Internal Trade[41] annexed to the EEC Treaty. Article 1 of this Protocol provides as follows:

> 'Since trade between the German territories subject to the Basic Law for the Federal Republic of Germany and the German territories in which the Basic Law does not apply is a part of German internal trade, the application of this Treaty in Germany requires no change in the treatment currently accorded this trade'.

This means that the Community may not impose or lift restrictions on trade between the two Germanies,[42] whether in the form of tariff or non-tariff barriers. Furthermore, it emerges clearly from Article 2 of the Protocol that the Member States other than the Federal Republic of Germany are entitled to make their own trade arrangements with East Germany, subject to certain conditions laid down in that Article.

However, the important provision for present purposes is in Article 3 of the Protocol, which reads:

> 'Each Member State may take appropriate measures to prevent any difficulties arising for it from trade between another Member State and the German territories in which the Basic Law for the Federal Republic of Germany does not apply'.

It seems clear that goods imported from the German Democratic Republic under the Protocol are in principle in free circulation [43] so that Article 3 constitutes an exception to Article 9 EEC. It is clear from its wording that this exception can be applied even before difficulties in trade actually exist, to prevent such difficulties arising.[44] Furthermore national measures under Article 3 do not require the approval of the Commission and a Member State taking such measures is not even required to inform the Commission. On the other hand, in accordance with general principles of Community law, it may be assumed that measures will not be 'appropriate' if

---

[41] Tomuschat, 'Rechtsfragen zum Handelspolitischen Arrangement zwischen der EWG und den sich um dem Beitritt bewerbenden Staaten' [1969] EuR. 287; Zuleeg 'Grundvertrag und EWG-Protokoll über den innerdeutschen Handel' [1973] EuR. 209; Ehlermann, Kupper, Lambrecht, Ollig, *Handelspartner DDR—Innerdeutsche Wirtschaftsbeziehungen* (1975); Case 14/74 *Norddeutsches Vieh- und Fleischkontor* v. *HZA Hamburg-Jonas* [1974] E.C.R. 899; Case 23/79 *Geflügelschlachterei Freystadt* v. *Hamburg-Jonas* [1979] E.C.R. 2789; written question 283/79 ([1980] O.J. C105/1).
[42] Ehlermann, *op. cit.* note 41 above, at 245. However, it would appear that Community legislation harmonising the conditions under which goods may be sold in the Community (see Chapter XII) can apply to imports from the GDR into the Federal Republic. The same would appear to apply to veterinary legislation.
[43] Laubereau, note 29 above, at 153; Ehlermann, *op. cit.* note 41 at 250.
[44] Ehlermann, *op. cit.* note 41, at 250.

they are more restrictive than is necessary to achieve their legitimate purpose.[45]

2.16   (iii) Another exception is contained in the Protocol to the EEC Treaty on goods originating in and coming from certain countries and enjoying special treatment when imported into a Member State. This Protocol provides in Article 1 that the application of the EEC Treaty

> 'shall not require any alteration in the customs treatment applicable, at the time of the entry into force of this Treaty, to imports: (a) into the Benelux countries of goods originating in and coming from . . . the Netherlands Antilles . . .'

The other countries and territories in the list all have traditional ties with the Netherlands, France or Italy as the case may be. Article 2 of the Protocol stipulates that

> 'goods imported into a Member State and benefiting from the treatment referred to above shall not be considered to be in free circulation in that State within the meaning of Article 10 of this Treaty when re-exported to another Member State'.

This Protocol may well be obsolete. Certainly it no longer applies to the Netherlands Antilles.[46] In addition, many of the third countries in question such as Morocco and Tunisia have now concluded agreements with the Community. At least as far as goods covered by such agreements are concerned the Protocol would appear to have been superseded or suspended.[47]

2.17   (iv) A further exception is contained in the Protocol to the first Act of Accession on the import of New Zealand butter and cheese into the United Kingdom. Article 1 (4) of that Protocol provides that the butter and cheese imported into the United Kingdom in accordance with that Protocol 'may not become the subject of intra-Community trade'. With regard to cheese the arrangements laid down by the Protocol lapsed on 31 December 1977 (Article 5 (3)). On the other hand, the Council has exercised its powers under Article 5 (2) to extend the arrangements for butter imports beyond that date.[48]

2.18   (v) Lastly, Articles 109 to 119 of the first Act of Accession contain various temporary exceptions relating to goods originating in certain developing countries and territories. These have all been superseded.[49]

---

[45] See para. 9.01.

[46] See para. 3.02 below and the notes thereto.

[47] In Case 26/69 E.C. Commission v. France [1970] E.C.R. 565, [1970] C.M.L.R. 444, which concerned this Protocol, the Court more or less tacitly accepted that such agreements could have this effect.

[48] See now Reg. 858/81 ([1981] O.J. L90/18).

[49] See Puissochet, L'élargissement des Communautés européennes (1974), 370; The enlargement of the European Communities (1975). The provisions of Arts. 109 to 115 were superseded by the Lomé Convention (note 28 above), to which all the developing countries concerned were party. Article 115 states that these provisions were to apply until 31 January 1975, with

III. THE NATIONALITY OF THE OWNER

2.19 It is only the status of the goods and not the nationality of their owner which is the determining factor for the application of the Treaty provisions on the free movement of goods. This has been emphasised by the court in relation to the prohibition on charges of equivalent effect in Article 12:

> '. . . The Treaty prohibits any pecuniary charge on imports and exports between Member States, irrespective of the nationality of the traders who might be placed at a disadvantage by such measures. Thus, in applying these provisions, there is no justification for a distinction to be made according to whether the measures in question adversely affect certain Member States and their nationals, or all the citizens of the Community, or only the nationals of the Member State which was responsible for the measures in question': *Sociaalfonds voor de Diamantarbeiders* v. *Brachfeld*.[50]

This statement also holds good for Articles 30 to 36.

In highly exceptional circumstances it may be otherwise when the owner of the goods is a national of a third state enjoying less than cordial relations with one or more Member States. It might then be possible for the Member States to have recourse to Article 224 to prohibit imports or exports in view of such tense relations.[51]

IV. THE TRANSACTIONS COVERED

2.20 The first two parts of this chapter considered what items benefit from the Treaty provisions governing the free movement of goods between Member States, and in particular Articles 30 to 36. This section is concerned with the relationship between these provisions and those relating to the other three freedoms enshrined in

---

the possibility of their being extended under certain conditions. In fact, the Council did extend the application of these provisions for a further period: Dec. 75/88 ([1975] O.J. L26/8), Reg. 1598/75 ([1975] O.J. L166/1), Reg. 1599/75 ([1975] O.J. L166/67), Reg. 405/76 ([1976] O.J. L50/1). From 1 January 1973 until that date products imported into the United Kingdom originating in the independent Commonwealth countries listed in Annex VI to the Act of Accession 'shall not, when they are re-exported to another new Member State or to the Community as originally constituted, be considered to be in free circulation within the meaning of Art. 10 of the EEC Treaty': Art. 112 (1). Conversely, goods imported into the Community as originally constituted originating from certain other developing countries, which had already concluded an association agreement with the Community, 'shall not, when re-exported to another Member State, be considered to be in free circulation in the Community as originally constituted, within the meaning of Art. 10 of the EEC Treaty': Art. 112 (2). Art. 112 (3) qualifies these rules: 'Where there is no risk of deflection of trade, and in particular in the event of minimal disparities in the import arrangements, the Commission may derogate from paragraphs 1 and 2.' By virtue of Art. 119 the same applies to goods originating in the New Hebrides and the Overseas Countries and Territories (OCTs) listed in Art. 24 (2) of the Act of Accession: Dec. 75/89 ([1975] O.J. 26/9), Reg. 1599/75 ([1975] O.J. L166/1), Reg. 1957/75 ([1975] O.J. 201/5), Reg. 405/76 ([1976] O.J. L50/1), Dec. 76/568 ([1976] O.J. L176/8). On OCTs generally see para. 3.02 below. Art. 116 in effect applied the rule in Art. 112 (1) to imports to the United Kingdom originating in Papua-New Guinea, until 31 December 1977. That territory has since become independent and acceded to the Lomé Convention: [1978] O.J. L271, [1978] O.J. L287/21.

[50] Cases 2–3/69 [1969] E.C.R., 211, [1969] C.M.L.R. 335, paras. 24–26 of the judgment.
[51] Para. 9.50.

the Treaty—the free movement of workers (Articles 48 *et seq.*), services (Articles 59–66) and capital (Articles 67–73). Lastly, we shall examine whether goods moving between Member States for non-economic purposes enjoy the benefit of the provisions on the free movement of goods.

2.21 First, however, it is helpful to set out certain movements which clearly fall under the provisions on the free movement of goods. As the reader will be aware, the classic case involves goods passing from one Member State to another to be sold in the second State.

The same applies where the goods merely transit through the second Member State to be sold in another Member State or even outside the Community. This can be deduced from the fact that transit is simply a particular type of importation and of exportation, but it is also expressly stated in Article 36, which begins: 'The provisions of Articles 30 to 34 shall not preclude prohibitions or restrictions on imports, exports or goods in transit. . . .'

Again, the same applies where goods are imported from one Member State to another, where they were produced or where they have already been put on the market. In other words, the provisions on the free movement of goods apply to re-imports.[52]

Lastly, it is submitted that the same holds true where an individual resident in one Member State seeks to import into it goods he has bought in another Member State. This point was made by Advocate General Warner in *R.* v. *Henn and Darby*[53]:

> 'There is trade between Member States [for the purposes of Articles 30 to 36] when an individual imports into a Member State for his own use goods that he has bought in another Member State.'

2.22 Having thus outlined the principal movements of goods to which Articles 30 to 36 apply, the relationship between these provisions and Articles 59 to 66 on the free provision of services may now be considered. The only stipulation in the Treaty as to this relationship is to the effect that the provisions on services only apply when those goods do not: Article 60.[54]

2.23 The 'grey area' of the greatest importance concerns import restrictions on goods such as tools required for the performance of a service under Article 59. In this connection Title III, Part B of the Council's General Programme for the abolition of restrictions on the freedom to provide services lists among the restrictions to be eliminated by that programme 'any prohibition of, or hindrance to, the movement of the item to be supplied in the course of the service

---

[52] An example is Case 78/70 *Deutsche Grammophon* v. *Metro* [1971] E.C.R. 487, [1971] C.M.L.R. 631, where, however, the Court did not mention the question of re-importation. As is frequent in such cases, the plaintiffs' object in seeking to prevent re-imports was to maintain differences in their prices between Member States.

[53] Case 34/79 [1979] E.C.R. 3795, [1980] 1 C.M.L.R. 246.

[54] Para. 2.05 above.

or of the materials comprising such item or of the tools, machinery, equipment and other means to be employed in the provision of the service'.[55] However, as Graf[56] points out, the opening words of Title III expressly state that this is subject to the Treaty provisions on the free movement of goods. Furthermore, when it adopted the General Programme, the Council adopted a declaration in which it recognised that customs duties on such goods could not be regarded as restrictions on services. Following this, the Commission addressed a recommendation to the Member States inviting them to abolish such duties, without prejudice to the obligations resulting from Articles 12 and 14 of the Treaty.[57]

The Council has adopted two Directives implementing this programme which concern the film industry and which provide for the abolition of certain import restrictions on films: Directives 63/607[58] and 65/264.[59] These Directives are expressed to be based on the EEC Treaty as a whole, and 'in particular Article 63 (2) thereof'.

It is submitted, therefore, that neither the Commission nor the Council has committed itself on this issue. Nor has the Court ever been called upon to rule on it.

2.24 Four possible solutions to this particular problem come to mind:

(i) One could apply the rules on the movement of goods in every case. This has the distinct advantage that there will be no need to enquire for what purpose goods are to be imported. Nevertheless, this theory overlooks the fact that some national restrictions on goods are precisely aimed at preventing the free provision of services;

(ii) The opposite solution—always to apply the rules on services—is also unsatisfactory, because in some cases a restriction on the transfer of goods may affect the provision of services only indirectly;

(iii) A more satisfactory test is the following: Is this restriction on the transfer of goods so closely related to services that the services aspect is predominant?

(iv) An alternative criterion is: Is this *movement* (or potential movement) of goods so closely related to services that the service aspect is predominant?

There is a slight difference of emphasis between solutions (iii) and (iv). If test (iii) is to be applied, then it may happen that a measure falls under Article 59 even though it incidentally covers some

---

[55] [1962] J.O. Spec.Ed. 3. Ehlermann in Groeben, Boeckh, Thiesing, note 18 above, Vol. I at 265.

[56] *Der Begriff 'Massnahmen gleicher Wirkung wie mengenmässige Einfuhrbeschränkungen' im EWG-Vertrag'* (1972), 88.

[57] Recommendation of 8 November 1962 ([1962] J.O. 2767/62). See also Rec. 64/412 ([1964] J.O. 1814/64) on the customs treatment of teaching materials.

[58] [1963] O.J.Spec.Ed. 2661/13.

[59] [1965] O.J.Spec.Ed. 1437/65.

movements of goods, which are quite unconnected with any service. On the other hand, the result of test (iv) will be that one and the same measure may fall under both Article 30 and 59, depending on the case—which would not appear to give rise to any problem. It is submitted, therefore, that the fourth test is the better one.

2.25 The same test can be applied in another area in which the question of the relationship between goods and services is posed: advertising. The Court has already delivered the following rulings with relation to advertising:

On the one hand, the Court has held in the Sacchi[60] and Debauve[61] cases considered earlier in this chapter that prohibitions or restrictions on television advertising fell to be considered under Articles 59 to 66.

On the other hand, Article 2 (3) (m) of Commission Directive 70/50[62] lists as measures of equivalent effect within the meaning of Article 30 those measures which 'prohibit or limit publicity in respect of imported products only, or totally or partially confine publicity to domestic products only.' In keeping with this, in 152/78 E.C. Commission v. France[63] the Commission maintained that certain French provisions restricting the advertising of alcoholic drinks contravened Article 30 in that they fell more heavily on imported drinks than on French drinks although such a distinction was not justified on health grounds. Without adverting to Article 59, the Court stated:

'As a preliminary point it should be observed that there is no dispute between the parties on whether a restriction on freedom of advertising for certain products may constitute a measure having an effect equivalent to a quantitative restriction within the meaning of Article 30 of the Treaty. Although such a restriction does not directly affect imports it is however capable of restricting their volume owing to the fact that it affects the marketing prospects for the imported products. The issue in point is therefore whether the prohibitions and restrictions on advertising laid down by the French legislation place a handicap on the importation of alcoholic products from other Member States.'[64]

It is submitted that there is no contradiction here: in the Sacchi and Debauve cases the restriction was more closely connected with services, while in E.C. Commission v. France it was more closely connected with goods.

2.26 In any case, it may be that the distinction between goods and services will not always be of great practical importance: it appears from the Court's judgments in Debauve and in Coditel v. Ciné Vog,[65] and more particularly from Advocate General Warner's joint conclusions in those cases, that the result of applying Article 59 to

[60] See note 10 above.
[61] See note 14 above.
[62] [1970] O.J. L13/29, see paras. 6.03 and 6.28 below.
[63] [1980] E.C.R. 2299, [1981] 2 C.M.L.R. 743.
[64] Para. 11 of the judgment.
[65] Case 62/79, [1980] E.C.R. 881, [1981] 2 C.M.L.R. 362.

23

a given case will often be the same as that of applying Articles 30 to 36. However, as March Hunnings points out,[66] only nationals of Member States can rely on Article 59 *et seq.*, whereas for the application of the Treaty provisions on the free movement of goods the nationality of the owner is irrelevant.[67] Again, where Community legislation is concerned, the difference could be of some consequence: Article 63 (services) only requires a qualified majority in the Council after the first stage of the transitional period, whereas Article 100 (which must be used in the case of goods for want of any more specific provision) requires a unanimous vote.

2.27 In determining the demarcation line between the free movement of goods and the free movement of workers, the same considerations should apply[68]: the test should be whether the goods or the workers aspect is predominant in the transaction concerned.

In practice, conflict between these two sets of provisions will rarely arise. Examples are:

- restrictions on the import or export between Member States of a worker's tools of trade, and
- restrictions on the transfer of an individual's personal effects for the purpose of settling in and taking up employment in another Member State.

2.28 The dividing line between the scope of the provisions on goods and those on capital is particularly difficult to draw. We saw in paragraph 2.06 that one and the same article—gold coins—is variously described as goods and as capital by different Community instruments. As already pointed out, some of the parties intervening before the Court in *Thompson*[69] concluded from this that in determining whether to apply the rules on goods or capital one must look to the purpose of the transfer. The Court held that coins which were a 'means of legal payment' were not 'goods' (though it did not decide whether such coins were capital under Article 67 or current payments under Article 106). It thus did not take into account the purpose for which the coins were transferred, but it did not thereby exclude the relevance of this factor. It is still probable that the same physical objects may be considered as 'goods' when their export is counterbalanced by a transfer of equivalent value to the exporting Member State, and 'capital' when there is no such transfer.[70]

Naturally, this whole question is of less practical importance if 'capital' only covers financial capital movements[71]—and not jewellery, furs or pictures or other objects of value.[72]

---

[66] *Op. cit.*, note 16 above, at 568.
[67] Para. 2.19 above.
[68] The similarity between Arts. 48 (workers) and 59 (services) has been stressed by the Court notably in Case 36/74 *Walrave* v. *Union Cycliste Internationale* [1974] E.C.R. 1405, [1975] 1 C.M.L.R. 320.
[69] See note 17 above.
[70] See Prout, note 17 above.

* Footnotes 71 and 72 are on p. 25.

2.29 Lastly, what of the individual wishing to cross a frontier to visit his relatives, to enjoy the sand and the sun or to attend a political demonstration[73] if he is prevented from bringing his car or his radio with him can he invoke the Treaty provisions on the free movement of goods? If the movement of an individual falls under Article 59 because he will almost inevitably receive a service during his stay,[74] then the problem is merely that already discussed of the interplay between goods and services. On the other hand, if we follow Advocate General Trabucchi[75] and Hartley[76] in saying that the movement of such an individual falls outside the Treaty altogether, then what about his goods? The situation then becomes assimilated to that of the man who sends a present to a friend in another Member State.[77]

One's immediate reaction is to say that if a person cannot enter a Member State, then his goods should not be able to do so either.

2.30 However, the contrary view was put most forcefully by Advocate General Warner in *Henn and Darby*.[78] The case involved the compatibility with Article 30 of the prohibition contained in section 42 of the (British) Customs Consolidation Act 1876 on importing indecent or obscene articles. In its observations before the

---

[71] For this view, see van Ballegooijen, note 18 above; *contra* Everling in Wohlfarth-Everling-Glaesner-Sprung *Die Europäische Wirtschaftsgemeinschaft, Kommentar zum Vertrag* (1960) 203. In Case 65/79 *Chatain* [1980] E.C.R. 1345, [1981] 3 C.M.L.R. 418, the French customs authorities considered that the purchase price paid for pharmaceuticals by the French subsidiary of Sandoz to its parent company in Switzerland had been artificially inflated in order to export capital to Switzerland. However, since this case involved imports from a third country, quite different provisions of Community law were in point so that it provides no assistance here.

[72] One quite different aspect of the relationship between goods and capital deserves a brief mention here. In *Thompson* the Commission claimed that where movements of capital were effected by the transfer of physical assets, such assets did not constitute capital for all purposes; thus they were still subject to customs formalities. The Court did not allude to this important point, but in any case it would appear to have no bearing on the application of Arts. 30 to 36.

[73] See generally Rec. 68/289 ([1968] J.O. L167/16), Reg. 1544/69 ([1969] J.O. L191/1) as amended, Reg. 1818/75 ([1975] O.J. L185/3) as amended; written question 289/79 on identity checks at the Community's internal frontiers ([1980] O.J. C116/1); Commission Proposal of 31 July 1979 for a Council Directive on a right of residence for nationals of Member States in the territory of another Member State ([1979] O.J. C207/14), as amended ([1980] O.J. C292/3).

[74] See Wyatt [1976] E.L.Rev. 558.

[75] Case 118/75 *Watson and Belmann* [1976] E.C.R. 1185 at 1204, [1976] 2 C.M.L.R. 552 at 559. Wyatt, note 74, above. Art. 1 (b) of Dir. 73/148 ([1973] O.J. L172/14) requires Member States to abolish restrictions on the movement and residence of 'nationals of Member States wishing to go to another Member State as recipients of services'. The Advocate General found that the structure of the Treaty and the wording of Art. 59 dictate that one should 'recognise freedom of movement for recipients of services also but only in so far as it appears to be indissolubly linked with the right to movement of those who have to provide those services'.

[76] In *EEC Immigration Law* (1978) 96, suggesting a solution on the same lines as that of Advocate General Trabucchi: 'recipients of services should be regarded as being within the scope of the provisions, but only if they are coming to the country concerned for the specific purpose of receiving the service'.

[77] If the present is a valuable one, then the Treaty provisions on capital might apply: see note 71 above.

[78] Note 53 above.

Court the United Kingdom suggested that Article 30 does not apply to import restrictions in so far as they affect only private individuals. The Advocate General rejected this submission, although the word 'trade' appears in a number of articles in Title I, such as Articles 9 and 36:

> 'No-one . . . would suggest that, because the word "trade" is occasionally used in Articles 12 to 17, relating to the elimination of customs duties between Member States, private individuals moving their possessions from one Member State to another may still be subjected to customs duties, or that, because that word is occasionally used in Articles 18 to 29, relating to the Common Customs Tariff, private individuals who bring their possessions into the Community from outside it are subject, not to the Common Customs Tariff, but to the erstwhile tariffs of Member States. By a parity of reasoning, Article 30, which is the leading Article on the elimination of quantitative restrictions between Member States, and which does not itself use the word "trade", cannot be interpreted as limited to transactions by or between traders'.[79]

Although the Court found that a measure could not constitute arbitrary discrimination within the meaning of Article 36 when there was no lawful trade in the goods at issue within the Member State concerned, that cannot be taken as a ruling on the point under consideration here.

The force of the Advocate General's reasoning—and, in particular, the analogy with the Common Customs Tariff—is considerable. It may well be that the free movement of goods is so central to the structure of the Treaty that all movements of goods between Member States are caught by its provisions except those covered by other parts of the Treaty—such as Articles 59 and 67.[80]

2.31 In conclusion, while the concept of 'goods' is reasonably clear, it is far from certain how the Treaty provisions on the free movement of goods relate to those concerning the other three freedoms enshrined in the Treaty; indeed it is not even certain whether some transfers of goods fall outside the Treaty altogether.

---

[79] At 3827.

[80] Dir. 69/196 ([1969] O.J. Spec.Ed. 232), which covers the harmonisation of exemptions from turnover tax and excise duty on travellers' personal luggage having no commercial character, is of no assistance. It is expressed to be based on the entire Treaty and 'in particular Art. 99 thereof'. This article falls within the Chapter of the Treaty on tax provisions and is not linked to any one of the four freedoms in particular.

CHAPTER III

Scope: Territory

3.01 For those with a taste for the obscure a consideration of the territorial application of the Treaty of Rome may afford a spree of intellectual satisfaction, involving as it does a glance at many a far-flung corner of the globe, both in Europe and beyond. Added to this is the fact that different parts of the Treaty have different territorial application, so that territories such as the Isle of Man are subject to some but not all of the provisions of the Treaty.[1] The question here, then, is to define the area to which Articles 30 to 36 apply, both as regards the benefit they confer and the burden they impose. In other words, what is the area in which the provisions of Articles 30 to 36 must be observed? There is a rebuttable presumption that this coincides with the area from which goods must be taken as originating in the Community to enjoy the benefit of these provisions.

3.02 Before considering this question mention should be made of Part IV of the Treaty entitled 'Association of the Overseas Countries and Territories' and running from Articles 131 to 136. These articles apply to the dependent territories listed in Annex IV to the Treaty as amended,[2] which include such non-European territories as Belize, Brunei, the Falkland Islands, the Netherlands Antilles and the French overseas territories (such as French Polynesia and the Wallis and Futuna Islands).[3] In fact, a number of territories appearing on the list have since attained independence so that Articles 131 to 136 no longer apply to them—even though none of them has been removed from the list. The court ruled to this effect in *Lensing* v. *Hauptzollamt Berlin-Packhof*,[4] which concerned the former French Colony of Guinea. Although Guinea remained on the list of OCTs, it had in fact become independent in 1958. Since it had never concluded any association agreement with the Community, the Court held that imports from Guinea were no longer exempt from

---

[1] For the application of Arts. 48 *et seq*. see Hartley, *EEC Immigration Law* 293(1978).
[2] By Art. 1 of the Convention of 13 November 1962 ([1964] J.O. 2414), which adds the Netherlands Antilles to this list, and Art. 24 (2) of the first Act of Accession.
[3] The Act of Accession added a sub-paragraph to Art. 227 (3), reading 'This Treaty shall not apply to those overseas countries and territories having special relations with the United Kingdom of Great Britain and Northern Ireland which are not included in [Annex IV to this Treaty].' This means that Hong Kong falls wholly outside the application of the Treaty, including Part IV.
[4] Case 147/73 [1973] E.C.R. 1543.

customs duties. At all events, these 'overseas countries and territories' are not in the Community at all, as the opening words of Article 131 show clearly: 'The Member States agree to associate with the Community the non-European countries and territories which . . .' Therefore, in the absence of any reference thereto in Articles 131 to 136, Articles 30 to 36 do not apply to the OCTs.[5]

3.03 Returning to Article 227, the most practical way of examining its effects with respect to Articles 30 to 36 is to consider them country by country. These can be summarised as follows:

(a) Belgium, the Republic of Ireland, Luxembourg and Italy are included in their entirety for all purposes. Since 1 January 1981 the same has applied to Greece by virtue of Article 20 of the Greek Act of Accession.

(b) The Treaty applies to Denmark, excluding the Faroe Islands. By virtue of Article 227 (5) (a) the Danish Government was entitled to make a declaration, at any time up to and including 31 December 1975, to the effect that the Treaty applied to those islands. No such declaration was ever made, so that the Faroes are outside the Community.

On the other hand, the Treaty does apply to Greenland. Annexed to the Act of Accession is a Protocol on Greenland, which contains an exception to the Community rules on establishment, but not to those on the free movement of goods.

(c) The Treaty also applies to the whole of the European territory of France. In addition Article 227 (2) provides that the rules on the free movement of goods apply to the French overseas departments, of which there are now five: Guadeloupe, Martinique, Réunion, French Guyana and, a more recent addition, St. Pierre and Miquelon.[6] These are to be distinguished from the French overseas *territories* which are OCTs.

More puzzlingly, Article 227 (2) still purports to apply certain parts of the Treaty, including that relating to free movement of goods, to Algeria. The reason for this is that, when the Treaty was signed, Algeria was part of French

---

[5] However, special arrangements have been made under Art. 136 in relation to quantitative restrictions and measures of equivalent effect in trade between the Community and the OCTs. These are now contained in Council Dec. 80/1186 ([1980] O.J. L361/1). Under this Decision the Community is bound by broadly similar rules with respect to imports as those set out in Arts. 30 and 36 EEC, except as regards the majority of agricultural products, for which the Community's obligations are less strict. Furthermore, Art. 5 provides that the Decision is not to prejudice the treatment applied by the Community to certain products in implementation of International Commodity Agreements to which the Community is a signatory. On the other hand the 'competent authorities' of an OCT may retain such restrictions as 'they consider necessary, in view of the present development needs' of that OCT (Art. 6); however, these authorities may not discriminate between Member States or apply treatment that is less favourable than the most-favoured-nation treatment—except that they may apply more favourable treatment to other OCTs and developing nations (Art. 8).

[6] See generally Case 148/77 *Hansen* v. *HZA Flensburg* [1978] E.C.R. 1787, [1979] 1 C.M.L.R. 604, where the Court delivered an almost revolutionary judgment on the application of certain other Treaty provisions—in this case Art. 95—to the French overseas departments.

territory. Yet common sense suggests that, that country having become independent on 1 July 1962, it is outside the scope of the Treaty. To this end one might call in aid the court's ruling in *Lensing* v. *HZA Berlin-Packhof*[7] already mentioned.

In any case, because of this peculiarity in Article 227 (2), the régime to be applied to imports from Algeria was unclear, and no agreement of any sort was signed with that country until the early 1970s.[8] Rather surprisingly the Co-operation Agreement between the Community and Algeria signed in April 1976[9] states in Article 56 that:

> 'This Agreement shall apply, on the one hand, to the territories to which the Treaty establishing the European Economic Community applies under the conditions laid down in that Treaty and, on the other, to the territory of the People's Republic of Algeria.'

(d) The Treaty applies to the entire area of the Federal Republic of Germany. By a 'Declaration on the application of the Treaties to Berlin' made at the time of signing the Treaty, the government of that State reserved the right to declare when depositing its instruments of ratification, that the Treaty of Rome applied to the Land Berlin (West Berlin). Such a declaration was in fact made so that the Treaty applies to West Berlin. Although inter-German trade is the subject of the special Protocol discussed in the previous chapter[10] the German Democratic Republic is nevertheless outside the scope of the Treaty.

(e) According to Dutch constitutional law the Kingdom of the Netherlands extends beyond the European territory of the Netherlands to cover the overseas territories. Although Article 227 (1) states without more that the Treaty applies to the Kingdom of the Netherlands, this is qualified by a special Protocol signed on the same day as the Treaty of Rome.[11] This Protocol entitled the Dutch Government, 'by way of derogation from Article 227', to ratify the Treaty on behalf of the Kingdom in Europe and Netherlands New Guinea. In fact, only the European part of the Kingdom became part of the Community and Netherlands New Guinea became an OCT

---

[7] See note 4 above.

[8] This curious question is examined in depth by Tavernier 'Aspects juridiques des relations économiques entre la CEE et L'Algérie' [1972] R.T.D.E. 1. See also Waelbroeck in *Le droit de la CEE*, (1970) Vol. 1, 146.

[9] [1978] O.J. L263/2.

[10] See para. 2.15 above. The Court has held that 'the dispensation thus granted does not have the result of making the German Democratic Republic part of the Community, but only that a special system applies to it as a territory which is not part of the Community': Case 14/74 *Norddeutsches Vieh- und Fleischkontor* v. *Hauptzollamt Hamburg-Jonas* [1974] E.C.R. 899.

[11] Protocol on the application of the Treaty establishing the EEC to the non-European parts of the Kingdom of the Netherlands.

subject to Part IV of the Treaty. Subsequently the Netherlands Antilles and Surinam also became OCTs.[12]

(f) In addition to Great Britain and Northern Ireland the Treaty also applies to various dependent territories of the United Kingdom. Article 227 (4) states that 'the provisions of this Treaty shall apply to the European territories for whose external relations a Member State is responsible'. This covers Gibraltar. The only exception provided for in the Treaties with respect to this territory is to be found in Article 28 of the Act of Accession, which states that:

> 'Acts of the institutions of the Community relating to the products in Annex II to the EEC Treaty and the products subject, on importation into the Community, to specific rules as a result of the implementation of the common agricultural policy, as well as the acts on the harmonisation of legislation of Member States concerning turnover taxes shall not apply to Gibraltar unless the Council, acting unanimously on a proposal from the Commission, provides otherwise.'

This would not appear to refer to the Articles of the Treaty, but only to the 'acts of the institutions of the Community'.[13] On this interpretation, Articles 30 to 36 would apply to Gibraltar, even as regards agricultural products. Yet it may be that these provisions do not apply to Gibraltar by virtue of Regulation 1496/68 discussed at the end of this chapter.

Furthermore, Article 227 (5) (c) provides that notwithstanding anything in paragraphs 1 to 4 of that Article 'This Treaty shall apply to the Channel Islands and the Isle of Man only to the extent necessary to ensure the implementation of the arrangements for those islands' set out in the Act of Accession. The Channel Islands and the Isle of Man are the subject of a special Protocol to the Act of Accession. Article 1 (1) of that Protocol begins: 'The Community rules on customs matters and quantitative restrictions, in particular those of the Act of Accession, shall apply to the Channel Islands and the Isle of Man under the same conditions as they apply to the United Kingdom.' Article 1 (2) in effect states that the same rules apply to agricultural products. Although only quantitative restrictions and not measures of equivalent effect are expressly mentioned in this provision, it is probable that this wording is sufficient to cover both types of measure.[14] This latter view is borne out by the Commission's answer to a recent written

---

[12] With respect to the Netherlands Antilles see note 2 above. On 14 August 1962 the Netherlands extended ratification to Surinam which became an OCT although it was never formally included in Annex IV. However, Surinam has since become an independent State and is therefore no longer an OCT. The same applies to Netherlands New Guinea, which has become part of Indonesia.

[13] See, however, Puissochet, *L'élargissement des Communautés européennes* (1974), 242, *The Enlargement of the European Community* (1975).

[14] Ehlerman in Groeben, Boeckh, Thiesing, *Kommentar zum EWG-Vertrag* (1974) Vol. I, 276. See para 5.09 below.

question in which it declared that 'In accordance with Protocol 3 of the Accession Treaty, the Community rules allowing free movement of goods apply in trade between the Isle of Man and other Member States.' In view of the subject-matter of the question the Commission's statement appears to embrace measures of equivalent effect as well as quantitative restrictions.[15]

On the other hand, the Treaty does not apply to the Sovereign Base Areas of the United Kingdom in Cyprus: Article 227 (5) (b).

(g) As already pointed out, Article 227 (4) lays down that: 'The provisions of this Treaty shall apply to the European territories for whose external relations a Member State is responsible.' It is unclear whether Monaco and San Marino fall within this provision.[16] In answer to a recent written question,[17] the Commission stated that as Monaco had not signed the Treaty of Rome, it did not form part of the EEC; it went on to state however, that the provisions on the free movement of goods in the Community apply to goods originating in Monaco, by virtue of Regulation 1496/68, discussed below. At all events, it seems clear that Article 227 (4) does not cover Andorra, because it is controlled jointly by the President of France and by the Bishop of Urgel in Spain.

3.04 What of the sea and the sea-bed?[18] Article 227 declares the Treaty to be applicable to the Member States without referring to their respective territories,[19] although the concept of territory does appear in Articles 48 to 52 covering the free movement of workers and the right of establishment respectively. Article 84 (2) provides that: 'The Council may, acting unanimously, decide whether, to what extent and by what procedure appropriate provisions may be laid down for sea and air transport.' The Court has held[20] that this provision refers only to the special provisions of the Title relating to transport, so that the 'general rules of the Treaty' such as Articles 48 to 51 apply to sea transport even in the absence of a specific decision by the Council.

---

[15] Written question 409/80 ([1980] O.J. C217). On the Channel Islands and the Isle of Man, see generally Simmonds 'The British Islands and the Community' [1968–9] C.M.L.Rev. 153 and [1970] C.M.L.Rev. 454. On Protocol 3 and the Isle of Man, see Case 32/79 *E.C.Commission* v. *United Kingdom* [1980] E.C.R. 2403, [1981] 1 C.M.L.R. 219 concerning fisheries, where, however, the Court avoided the issue.

[16] See Bathurst in *Legal Problems of an Enlarged European Community* (1972) 162; Smit and Herzog, *Law of the European Economic Community* para 6-210; Campbell, *Common Market Law* Vol. III, para. 8-5; Thiesing in Groeben, Boeckh, Thiesing, *op. cit.* note 14 above, Vol. 2, 691

[17] Written question 1215/80 ([1980] O.J.C335/10).

[18] See generally the Draft Regulation in [1980] O.J. C305/4, see note 26 below.

[19] Brouir, 'Le réglement du Conseil de la CEE de 1970 sur les pêcheries' [1973] C.D.E. 20; Koers 'The external authority of the EEC in regard to marine fisheries' [1977] C.M.L.Rev. 269.

[20] Case 167/73 *E.C. Commission* v. *France* [1974] E.C.R. 359, [1974] 2 C.M.L.R. 216.

Although the Treaty contains no provision dealing specifically with maritime fishing, its provisions on agriculture (Articles 39 to 46) provide an appropriate basis for a common fisheries policy and accordingly legislation on maritime fishing has been passed on the basis of those provisions.[21] Furthermore Articles 100 to 103 of the first Act of Accession are devoted to this matter. The Court has also had occasion to consider it in a series of cases brought before it.[22] In the present context the first of these cases, *Kramer,* is the most important because one of the questions put to the Court was whether fishing quotas not fixed under Community auspices infringed Article 30. The Court found that such quotas were compatible with Article 30 on the grounds that, although restricting 'production' in the short term, they ensured supplies in the long term.[23] In so doing the Court made no allusion to the geographical scope of Article 30, but there can be no doubt from the judgment that it applies to the resources of the sea: in answer to another question the Court held that the Community has power to 'take any measures for the conservation of the biological resources of the sea', even as regards the high seas.

It appears that Articles 30 to 36 apply to fish and other products caught on the high seas by a vessel lawfully flying the flag of a Member State as is shown by Regulation 802/68[24] defining the concept of origin of goods. By virtue of Article 4 (2) (f) thereof 'products of sea-fishing and other products taken from the sea by vessels registered or recorded in [a] country and flying its flag' are taken to originate in that country.

Moreover, it is submitted that Articles 30 to 36 also apply to resources extracted from that part of the sea-bed over which Member States exercise sovereign rights[25]—a matter of considerable practical importance, not least for the British economy.

3.05 Finally, mention should be made of Regulation 1496/68 on the definition of the customs territory of the Community.[26] This Regulation, which is based on Article 235 and which defined the

---

[21] See in particular Regs. 100/76 and 101/76 ([1976] O.J. L20/1 and 19).

[22] In particular, Cases 3, 4 and 6/76 *Kramer* [1976] E.C.R. 1279, [1976] 2 C.M.L.R. 440, noted by Wyatt [1977] E.L.Rev. 41; Case 61/77 *E.C. Commission* v. *Ireland* [1978] E.C.R. 937, [1978] 2 C.M.L.R. 466; Case 88/77 *Minister for Fisheries* v. *Schonenberg* [1978] E.C.R. 473, [1978] 2 C.M.L.R. 519; Cases 185–204/78 *van Dam* [1979] E.C.R. 2345, [1980] 1 C.M.L.R. 350; Case 141/78 *France* v. *U.K.* [1979] E.C.R. 2923, [1980] 1 C.M.L.R. 6.

[23] See para. 7.63 below.

[24] [1968] J.O. L148/1, see para. 2.10.

[25] See the Commission memorandum of 18 September 1970 SEC(70) 3095 Final, reprinted in CCH CMR, para. 9625. In case 8/79 *Filby* v. *Insurance Officer* the National Insurance Commissioner referred a number of questions requiring the Court to rule on the application of the Community legislation on social security for migrant workers to the continental shelf. However, the British Government amended its legislation and the case was struck out.

[26] [1968] J.O. L238/1; on this Regulation as it applied to the Six see Daillier 'Les frontières douanières de la CEE' *Annuaire Français de Droit International* [1968] 789; Vaulont, 'Das Zollgebiet der Gemeinschaft' *Zeitschrift für Zölle* (1971) 105. See also the draft Regulation intended to replace it, note 18 above.

customs territory of the Community as orginally constituted, was amended by Annex I to the first Act of Accesssion and by Annex I of the Act of Accession of Greece. The customs territory so described varies from the territory set out in paragraph 3.03 above in the following respects:

— the Austrian territories of Jungholz and Mittelberg are included, although they are clearly not in the Community;

— Monaco and San Marino are also included although they are probably not in the Community;

— certain German and Italian territories such as Heligoland and the commune of Livigno are excluded although they are clearly in the Community; the situation of Gibraltar is anomalous since it is neither expressly included nor expressly excluded.[27]

Most of these exceptions are based on treaties between the Member State in question and a third state. The purposes for which this definition is to apply are not set out in the Articles of the Regulation. It is clear that it relates to the common customs tariff and also to such technical customs matters as the determination of the value of goods for customs purposes[28]: such value is to be determined at the moment when the goods are introduced into the customs territory of the Community. The Commission has now stated in answer to a written question[29] that by virtue of the Regulation goods originating in Monaco are subject to the Treaty provisions on the free movement of goods within the Community. The same will presumably apply to San Marino.

On the other hand, the position of goods originating in third countries is different: these will not be in free circulation within the meaning of Articles 9 and 10 EEC unless they have undergone the appropriate customs formalities.[30] This can presumably not occur if the goods remain outside the customs territory as defined by Regulation 1496/68 as amended. It may be, therefore, that to this extent Articles 30 to 36 do not apply to Gibraltar or the territories expressly excluded from the Community customs territory by Regulation 1496/68.[31]

---

[27] For the purposes of Reg. 926/79 on common rules for imports from third countries, Gibraltar is 'in the same position as' the third countries and territories whose exports were liberalised by that Regulation ([1979] O.J. L131/15 at 407). See, however, note 58 to Chapter IX.

[28] See Reg. 803/68 ([1968] J.O. L148/6) replaced by Reg. 1224/80 ([1980] O.J. L134/1).

[29] See note 17 above.

[30] See para. 2.11.

[31] Dir. 69/73 ([1970] O.J. Spec.Ed. L58/11) on free zones, amended by the two Acts of Accession and by Dir. 76/634 ([1976] O.J. L223/17) does not alter the customs territory of the Community, although goods from third countries may enter such free zones without being subject to Community customs duties or taxes of equivalent effect, quantitative restrictions or measures of equivalent effect (Dir. Art. 1 (2)). The directive lays down the operations which may be carried out in such free zones.

CHAPTER IV

Scope: Persons bound

4.01 The question to be examined in this chapter is what persons or bodies are bound by Articles 30 to 36. This question arises with respect to the Member States, the Community institutions and, finally, private parties (individuals or non-State bodies). Each of these will be examined in turn. Since Articles 30 to 36 must in this respect be construed in the same way as Articles 12 to 17 prohibiting customs duties and taxes of equivalent effect, some of the cases discussed in this chapter relate to the latter set of provisions.

I. MEMBER STATES

4.02 The very terms of these articles show beyond doubt that they cover State measures. Thus the first paragraph of Article 31 reads: 'Member States shall refrain from introducing between themselves any new quantitative restrictions or measures having equivalent effect'. Similarly the first paragraph of Article 32 stipulates that 'in their trade with one another Member States shall refrain from making more restrictive the quotas and measures having equivalent effect existing at the date of entry into force of this Treaty'. Further clear references to the fact that State measures are concerned are to be found in Articles 33, 34 and 35.

4.03 What is meant by the 'State' in this context? This concept is to be interpreted widely to cover the public authorities of a Member State in general.[1] This embraces not only central government but also regional and local government[2]: it is irrelevant to the Community whether discrimination against a product from another Member State emanates from the federal, the provincial or the parish authorities, so long as that discrimination exists.[3] Thus the Commission has brought proceedings against Belgium with respect to a measure adopted by the city of Liège under which that city granted preferential treatment for material manufactured in Belgium.[4]

---

[1] Béraud 'Les mesures d'effet équivalent au sens des articles 30 et suivants du Traité de Rome' [1968] R.T.D.E. 265 at 278.

[2] Graff, *Der Begriff, 'Massnahmen gleicher Wirkung wie mengenmässige Einfuhrbeschränkungen in dem EWG-Vertrag'* (1972) 125 *et seq.*

[3] Dir. 70/32 of the Commission ([1970] J.O. L13/1) describes as measures of equivalent effect provisions which discriminate against the purchase of imported goods by the State or local authorities. However, it does not state expressly whether it covers *measures emanating* from local authorities.

[4] E.C.Bull. 1–1978, point 3.31.

34

4.04 Likewise, Articles 30 to 36 apply not only to measures of the executive, but also of the legislature or of the judiciary. This has now been made clear by the Court in *Dansk Supermarked* v. *Imerco*[5] where it held that:

> 'Articles 30 and 36 of EEC Treaty must be interpreted to mean that the judicial authorities of a Member State may not prohibit, on the basis of a copyright or of a trade mark, the marketing on the territory of that State of a product to which one of those rights applies . . . .'

In addition, it is generally accepted [6] that an action can be brought under Article 169 against a Member State with respect to judicial acts. However, this is not to say that a single decision by a national court will necessarily render a Member State liable to a declaration under Article 169.

In this connection the following statement by Advocate General Warner in *R.* v. *Bouchereau* deserves mention:

> 'It is obvious . . . that a Member State cannot be held to have failed to fulfil an obligation under the Treaty simply because one of its courts has reached a wrong decision. Judicial error, whether due to the misapprehension of facts or to misapprehension of the law, is not a breach of the Treaty. In the judicial sphere, Article 169 could only come into play in the event of a court of a Member State deliberately ignoring or disregarding Community law'.[7]

4.05 When the power to pass binding acts of a legislative or administrative nature is delegated by the public authorities to a non-government body such as a trade organisation, those acts are attributable to the State for the purposes of Articles 30 to 36.[8] In addition there exists in the Community a myriad of different types of public undertakings, semi-public bodies and 'quangos' (quasi-autonomous national governmental organisations), fulfilling a host of different functions and roles, ranging from the social and cultural to the commercial and industrial. Little clear indication exists as to which acts of such bodies are to be attributed to the State for the present purposes. What is more, an already confused picture is complicated by the existence of Article 37, which relates specifically to State monopolies of a commercial character and which is the

---

[5] Case 58/80 [1981] E.C.R. 181, [1981] 3 C.M.L.R. 590.
[6] Written question 100/67 ([1967] J.O. 270/3); written question 349/69 ([1970] J.O. C20/3). In Cases 77/69 *E.C. Commission* v. *Belgium* [1970] E.C.R. 237 and 8/70 *E.C. Commission* v. *Italy* [1970] E.C.R 961 the Court held that: 'The obligations arising from the Treaty devolve upon States as such and the liability of a Member State under Art. 169 arises whatever the agency of the State whose action or inaction is the cause of the failure to fulfil its obligations, even in the case of a constitutionally independent institution'.
[7] Case 30/77 [1977] E.C.R. 1999 at 2020, [1977] 2 C.M.L.R. 800 at 810.
[8] See Béraud note 1 above; see also Case 190/73 *Van Haaster* [1974] E.C.R. 1123, [1974] 2 C.M.L.R. 521, where the defendant in the main case was charged before the Dutch courts with infringing a provision of a binding regulation adopted by the Produktschap voor Siergewassen, an organisation of producers of ornamental plants; the Court held this provision to be a measure of equivalent effect to a quantitative restriction. However, the court did not refer expressly to the question in point here. Also, after its adoption by the Produktschap, the regulation received the approval of the Minister of Agriculture. A similar ruling with respect to a levy imposed by the same body was delivered in Case 51/74 *Van der Hulst's Sonen* v. *Produktschap voor Siergewassen* [1975] E.C.R. 79, [1975] 1 C.M.L.R. 236.

subject of Chapter XI of this book, of Article 90 on public undertakings and other undertakings on which the Member States confer special rights,[9] and of Article 222.[10] None of these provisions is particularly straightforward. Accordingly it is not possible to do more than very tentatively suggest that the following test should be applied to determine whether a particular act of such a body is to be regarded as a State measure: is this body with respect to this act exercising public authority flowing from the State? It must be emphasised that this is only a very tentative suggestion, which will not necessarily be applicable or sufficient in all cases.

4.06 Finally, if a restriction on trade between Member States is provided for by a State measure, it is of no consequence that an individual or other private party must apply to the authorities to obtain the benefit of that restriction.[11] This is because the measure still flows from the State.

It will be clear from the above that State measures do not necessarily have to be binding to fall foul of Articles 30 to 36. This point is discussed at greater length at paragraph 6.07 below.

II. THE COMMUNITY INSTITUTIONS[12]

4.07 Can Community legislation validly prohibit or restrict trade between Member States? Alternatively, can such legislation authorise Member States to take such action?

The concept of harmonisation of national rules by the Community (whether under Article 100 or any other Article of the Treaty such as Article 43 on the common agricultural policy) presupposes the power to adopt standards with which products from all the Member States must comply. This will involve the submission of certain

---

[9] Art. 90, which falls outside the purview of this book, reads as follows:

'1. In the case of public undertakings and undertakings to which Member States grant special or exclusive rights, Member States shall neither enact nor maintain in force any measure contrary to the rules contained in this Treaty, in particular to those rules provided for in Article 7 and Articles 85 to 94.

2. Undertakings entrusted with the operation of services of general economic interest or having the character of a revenue-producing monopoly shall be subject to the rules contained in this Treaty, in particular to the rules on competition, in so far as the application of such rules does not obstruct the performance, in law or in fact, of the particular tasks assigned to them. The development of trade must not be affected to such an extent as would be contrary to the interests of the Community.

3. The Commission shall ensure the application of the provisions of this Article and shall, where necessary, address appropriate directives or decisions to Member States'.

See also Chap. XI, note 45.

[10] See para. 9.45 below.

[11] Matthies 'Herkunftsangaben und Europäisches Gemeinschaftsrecht' *Festschrift für Schiedermair* (1976) 395.

[12] See Mertens de Wilmars, 'De heffingen van gelijke werking als de douanerechten' in *Liber Amicorum J. Van Houtte* at 697; Matthies 'Die Verfassung des Gemeinsamen Marktes' in *Das Europa der Zweiten Generation, Gedächtnisschrift* (1981), Vol. I, 115; Oliver, 'La législation communautaire et sa conformité avec la libre circulation des marchandises' [1979] C.D.E. 245.

goods to particular conditions, such as labelling or packaging requirements, and will sometimes entail the complete prohibition of goods
falling within certain categories. While a standard laid down in some
but not all Member States may restrict interstate trade, it will cease
to do so once it is introduced throughout the Community: all
Member States will then apply the same standard so that goods from
one Member State can be imported and sold in all the others. In
such a case no problem arises as to the compatibility of the
Community legislation with the Treaty provisions on the free
movement of goods.

Nevertheless it may happen that the Community institutions
decide to subject movements of certain goods between Member
States to certain taxes or procedures or even to prohibit them
altogether.

4.08 The starting point for the consideration of this type of case
must be the court's statement in *Ramel* v. *Receveur des Douanes*[13]
to the effect that:

'the extensive powers, in particular of a sectoral or regional nature, granted to
the Community institutions in the conduct of the Common Agricultural Policy
must, in any event as from the end of the transitional period, be exercised from
the perspective of the unity of the market to the exclusion of any measure
comprising the abolition between Member States of customs duties and.
quantitative restrictions or charges or measures having equivalent effect.'

The case had arisen out of the 'wine war' between France and
Italy, which flared up at the end of 1975. Article 31 (1) of Regulation
816/70[14] laying down additional provisions for the common market
organisation in wine prohibited charges of equivalent effect to
customs duties in the internal trade of the Community, subject to
one exception not material here. However, Article 31 (2) stated that

'by way of derogation from the provisions of paragraph 1, so long as all the
administrative mechanisms necessary for the management of the market in wine
are not in application. . . producer Member States shall be authorised in order
to avoid disturbances on their markets to take measures that may limit imports
from another Member State.'

In 1975 there was an exceptional influx of Italian wine into the
French market owing to a particularly good harvest as well as to
successive devaluations of the lira. With a view to limiting that influx
the French Government levied a charge on certain Italian wines in
September of that year. The Commission brought an action under
Article 169 against France for failure to comply with its Treaty
obligations, but discontinued it when the French measure was
repealed with effect from 1 April 1976.

However, the plaintiffs in the main proceedings had been required
to pay the charges at issue on various consignments of wine from
Italy and now sought to recover those sums in actions against the

[13] Cases 80–81/77 [1978] E.C.R. 927.
[14] [1970] O.J.Spec.Ed. (I) 234.

French customs authorities. The Tribunal d'Instance of Bourg-en-Bresse, before which these actions were brought, accordingly asked the Court of Justice whether Article 31 (2) of the Regulation was compatible with the Treaty and, if so, whether it continued to be applicable.

The Court began by considering Article 38 (2) of the Treaty, which reads:

> 'Save as otherwise provided in Articles 39 to 46, the rules laid down for the establishment of the common market shall apply to agricultural products'.

The court found nothing in Articles 39 to 46—the provisions of the Treaty dealing with agriculture—which either expressly or by necessary implication provided for or authorised the introduction of charges of equivalent effect to customs duties in intra-Community trade at the end of the transitional period.[15]

After making the statement already quoted, the Court therefore concluded that

> 'Article 31 (2) of Regulation 816/70 in so far as it authorises producer Member States to prescribe and levy, in intra-Community trade in the products covered by the organisation of the market which that regulation sets up, charges having an effect equivalent to customs duties, is incompatible with Article 13, in particular paragraph (2) thereof, and with Articles 38 to 46 of the Treaty and is consequently invalid.'

4.09 The case concerned taxes but it is expressly stated in the passage first quoted here that the same result will apply to quantitative restrictions and measures of equivalent effect. Indeed, this is also clear from a *dictum* in *Rivoira*.[16] There the court was called upon to interpret Regulation 2513/69 [17] on the co-ordination and standardisation of the treatment accorded by each Member State to imports of fruits and vegetables from non-member countries, and Regulation 1524/70[18] implementing the Agreement between Spain and the EEC of 1970. It held that the power conferred by those Regulations on Member States to impose quantitative restrictions on Spanish grapes over a certain period was limited to direct imports from third countries, on a proper reading of Article 1 of Regulation 2513/69. It added that:

> 'the said Article 1 could not have covered the application by a Member State of restrictions on the importation of products in free circulation within the Community from other Member States, because such an ambit would have constituted a derogation from the fundamental rules of the Treaty on the free movement of goods'.[19]

---

[15] A similar approach to the interpretation of Art. 38 (2) had been used by the Court in Cases 90–91/63 *E.C. Commission* v. *Belgium and Luxembourg* [1964] E.C.R. 625, [1965] C.M.L.R. 58 and Case 48/74 *Charmasson* v. *Minister of Economic Affairs* [1974] E.C.R. 1383, [1975] 2 C.M.L.R. 208 discussed at para. 10.02 below.

[16] Case 179/78 [1979] E.C.R. 1147, [1979] 3 C.M.L.R. 456.

[17] [1970] J.O. L318/6.

[18] O.J.Spec.Ed. Second Series I External Relations (1), 269.

[19] See also the Advocate General in Case 34/78 *Yoshida* v. *Kamer van Koophandel* [1979] E.C.R. 115 at 147, [1979] 2 C.M.L.R. 747 at 752.

4.10 It is established, then, that the Community institutions must have regard to the principle of the free movement of goods in framing their legislation. However, two judgments of the Court indicate that in this matter the Community institutions enjoy a greater measure of freedom than the Member States.

The first of these, *REWE-Zentral* v. *HZA Kehl*,[20] was one of a series of three cases[21] decided on the same day, all of which concerned the validity of Regulation 974/71[22] establishing the system of monetary compensatory amounts.[23] Of these only the *REWE* case concerned interstate trade and thus raised the question of the compatibilty of these levies with Articles 9, 12 and 13 of the Treaty prohibiting charges of equivalent effect to customs duties. In answer to a question raised by a national court under Article 177, the Court ruled that:

'Although the compensatory amounts do constitute a partitioning of the market, here they have a corrective influence on the variations in fluctuating exchange rates which, in a system of market organisation for agricultural products based on uniform prices, might cause disturbances in trade in these products.

Diversion of trade caused solely by the monetary situation can be considered more damaging to the common interest, bearing in mind the aims of the common agricultural policy, than the disadvantages for the measures in dispute.

Consequently these compensatory amounts are conducive to the maintenance of a normal flow of trade under the exceptional circumstances created temporarily by the monetary situation.

They are also intended to prevent the disruption in the Member State concerned of the intervention system set up under Community regulations.

Furthermore, these are not levies introduced by some Member States unilaterally, but Community measures which, bearing in mind the exceptional circumstances of the time, are permissible within the framework of the common agricultural policy.

Thus, the Council, by adopting them, did not contravene the provisions referred to by the national court'.

4.11 In the second case, *Bauhuis* v. *Netherlands*,[24] the Court was confronted with a rather different type of tax, although it was also confined to agricultural products. In accordance with the provisions of the Dutch law relating to livestock, the plaintiff in the main action was required to pay fees for public health inspection, *inter alia*, on export of pigs, 'bovine animals' and horses. Directive 64/432[25] required the exporting Member State to carry out certain veterinary and public health inspections of pigs and 'bovine animals', without stating whether a charge might be levied for such inspections. The

---

[20] Case 10/73 [1973] E.C.R. 1175.
[21] The other two cases were Cases 5/73 *Balkan-Import-Export* v. *HZA Berlin-Packhof* [1973] E.C.R. 1091 and Case 9/73 *Carl Schlüter* v. *HZA Lörrach* [1973] E.C.R. 1135.
[22] [1971] O.J. L106/1.
[23] This is the mechanism informally known as 'green currencies'. See Gilsdorf 'The system of Monetary Compensation from a Legal Standpoint' [1980] E.L.Rev. 341 and 433.
[24] Case 46/76 [1977] E.C.R. 1.
[25] [1964] O.J.Spec.Ed. 164.

object of the Directive was to shift supervision to the exporting Member State so as to avoid the need for multiple inspections at subsequent frontiers, and thereby to facilitate intra-Community trade. The Directive does not apply to horses.

In an action before it in which the plaintiff contested the compatibilty of these charges with Community law, the Arrondissementsrechtbank of The Hague asked the Court of Justice to decide whether charges of this kind constituted charges of equivalent effect to customs duties on exports contrary to Article 16 of the Treaty.

The Court had already held[26] that, even when an inspection is justified under Article 36 on human or animal health grounds, any sum charged for that inspection constitutes a prohibited charge of equivalent effect to a customs duty if it is levied according to criteria not comparable with those employed in fixing charges on similar domestic products. Consequently, in *Bauhuis* the Court held that the charges for the inspection of horses were contrary to Article 16, such inspections not being provided for by Community legislation.

Yet the Court adopted a radically different approach to the other charges, since they related to inspections which:

> 'are not[27] laid down unilaterally by each Member State but have been made obligatory and uniform in the case of all the products in question whichever the exporting Member State or the Member State of destination may be.
>
> On the other hand they are not prescribed by each Member State in order to protect some interest of its own but by the Council in the general interest of the Community'.
>
> They cannot therefore be regarded as unilateral measures which hinder trade but rather as operations intended to promote the free movement of goods, in particular by rendering ineffective the obstacles to this free movement which might be created by the measures for veterinary and public health inspections adopted pursuant to Article 36.
>
> In these circumstances fees charged for veterinary and public health inspections, which are prescribed by a Community provision, which are uniform and are required to be carried out before despatch within the exporting country do not constitute charges having an effect equivalent to customs duties on exports, provided that they do not exceed the actual cost of the inspection for which they are charged.[28]

4.12   One may tentatively deduce from these cases that Community legislation restricting trade between Member States is lawful if it satisfies the following cumulative conditions:

---

[26] Case 29/72 *Marimex* v. *Italian Finance Administration* [1972] E.C.R. 1309, [1973] C.M.L.R. 486.

[27] Unfortunately the word 'not' appears to be missing in the English text, but the other language versions indicate that it should be there.

[28] For criticisms of this ruling see Barents 'Charges of Equivalent Effect to Customs Duties' [1978] C.M.L.Rev. 415 and Kohler, *Abgaben zollgleicher Wirkung im Recht der Europäischen Gemeinschaften* (1978).

It should also be pointed out that in Case 89/76 *E.C. Commission* v. *Netherlands* [1977] E.C.R. 1355, [1978] 3 C.M.L.R. 630 the Court reached a similar conclusion with respect to fees charged for the phytosanitary inspection of plant exports provided for not by Community legislation, but by an international convention to which all the Member States were party.

(i) It must be uniform throughout the Member States. This must, however, be subject to the rule that objectively different situations require different treatment.[29] Otherwise the validity of the Community's regional policy would be in serious doubt.

(ii) It must be adopted 'in the general interest of the Community'. It is not clear quite what is meant by this, but in *REWE-Zentral* v. *Bundesmonopolverwaltung für Branntwein*[30] (the 'Cassis de Dijon' case), discussed at length in Chapter VI of this book, the Court found that national measures constituting obstacles to interstate trade must be accepted in so far as those provisions may be recognised as being necessary in order to satisfy mandatory requirements relating in particular to the effectiveness of fiscal supervision, the protection of public health, the fairness of commercial transactions and the defence of the consumer. The concept of general interest for the purposes of Community legislation must be at least as wide as that obtaining for national measures. At all events, the provisions of Articles 2 and 3 of the Treaty will serve as a general guide to the concept of general interest for these purposes.

(iii) It must be 'intended to promote the free movement of goods' although in itself it is restrictive of trade between Member States. This requirement may in fact merge with (ii) above. In many cases, it is something of a misnomer to describe such measures as restrictive of interstate trade, because they are in fact less restrictive than the measures which would be necessary in their absence. Such is the case, for example, with the public health inspections at issue in *Bauhuis*: in the absence of the export inspections laid down by the Directive, the Member States would in practice have been obliged to carry out checks on imports, which would be justified under Article 36 of the Treaty but which would constitute a greater restriction on trade.

Although the case law does not provide for it, it may be that the following additional condition must be met:

(iv) The restrictive effects of the Community measure must not be greater than is necessary to attain the legitimate end in view. The Court has held in other contexts that, since the principle of the free movement of goods is a fundamental principle of the Treaty, exceptions to it may only be allowed in so far as they are necessary.[31]

4.13 It is probable, though, that the burden of proof is different in the case of Community legislation than in the case of national measures. While there is a presumption that national measures

---

[29] Case 13/63 *E.C. Commission* v. *Italy* [1963] E.C.R. 165, [1963] C.M.L.R. 289.
[30] Case 120/78 [1979] E.C.R. 649, [1979] 3 C.M.L.R. 494.
[31] With respect to Art. 36, see Case 104/75 *de Peijper* [1976] E.C.R. 613, [1976] 2 C.M.L.R. 271 discussed at para. 8.10 below; see also para. 9.01 below.

creating restrictions on interstate trade are unjustified,[32] the opposite should apply to Community legislation. Indeed as already pointed out, an apparent obstacle to interstate trade contained in Community legislation will often turn out not to be an obstacle at all by comparison with the situation which would have existed in its absence.

4.14 In any case, it can be concluded that the Community institutions are bound to have regard in adopting legislation to the principle of the free movement of goods. Having established this, the question arises whether these institutions are bound by Articles 9 to 17 and 30 to 36 EEC themselves or rather by rules which are analogous to them. No clear indication can be found in the Treaty itself. Although in some instances it states simply that the restrictions in question are prohibited 'between Member States' (as in Articles 9 (1), 30 and 34 (1)), in others the obligations in point are expressed to be addressed to the Member States (as in Article 31, which states that 'Member States shall refrain from introducing . . .'). Little if any conclusion can be drawn from the existence of these two forms of words.

In *Ramel*[33] it was held that the Community provision concerned was contrary to Article 13 itself, but according to Matthies[34] this was merely because the provision did not itself impose an import duty but merely permitted the Member States to do so. He firmly takes the view that the Community legislator is bound by the *principle* of the free movement of goods, and not by Articles 9 to 17 or 30 to 36 as such. In his view, the free movement of goods is a fundamental principle of Community law to be observed by the Community institutions in the performance of their tasks much in the same way as the principles of non-discrimination and of proportionality.

4.15 Whatever attitude one adopts to this particular problem, it seems clear that the Court has plotted a middle course: while setting bounds to the freedom enjoyed by the Community institutions in this regard, it has ensured that this freedom is greater than that permitted to the Member States in view of the special tasks which the Community is called upon to perform. In addition, the Community institutions possess special powers under exception or escape clauses such as Articles 103, 108 and 115 of the EEC. These are discussed in Chapter IX below.

III. PRIVATE PARTIES

4.16 There remains the difficult question as to whether private parties—individuals and non-State bodies—are bound by the pro-

---

[32] See para. 8.03 below.
[33] See note 13 above.
[34] See note 12 above.

visions of Articles 30 to 36.[35] Frequently, restrictions on interstate ✕
trade resulting from the action of private parties will fall under
Articles 85 and 86 of the Treaty relating to competition. But these ✕
provisions only apply in the case of agreements between undertakings
(Article 85) or action taken by one undertaking acting alone where
that undertaking has a dominant position (Article 86). Other restrictions on imports and exports due to the actions of private parties fall
outside Articles 85 and 86. Let us take two examples:

- an insurance company without any dominant position refuses
  to insure imported cars, without being party to any agreement
  to that effect;
- a dockers' union takes industrial action with the specific aim of
  preventing imports (it is generally considered that trade unions
  fall outside the scope of the concept of 'undertakings' in Articles
  85 and 86).

In each case it will be assumed that no Member State has in any way
supported the action in question.[36]

4.17 Clearly such behaviour is contrary to the spirit of the Treaty
but is it unlawful? Put in more technical terms, do Articles 30 and
34 have 'horizontal effect'? Perhaps surprisingly, the Court has not
yet been called upon to decide the point. On the other hand, in
Written Question 909/79 the Commission was asked whether industrial action which prevents goods from crossing national frontiers
was contrary to the letter of the Treaty. The Commission replied[37]
in the following somewhat non-committal terms:

'. . . the Commission agrees that, although the type of action described by the
Honourable Member does not contravene Article 30 of the EEC Treaty, it
could under certain circumstances disrupt trade within the Community'.

4.18 Proponents of the view that such action is contrary to Article
30 would rely on the following arguments:
First, they would rely on the Court's case law[38] stating that the
exercise of industrial property rights to exclude imports from other
Member States can in certain circumstances be contrary to Article
30. They would rely in particular on certain passages in these
judgments suggesting that such exercise is to be regarded as the act
of the private party concerned. An example is the following passage
in *Deutsche Grammophon* v. *Metro*[39]:

'. . . the essential purpose of the Treaty, which is to unite national markets
into a single market . . . could not be attained if, under the various legal

---

[35] See van Gerven 'The Recent Case Law of the Court of Justice concerning Arts. 30 and
36 of the EEC Treaty' [1977] C.M.L.Rev. 5; Matthies, *op. cit.* note 12 above; VerLoren van
Themaat 'De artikelen 30–36 van het EEG-verdrag' [1980] *RM Themis* 4–5 378; Barents,
'New Developments in Measures Having Equivalent Effect' [1981] C.M.L.Rev. 271, at 275.
[36] Any action encouraged by the State, even in a non-binding form, constitutes a State
measure for this purpose: para. 6.07 below.
[37] [1980] O.J. C156/10.
[38] See paras. 8.53 *et seq.* below.
[39] Case 78/70 [1971] E.C.R. 487 at 500, [1971] C.M.L.R. 631 at 657.

systems of the Member States, nationals of those States were able to partition the market and bring about arbitrary discrimination or disguised restrictions on trade between Member States'.

4.19   Secondly, they would advert to the Court's decision in *Walrave* v. *Union Cycliste Internationale*.[40] That case concerned alleged discrimination on the grounds of nationality within a private sporting organisation. One of the points which arose for decision was whether a private body was bound by Article 48 of the Treaty on the free movement of workers and Article 59 on the free provision of services. The Court ruled as follows:

'Articles 7, 48, and 59 have in common the prohibition, in their respective spheres of application, of any discrimination on grounds of nationality.

Prohibition of such discrimination does not only apply to the action of public authorities but extends likewise to rules of any other nature aimed at regulating in a collective manner gainful employment and the provision of services . . .

It follows that the provisions of Articles 7, 48 and 59 of the Treaty may be taken into account by the national court in judging the validity or the effects of a provision inserted in the rules of a sporting organisation'.[41]

This ruling was subsequently confirmed in *Donà* v. *Mantero*.[42]

4.20   This case law is particularly interesting in that the structure of Articles 59 to 66 on services is in one sense analogous to those relating to goods. While Article 59 simply states that 'restrictions on freedom to provide services within the Community shall be progressively abolished during the transitional period in respect of nationals of Member States', the third paragraph of Article 60 as well as Articles 62 and 64 are expressed to be addressed to the Member States (as in Article 62, which states that 'Member States shall not introduce any new restrictions . . .').[43] In *Walrave* the Court addressed itself to this question in the following terms:

'Although the third paragraph of Article 60, and Articles 62 and 64 specifically relate, as regards the provision of services to the abolition of measures by the State, this fact does not defeat the general nature of the terms of Article 59, which makes no distinction between the source of the restrictions to be abolished'.

4.21   The third argument is based on *Defrenne* v. *Sabena*.[44] That case concerned the interpretation of Article 119 of the Treaty, the first paragraph of which reads:

'Each Member State shall during the first stage ensure and subsequently maintain the application of the principle that men and women should receive equal pay for equal work.'

In reply to a preliminary question the Court ruled that Article 119 prohibited discrimination in pay between men and women whether

---

[40] Case 36/74 [1974] E.C.R. 1405, [1975] 1 C.M.L.R. 320.
[41] At 1418–1419.
[42] Case 13/76 [1976] E.C.R. 1333, [1976] 2 C.M.L.R. 578.
[43] See para. 4.14 above.
[44] Case 43/75 [1976] E.C.R. 455, [1976] 2 C.M.L.R. 98.

by private or by public organisations. The following passages of the judgment are particularly illustrative in the present context:

'It is also impossible to put forward arguments based on the fact that Article 119 only refers expressly to "Member States".

Indeed, as the Court has already found in other contexts, the fact that certain provisions of the Treaty are formally addressed to the Member States does not prevent rights from being conferred at the same time on any individual who has an interest in the performance of the duties thus laid down . . .

. . . in its reference to "Member States", Article 119 is alluding to those States in the exercise of all those of their functions which may usefully contribute to the implementation of the principle of equal pay . . .

Therefore, the reference to "Member States" in Article 119 cannot be interpreted as excluding the intervention of the courts in direct application of the Treaty'.[45]

In other words, the judiciary is one of the organs of the Member States and is bound by Article 119 in the same way as the other organs of the States.

4.22 The first argument[46] should, it is submitted, be rejected: the exercise of industrial rights by a private person merely constitutes reliance on measures adopted by the Member States; without legislation, patent, trade mark and copyright protection would simply not exist.[47] However, the second and third arguments have considerable force.

It is submitted therefore that Articles 30 to 36 or, more probably, certain analogous principles[48] can bind private parties in certain circumstances. However, it is not clear how wide this rule is:

(a) first, it would be extremely cumbersome if most acts caught by Article 85 or 86 simultaneously contravened Articles 30 to 36 (or analogous principles);

(b) measures attributable to the State discriminating against imported goods in public supply contracts are contrary to Article 30[49]; yet it would clearly be far-fetched to hold that a private person with no dominant position and acting alone would fall foul of Article 30 (or an analogous principle) if he chose not to purchase imported goods.[50]

4.23 At all events, it is submitted, the acts of private parties not attributable to the State cannot give rise to infringement proceedings under Article 169 of the Treaty. Such actions can only be brought against the Member States and not against private parties; and there is no reason to suppose that a Member State can be held responsible

---

[45] At 475.
[46] See para. 4.18 above.
[47] VerLoren van Themaat, *op. cit.* note 35 above.
[48] For this view see Matthies, *op. cit.* note 12 above.
[49] See paras. 7.20 *et seq.* below.
[50] Matthies, *op. cit.* note 12 above.

in this way for the act of a private person which that Member State has neither required nor in any way incited.

Finally, it should be emphasised that the other chapters of this book in principle concern only those measures which are attributable to the Member States. Measures attributable to the Community institutions or to private parties are only referred to incidentally.

CHAPTER V

Quantitative restrictions

Quantitative restrictions on imports and exports are prohibited by Articles 30 and 34 respectively, unless they are justified under Article 36.

This chapter is divided into three sections covering respectively the timetable for the abolition of these restrictions, the direct applicability of the prohibition, and the definition of the concept of quantitative restrictions. Article 36 is not considered in this chapter, since it is the subject of Chapter VIII.

I. THE TIMETABLE

5.01 With respect to imports, the basic prohibition on quantitative restrictions is to be found in Article 30, which provides

> 'Quantitative restrictions and measures having equivalent effect shall, without prejudice to the following provisions, be prohibited between Member States'.

The timetable for the abolition of these measures is governed by the subsequent provisions. Articles 31 and 32 EEC lay down a 'standstill' rule as from the date of entry into force of the Treaty of Rome. The former provision states that Member States shall refrain from introducing new quantitative restrictions as between themselves, whereas, the first paragraph of Article 32 prohibits Member States from making existing quotas more restrictive. The second paragraph of Article 32 declares that quotas shall be abolished by the end of the transitional period, 31 December 1969, at the latest and Article 33 sets out the system for their progressive abolition during this period. Article 35 states that the abolition of quantitative restrictions may be effected more rapidly than is provided for in Article 33, and indeed by Article 3 of Council Decision 66/532 of 26 July 1966[1] such restrictions were to be abolished immediately. In accordance with Article 191 of the Treaty, that provision took effect when the decision was notified to the Member States.

However, Article 3 of that decision expressly excludes agricultural products from its scope. All the regulations establishing common market organisations[2] for agricultural products during the transitional period prohibited quantitative restrictions with respect to

---

[1] [1966] J.O. 165. This was preceded by two earlier acceleration decisions: those of 12 May 1960 (J.O. 12.9.1960) and 15 May 1962 (J.O. 28.5.1962).

[2] For the meaning of this term see para. 10.01 below.

those products from the date of their entry into force. For agricultural products not yet subject to a common market organisation the prohibition took effect at the end of the transitional period.[3]

Article 34 EEC prohibits quantitative restrictions on exports as from the end of the first stage of the transitional period, namely 31 December 1961. The better view is that the prohibition applied to agricultural products as from the same date.[4] Although Article 34 does not expressly require Member States to refrain from introducing new restrictions on exports during the first stage of the transitional period, such an obligation can be deduced from its general structure.[5]

5.02 The first Act of Accession provides for the abolition of quantitative restrictions on imports and exports between the old and the new Member States as from its entry into force on 1 January 1973: Article 42. However, the prohibition took effect one month later for agricultural products subject to a common market organisation at the date of accession: Articles 60 (1) and 151. For other agricultural products quantitative restrictions have been prohibited since 1 January 1978.[6] In addition, Article 43 entitled Member States to retain restrictions on exports of waste and scrap metal of iron and steel for a two-year period, except Denmark and the Republic of Ireland, which were granted periods of three and five years respectively. Finally two Protocols to the Act of Accession lay down exceptions for the Republic of Ireland. Protocol 6 sets out a timetable for the abolition of Irish import quotas of stockings, brushes and brooms, superphosphate and certain vehicle parts, which exception expired on 1 July 1975. It also authorises the retention until 1 July 1975 of quantitative restrictions on exports from that State of certain hides and skins, certain types of woods and certain metals. Protocol 7—the only one of these exceptions still in force—entitles the Irish government to maintain until 1 January 1985 its quota system applicable to the assembly and import of motor vehicles applied in accordance with the Motor Vehicles (Registration of Importers) Act 1968.

5.03 The Act of Accession of Greece[7] to the Communities likewise provides for the immediate abolition of quantitative restrictions on imports or exports between the Nine and Greece as from the date of accession, namely 1 January 1981: Article 35. This applies also to agricultural products covered by a common organisation of the market: Article 65 (1). On the other hand, Annex III to the Act lists

---

[3] See para. 10.02 below.
[4] See para. 10.04 below.
[5] This can be deduced in particular from the fact that Art. 34 (2) requires Member States to abolish, by the end of the first stage of the transitional period, export restrictions 'which are in existence when this Treaty enters into force', see Waelbroeck in *Le Droit de la Communauté Economique Européenne* (1970), Vol. 1, 113; Ehlermann in Groeben, Boeckh, Thiesing—*Kommentar zum EWG-Vertrag* (1974), Vol. 1, 283–284.
[6] See para. 10.05 below.
[7] [1979] O.J. L291.

a number of industrial products for which Greece may gradually reduce quantitative restrictions and must abolish them on 31 December 1985 by virtue of Article 36 of the Act. Also, as in the first Act of Accession, there is a special provision for export restrictions on waste and scrap metal of iron or steel falling within heading no. 73.03: Article 37 provides that such arrangements may be maintained for a period of two years from 1 January 1981, in so far as they are not more restrictive than those applied to exports to third countries.[8] Finally, Article 65 (2) provides that

> 'in respect of products not covered, on the date of accession, by a common organisation of the market, the provisions of Title II concerning the progressive abolition of charges having equivalent effect to customs duties and of quantitative restrictions and measures having equivalent effect shall not apply to those charges, restrictions and measures if they form part of a national market organisation on the date of accession. This provision shall only apply until the common organisations of the market for these products is implemented and not later than 31 December 1985 and to the extent strictly necessary to ensure the maintenance of the national organisation'.

The better view is that both Greece and the other Member States may rely on this provision.[9]

Thus no transitional exemption from the prohibition on quantitative restrictions on imports or exports is to apply after the end of 1985. Permanent exceptions to that prohibition are considered in Chapters VIII and IX.

II. DIRECT EFFECT

5.04 In *Salgoil* v. *Italian Ministry for Foreign Trade*[10] an Italian court asked the Court of Justice to 'determine whether the provisions of Article 30 *et seq*. of the Treaty, especially Article 31, also produce effects on the relationship between a Member State and its nationals'. Since this question was posed during the transitional period, the Court saw no need to decide the question in relation to Article 30 itself, but only in relation to Articles 31 to 33.

In this connection the Court found that the initial paragraphs of Articles 31 and 32—the contents of which were discussed at the beginning of this chapter—did produce 'direct effects on the legal relationships between Member States and those subject to their jurisdiction'.[11] On the other hand, the second paragraph of Article 32 and Article 33, both of which concerned the gradual elimination of existing quotas, did not produce such effects.

---

[8] It appears from other language texts that the reference to import restrictions in the English text of Art. 37 is erroneous and that the article is intended to cover *export* restrictions.

[9] See paras. 10.05 and 10.06 below.

[10] Case 13/68 [1968] E.C.R. 453, [1969] C.M.L.R. 181.

[11] In the case of Art. 31 the Court held that such effects were delayed for a period of up to six months, by virtue of the second paragraph of that Article.

5.05 Not until 1977 did the Court decide this point with respect to Article 30 itself, in *Iannelli* v. *Meroni*.[12] It did so in the following terms:

> 'The prohibition of quantitative restrictions and measures having equivalent effect laid down in Article 30 of the Treaty is mandatory and explicit and its implementation does not require any subsequent intervention of the Member States or Community institutions.
>
> 'The prohibition therefore has direct effect and creates individual rights which national courts must protect; this occurred at the end of the transitional period at the latest, that is to say on 1 January 1970 as the provisions of the second paragraph of Article 32 of the Treaty indicate'.

Likewise in *Pigs Marketing Board* v. *Redmond*[13] the Court held that Articles 30 and 34 were 'directly applicable and that as such they confer on individuals rights which the courts of Member States must protect'.

It is clear that these pronouncements apply equally to quantitative restrictions and to measures of equivalent effect.

III. THE DEFINITION OF QUANTITATIVE RESTRICTIONS

5.06 The Court of Justice has held that 'the prohibition on quantitative restrictions covers measures which amount to a total or partial restraint of, according to the circumstances, imports, exports or goods in transit': *Geddo* v. *Ente Nazionale Risi*.[14] In that case it was clear beyond all doubt that the national measure at issue did not fall within that definition.

However, this matter was raised subsequently with respect to section 42 of the Customs Consolidation Act 1876 prohibiting the importation into the United Kingdom of indecent or obscene articles. The case in question was *R.* v. *Henn and Darby*[15] in which the defendants had been convicted before the English courts of contravening this section.

When it was contended before it that this provision was contrary to Article 30, the Court of Appeal[16] rejected this argument, *inter alia*, on the grounds that the term 'quantitative restrictions' connoted restrictions 'concerned with quantity' and not total prohibitions. This ruling caused some surprise in that one of the principal aims of the Treaty of Rome was to guard against protectionism between the Member States—an aim which would be completely undermined if the Court of Appeal's interpretation were followed. More concretely, the Court of Appeal's judgment was contrary to the ruling

---

[12] Case 74/76 [1977] E.C.R. 557, [1977] 2 C.M.L.R. 688.
[13] Case 83/78 [1978] E.C.R. 2347, [1979] 1 C.M.L.R. 177.
[14] Case 2/73 [1973] E.C.R. 865 at 879, [1974] 1 C.M.L.R. 13 at 42.
[15] Case 34/79 [1979] E.C.R. 3795, [1980] 1 C.M.L.R. 246, see Chap. 8, note 19 below.
[16] [1978] 1 W.L.R. 1031.

of the Court of Justice in the *Geddo* case and failed to take account of the opening words of Article 36:

'The provisions of Articles 30 to 34 shall not preclude *prohibitions*[17] or restrictions on imports, exports or goods in transit justified on grounds of public morality . . .'.

The defendants then appealed to the House of Lords, which made its first reference ever to the Court of Justice on this and other points arising out of the case. It was not contended by any party before the Court of Justice that the Court of Appeal's interpretation had been correct and it was virtually a foregone conclusion that the Court would hold, as indeed it did, that a prohibition on imports of pornographic articles fell under Article 30 (as indeed it was virtually a foregone conclusion that the Court would rule that such a measure was justified under Article 36).[18] Nevertheless it is interesting to note that although the reference only contemplated the possibility that the prohibition was a measure of equivalent effect, both the Advocate General and the Court specifically found that it was a quantitative restriction pure and simple.

Thus the concept of quantitative restrictions covers not only 'quotas', which term appears in Articles 32 and 33, but also absolute prohibitions on imports or exports, as the case may be. This is so whatever the nature of the imports or exports, be they reimports or goods in transit,[19] or re-exports.[20] Furthermore, a quantitative restriction may be based on legislation or merely be an administrative practice.[21] On the other hand, the Articles in question only cover non-tariff quotas; under these import or export bans are imposed once the ceiling has been reached. Tariff quotas (under which customs duties are imposed on goods exceeding the ceiling laid down) infringe Article 12 *et seq.* if they are imposed between Member States.

5.07 Nevertheless, the exact dividing line between quantitative restrictions and measures of equivalent effect is not yet fully clear. For instance, the requirement of import or export licences has been held to constitute a measure of equivalent effect.[22] Yet such a requirement amounts to a prohibition on import or export without the requisite licence. The same applies with respect to the obligation to produce sanitary or veterinary certificates for imports or exports.[23]

The distinction might perhaps be made in the following manner:

---

[17] The italics are those of the author.
[18] See para. 8.20
[19] See para. 2.21 above.
[20] See para. 6.53 below.
[21] See para. 6.07 below.
[22] See para. 7.03 below.
[23] See para. 7.04 below.

- when an import or export prohibition relates to the goods themselves (*i.e.* their size, weight, composition, presentation, etc. . . .), then it constitutes a quantitative restriction[24];
- when the prohibition relates to factors extraneous to the goods themselves (*e.g.* the failure to obtain an import or export licence, or to produce a certificate), then it constitutes a measure of equivalent effect.

5.08 On this view an import prohibition designed to protect industrial property rights constitutes a quantitative restriction rather than a measure of equivalent effect.[25] On this view also the national provision at issue in Case 153/78 *E.C. Commission* v. *Germany*[26] would be considered a quantitative restriction. That case arose out of proceedings brought under Article 169 of the Treaty with respect to a German provision prohibiting the importation of meat products processed in a country other than the one in which the original animals were slaughtered. In ruling that this measure was contrary to Article 30, the Court did not decide whether it was a quantitative restriction or a measure of equivalent effect, as it was not necessary to decide this.

5.09 In any case, it would seem that the distinction between quantitative restrictions and measures of equivalent effect is only material with respect to the transitional periods laid down by the Treaty of Rome and the Acts of Accession, in the following manner:

- whereas quantitative restrictions were to be abolished as between the original Member States in 1966,[27] this did not occur for measures of equivalent effect until 1 January 1970[28];
- the first Act of Accession provided for the immediate abolition of quantitative restrictions,[29] while measures of equivalent effect were subject to a two-year period of grace[30];
- Article 36 of the Act of Accession of Greece[31] entitles that country to retain quantitative restrictions on certain industrial products for a certain period, without creating a corresponding exception with respect to measures of equivalent effect.

However, it should be recalled[32] that Protocol 3 to the first Act of Accession on the Channel Islands and the Isle of Man begins:

'The Community rules on customs matters and quantitative restrictions, in particular those of the Act of Accession, shall apply to the Channel Islands and

---

[24] It is submitted that this applies even to an import prohibition coupled with a prohibition on sale within the Member State concerned. On the other hand, a prohibition on sale in itself constitutes a measure of equivalent effect: para. 7.39 below. See generally Ehlermann, *op. cit.* note 5 above, at 253–254.
[25] As to justification, see para. 8.53 *et seq.* below.
[26] [1979] E.C.R. 2555, [1980] 1 C.M.L.R. 198.
[27] See para. 5.01 above.
[28] See para. 6.02 below.
[29] See para. 5.02 above.
[30] See para. 6.02 below.
[31] See para. 5.03 above.
[32] See para. 3.03 above.

the Isle of Man under the same conditions as they apply to the United Kingdom.'

Although measures of equivalent effect are not expressly mentioned, it is probable that this Protocol covers such measures[33]—particularly in the light of the Court's ruling in *Iannelli* v. *Meroni* which suggests that 'quotas' in Article 32 covers measures of equivalent effect.[34]

Unless otherwise stated, the rules discussed in this book apply in the same way to quantitative restrictions as to measures of equivalent effect.[35] In particular, the prohibition on quantitative restrictions is subject to the exception clauses discussed in Chapters VIII and IX.

---

[33] See para. 3.03 above.
[34] See the passage quoted at para. 5.05 above.
[35] See note 97 to Chap. VI.

CHAPTER VI

Measures of equivalent effect: General

6.01 Article 30 provides that: 'Quantitative restrictions on imports and all measures having equivalent effect shall . . . be prohibited between Member States'. Article 34 is couched in the same terms, except that it applies to restrictions on exports. These prohibitions are subject to the exception contained in Article 36, which is discussed in Chapter VIII.

As will be seen, the concept of measures of equivalent effect to quantitative restrictions differs from that of quantitative restrictions themselves in that it is considerably wider and more complex. Indeed the definition of this concept forms the crux of this book. For this reason this chapter contains more sections than Chapter V. These are: the timetable for the abolition of measures of equivalent effect, the definition of measures of equivalent effect on imports, the definition of such measures relating to exports and, finally, 'purely national' restrictions. The direct applicability of the prohibition of measures of equivalent effect on imports and exports has already been dealt with in paragraph 5.05 above.

The compatibility of specific national measures with Articles 30 and 34 will be considered in Chapter VII.

I. THE TIMETABLE

6.02 The reader is referred to paragraphs 5.01 to 5.03 above which cover the timetable for the abolition of quantitative restrictions, since the rules are broadly the same.

As between the original Member States the only difference in the timetable of abolition of quantitative restrictions and measures of equivalent effect is that Decision 66/532[1] only applies to quantitative restrictions.

Consequently the prohibition on measures of equivalent effect on imports did not take effect until the end of the transitional period[2]—except as regards products already covered by a common

---

[1] [1966] J.O. 165.
[2] By some quirk of drafting the Treaty does not actually state that measures of equivalent effect on imports were to be abolished at the end of the transitional period. The second paragraph of Art. 32 stipulates that 'quotas shall be abolished by the end of the transitional period at the latest'. It appears that the term 'quotas' must be stretched beyond its natural meaning to include measures of equivalent effect; this appears to be the approach adopted by the Court in Case 74/76 *Iannelli* v. *Meroni* [1977] E.C.R. 557, [1977] 2 C.M.L.R. 688, see para. 5.05 above. In any case, there cannot be a shadow of a doubt that the prohibition on

market organisation or by a Directive based on Article 33 (7). That paragraph provides:

'The Commission shall issue directives establishing the procedure and timetable in accordance with which the Member States shall abolish, as between themselves, any measures in existence when this Treaty enters into force which have an effect equivalent to quotas'.

6.03 It is clear from the context, and in particular the second paragraph of Article 32, that Article 33 (7) lapsed at the end of the transitional period. During that period the Commission adopted five directives on the basis of this provision:

- Directive 64/486[3] requiring the Federal Republic of Germany progressively to abolish its import restrictions on potatoes; this Directive is exceptional in that it is addressed to one Member State only, the others being addressed to all the Member States;
- Directive 66/682[4] requiring the Member States to abolish, save for certain listed products, measures by which the importation of a product is made conditional on the exportation or purchase or sale of a domestic product;
- Directive 66/683[5] requiring the Member States to abolish, other than for certain products listed in the annex to the Directive, measures which partially or totally prohibit the use of an imported product; or which require the partial or total use of a domestic product; or subject the entitlement to a benefit, other than an aid within the meaning of Article 92 of the Treaty, to the total or partial use of a national product;
- Directive 70/32[6] requiring the Member States to abolish legislative provisions and put an end to administrative practices discriminating against the supply of imported goods to public authorities;
- Directive 70/50[7] is by far the most important of the five Directives; it is not limited to any particular type of measure like the other Directives, but sets out a lengthy list of measures which it requires the Member States to abolish as being measures of equivalent effect; it also sets out the Commission's general thinking at that time as to the scope and meaning of this concept; it will be described in greater detail during the course of this chapter.

6.04 During the transitional period these Directives may well have been directly effective[8] and thus been capable of being relied on by

measures of equivalent effect on imports did take effect at the end of the transitional period: see, *e.g.* the *Iannelli* case.
[3] [1964] J.O. 2253.
[4] [1966] J.O. 3745.
[5] [1966] J.O. 3748.
[6] [1970] J.O. L13/1, para. 7.20 below.
[7] [1970] J.O. L13/29. See Annexe II to this book.
[8] See generally Case 33/70 *SACE* v. *Italian Ministry of Finance* [1970] E.C.R. 1213, [1971] C.M.L.R. 123.

55

individuals before the national courts. However, at the end of the transitional period Article 30 itself acquired direct effect,[9] so that this function of these Directives has been superseded. Also, any clauses in the Directives exempting particular products or measures lapsed at the end of the transitional period.

In addition, Article 33 (7) empowers the Commission to issue Directives relating only to measures 'in existence when this Treaty enters into force'.[10] However, it would be anomalous if different criteria were to apply as regards measures adopted after the Treaty came into force. Moreover, in Case 12/74 *E.C. Commission* v. *Germany*,[11] the Court cited Directive 70/50 with approval with respect to a German statute of 1971, although it did not refer to this particular issue.

Moreover, while the Court has often quoted and followed Directive 70/50, it has also, as we shall see later,[12] implicitly rejected certain aspects of it, in particular its approach to 'indistinctly applicable' measures.

In summary, while in legal theory these directives may have been directly effective since their adoption, as a matter of practice they have been relegated in importance since the end of the transitional period, when Article 30 itself acquired direct effect. Since then the Court has delivered a considerable body of case law on the concept of measures of equivalent effect under Article 30. This case law has largely superseded the Directives so that *in practice* they merely serve as non-binding guidelines to the interpretation of Article 30[13]—in so far as they have not been implicitly set aside by the case law of the Court. The non-exhaustive list of measures of equivalent effect set out in Article 2 (3) of Directive 70/50 is of particular use.

6.05   Under the first Act of Accession, measures of equivalent effect to quantitative restrictions on imports and exports were to be abolished by 1 January 1975 by virtue of Article 42 (2) of that Act. The exceptions to that rule are those set out above at paragraph 5.02.

Centrafarm v. *Sterling Drug Inc.*[14] and *Centrafarm* v. *Winthrop*[15] concerned the use of patents and trade marks respectively to prevent imports into a Member State of goods put on to the market of

---

[9] Para. 5.05 above.

[10] See Graf *Der Begriff 'Massnahmen gleicher Wirkung wie mengenmässige Einfuhr-beschränkungen' im EWG-Vertrag* (1972), 25.

[11] [1975] E.C.R. 181 at 193, [1975] 1 C.M.L.R. 340 at 364 *et. seq.* See para. 7.27 below.

[12] See paras. 6.38 and 7.03 below.

[13] Matthies, 'Herkunftsangaben und Europäisches Gemeinschaftsrecht' in *Festschrift für Schiedermair* (1976), 397, Mestmäcker, *Die Vereinbarkeit von Preisregelungen und dem Arzneimittelmarkt mit dem Recht der Europäischen Wirtschafsgemeinschaft* (1980), 29; for the view that Dir. 70/50 is binding see Sabiani, 'L'incidence du droit de la communauté économique européenne sur la réglementation française de prix' [1975] R.T.D.E. 496, Winkel 'Die Vereinbarkeit staatlicher Preislenkungsmassnahmen mit dem EWG-Vertrag' [1976] N.J.W. 2050; see generally the Advocate General in Case 12/74 *E.C. Commission* v. *Germany* [1975] E.C.R. 181 at 208, [1975] 1 C.M.L.R. 340 at 343.

[14] Case 15/74 [1974] E.C.R. 1147, [1974] 2 C.M.L.R. 480.

[15] Case 16/74 [1974] E.C.R. 1183, [1974] 2 C.M.L.R. 480.

another Member State by the patentee or with his consent. In each case the Court held that such use was contrary to Article 30 without being justified under Article 36. The Court then turned to the interpretation of Article 42 of the Act of Accession: since these cases concerned imports from the United Kingdom and the Netherlands and the reference to the Court of Justice occurred in 1974, the national court asked in effect whether the prohibition could be invoked with respect to such imports before 1975.

On this point the Court replied:

> 'In the context, [Article 42 (2)] can refer only to those measures having an effect equivalent to quantitative restrictions which, as between the original Member States, had to be abolished at the end of the transitional period, pursuant to Articles 30 and 32 to 35 of the EEC Treaty.
>
> It therefore appears that Article 42 of the Act of Accession has no effect upon prohibitions on importation arising from national legislation concerning industrial and commercial property.
>
> It follows that Article 42 of the Act of Accession cannot be invoked to prevent importation into the Netherlands, even before 1 January 1975, of goods put on to the market in the United Kingdom under the conditions set out above by the patentee or with his consent'.

This reasoning is apparently based on two premises. The first is that Article 36 is to be treated quite separately from Article 30; yet how could this be so? The second is that measures of equivalent effect, which are *prima facie* covered by Article 36 but on closer examination are not so covered, are to be abolished earlier than their brethren measures of equivalent effect which correspond to none of the heads of justification under Article 36; why? The Advocate General took the opposite view[16] from the Court on this point.

6.06   The provisions of the Greek Act of Accession already set out in paragraph 5.03 above also apply to measures of equivalent effect. The exception is Article 36 of this Act, which sets out a timetable for the gradual elimination of quantitative restrictions on products listed in Annex III thereto but which does not apply to measures of equivalent effect. In addition, Article 38 gives Greece a three-year period starting on 1 January 1981 to eliminate its import deposits and cash payments in force in Greece on 31 December 1980. Finally, by Article 39 the 8 per cent. general preference applied in Greece on public contracts is to be progressively eliminated over a five-year period starting on 1 January 1981.

II. THE MEANING OF 'MEASURES'

6.07   Even non-binding acts may be caught by Article 30 or 34. This is shown by the preamble to Directive 70/50 where the Commission stated:

---

[16] At 1178.

'Whereas for the purpose of Article 30 *et seq.* "measures" means laws, regulations, administrative provisions, administrative practices, and all instruments issuing from a public authority, including recommendations;

Whereas for the purposes of this Directive "administrative practices" means any standard and regularly followed procedure of a public authority; whereas "recommendations" means any instruments issuing from a public authority which, while not legally binding on the addressees thereof, cause them to pursue a certain conduct . . .'

Cases of this kind are rife in the field of public supply contracts. An example is the circulars addressed by the United Kingdom Government to public authorities urging them to buy national products in connection with textiles, clothing and footwear; the Commission has commenced infringement proceedings under Article 169 against these circulars[17].

The financing of a scheme or project or the grant of a loan by public authorities may constitute a 'measure'—for example in the case of a publicity campaign in favour of national goods, or the grant of a loan to public officials for the purchase of cars on condition that they buy national cars. Furthermore, a Treaty concluded by a Member State can also be a 'measure'[18].

6.08 A legislative measure kept on the statute book will be a 'measure', even if it is not applied or has not entered into force; this is not least because it will cause confusion and might deter potential importers[19]. Conversely, a legislative measure, which has not yet been formally adopted, will constitute a measure if it is applied in practice. What is more, importers may be deterred from importing certain goods if they know that their sale is soon to be prohibited by the Member State in question. Thus, even if it were not applied, a draft legislative measure might contravene Articles 30 or 34, at least if it were used by a Member State to deter potential importers from importing goods which do not conform to the draft measure[20].

6.09 As has been explained earlier in this book[21], measures falling under Article 30 or 34 may emanate not only from central govern

---

[17] E.C. Bull. 4/1979, 118.

[18] See, however, Art. 234 discussed at para. 9.53 *et seq.* below.

[19] See the Advocate General in case 68/76 *E.C. Commission* v. *France* [1977] E.C.R. 515 at 541, [1977] 2 C.M.L.R. 161 at 175.

[20] In its Communication on the *Cassis de Dijon* case discussed below (para. 6.35), the Commission stated that:

'To forestall later difficulties, the Commission will be informing Member States of potential objections, under the terms of Community law, to provisions they may be considering introducing which come to the attention of the Commission'.

This does not mean that any instrument is capable of infringing Art. 30, even when that instrument is in draft form. Presumably, it is designed primarily to show that the Commission reserves the right to point out to a Member State that a draft which that State is considering adopting would, if adopted, infringe Art. 30.

See also the Commission's proposal for a Decision laying down a procedure for the provision of information in the field of technical standards and regulations ([1980] O.J. C253/2), discussed at para. 12.12 below.

[21] Para. 4.03 above.

ment but also from regional or local government. They may also emanate from the executive, the legislature or the judiciary[22].

6.10 A measure is not rendered compatible with Articles 30 and 34 simply because a procedure is provided under national law for obtaining an exemption. Thus in *International Fruit Company* v. *Produktschap voor Groenten en Fruit*[23] the Court held that a 'national measure, which requires, *even purely as a formality*[24], import or export licences or any other similar procedure' was precluded by Articles 30 and 34. Also, in *Openbaar Ministerie* v. *Van Tiggele*[25], having held that a particular system of minimum prices was contrary to Article 30, the Court continued:

> 'This is the conclusion which must be drawn even though the competent authority is empowered to grant exemptions from the fixed minimum price and though this power is freely applied to imported products, since the requirement that importers and traders must comply with the administrative formalities inherent in such a system may in itself constitute a measure having an effect equivalent to a quantitative restriction'.

This was confirmed in *Fietje*[26].

6.11 Also, unlike Articles 85 and 86 relating to competition Articles 30 and 34 are subject to no *de minimis* rule. This is shown by the *International Fruit* case just mentioned. Again in the *Van Tiggele* case referred to in the preceding paragraph it was held that even a temporary measure could be contrary to Article 30. As Barents[27] points out, the rule that Articles 30 and 34 are subject to no *de minimis* rule may be justified on the grounds that *State* interventions on the market may be said to have an appreciable effect by their very nature.

III. MEASURES OF EQUIVALENT EFFECT ON IMPORTS

A. General

6.12 Quantitative restrictions always take effect at the borders of the Member State which imposes them. Measures of equivalent effect may do so, but need not. Some classic examples of measures of equivalent effect may be cited from Directive 70/50 already referred to:

> 'measures which: . . .
> (f) lower the value of an imported product, in particular by causing a reduction in its intrinsic value, or increase its costs;
>   . . .
> (h) . . . subject imported products to conditions which are different from

---

[22] Para. 4.04 above.
[23] Cases 51–54/71 [1971] E.C.R. 1107, see para. 7.03 below.
[24] The italics are those of the author.
[25] Case 82/77 [1978] E.C.R. 25, [1978] 2 C.M.L.R. 528; see, however, para. 8.13 below.
[26] Case 27/80 [1980] E.C.R. 3839, [1981] 3 C.M.L.R. 722.
[27] 'Measures of Equivalent Effect: Some Recent Developments' [1981] C.M.L. Rev. 271 at 287.

those laid down for domestic products and more difficult to satisfy;

. . .

(j) subject imported products only to conditions, in respect, in particular of shape, size, weight, composition, presentation, identification or putting up, or subject imported products to conditions which are different from those for domestic products and more difficult to satisfy;

(k) hinder the purchase by private individuals of imported products only, or encourage, require or give preference to the purchase of domestic products only;

. . .

6.13 That the concept of measures of equivalent effect is indeed a wide one is confirmed by the classic definition of such measures set out in *Procureur du Roi* v. *Dassonville*:

'All trading rules enacted by Member States, which are capable of hindering, directly or indirectly, actually or potentially, intra-Community trade are to be considered as measures having an effect equivalent to quantitative restrictions'[28].

Time and again this definition has been repeated in the Court's case law, though with minor variations: for instance, the term 'trading rules' does not always appear; and the Court sometimes speaks of obstacles 'to imports between Member States' rather than to 'intra-Community trade'[29]. At all events, it is clear from this formula that one must look to the *effects* of a measure and not to its aims in deciding whether it falls under Article 30[30]. Furthermore, it is not necessary to show that a measure actually restricts imports, but only that it *potentially* does so.

It follows that it is inappropriate to consider statistical evidence as to the volume of imports of products subject to the national measure in question; even if imports have actually increased since the measure was introduced, they might have increased more in the absence of such a measure. These are obviously factors of fundamental importance in the interpretation of Article 30.

6.14 What is more, Article 30 does not only cover restrictions on imports pure and simple, but also restrictions on:

(a) re-imports[31]; or

(b) goods in transit[32]; or

(c) indirect imports[33]; or

(d) parallel imports. This was spelt out by the Court in *De Peijper*[34] where it held that 'rules or practices which result in imports being channelled in such a way that only certain

---

[28] Case 8/74 [1974] E.C.R. 837 at 852, [1974] 2 C.M.L.R. 436 at 453.

[29] *e.g.* 'a direct or indirect, real or potential hindrance to imports between Member States', Case 4/75 *Rewe-Zentralfinanz* v. *Landwirtschaftskammer* [1975] E.C.R. 843 at 858, [1977] 1 C.M.L.R. 599 at 618; see also Case 104/75 *De Peijper* [1976] E.C.R. 613 at 635, [1976] 2 C.M.L.R. 271 at 304.

[30] The intention of the author of a measure may be relevant, however, in deciding whether it constitutes a disguised restriction on trade under Art. 36. See para. 8.09 below.

[31] Para. 2.21 above.

[32] Para. 2.21 above.

[33] Para. 7.04 *et seq.* below.

[34] Note 29 above.

traders can effect these imports, whereas others are prevented from doing so' are measures of equivalent effect under Article 30;

(e) imports of raw materials or semi-finished products, even where the finished product is subject to no restrictions. This emerges clearly from the recitals to Directive 70/50, which state that measures of equivalent effect can apply 'at any marketing stage'. It emerges also from the Court's judgment in *Eggers* v. *Freie Hansestadt Bremen*[35].

6.15 In addition, it is clear that to comply with Article 30 Member States must not only refrain from imposing restrictions on imports. In some cases Article 30 imposes an obligation on Member States to take positive steps.[36] Thus, they are required to provide reasonable customs facilities,[37] for instance in keeping customs posts open during reasonable hours and in providing adequate staff and equipment to carry out veterinary and public health checks with due speed. Similarly, in *De Peijper*[38] the Court ruled that Member States were under an active duty to co-operate with one another so as to ensure that registration formalities with respect to parallel imports of pharmaceuticals be reduced to the minimum; and in *Denkavit Futtermittel* v. *Minister of Agriculture*[39] it found a similar duty to co-operate with respect to veterinary checks on animal feed.

6.16 On the other hand, the prohibition on measures of equivalent effect like that on quantitative restrictions is subject to the specific exception contained in Article 36, which reads as follows:

'The provisions of Articles 30 to 34 shall not preclude prohibitions on imports, exports or goods in transit justified on grounds of public morality, public policy or public security; the protection of health and life of humans, animals or plants; the protection of national treasures possessing artistic, historic or archeological value; or the protection of industrial and commercial property. Such prohibitions or restrictions shall not, however, constitute a means of arbitrary discrimination or a disguised restriction on trade between Member States'.

A detailed examination of this provision is to be found in Chapter VIII of this book.

6.17 What is more the concept of measures of equivalent effect is not so wide as to cover restrictions on movements of goods falling under other provisions of the Treaty. This was clearly stated by the Court in *Iannelli* v. *Meroni*[40], in the following terms:

---

[35] Case 13/78 [1978] E.C.R. 1935, [1979] 1 C.M.L.R. 562.
[36] For this view see Schiller 'Gewährt Art. 30 des EWG-Vertrages dem Gemeinschaftsbürger neben einem subjektiven Abwerhrrecht auch ein subjektiven Leistungsrecht?' [1980] R.I.W./A.W.D. 569.
[37] Para. 7.15 below.
[38] Note 29 above.
[39] Case 251/78 [1979] E.C.R. 3369, [1980] 3 C.M.L.R. 513 para. 8.27 below.
[40] Case 74/76 [1977] E.C.R. 557, [1977] 2 C.M.L.R. 688.

'However wide the field of application of Article 30 may be, it nevertheless does not include obstacles to trade covered by other provisions of the Treaty.

In fact, since the legal consequences of the application or of a possible infringement of these various provisions have to be determined having regard to their particular purpose in the context of all the objectives of the Treaty, they may be of a different kind and this implies that their respective fields of application must be distinguished, except in those cases which may fall simultaneously within the field of application of two or more provisions of Community law'.

Consequently, the following fall outside the scope of Article 30:
- customs duties and charges of equivalent effect (Articles 9 to 16)
- aids (Articles 92 to 94)
- internal taxation (Articles 95 to 99)
- restrictions on current payments (Article 106).

Each of these will be examined in turn, after which the relationship between Article 30 and Articles 85 and 86 will be considered.

On the other hand, the relationship between Articles 30 and 37 is discussed in Chapter XI and that between Articles 30 and 100 in Chapter XII so that there is no need to consider them at this juncture. Likewise, the relationship between Article 30 and the Treaty provisions relating to the free movement of persons, services and capital has been covered in Chapter II.

6.18   In *Iannelli* the Court held that customs duties and charges of equivalent effect within the meaning of Articles 9 to 16 EEC did not fall under Article 30. This ruling was recently confirmed in *Kortmann*[41], in which a parallel importer of pharmaceutical products claimed that costs incurred in registering these products as required under Dutch law were contrary to Article 30, on the grounds that the registration was superfluous as the 'official' importer had already effected such registration. The Court held that such costs fell to be examined under Articles 9 to 13 and 95 and not under Article 30.

This is not to say, however, that every measure requiring importers or persons selling imported goods to pay a sum of money falls automatically outside Article 30. We shall see in the next chapter that the obligation to pay a deposit when importing goods[42] is caught by Article 30, as are certain types of fines[43]. Furthermore, in *Musik-Vertrieb Membran* v. *GEMA*[44] the Court classified copyright royalties as measures of equivalent effect rather than taxes of equivalent effect on the grounds that they were really damages paid for the infringement of copyright.

---

[41] Case 32/80 [1981] E.C.R. 251.
[42] Para. 7.24 below.
[43] Para. 7.10 below.
[44] Cases 55/80 and 57/80, [1981] E.C.R. 147, [1981] 2 C.M.L.R. 44, para. 8.74 below.

6.19 In the *Iannelli* case the Court also considered the relationship between Article 30 and Articles 92 to 94 relating to State aids.[45] Those provisions stipulate that such aids are in principle incompatible with the common market, but lay down a number of exceptions to that rule and give the Commission a wide discretion to accept a State aid in derogation of this principle. Consequently, the Court held that this principle of incompatibility did not have direct effect, whereas Article 30 did have such effect. In the light of this the Court ruled that:

'The effect of an interpretation of Article 30 which is so wide as to treat an aid as such within the meaning of Article 92 as being similar to a quantitative restriction referred to in Article 30 would be to alter the scope of Articles 92 and 93 of the Treaty and to interfere with the system adopted in the Treaty for the division of powers by means of the procedure for keeping aids under constant review as described in Article 93'.

6.20 Yet the Court at once proceeded to qualify this ruling as follows:

'Nevertheless the position is different if it is possible when a system of aid is being analysed to separate those conditions or factors which, even though they form part of this system, may be regarded as not being necessary for the attainment of its object or for its proper functioning.

In the latter case there are no reasons based on the division of powers under Articles 92 and 93 which permit the conclusion to be drawn that, if other provisions of the Treaty which have direct effect are infringed, those provisions may not be invoked before national courts simply because the factor in question is an aspect of aid'.

It might have been preferable for the Court to follow the Advocate General and rule that the principle that an aid could not fall under Article 30 was unqualified: as Dashwood has pointed out,[46] the test which the Court laid down lacks clarity and may prove very hard to apply. This is perhaps borne out by the Court's attempt to apply its severability test to the case in hand: it ruled that Article 30 would apply to that aspect of an

'arrangement whereby aid is granted to traders who obtain supplies of imported products through a State agency but is withheld when the products are imported direct, if this distinction is not clearly necessary for attainment of the objective of the said aid or for its proper functioning'.

6.21 As regards internal taxation, in *Fink-Frucht* v *Hauptzollamt-München*,[47] one of its earliest cases on Article 30, the Court held that one and the same national provision could not fall to be considered under Article 30 and Article 95. This was subsequently confirmed in the *Iannelli* case already referred to. Further enlighten-

---

[45] See also Case 82/77, note 25 above. Some guidance is perhaps also to be derived from Case 73/79 *E.C. Commission* v. *Italy* [1980] E.C.R. 1533, [1982] 1 C.M.L.R. 1, although that case concerns the relationship between Arts. 92–93 and 95; see Gilmour 'The Enforcement of Community Law by the Commission in the Context of State Aids: the Relationship between Arts. 93 and 169 and the Choice of Remedies' [1981] C.M.L. Rev. 63.
[46] [1977] E.L. Rev. 367.
[47] Case 27/67 [1968] E.C.R. 223, [1968] C.M.L.R. 228.

ment on the relationship between the two articles can perhaps be gleaned from Case 55/79 *E.C. Commission* v. *Ireland*[48] concerning Irish provisions whereby payment of excise duty on Irish spirits, beer and made wine could be deferred for a certain period, whereas no such deferment was allowed in the case of the same products from other Member States. The Commission claimed that these measures infringed Community law, basing its claim on Article 95 and, in the alternative, on Article 30. Having ruled that these measures were contrary to Article 95, the Court stated that 'in view of this conclusion, it is unnecessary to examine the Commission's alternative conclusions based on the application of Article 30'.

What is more, in a dictum in case 159/78 *E.C. Commission* v. *Italy*[49] the Court held that

> 'frontier controls remain justified . . . in so far as they are necessary . . . for the levying of internal taxation within the meaning of Article 95 of the Treaty when the crossing of the frontier may legitimately be assimilated to the situation which, in the case of domestic goods, gives rise to the levying of the tax . . .'[50]

6.22   Finally, it would seem clear that Article 30 does not cover measures caught by Article 106 which obliges the Member States to authorise 'any payments connected with the movement of goods, services or capital' as and when those movements themselves are liberalised. The concept of 'payments connected with the movement of goods' appears to cover not only the price of the goods, but the payment of a deposit by the buyer, or of damages for late or imperfect performance of a contract.[51]

6.23   It is appropriate at this stage to turn to the relationship between Articles 30 and 34 on the one hand and Articles 85 and 86 on the other. We saw in an earlier chapter[52] how in principle Articles 30 and 34 covered State measures whereas Articles 85 and 86 cover the agreements and practices of private undertakings. Indeed, Ver-Loren van Themaat,[53] Matthies[54] and Barents[55] have focused on the similarities between the two sets of provisions: both prohibit restrictions on imports (or exports, as the case may be), subject to a justification clause (Articles 36 and 85 (3)). Yet there are notable differences. For instance, no *de minimis* rule exists under Articles 30 to 36. Moreover, economic evidence will rarely be pertinent under Articles 30 and 34: the question as to whether a measure constitutes

---

[48] [1980] E.C.R. 481, [1980] 1 C.M.L.R. 734.
[49] [1979] E.C.R. 3247, [1980] 3 C.M.L.R. 446.
[50] See paras. 7.61 and 8.42 *et seq.*
[51] Börner 'Rechtsfragen des Zahlungs- und Kapitalverkehrs in der EWG' [1966] EuR. 97; see also generally paras. 2.07 above and 7.24 below.
[52] Paras. 4.16 *et seq.* above.
[53] 'Zum Verhältnis zwischen Artikel 30 and Artikel 85 EWG-Vertrag', *Festschrift für Gunther*, (1976) 373, 'De artikelen 30–36 van het EEG-verdrag' [1980] R.M. Themis 4/5, 378 at 399.
[54] 'Die Verantwortung der Mitgliedstaaten für den freien Warenverkehr im Gemeinsamen Markt' in *Festschrift fur Ipsen* (1977), 669 at 672 *et seq.*
[55] See note 27 above.

a restriction on imports or exports is rarely an economic one,[56] and the question of justification never is.[57] Consequently, while a comparison between the two sets of provisions will yield results of great practical importance, the reader well versed in competition law should not be lulled into thinking that the principles he knows can quite simply be applied unaltered to State measures under Articles 30 to 36.

6.24   Can the two sets of provisions apply to one and the same set of circumstances? It would appear that they can, since in *GB-Inno* v. *ATAB*[58] the Court held that:

> 'While it is true that Article 86 is directed at undertakings, nonetheless it is also true that the Treaty imposes a duty on Member States not to adopt or maintain in force any measure which could deprive that provision of its effectiveness . . .
>
> In any case, a national measure which has the effect of facilitating the abuse of a dominant position capable of affecting trade between Member States will generally be incompatible with Articles 30 and 34, which prohibit quantitative restrictions on imports and all measures having equivalent effect'.

It seems clear that the same would apply to national measures facilitating the conclusion of agreements contrary to Article 85, especially as the Court also held in that judgment that 'Member States may not enact measures enabling private undertakings to escape from the constraints imposed by Articles 85 to 94 of the Treaty'. In addition, if Articles 30 and 34 cover measures facilitating agreements or abuses by undertakings contrary to Articles 85 and 86, then *a fortiori* Articles 30 and 34 must apply to measures requiring such agreements or abuses.

No doubt the Commission and the Court will in due course have occasion to consider more closely the relationship between Articles 30 to 36 on the one hand and Articles 85 and 86 on the other.

B. 'Indistinctly applicable' measures under Articles 30 and 36

6.25   Two questions are of central importance to this book:
- to what extent does Article 30 cover measures applying in the same way to domestic and imported goods ('indistinctly applicable' measures)?
- what is the relationship between Articles 30 and 36 to the extent that Article 30 does cover such measures?

6.26   The Commission encountered the problem of 'indistinctly applicable' measures at a very early stage. The first case concerned fertilisers.[59] By a Belgian Royal Decree of 1961 only ammonium nitrate containing at least 22 per cent. nitrogen could be sold in

---

[56] Para. 6.13 above.
[57] Para. 8.18 below.
[58] Case 13/77 [1977] E.C.R. 2115, [1978] 1 C.M.L.R. 283: see also the Advocate General in Case 82/77, note 25 above, at 47, and Case 5/79 *Buys* [1979] E.C.R. 3203, [1980] 2 C.M.L.R. 99.
[59] Written question 118/66 ([1966] J.O. 901 at 903).

Belgium, be it domestically produced or imported ammonium nitrate. The normal nitrogen content in the Community was 20.5 per cent. This meant that producers of ammonium nitrate in other Member States were faced with the choice of making a special production for Belgium or stopping exports to that country. The Belgian authorities were unable to show any convincing reason for this measure and it was clear that it was designed to protect Belgian producers. The Commission prevailed upon the Belgian authorities to repeal the measure by a Royal Decree of 1962.

6.27   Perhaps more telling to the non-scientist was the French blankets case. A French Ministerial Decree of 1968 provided that only blankets of particular sizes could be sold in France. It was no accident that the decreed sizes were those already applied by French producers. This meant that blanket manufacturers in other Member States were obliged to stop exporting to France or to have a special production for the French market with all the resulting expense, whereas French manufacturers continued to produce as before. The French Government was unable to show that the measure was justified under any grounds known to Community law, since its object was clearly to protect French manufacturers. The French authorities therefore bowed to pressure from the Commission and repealed the Decree. This case shows with the utmost clarity how an 'indistinctly applicable' measure can be blatantly protectionist in its effects.

6.28   In the light of these cases, the Commission set out a twofold definition of measures of equivalent effect under Article 30 in its Directive 70/50[60]:

 - overtly discriminatory ('distinctly applicable') measures: those which apply to imported products only and make importation more costly or more difficult, and those which impose on imported products a condition differing from that required for domestic products and more difficult to satisfy (Article 2 of the Directive);
 - 'indistinctly applicable' measures: those which are equally applicable to domestic and to imported products; these were lawful unless their restrictive effect exceeded the effects intrinsic to trade rules. This would be the case in particular where the restrictive effects on the free movement of goods were out of proportion to their purpose, or where the same objective could be achieved by other means less restrictive of trade (Article 3).

Thus while overtly discriminatory measures were automatically considered to be measures of equivalent effect, there was a presump-

---

[60] Para. 6.03 above; prior to this Directive, the Commission also gave indications of its views in its answers to written question 118/66, note 59 above; written question 64/67 ([1967] J.O. 169/11) and written question 185/67 ([1968] J.O. C 5/5).

tion that 'indistinctly applicable' measures were compatible with Article 30.

The Directive is expressed to apply without prejudice to Article 36: Article 5 (2).

6.29 The views of legal authors as to the concept of measures of equivalent effect can be divided into three categories[61]:

- the narrow definition (Seidel, Graf, Marx, to a certain extent also Meier);
- the wide definition (VerLoren van Themaat, Waelbroeck);
- the intermediate approach, some of whose proponents support Directive 70/50 (Béraud, Donâ-Viscardini), while others criticise that Directive (Ulmer, Steindorff).

6.30 According to the narrow view only 'distinctly applicable' measures[62] fall to be considered as measures of equivalent effect under Article 30. Seidel,[63] the first author to take this approach, relied on an analogy with quotas. Graf[64] reached this conclusion on the basis of a comparison between the four freedoms, while Marx[65] based his theory on an analysis of Article 100. Meier's[66] approach was particularly restrictive: according to him, only those measures that operated at the frontier were measures of equivalent effect. Measures operating at a later stage, and in particular at the point of sale, fell outside Article 30 altogether in his view.

The overwhelming disadvantage of this school of thought was that it would lead to Article 30 being circumvented simply by careful drafting of national legislation. In any case, it has become untenable at least since the *GB-Inno*[67] ruling.

6.31 According to VerLoren van Themaat[68] and Waelbroek,[69] the proponents of the wide definition, Article 30 did not only apply to

---

[61] The views of the authors listed here have evolved over the years in accordance with changing events, in particular the Court's case law. For summaries of the various views see Ehlermann in Groeben, Boeckh, Thiesing, *Kommentar zum EWG-Vertrag* (1974), Vol. I, 263, Waelbroeck *Les réglementations nationales de prix et le droit communautaire* (1975), 23 *et seq.*; Meij and Winter, 'Measures having an effect equivalent to quantitative restrictions' [1976] C.M.L. Rev. 79; van Gerven, 'The Recent Case Law of the Court of Justice concerning Arts. 30 and 36 of the EEC Treaty' [1977] C.M.L. Rev. 5; Ehlermann, 'Das Verbot der Massnahmen gleicher Wirkung in der Rechtsprechung des Gerichtshofes' in *Festschrift für Ipsen*, (1977), 579; Veelken, 'Massmahmen gleicher Wirkung wie mengenmässige Beschränkungen' [1977] EuR. 311; VerLoren van Themaat, 'De artikelen 30–36 van het EEG-Verdrag,' *op. cit.* note 53 above.

[62] See para. 6.28 above.

[63] 'Der EWG-rechtliche Begriff der 'Massnahmen gleicher Wirkungen wie eine mengenmässige Beschränkung'' [1967] N.J.W. 2081.

[64] *Op. cit.* note 10 above.

[65] *Funktion und Grenzen der Rechtsangleichung nach Art. 100 EWG-Vertrag* (1976) in particular at 84 *et seq.*

[66] In Ehle and Meier *EWG-Warenverkehr* (1971), 158 *et seq.*

[67] Note 58 above; see also para. 7.53 below.

[68] 'Bevat art. 30 van het EEG-Verdrag slechts een non-diskriminatie-beginsel ten aanzien van invoerbeperkingen' 15 S.E.W. 632; see also his comments on Dirs. 70/32 and 70/50 in (1970) 18 S.E.W. 258.

[69] *Le droit de la Communauté économique européenne* (1970) Vol. I, 102.

measures discriminating against imports. In their view, all measures restricting inter-State trade were prohibited by Article 30, unless they were justified under Article 36 or were governed by other provisions of the Treaty. In support of this view, they pointed to the wide formulation of Article 30, which makes no mention of discrimination. Meij and Winter,[70] who adhered to this theory in a qualified form, also criticised Article 3 of Directive 70/50 on the grounds that it purports to deprive Article 36 of its proper scope by using the test of justification to decide whether a measure fell under Article 30 in the first place.[71]

On the other hand, the effect of this wide definition of measures of equivalent effect was to overstretch Article 36, which only applies to measures pursuing goals of a non-economic nature.[72] In consequence, Waelbroeck[73] added the rider that to come under Article 30 a measure must have direct causal effect on imports or on the marketing or use of an imported product so that economic policy measures affecting such matters as interest rates and incomes[74] fall outside Article 30. However, as has been pointed out,[75] the test of directness is no easier to apply than that of discrimination. Nor does it accord with the *Dassonville*[76] formula according to which measures capable of hindering intra-Community trade 'directly or indirectly, actually or potentially' constitute measures of equivalent effect. Similarly, Meij and Winter sought to overcome the same difficulty by putting forward the view that the concept of measures of equivalent effect only covered 'trading rules'. However, as they themselves admitted, it is not at all clear what is meant by 'trading rules'.[77]

6.32 The intermediate approach has been followed by those authors[78] who advocate the definition laid down by Directive 70/50. A second form of intermediate approach was adopted by Steindorff[79] who stated that the concept of measures of equivalent effect only applied to discriminatory measures but, unlike the proponents of the narrow definition, he considered that discrimination in this context covered not only discrimination of form but also discrimi-

---

[70] *Op. cit.* note 61 above.
[71] See para. 7.33 below; by a parity of reasoning Art. 5 (2) of Dir. 70/50, in so far as it provides that the Directive applies without prejudice to Art. 36 EEC, is meaningless as far as 'indistinctly applicable' measures are concerned.
[72] See para. 8.18 below.
[73] *Op. cit.* note 61 above, at 19 *et seq.*
[74] See para. 7.64 below.
[75] Van Gerven, *op. cit.* note 61 above, at 9.
[76] See para. 6.13 above.
[77] In addition, the Court does not always use the term 'trading rules'; see para. 6.13 above.
[78] Béraud, 'Les mesures d'effet équivalent au sens des articles 30 et suivants du Traité de Rome' [1968] R.T.D.E. 265; Dona, 'Les mesures d'effet équivalent à des restrictions quantitatives' [1973] R.M.C. 224; Mattera, 'Libre circulation des marchandises et articles 30 à 36 du Traité CEE' [1976] R.M.C. 500.
[79] In *Dienstfreiheit und Versicherungsaufsicht im Gemeinsamen Markt* (1971), 79 at 82.

nation of substance. This meant that one must look behind a measure which is not discriminatory 'on its face' to see whether it is discriminatory in practice. Unfortunately the practical difficulties of applying such a test are very considerable[80] since it may involve consideration of complicated statistical data. What is more, on this test a measure may constantly oscillate between being discriminatory and not being discriminatory.[81]

This prompted Ulmer[82] to suggest yet another intermediate position. He criticised the test of discrimination, claiming that it was often hard to determine what was meant by this concept, and thus to apply the test. He gave as an example the requirement that goods of a certain kind, domestic and imported, bear an indication of origin likely to reduce the attraction of the imported product for the consumers. Furthermore, the test could not be applied at all to measures concerning products for which no national production exist. His solution was to suggest that the test set out in Article 3 of the Directive was to be applied to *all* measures whether discriminatory or not.

6.33   Ulmer's view may have influenced the Advocate General and the Court in the leading case of *REWE-Zentral* v. *Bundesmonopolverwaltung für Branntwein*[83] (commonly called the '*Cassis de Dijon*' case). The plaintiffs, who sought to import the French blackcurrant-based drink known as 'Cassis de Dijon', contested the validity of a provision of German law requiring spirits to have a minimum alcohol content. Cassis de Dijon, which in France has a content of between 15 per cent. and 20 per cent. fell into the category of products required to have 25 per cent. under the German provision. The German Court referred two questions on the compatibility of such a measure with Articles 30 and 37[84] respectively.

Advocate General Capotorti's conclusions are of particular interest

---

[80] Peter Ulmer 'Zum Verbot mittelbarer Einfuhrbeschränkungen im EWG-Vertrag' [1973] G.R.U.R. Int. 502 at 507.

[81] With respect to one category of measures, namely certain price controls, the Court does appear to apply the test of discrimination of substance: para. 7.47 *et seq.* below. The result is that it is extremely difficult to determine whether a given maximum price control is compatible with Art. 30 or not: para. 7.57 below.

[82] *Op. cit.* note 80 above.

[83] Case 120/78 [1979] E.C.R. 649, [1979] 3 C.M.L.R. 494; case notes, *inter alia*, by Millarg [1979] EuR. 420; Deringer and Sedemund [1979] N.J.W. 1079; Oliver [1980] C.M.L. Rev. 109; Wyatt [1981] E.L. Rev. 185; see also Meier, 'Zur Kombination von nationalen Lebensmittel-Begriffsbestimmungen und Vorschriften zum Schutz des Verbrauchers gegen Irreführungen als Rechtfertigungsgründe nach Art. 36 EWGV' [1980] W.R.P. 59; Meier, 'Kennzeichnung statt Verkehrsverbote—Die Rechtsprechung als Schrittmacher des Lebensmittelrechts' *Schriftenreihe des Bundes für Lebensmittelrecht und Lebensmittelkunde* (1980) 94 Heft 47; Dashwood 'Cassis de Dijon: A major step in the liberalization of trade' (1981) 9 E.I.P.R. 268; Capelli, 'Les malentendus provoqués par l'arrêt sur le "Cassis de Dijon"' [1981] R.M.C. 421; Masclet, 'Les articles 30, 36 et 100 du Traité CEE a la lumière de l'arrêt "Cassis de Dijon"' [1980] R.T.D.E. 64; Mattera, 'L'arrêt "Cassis de Dijon": une nouvelle approche pour la réalisation et le bon fonctionnement du marché intérieur' [1980] R.M.C. 505; VerLoren van Themaat, *op. cit.* note 61 above; Barents, *op. cit.* note 27 above.

[84] As regards Art. 37, see para. 11.12 below.

since, it is submitted, they throw light on certain aspects of the Court's judgment. He rejected the presumption contained in Directive 70/50 that 'indistinctly applicable' measures were compatible with Article 30. In his view this presumption was based on an 'attitude of prudence' which ceased to be justified after the end of the transitional period. On the other hand, he considered that consumer protection, though it did not expressly figure in the heads of justification in Article 36, did in fact fall under that provision. Applying both Article 36 EEC and Article 3 of the Directive, he found that a minimum alcohol requirement constituted an unjustified restriction on imports contrary to Article 30.

6.34   The Court's starting point was that 'in the absence of common rules relating to the production and marketing of alcohol' it is for the Member States to regulate these matters on their own territory.[85] Thereupon the Court stated that:

> 'Obstacles to movement within the Community resulting from disparities between the national laws relating to the marketing of the products in question must be accepted in so far as those provisions may be recognised as being necessary in order to satisfy mandatory requirements relating in particular to the effectiveness of fiscal supervision, the protection of public health, the fairness of commercial transactions and the defence of the consumer'.

It is clear from the words 'in particular' that the 'mandatory requirements' listed are merely examples. The list given in the judgment is therefore not exhaustive.[86]

The Court then proceeded to reject the German Government's arguments to the effect that the restriction in question was justified on the grounds of public health and consumer protection. In particular, as regards consumer protection it held that a reasonable labelling requirement would constitute an adequate guarantee for the consumer so that the imposition of a minimum alcohol requirement for drinks intended for human consumption constituted a measure of equivalent effect contrary to Article 30, if it applied to the importation of alcoholic beverages lawfully produced and marketed in another Member State.

6.35   This ruling is clearly a landmark in the Court's case law on Article 30, especially as it has now been confirmed in a series of subsequent judgments.[87] To underline the importance of this ruling the Commission has taken the unusual step of issuing a Communication[88] setting out the consequences flowing from it.

---

[85] On this part of the judgment see paras. 10.08 and 12.17 below.
[86] See para. 8.56 *et seq.* below.
[87] See para. 7.40 *et seq.* below.
[88] [1980] O.J. C256/2, see Annexe II to this book. Barents, *op. cit.* note 27 above, criticises this Communication, notably on the grounds of lack of clarity. Moreover, he objects to the fact that the Communication does not state whether the approach set out in Dir. 70/50 is henceforth to be abandoned by the Commission. Judge Touffait in 'Les entraves techniques à la libre circulation des marchandises' (Recueil Dalloz-Sirey 1982, Chronique 37) is also critical of the Communication; see Chap. XII, note 34. For a less critical view see Gormley [1981] E.L. Rev. 454.

On the other hand, it would be wrong to describe *Cassis de Dijon* as a 'revolutionary' judgment. Rather it has brought together in a new form strands that were to be found in various earlier cases.[89]

6.36 At all events it is generally considered that in view of the *Cassis de Dijon* judgment the test of whether a measure constitutes a measure of equivalent effect is not whether it discriminates against imports, but whether it *restricts* imports. This approach is entirely in keeping with the definition of measures of equivalent effect laid down in *Dassonville*[90]:

> 'all trading rules enacted by Member States, which are capable of hindering, directly or indirectly, actually or potentially, intra-Community trade'.

Yet discrimination continues to be relevant in two ways. First, a measure discriminating against imports constitutes *per se* an actual or potential, direct or indirect restriction on them. Secondly, with certain categories of measure of equivalent effect, discrimination is an inherent element. Examples are discrimination in the award of public supply contracts or measures inciting the purchase of national products. In these cases, discrimination is the very essence of the measure, and if it were removed, there would be no restriction on imports left. For these reasons, the continued mention of discrimination in some of the Court's judgments on Article 30 is quite consistent with *Cassis de Dijon*[91].

An alternative view has tentatively been put forward by Wyatt.[92] On this view, discrimination is merely 'presumed to be present where the sale of a product in free circulation in one Member State is prohibited in another' so that 'it will still be open to a party to proceedings to adduce evidence that the measure does not or is not likely in fact to have a discriminatory effect'. This view does not appear to be at variance with the Court's case law. On the other hand, the case law does not appear to afford any particular support to this view.

6.37 Also, reference should be made to a passage of the Court's judgment in Case 193/80 *E.C. Commission* v. *Italy*,[93] which may constitute the beginning of a new trend in its case law. The case arose out of infringement proceedings concerning an Italian Decree, which prohibited the sale in Italy of all vinegar, be it Italian or imported, other than wine vinegar. In its defence, the Italian Government claimed that the Decree was compatible with Article 30 because it applied to domestic products and to imports in the same way. The Court rejected this argument on the grounds that, even

---

[89] *e.g.* Case 13/77, note 58 above, see para. 7.53 below; Case 82/77, note 25 above, see para. 7.55 below.

[90] Para. 6.13 above.

[91] It appears, furthermore, that discrimination is decisive with respect to maximum price controls: para. 7.47 *et seq.* below.

[92] *Op. cit.* note 83 above, at 189.

[93] Judgment of 9 December 1981.

though the Decree applied to domestic products and to imports in the same way, it was nevertheless protectionist in its effects because it operated in favour of a typically Italian product, namely wine vinegar.

It may be that this phrase is simply a declaration of fact by the Court, in which case no significance is to be attached to it. On the other hand, it is open to criticism if it is intended to pave the way for a later judgment in which a new rule is to be laid down that a measure applying to domestic products and to imports in the same way only falls under Article 30 if it serves to protect a 'typical product' of the Member State concerned. It is hard to see how such a test of 'typicalness' could be workable. This is why it is submitted that it is preferable that all measures restricting imports, be they discriminatory or not, should be held to fall within Article 30— subject, of course, to the normal rules of 'justification'.

6.38   Be that as it may, another feature of *Cassis de Dijon* is that, following the Advocate General, the Court appears to have reversed the presumption of legality contained in Article 3 of Directive 70/ 50; consequently the burden of proof is now borne by the party seeking to show that a measure restricting trade is justified[93a]. This is shown by the wording of the Court's judgment in *Gilli and Andres*,[94] the first to confirm *Cassis de Dijon*. There the Court held that

> 'it is only where rules, which apply without discrimination to both domestic and imported products, may be justified as necessary in order to satisfy imperative requirements . . . that they may constitute an exception to the requirements arising under Article 30'.

Yet the mere fact that Directive 70/50 has been implicitly overruled to this extent does not mean that it ceases to have any value. It is submitted that parts of the Directive are still of value as a guide to the interpretation of Article 30.[95]

6.39   One question left open by *Cassis de Dijon* was the relationship between the 'mandatory requirements' laid down by that judgment[96] and Article 36. That provision is not mentioned at all in the *Cassis de Dijon* judgment. Two schools of thought have evolved on this matter:

> (i) According to the first view, the dichotomy between 'distinctly' and 'indistinctly applicable' measures lives on so that,

---

[93a] However, the Court referred once again to Article 3 of Directive 70/50 in Case 75/81 *Blesgen* v. *Belgian State*, see Annexe I.

[94] Case 788/79 [1980] E.C.R. 2071 at 2078, [1981] 1 C.M.L.R. 146 at 154; see para. 8.03 below.

[95] Para. 6.04 above.

[96] Para. 6.34 above.

- 'distinctly applicable' measures may only be justified on the grounds expressly set out in Article 36, whereas
- 'indistinctly applicable' measures may be justified *in addition* under the mandatory requirements.

This means that the question whether an 'indistinctly applicable' measure is necessary to satisfy a 'mandatory requirement' is to be weighed up *within* Article 30. Only if an 'indistinctly applicable' measure is found to be unjustified according to this test does it fall to be considered as a measure of equivalent effect at all.

On this view moreover—and this perhaps is the crucial point—'indistinctly applicable' measures are granted more favourable treatment in that the 'mandatory requirements' apply to them alone.

6.40   (ii) According to the second view, the 'mandatory requirements' are regarded as being subsumed under Article 36, either on the grounds that they fall under the heading of public policy[97] or that they constitute additions to the list of grounds of justification set out in Article 36.[98] On this view, *all* measures whether 'distinctly' or 'indistinctly' applicable' are subject to the same twofold test:
- does this measure actually or potentially, directly or indirectly restrict imports so as to fall under Article 30?
- if so, is it justified under Article 36 as extended by the 'mandatory requirements'?[99]

6.41   In support of the first theory, it should be said that the Court has repeatedly held that Article 36 must be interpreted narrowly since it constitutes an exception to a fundamental principle of Community law.[100]

6.42   On the other hand the following points can be made in support of the second theory:
   (i) This theory avoids the undue harshness resulting from the first theory with respect to 'distinctly applicable' measures *necessary* on, for instance, consumer protection grounds. According to the first theory, even though they are necessary, such measures are contrary to Article 30. According to the second theory, such measures are considered to fall under Article 30, but they may be justified under Article 36.
   (ii) It is submitted that the 'mandatory requirements' have the same properties as the grounds of justification in Article 36. Thus, for instance the Member State bears the burden of proof

[97] Meier, *op. cit.* note 83 above.
[98] Masclet, *op. cit.* note 83 above, at 624.
[99] A logical and consistent application of this theory would mean that quantitative restrictions would also be subject to the exceptions contained in 'mandatory requirements'.
[100] Para. 8.02 below.

that its measure is justified as with Article 36.[101] Also, as the Court expressly stated in *Cassis* in the passage quoted above, a measure will only be justified by a 'mandatory requirement' if it is necessary to attain that end—just as with Article 36.[102] Again, it is submitted that the 'mandatory requirements' cannot justify a national measure where Community legislation containing sufficient guarantees with respect to those requirements has come into force, just as with Article 36.[103]

(iii) Public health is expressly covered by Article 36 and is also mentioned in Case 120/78 as a 'mandatory requirement'. According to the second theory, this gives rise to no difficulty. Yet if the first theory is adopted, there is something of a logical impasse.[104]

(iv) It is not clear whether the protection of appellations of origin falls under industrial and commercial property within the meaning of Article 36 or whether it falls under the fairness of commercial transactions ('mandatory requirements').[105] It does not seem right that any consequences should flow from this classification.

(v) The first theory keeps in being the dichotomy between 'distinctly' and 'indistinctly applicable' measures, and we have seen how difficult this distinction is to apply.[106]

In view of these arguments, is it really decisive that Article 36, as an exception to a fundamental principle of Community law, is to be strictly construed? After all, once it has been decided that the 'mandatory requirements' justify import and export restrictions, a breach has inevitably been made in that principle; this is so regardless of which Treaty provision is said to contain those requirements. One wonders, therefore, whether it is really consistent to use this argument for excluding the 'mandatory requirements' from Article 36—and then to read the 'mandatory requirements' into Article 30.

6.43   It was not until its ruling in Case 113/80 *E.C. Commission* v. *Ireland*[107] that the Court ruled on this question. That case arose out of proceedings brought by the Commission under Article 169 of the

---

[101] Para. 6.38 above and para. 8.03 below.

[102] Para. 8.10 below.

[103] Para. 8.14 below.

[104] In para. 21 of its judgment in Case 193/80 (see note 93 above), the Court speaks of 'mandatory requirements such as the protection of public health referred to in Article 36'. It is unclear how this phrase is to be interpreted. In addition, in Case 272/80 *Frans-Nederlandse Maatschappij voor Biologische Producten* (judgment of 17 December 1981), the national court asked whether a national statute prohibiting the sale of pesticide without prior Government approval was contrary to Art. 30 or was justified on health grounds. The law applies in the same way to domestic products and to imports. Although the national court did not refer to Art. 36 in its question, the Court based its judgment on both Art. 30 and Art. 36.

[105] Para. 8.57 below.

[106] Para. 6.32 above.

[107] Judgment of 17 June 1981 [1982] 1 C.M.L.R. 706; see Judge Touffait, *op. cit.* note 88 above.

Treaty with respect to two Irish Orders requiring certain metal objects to bear an origin marking. The Orders only applied to imported goods and were thus 'distinctly applicable'. The Irish Government contended that these measures were justified on the grounds of consumer protection, a 'mandatory requirement'. Thus the question of whether the 'mandatory requirements' applied to 'distinctly applicable' measures was squarely posed. The Court ruled in the following terms:

'The orders concerned in the present case are not measures which are applicable to domestic products and to imported products without distinction but rather a set of rules which apply only to imported products and are therefore discriminatory in nature, with the result that the measures in issue are not covered by the decisions cited above which relate exclusively to provisions that regulate in a uniform manner the marketing of domestic products and imported products'.

It is submitted that this statement is open to the objections set out in paragraph 6.42. But the Court then proceeded to rule that it is 'necessary to consider whether the contested measures are indeed discriminatory or whether they constitute discrimination in appearance only'. The Court then examined the measures to see if they were justified on consumer protection grounds (and found they were not). This appears to go back on the passage of this judgment just quoted. The idea that a 'distinctly applicable' measure may be justified on the grounds of consumer protection has been put out by the door[108] and let in through the window! What is more, this constitutes a major departure from the well-established principle that a measure constituting 'discrimination in appearance only' (that is, a measure applying to imports only or in a more onerous way, but which is nevertheless objectively justified) falls under Article 30 but is justified under Article 36.[109]

Consequently it is to be feared that the judgment in *E.C. Commission* v. *Ireland* will lead to considerable legal uncertainty.

6.44 The Court's judgment in *E.C. Commission* v. *Ireland* has now been followed up by a Commission answer to a written question[110] in which it stated that the 'mandatory requirements' apply 'if (and only if) the measure in question applies equally to domestic and imported goods'. In other words, it has come out in favour of the first of the two theories set out above. The same approach was followed by Advocate General VerLoren van Themaat in his conclusions in *Industrie Diensten Groep* v. *Beele*.[111] His view appears to be that the 'mandatory requirements' fall under Article 30, but that the general principles of Article 36 nevertheless apply to the 'mandatory

---

[108] See para. 6.42 point (i) above.
[109] Para. 8.06 below.
[110] Written question 874/81 ([1981] O.J. C295/29). See also generally written question 749/81 ([1981] O.J. C309/7).
[111] Case 6/81, judgment of 2 March 1982.

requirements': thus a measure will not be justified if it constitutes arbitrary discrimination or a disguised restriction on trade between the Member States, or if it is more restrictive of imports than is necessary, having regard to the object to be achieved. In this connection he points out that the 'mandatory requirement' at issue in that case, namely the prevention of unfair competition, is very close to the protection of industrial and commercial property under Article 36.

What is more, in a recently published article,[112] Judge Touffait has taken a similar view. For him, the 'mandatory requirements' are subject to broadly the same criteria as the grounds of justification under Article 36, but there are differences: whereas with Article 36 the measure must not constitute a means of arbitrary discrimination or a disguised restriction on trade between Member States, with the 'mandatory requirements' it must be shown that the measure concerned is necessary to meet such a requirement, that it applies in the same way to domestic products and imports, and that it is 'neither discriminatory, nor disproportionate'.

C. The principle of equivalence

6.45   In its penultimate ground of judgment in *Cassis de Dijon* the Court ruled that:

> 'There is . . . no valid reason why, provided that they have been lawfully produced and marketed in one of the Member States, alcoholic beverages should not be introduced into any other Member State; the sale of such products may be subject to a legal prohibition on the marketing of beverages with an alcohol content lower than the limit set by national rules'.

Consequently, in the operative part of its judgment, the Court ruled that a measure of the kind in question was contrary to Article 30 'where the importation of alcoholic beverages lawfully produced and marketed in another Member State is concerned'.[113]

Although the Court did not spell out the principle of equivalence expressly in *Cassis de Dijon*, it did do so in its subsequent ruling in *Fietje*.[114] There, the Court held in effect that the obligation to declare the nature of goods on their label was, in principle, justified on consumer protection grounds. However, it added that:

> 'There is no longer any need for such protection if the details given on the original label of the imported product have as their content information on the nature of the product and that content includes at least the same information and is just as capable of being understood by the consumers in the importing State as the description prescribed by the rules of that State. . . .'

6.46   The Commission attached particular importance to the passage quoted from *Cassis de Dijon* communication[115] on that case. It drew

---

[112] 'Les entraves techniques à la libre circulation des marchandises' [1982] Recueil Dalloz-Sirey, Chronique 37.
[113] See also Case 788/79, note 94 above; and Case 130/80 *Kelderman* [1981] E.C.R. 527.
[114] Note 26 above.
[115] Note 88 above.

the conclusion that this passage was of general application, asserting that:

> '*Any product*[116] imported from another Member State must in principle be admitted to the territory of the importing Member State if it has been lawfully produced, that is, conforms to rules and processes of manufacture that are customarily and traditionally accepted in the exporting country, and is marketed in the territory of the latter . . .
>
> The principles decided by the Court imply that a Member State may not in principle prohibit the sale in its territory of a product lawfully produced according to technical or quality requirements which differ from those imposed on its domestic products. Where a product "suitably and satisfactorily" fulfils the legitimate objective of a Member State's own rules (public safety, protection of the consumer or the environment, etc.) the importing country cannot justify prohibiting its sale in its territory by claiming that the way it fulfils the objective is different from that imposed on domestic products'.

6.47 This calls for a number of comments:

(i) The judgments do not define what is meant by lawful marketing in the Member State of production. Nor does the Commission's Communication. Presumably it will be enough if, on production, the goods are lawfully sold for export. There would appear to be no need for an initial sale entirely within the producing Member State before the goods are sold for export. Mattera[117] reaches the same conclusion by a different route. For him the requirement means that while Member States must allow typical and traditional products from other Member States, they may prohibit products which do not match up to their traditional image and thus do not possess the characteristics which the consumer expects.

6.48 (ii) As the Commission pointed out in its Communication, even if a product is lawfully produced and marketed in a Member State, it may not be sold within another Member State which has higher standards than the Member State of production—provided always that those higher standards are justified as being necessary to satisfy mandatory requirements. Thus if the optimal standard for a given product is 100 and the importing Member State requires 80, then it may justifiably prohibit the sale of goods conforming to the standard of only 70 imposed by the producing Member State. The same applies *a fortiori* if the producing Member State imposes no minimum standards at all. But, as already explained,[118] there is always a rebuttable presumption that the higher standard is not necessary.

---

[116] The italics are those of the author.
[117] *Op. cit.* note 83 above.
[118] Para. 6.38 above.

On the other hand, if two Member States both require a standard of 80 but lay down different means of reaching that result, then each must permit the sale of the other's product. That is what we have called the principle of equivalence.

It will not always be clear whether two standards are in fact equivalent. It is submitted that Member States are under a duty to take active steps[119] to establish whether this is so.

6.49   (iii) What is important in this context is not whether the producing Member State imposes a standard equivalent to that of the importing Member State. What matters, rather, is whether the product in question *in fact* meets a standard equivalent to that of the importing Member State—assuming that the product was lawfully produced in the Member State of production. This is illustrated by *Fietje* which in essence concerned the compatibility with Articles 30 to 36 of the obligation to indicate the denomination 'liqueur' on goods of a particular kind. The Court found that such a requirement fell foul of Article 30 if the goods *in fact* bore a label containing information of equivalent value to the consumer. The Court did not state that it was necessary to look into the legislation of the producing Member State to consider whether it required such labelling.

6.50   Does the mention in *Cassis de Dijon* of goods lawfully produced and marketed *in a Member State* mean that the principle of equivalence does not apply to goods originating in a third State but in free circulation in the Community?[120] It is submitted that it does not mean this: the wording of the judgment is determined by the fact that in the case itself the goods in question did originate in a Member State.

Let us take the following example: a product is manufactured in a third country and is then put in free circulation in Member State A, whereupon it is imported into Member State B.[121] The following solution is tentatively proposed:

(a) the principle of equivalence has no bearing within Member State A. For the question whether Member State A can prevent

---

[119] Paras. 6.15 above and 12.17 below.

[120] Some language versions of the initial cyclostyled text of the judgment in Case 788/79 *Gilli* (see note 94 above) stated that it was enough that goods were lawfully marketed in a Member State. However, a corrigendum was then published adding the requirement of lawful *production* in a Member State thus bringing it into line with *Cassis*. The remarks of Meier on this aspect of the *Gilli* judgment in [1981] EuR. 43 at 46 concern the unamended version of the judgment.

[121] This is quite different from the case where restrictions are imposed on direct imports into the Community, a subject which falls outside the scope of this book. See generally, however, para. 9.23 below. On quantitive restrictions and measures of equivalent effect in direct trade with third countries see Cases 51–54/71, note 23 above; Case 51/75 *EMI* v. *CBS* [1976] E.C.R. 811, [1976] 2 C.M.L.R. 235; Case 86/75 *EMI* v. *CBS* [1976] E.C.R. 871, [1976] 2 C.M.L.R. 235; Case 96/75 *EMI* v. *CBS* [1976] E.C.R. 913, [1976] 2 C.M.L.R. 235; Case

the product being put into free circulation, Article 30 is not relevant at all. As regards a prohibition on sale, it is submitted that the principle of equivalence does not apply either and it is therefore not enough that the product presents guarantees equivalent to the norms laid down by Member State A; the product must conform to those norms themselves. This is because the concept of putting in free circulation is essentially a customs concept: it does not mean that goods from third countries put into free circulation in the Community are assimilated to Community goods in every respect;

(b) when the goods are then imported from Member State A to Member State B, there will of course be no problem if they actually meet the standards laid down by Member State B. But, in any case, if the goods comply with the norms of Member State A, then they are assimilated to goods originating in Member State A for this purpose.

6.51 What are the practical consequences for the non-specialist of the principle of equivalence? Potentially these are enormous. Mattera[122] sees this ruling as a step away from the faceless world of Euro-bread, Euro-beer and Euro-toys. Instead, local specialities from every Member State can in principle be bought and sold in their traditional form all over the Community. This gives the consumer a wide range of products to choose from.

On the other hand, this ruling has been criticised on the grounds that it will result in a lowering of standards: as has just been explained, the effect of the ruling is that a Member State may prohibit the sale of goods complying with a lower standard than its own, provided the higher standard is justified. Thus, for instance, it cannot seriously be argued that the judgment in *Gilli*—in which the Court held that the prohibition in a Member State on the sale of cider vinegar was contrary to Article 30—resulted in any lowering of standards. It is not the *principles* laid down in *Cassis de Dijon* but their possible *application* which could lead to a lowering of standards; it all depends how wide the Court makes the exceptions (in particular consumer protection[123] and the prevention of unfair competition).

IV. MEASURES OF EQUIVALENT EFFECT ON EXPORTS

6.52 Before examining the concept of measures of equivalent effect falling under Article 34, it is as well to consider why Member States

---

52/77 *Cayrol* v. *Rivoira* [1977] E.C.R. 2261, [1978] 2 C.M.L.R. 253; Case 179/78 *Procureur de la République* v. *Rivoira* [1979] E.C.R. 1147, [1979] 3 C.M.L.R. 456; Case 225/78 *Procureur de la République* v. *Bouhelier* [1979] E.C.R. 3151, [1980] 2 C.M.L.R. 541; Case 65/79 *Procureur de la République* v. *Chatain* [1980] E.C.R. 1345, [1981] 3 C.M.L.R. 418; Case 270/80 *Polydor* v. *Harlequin Record Shops* [1982] 1 C.M.L.R. 677,

[122] *Op. cit.* note 83 above, at 50.
[123] See para. 8.49 below.

impose restrictions on exports at all. A Member State will normally be moved to take such action by one or more of the following motives[124]:

- a desire to ensure supplies;
- the protection of jobs in processing industries (in this case the export restriction will cover the raw material or component part, but not the finished product);
- the prevention of parallel exports (so that manufacturers established in the Member State in question will be able to obtain higher profits in their export trade);
- the preservation of works of art for the nation.[125]

6.53   The timetable for the abolition of such measures is that set out in paragraphs 5.01 to 5.03 above: Article 33 (7) and the Directives[126] adopted under it apply only to measures of equivalent effect on imports.

Sections II and III (A) of this chapter apply *mutatis mutandis* to Article 34. In so far as discrimination is at all relevant, it is discrimination against goods intended for export in favour of goods intended for the domestic market. This applies whether these goods were produced in the Member State in question or are merely in free circulation there; it is clear that the prohibition in Article 34 applies to re-exports.[127] Like measures of equivalent effect on imports, such measures relating to exports may take effect at the border but do not necessarily do so. Classic examples are: export licences[128]; measures which lower the value of a product intended for export or increase its costs; and measures which discourage the sale of products for export. Once again, a measure will not fall under Article 34 if it is caught by another prohibition in the Treaty, such as Article 16, 92 or 95.

6.54   As we have seen,[129] a measure restricting imports will fall under Article 30, even if it applies to domestic and imported products in the same way. The fundamental question concerning Article 34 which remains to be answered is: can measures fall within the concept of measures of equivalent effect under Article 34, even if they apply in the same way to exports and to goods intended for the domestic market? In other words, does a measure restricting exports fall under Article 34 even if it does not discriminate against exports? At first sight, there would appear to be no obstacle to Article 34 covering this type of measure, especially as the *Dassonville*[130] formula does not purport to be limited to measures of equivalent effect on

---

[124] As to the relevance of the object of the measure, see para. 6.57 and note 139 below.
[125] Measures adopted for the latter motive will often be justified under Art. 36: see paras. 8.33 *et seq.* below.
[126] Paras. 6.02 *et seq.* above.
[127] Restrictions on re-exports will generally infringe both Art. 30 and Art. 34.
[128] Para 7.67 *et seq.* below.
[129] Para. 6.36 above.
[130] Para. 6.13 above.

imports.[131] Nevertheless on closer examination the problem becomes more complex.

In this context it is necessary to distinguish between:
- restrictions on production; and
- restriction on sale.

These will be taken in turn.

6.55 In *Groenveld* v. *Produktschap voor Vee en Vlees*,[132] which concerned a prohibition on producing horse meat, the Court held that Article 34 'concerns national measures which have as their specific object or effect the restriction of patterns of exports and thereby the establishment of a difference between the domestic trade of a Member State and its export trade in such a way as to provide a particular advantage for national production or for the domestic market of the State in question'. This was the first case concerning the compatibility with Article 34 of a restriction on the production of goods not covered by an agricultural organisation of the market.[133] Yet this ruling was delivered by a Chamber of the Court and constituted such a radical break from the previous case law on Articles 30 and 34 that there was reason to think that it would not be followed by the full Court.[134]

6.56 Nevertheless, VerLoren van Themaat[135] has expressed the view that this ruling is correct. In his view Article 34 only applies to restrictions imposed on exports alone or falling more heavily on exports than on goods put on the national market: in other words, he takes the view that Article 34 only covers 'distinctly applicable' measures.[136] It is indeed true that if all restrictions on production were held to fall under Article 34, that provision would be very wide indeed. For instance, legislation imposing the requirement to obtain planning permission before building a factory would fall under Article 34, as would legislation relating to health and safety at work. Such measures would then be incompatible with the Treaty unless it could be shown that they were justified.

VerLoren van Themaat deduces from Article 52 that Article 34 cannot be so wide. Article 52, relates to the right of establishment and provides in particular that

'freedom of establishment shall include the right to take up and pursue activities as self-employed persons and to set up and manage undertakings . . . under

---

[131] The *Dassonville* formula was incorporated (though in rather an oblique way) in para. 16 of the judgment in Case 53/76 *Procureur de la République* v. *Bouhelier* [1977] E.C.R. 197 at 205, [1977] 1 C.M.L.R. 436 at 444; that judgment concerned Art. 34.
[132] Case 15/79 [1979] E.C.R. 3409, [1981] 1 C.M.L.R. 207.
[133] See paras. 7.63 and 10.12 and 10.13.
[134] See also para. 7.69 below.
[135] *Op. cit.* note 61 above.
[136] He points out (*op. cit.* at 391) that on the basis of *Groenveld*, the United Kingdom and the Netherlands would be entitled to restrict production of North Sea oil and gas respectively without falling foul of Art. 34—provided that such restrictions applied in the same way to products intended for the domestic market and for export.

the conditions laid down for its own nationals by the law of the country where such establishment is effected . . .'.

That provision thus appears to be a prohibition on discrimination rather than on restrictions on the freedom of establishment. Ver-Loren van Themaat takes the view that Article 52 would be undermined if all restrictions on establishment simultaneously fell under Article 34. He therefore regards such a wide definition of measures of equivalent effect under Article 34 as contrary to the 'system of the Treaty'. This leads him to the conclusion that the *Groenveld* judgment is of general significance, since it avoids this potential conflict between Articles 34 and 52.

6.57 Against this background, the *Groenveld* formula was reiterated by the full Court in *Oebel*[137] with respect to a prohibition on baking at night. Under these circumstances, the formula requires dissection here. For a measure to constitute a measure of equivalent effect under Article 34, it appears to lay down two cumulative conditions:

– the measure must have as its specific object[138] or effect the restriction of patterns of export; and
– it must discriminate in favour of goods intended for the domestic market against exports so as to favour national production[139] or the domestic market of the State in question.

This would be a very onerous burden of proof to discharge. For instance, on this test a measure applying in the same way to goods intended for the national market and for export will fall outside Article 34 altogether even if it restricts exports and its sole object is to restrict exports without there being any objective justification for this. Thus the prohibition contained in Article 34 could often be circumvented simply by careful drafting of national legislation. Read literally this ruling would have the effect of excluding from the scope of Article 34 all but the most flagrant measures such as export licences.

6.58 In fact, any measure which discriminates against exports must *per se* have as its specific object or effect to restrict patterns of exports. Consequently, it is preferable not to construe the formula as containing two separate and cumulative conditions. Perhaps the test itself is contained in the first part of the formula: to constitute a measure of equivalent effect under Article 34 a measure must have as its specific object or effect to restrict patterns of exports. On this view, the second limb is merely a gloss on the first and simply gives an example of a measure having as its specific object or effect the

---

[137] Case 155/80 [1981] E.C.R. 1993.
[138] Until *Groenveld* it had been thought that the *object* of a measure was always irrelevant in determining whether it fell under Art. 30 or 34: para. 6.13 above.
[139] It is not entirely clear how a restriction on exports could favour national production, unless it be national production of finished products where the restriction applies to the raw material or component parts.

restoration of patterns of export. All this is purely hypothetical, but in any event the *Groenveld* formula may need further refinement if improper restrictions on exports are not to slip through the net of Community law.

6.59   So much for restrictions on production. What of restrictions on sale? The *Groenveld* formula purports to apply to all restrictions on export whether they apply at the stage of production or of sale. Yet it is interesting to note that *Groenveld* itself concerned a restriction on production, as did that aspect of *Oebel* to which the Court applied that formula (namely the prohibition on night baking). In *Oebel* itself, as regards the prohibition on night delivery of bread—a restriction on sale—the Court applied the same test for Articles 30 and 34.[140]

Indeed, there appears to be no reason why *Cassis de Dijon* cannot be applied *mutatis mutandis* to Article 34 as regards restrictions on sale. This category of measures comprises provisions of the type at issue in *Cassis de Dijon* itself: measures prohibiting the sale of certain products; or relating to the presentation of products. Frequently, national measures of this kind do not apply to sales for export.[141] Nevertheless, to the extent that such measures do cover sales for export, there appears to be no real reason why *Cassis de Dijon* should not apply to them; in other words, in the absence of justification such restrictions may be contrary to Article 34 even though they apply in the same way to exports and to goods put on the national market.

6.60   Lastly, do the 'mandatory requirements' laid down in *Cassis de Dijon*[142] apply to measures of equivalent effect on exports? There is every reason to suppose that they do. In his observations in *Groenveld* and *Oebel* Advocate General Capotorti propounded the view that the 'mandatory requirements' did apply to export restrictions.[143] Moreover, the Court in *Oebel* more or less implied this to be so.[144]

Nonetheless it is difficult to see how there could be room for the 'mandatory requirements' to apply to export restrictions if the Court continues to rule that:

- the 'mandatory requirements' do not apply to 'distinctly applicable' measures[145]; and
- the concept of measures of equivalent effect under Article 34 only covers measures discriminating against exports ('distinctly applicable' measures).

[140] Para. 7.46 below.
[141] See note 159 below.
[142] Paras. 6.34 *et seq.* above.
[143] However, he took the view that *Cassis de Dijon* could quite generally be applied *mutatis mutandis* to Art. 34, so that 'indistinctly applicable' measures fell under that provision. As we have seen, the Court held otherwise in *Groenveld* and *Oebel*.
[144] Para. 8.55 below.
[145] Para. 6.43 above.

V. DE FACTO HARMONISATION

6.61 We saw in an earlier part of this chapter[146] how the Court held in the *Cassis de Dijon* case that in the absence of a mandatory requirement a Member State is bound to admit goods lawfully produced and marketed in another Member State. If all the Member States impose precisely the same technical standard for a particular product, then goods not complying with that standard cannot be lawfully produced or marketed in any Member State of the Community. There will then be no restriction on imports or exports between Member States so that neither Article 30 nor Article 34 will be infringed. It is submitted then, that as regards technical standards, *de facto* harmonisation is compatible with Articles 30 to 36.[147] To hold otherwise would be to interpret Articles 30 to 36 as guaranteeing access to the market or, in other words, creating a fundamental right to sell goods commercially.[148] This goes considerably further than the mere prohibition on unnecessary restrictions on inter-State trade.

To take one example, should all Member States require a particular drink to have an alcohol content of at least 15 per cent. there will be no infringement of Article 30 or 34, simply because there will be no restrictions on imports or exports between Member States. This will be so whether or not Member States have acted in concert. It will be otherwise, however, if one single Member State imposes a different minimum alcohol requirement or none at all: trade between that State and the others will then be restricted. This shows that *de facto* harmonisation is no lasting substitute for Community legislation.

6.62 However, it must not be overlooked that as a general rule if all Member States enact the same restriction they will all be infringing Article 30. Thus, for instance, if they all subject imports of a certain product to unnecessary import controls, then they are all committing an infringement. Only technical standards cease to constitute import restrictions once they are adopted by all the Member States.

VI. "PURELY NATIONAL" MEASURES

6.63 Do Articles 30 and 34 prohibit restrictive national measures relating to goods, which affect neither imports nor exports? Similarly, can a domestic producer supplying only the domestic market invoke either of these provisions against a measure on the grounds that the measure also restricts imports or exports? For example:

---

[146] Paras. 6.45 *et seq.* above.

[147] In a rather different context Case 89/76 *E.C. Commission* v. *Netherlands* [1977] E.C.R. 1355, [1978] 3 C.M.L.R. 630, which concerned phytosanitary controls on exports, shows that the Court attaches importance to *de facto* harmonisation.

[148] See Schiller, *op. cit.* note 36 above; this theory is also discussed by Grabitz 'Das Recht auf Zugang zum Markt nach dem EWG-Vertrag' in *Festschrift für Ipsen*, (1977), 645.

- can a producer of goods in a Member State invoke Article 30 or 34 against a restriction on sale in that Member State in respect of goods put on the national market?
- can an importer of goods originating in England, Scotland or Wales rely on Article 30 with respect to a restriction on importing those goods to Northern Ireland?

These are open questions.[149] But it would seem that the result for national goods must be the same whether the measure complained of applies only to national goods or applies also to goods from other Member State.[150]

6.64 Nevertheless, it is contended here that 'purely national' measures are not caught by these provisions at all. Article 30 prohibits 'quantitative restrictions on imports and all measures having equivalent effect' while Article 34 prohibits the same measures with respect to exports. Consequently, it can be deduced from the wording of these provisions that a measure applying neither to imports nor to exports but applying only to domestic goods put on the national market falls outside Articles 30 and 34 altogether. This view corresponds with the thesis already put forward to the effect that the function of these provisions is to prohibit (subject to exceptions) restrictions on trade between Member States, and not to create some sort of fundamental right to sell goods commercially.[151] On this view the only means provided by the Treaty for removing any disparities that might result from differences between different 'purely national' measures is by harmonisation under Article 100[152] or action under Article 101.[153] This thesis also corresponds to the wording of the Court's judgments in *Fietje*[154] and *Keldermann*[155] where the Court held that the *extension to imports* of the measures at issue was contrary to Article 30.[156] This implies that had those measures not extended to imports, they would have been compatible

---

[149] To some extent, this is the question of reverse discrimination, which has been examined by the Court with respect to other provisions in the Treaty. See Case 1/78 *Kenny* v. *Insurance Officer* [1978] E.C.R. 1489, [1978] 3 C.M.L.R. 651 (social security); Case 175/78 *R.* v. *Saunders* [1979] E.C.R. 1129, [1979] 2 C.M.L.R. 216 (Art. 48); Case 115/78 *Knoors* v. *Secretary of State for Economic Affairs* [1979] E.C.R. 399, [1979] 2 C.M.L.R. 357 (Arts. 52 and 59); Case 136/78 *Ministère Public* v. *Auer* [1979] E.C.R. 437, [1979] 2 C.M.L.R. 373 (Art. 52); Case 86/78 *Peureux* v. *Directeur des Services Fiscaux* [1979] E.C.R. 897, [1980] 3 C.M.L.R. 337 (Art. 95). The articles by Mortelmans, 'La discrimination à rebours et le droit communautaire' [1979] S.E.W. 654 and [1980] Dir. Scamb. Int. 1 and by Kon, 'Aspects of Reverse Discrimination in Community Law' [1981] E.L. Rev. 75 show that whether reverse discrimination is prohibited depends on the Treaty provision in question.

[150] See Case 68/79 *Just* v. *Ministry for Fiscal Affairs* [1980] E.C.R. 501, [1981] 2 C.M.L.R. 714 (on Art. 95).

[151] See para. 6.61 above.

[152] See para. 12.02 below.

[153] See para. 12.06 below.

[154] Note 26 above.

[155] Note 113 above.

[156] In *Fietje* this finding was only conditional (see para. 8.47 below) but that is not relevant in this context.

with Article 30. However, the question of 'purely national measures' did not arise in these cases.

6.65   The only case to date in which this matter has arisen is *Officier van Justitie* v. *Koninklijke Kaasfabriek Eyssen.*[157] That case concerned a Dutch measure prohibiting the use of a preservative called nisin in processed cheese while creating an exemption for exports. The defendant company, which produced processed cheese in the Netherlands, was charged before the Dutch courts with contravening that regulation. On a reference for a preliminary ruling, the Dutch court in effect asked whether such a measure was compatible with Articles 30 to 36. In its submissions the Commission invited the Court to rule, *inter alia*, that the defendant company could not invoke these provisions at all: it could not invoke Article 30, because the goods at issue were domestically produced and not imported; it could not invoke Article 34 either because the national legislation contained a special exemption for exports.

The Advocate General gave this argument short shrift:

> 'In the familiar words of the judgment of the Court in the *Dassonville* case [Article 30] "forbids all trading rules enacted by Member States which are capable of hindering, directly or indirectly, actually or potentially, intra-Community trade". Thus Article 30 does not merely forbid discrimination against goods from other Member States. It can apply even where there is not such discrimination'.

Nevertheless, it is not certain that such a specific proposition can be deduced from the *Dassonville* formula. In any case, the Court sometimes speaks of Article 30 as covering obstacles 'to imports between Member State' rather than to intra-Community trade.[158] The Court found that the measure was justified under Article 36 and therefore did not rule on the question at issue here.[159]

6.66   One objection can be levelled against the view that 'purely national' measures fall outside Articles 30 and 34: the concept of the domestic products of a Member State must be defined. Yet there appears to be no reason for not applying by analogy the principles laid down in the Community Regulations on origin.[160]

6.67   Lastly, a common market organisation may widen the prohibitions contained in Articles 30 and 34[161] so as to prohibit even 'purely national' measures.

---

[157] Case 53/80 [1981] E.C.R. 429.

[158] Para. 6.13 above.

[159] Para. 8.29 below. Also the defendants in the main case alleged that even though there was an express exemption in the Dutch legislation with respect to exports, the legislation fell under Art. 34, because they had to establish two production lines: one for the domestic market (without nisin) and one for export. Neither the Court nor the Advocate General found it necessary to decide the point. In any case, the view put forward by the defendant does not seem compatible with the Court's new case law on Art. 34: see para. 6.55 above.

[160] See para. 2.10 above.

[161] Para. 10.14 below.

VII. CONCLUSION

6.68 It is submitted then that with certain exceptions,[162] the concept of measures of equivalent effect under Article 30 embraces all restrictions on imports not covered by other provisions of the Treaty—even if they do not discriminate against imports.[163]

On the other hand, as regards restrictions on production, the concept of measures of equivalent effect under Article 34 is considerably narrower. It remains to be seen whether the same applies to other types of export restrictions, although there is no reason why it should do so.

Once it has been established that a particular measure falls under Article 30 or 34, then it must be considered whether that measure is justified under Article 36. A distinction must always be made between the question whether a measure constitutes a measure of equivalent effect and whether it is justified. Thus the question whether a measure is compatible with Article 30 or 34 must always be examined in two stages. At all events, it is submitted that the grounds of justification are the same whether a measure falls under Article 30 or Article 34 and whether it is 'distinctly applicable' or 'indistinctly applicable'.

---

[162] See para. 7.56 below.
[163] See para. 6.36 above.

CHAPTER VII

Measures of Equivalent Effect: II

7.01 In the previous chapter we considered the general principles relating to measures of equivalent effect. The purpose of the present chapter is to consider specific measures with a view to establishing whether or not they constitute measures of equivalent effect under Article 30 or 34 as the case may be. Articles 30 and 34 will be examined in turn. Naturally we shall leave out of account those measures which fall to be considered under other provisions of the Treaty.[1]

As we saw in the previous chapter, the compatibility of a national measure with Article 30 or Article 34 must be tested in two stages, by asking two fundamental questions:
- Does this measure constitute a measure of equivalent effect falling under Article 30 or Article 34?
- If so, is it justified under Article 36 as widened by *Cassis de Dijon*?

This chapter is concerned with the first of these two questions, while the second is dealt with in the following chapter. However, it has not been found possible to avoid mentioning Article 36 altogether.

7.02 Lastly, it should be pointed out that a large number of the Court's rulings discussed here concern agricultural products falling under a common market organisation.[2] As will be explained later in this book,[3] it is not always clear whether rulings of this kind are in fact interpretations of the common market organisation in question rather than of Articles 30 and 34. This means that it is not clear whether such rulings apply to all products.

I. MEASURES OF EQUIVALENT EFFECT UNDER ARTICLE 30

Import licences

7.03 The obligation to obtain an import licence or permit from the importing Member State before importing goods is a clear example of a measure of equivalent effect. In one of the first cases on Article

---

[1] Paras. 6.17 *et seq.* above.
[2] On the meaning of this concept of common market organisations, see para. 10.01 below.
[3] Paras. 10.08 *et seq.* below.

30 to come before it, *International Fruit Company* v. *Produktschap voor Groenten en Fruit*,[4] the Court decided that this held good even where licences were granted automatically and the Member State concerned did not purport to reserve the right to withold a licence. It did so in the following terms:

> 'Apart from the exception for which provision is made by Community law itself [Articles 30 and 34 (1)] preclude the appplication to intra-Community trade of a national provision which requires, even purely as a formality, import or export licences or any other similar procedure'.

The reason clearly is that even automatic licences can give rise to delay and abuse on the part of the importing Member State. The effect of this ruling was implicitly to strike down Article 2 (2) of Commission Directive 70/50[5] in so far as that provision suggests that a mere formality is compatible with Article 30.

This ruling has been repeated in a number of subsequent cases, notably *Donckerwolcke* v. *Procureur de la République*,[6] which show that such measures constitute measures of equivalent effect rather than quantitative restrictions. It is not clear whether such measures could ever be justified under Article 36.

The obligation to produce certain certificates

7.04 We are concerned here with the requirement that an importer produce certain types of certificate on importation, whether furnished by the authorities of an exporting Member State or by any other public or private body outside the importing Member State. This is to be distinguished from the case of import licences granted by the importing Member State itself, which was discussed in the previous section.

The first major case on Article 30, *Procureur du Roi* v. *Dassonville*,[7] was concerned with this type of measure. That case concerned a Belgian Royal Decree of 1934 prohibiting the importation into Belgium of spirits bearing a designation of origin officially recognised by the Belgian Government without an official document certifying their entitlement to such designation. The designation of origin 'Scotch Whisky' had been duly adopted by the Belgian Government. In 1970 (before Britain joined the Community) the defendants in the main case were parallel importers who had imported into Belgium various quantities of Scotch whisky from France, where they were in free circulation. They were charged with forging the official certificates of authenticity. In a reference for a preliminary ruling

---

[4] Cases 51–54/71 [1971] E.C.R. 1107.

[5] [1970] O.J. Spec. Ed. L13/29; see paras. 6.03 *et seq.* above.

[6] Case 41/76 [1976] E.C.R. 1921, [1977] 2 C.M.L.R. 535; see also Case 53/76 *Bouhelier* [1977] E.C.R. 197, [1977] 1 C.M.L.R. 436; Case 68/76 *E.C. Commission* v. *France* [1977] E.C.R. 515, [1977] 2 C.M.L.R. 161. The following cases concern export licences: Case 52/77 *Cayrol* v. *Rivoira* [1977] E.C.R. 2261, [1978] 2 C.M.L.R. 253.

[7] Case 8/74 [1974] E.C.R. 837, [1974] 2 C.M.L.R. 436, noted by Joliet [1975] M.L.R. 200 and Wellinghausen [1975] EuR. 322.

the Brussels court asked the Court of Justice, *inter alia*, whether measures of this kind were compatible with Article 30. In its reference the Brussels court pointed out that the effect of the Belgian provisions was to make imports of whisky from France impossible, since France did not require such certificates of authenticity.

The Court replied as follows:

> 'All trading rules enacted by Member States which are capable of hindering, directly or indirectly, actually or potentially, intra-Community trade are to be considered as measures having an effect equivalent to quantitative restrictions.
>
> In the absence of a Community system guaranteeing for consumers the authenticity of a product's designation of origin, if a Member State takes measures to prevent unfair practices in this connection, it is however subject to the condition that these measures should be reasonable and that the means of proof required should not act as a hindrance to trade between Member States and should, in consequence, be accessible to all Community nationals.
>
> Even without having to examine whether or not such measures are covered by Article 36, they must not, in any case, by virtue of the principle expressed in the second sentence of that Article, constitute a means of arbitrary discrimination or a disguised restriction on trade between Member States.
>
> That may be the case with formalities, required by a Member State for the purpose of proving the origin of a product, which only direct importers are really in a position to satisfy without facing serious difficulties.
>
> Consequently, the requirement by a Member State of a certificate of authenticity which is less easily obtainable by importers of an authentic product which has been put into free circulation in a regular manner in another Member State than by importers of the same product coming directly from the country of origin constitutes a measure having an effect equivalent to a quantitative restriction as prohibited by the Treaty'.

7.05   It is clear from this passage that Article 30 prohibits not only restrictions on imports as such, but also measures discriminating in favour of direct imports against indirect imports. As already explained, the facts in *Dassonville* arose before Britain had acceded to the Community, so that it is manifest that this principle applies even where the country of origin is not a Member State.

7.06   Indeed, the wording of this passage suggests that the requirement that imports be accompanied by a certificate of authenticity is not in itself a measure of equivalent effect. The wording suggests, rather, that this requirement only constituted a measure of equivalent effect because the certificates were harder to obtain for indirect imports than for goods coming directly from the country of origin.

However, this is merely due to the fact that *Dassonville* was the first major judgment of the Court on Article 30 and the Court's case law has evolved considerably since then. That the obligation to produce a certificate on importation in itself constitutes a measure of equivalent effect is shown by later cases. In particular, in *Denkavit Futtermittel* v. *Minister für Ernährung*[8] concerning imports of animal feed the Court held that

---

[8] Case 251/78 [1979] E.C.R. 3369, [1980] 3 C.M.L.R. 513; see also Case 53/76, note 6 above, as regards exports.

> 'the concept of a measure having an effect equivalent to a quantitative restriction
> . . . applies to the obligation to produce a certificate to the effect that the
> imported feeding-stuffs have undergone specified treatment in the exporting
> country'.

It is submitted, then, that any requirement to produce a document on importation[9] constitutes a measure of equivalent effect under Article 30. This applies whatever the nature of the document, be it a certificate of authenticity, or origin,[10] or a sanitary, veterinary or phytosanitary certificate. However, this is perhaps subject to the proviso that import controls fall outside Article 30 in so far as they are inherent in the customs procedure.[11] Again, inasmuch as such requirements do fall under Article 30, they will frequently be justified under Article 36 particularly on health grounds—although it is not clear that certificates of origin could ever be justified,[12] except for the limited category of products for which origin is essential.[13]

7.07 An element of confusion has, however, been caused by the Court's ruling in *E.C. Commission* v. *Belgium*[14] (sometimes known as *'Dassonville II'*). Since imports of Scotch whisky into Belgium were still subject to the restriction at issue in the first *Dassonville* case—except for certain 'liberalising measures' introduced as a matter of practice—the Commission brought proceedings under Article 169 of the Treaty against Belgium for infringement of Article 30. Yet the Court rejected the Commission's action.

The Court held that the test to be applied was: Do those measures create for the indirect importer 'difficulties in obtaining certificates which are unreasonable in relation to those which that State imposes on a direct importer'? It went on to rule as follows:

> 'The Commission has not satisfactorily refuted the argument of the Belgian
> Government that those liberalising measures have contributed to an appreciable
> improvement in the position in relation to direct importers or traders wishing
> to import spirits bearing a protected designation of origin into Belgium from
> another Member State where they are in free circulation, but has confined itself
> to stating that in spite of the said measures the system of control adopted by
> the Belgian Government still involves the importer of those products into
> Belgium in more difficulties than would result from the system of sealing and
> labelling which it advocates.
>
> That fact relied on by the Commission nevertheless cannot in itself constitute
> a failure by the Kingdom of Belgium to fulfil its obligations under Article 30
> of the Treaty.

---

[9] Similar restrictions operating at a later stage, *e.g.* sale, also constitute measures of equivalent effect: para. 7.39 below.

[10] A measure requiring certificates of origin has not yet come before the Court. But in view of the Court's rulings on declarations of origin (para. 7.13 below), the requirement of certificates of origin must *a fortiori* constitute a measure of equivalent effect. See written question 1288/81 [1982] O.J. C53/7).

[11] Para. 7.61 below.

[12] Para. 9.41 below.

[13] Para. 7.36 below.

[14] Case 2/78 [1979] E.C.R. 1761, [1980] 1 C.M.L.R. 216.

It is clear from those considerations that, even if the system for checking the authenticity of products bearing a designation of origin as applied by the Belgian Government involves the importer of those products into Belgium in more difficulties than would result from a system of sealing and labelling, that fact cannot in itself constitute a failure by the Kingdom of Belgium to fulfil its obligations under Article 30 of the Treaty.

For those reasons the action must be dismissed'.

7.08   This ruling appears to be irreconcilable with the rest of the Court's case law on Article 30, for two reasons:

Firstly, the first question to be asked in each case is, it is submitted, whether the measure in question restricts imports. In this connection it is not enough to consider whether the measure puts the direct importer in a more favourable position than the indirect importer. Otherwise a separate category of measures is created to which this (less stringent) test is applied—and how is this category to be circumscribed? In laying down this 'direct/indirect importer' test the Court was presumably influenced by the wording of the first *Dassonville* judgment,[15] yet it cannot be deduced from that earlier judgment that this is necessarily the test to be applied. What is more, the 'direct/indirect importer' test runs counter to the rest of the case law on Article 30.

Secondly, as will be seen in the following chapter,[16] it is a golden rule that a measure cannot be justified under Article 36 if it is unnecessarily restrictive on imports having regard to the purpose to be achieved. Yet by declining to have regard to the system of sealing and labelling advocated by the Commission, the Court in effect refused to apply this well established principle in *E.C. Commission* v. *Belgium*.

Import inspections

7.09   The obligation to submit imports or exports to veterinary, sanitary, phytosanitary and other similar inspections on imports or exports constitutes a measure of equivalent effect within the meaning of Articles 30 and 34 respectively. This was established with respect to phytosanitary controls on apple imports (designed to track down the formidable San José scale insect) in *Rewe-Zentralfinanz* v. *Landwirtschaftskammer*[17] and with respect to veterinary and public health inspections on veal imports in *Simmenthal* v. *Minister for Finance*.[18] Frequently such inspections will be justified under Article 36 on the grounds of the protection of the health and life of humans,

---

[15] See the last paragraph of the passage of *Dassonville* quoted at para. 7.04 above.
[16] Para. 8.10.
[17] Case 4/75 [1975] E.C.R. 843, [1977] 1 C.M.L.R. 599.
[18] Case 35/76 [1976] E.C.R. 1871, [1977] 2 C.M.L.R. 1; see also the following cases—Case 251/78, note 8 above; Case 132/80 *United Foods and Van den Abeele* v. *Belgian State* [1982] 1 C.M.L.R. 273; Case 42/82R *E.C. Commission* v. *France*, Order of 4 March 1982 (since this was an order for interim measures, it is of necessity couched in procedural rather than substantive terms and is thus of limited assistance in the understanding of Art. 30; see para. 7.18 below).

animals or plants, as the case may be. It is also probable that frontier controls inherent in the customs procedure fall outside Article 30 altogether.[19]

Certain sanctions or fines

7.10 There are three ways in which fines or other sanctions imposed for an offence under national law with respect to imported goods may fall under Article 30:

(i) It is clear that a sanction attached to a restriction on imports will be contrary to Article 30 if the restriction itself is: *Procureur de la République* v. *Rivoira*.[20]

(ii) It is also evident that criminal penalties discriminating against imported goods are contrary to Article 30: *Cayrol* v. *Rivoira*.[21] This may occur where national law either lays down no such penalties with respect to domestic goods or lays down lighter penalties with respect to domestic goods.

(iii) Lastly there is a measure of equivalent effect under Article 30 when a Member State imposes a penalty for a customs irregularity, which penalty is disproportionately high in view of the fact that the Member State is not entitled to prohibit the importation of the goods in question.

7.11 This last point was established in *Donckerwolcke* v. *Procureur de la République*[22] and in *Cayrol* v. *Rivoira*. In each case criminal proceedings had been brought against persons who had imported goods into France and falsely declared them to originate in a Member State. In each case, however, although the goods were in free circulation in the Community, they had in fact originated in a third country. The object of the reference was to ascertain whether the requirement of a declaration of origin imposed by the French authorities, and connected measures, were contrary to Article 30. As regards penalties the Court held:

> 'The fact that the importer did not comply with the obligation to declare the real origin of the goods cannot give rise to the application of penalties which are disproportionate taking account of the purely administrative nature of the contravention . . .
>
> In general terms any administrative or penal measure which goes beyond what is strictly necessary for the purposes of enabling the importing Member State to obtain reasonably complete and accurate information on the movement of goods falling within specific measures of commercial policy[23] must be

---

[19] Para. 7.61 below.

[20] Case 179/78 [1979] E.C.R. 1147, [1979] 3 C.M.L.R. 456, para. 14 of judgment; for the facts, see para. 9.35 below.

[21] Case 52/77 [1977] E.C.R. 2261, [1978] 2 C.M.L.R. 253, para. 5 of judgment; for the facts, see para 9.34 below.

[22] Note 6 above, discussed also at para. 9.33 below; see generally Case 65/79 *Procureur de la République* v. *Chatain* [1980] E.C.R. 1345, [1981] 3 C.M.L.R. 418.

[23] The phrase 'specific measures of commercial policy' would appear to be a reference to Art. 115; see paras. 7.14 and 9.33 below.

regarded as a measure having an effect equivalent to a quantitative restriction prohibited by the Treaty'.

7.12 It is submitted that this principle must apply equally to penalties imposed for the contravention of other customs requirements imposed by the Member States. The principle does not apply, however, where the Member State is entitled to prohibit or restrict the importation of the goods in question, since in such a case the offence is not 'purely administrative': this was made clear in *Procureur de la République* v. *Rivoira* where the Court held that criminal penalties 'cannot be applied without regard being had to the fact that the present case did not concern prohibited imports'. As will be explained in the next two chapters of this book, the reasons why a Member State may be entitled to restrict or prohibit imports are manifold: for instance, the restrictions may be justified under Article 36 or the Member State may have obtained an authorisation under Article 115 to prohibit the importation of the goods. Thus, to take but one example, if an importer evades a compulsory sanitary or veterinary control justified by Article 36, that is not an offence of a 'purely administrative nature'—even, it is submitted, if the goods in fact presented no danger to health and so would have had to be admitted after the sanitary or veterinary control had been carried out.

When the offence is of a 'purely administrative' nature, what types of penalty are excessive? In *Donckerwolcke* and *Cayrol* the Court gave two examples: firstly, seizure of the goods and, secondly, any pecuniary penalty fixed according to the value of the goods.

It is hard to imagine how any penalties falling under Article 30 could be justified under Article 36.

Certain obligatory declarations of origin

7.13 In certain circumstances the requirement that the importer make a declaration of origin at the time of importation is contrary to Article 30. This was laid down in the *Donckerwolcke* judgment already discussed where the Court held that:

> 'The requirement by the importing Member State of the indication of the country of origin on the customs declaration document for products in free circulation . . . does not in itself constitute a measure of equivalent effect . . . if the goods in question are covered by measures of commercial policy adopted by that State in conformity with the Treaty.
>
> Such a requirement would, however, fall under the prohibition contained in Article 30 of the Treaty if the importer were required to declare, with regard to origin, something other than what he knows or may reasonably be expected to know . . .'.

This was confirmed in *Cayrol* v. *Rivoira* and *Procureur de la République* v. *Rivoira*, both of which have also been discussed.

It is clear, then, that the obligation to make a declaration of origin constitutes a measure of equivalent effect under Article 30 where such obligation applies to an importer who does not know and cannot reasonably be expected to know the origin of the goods.

7.14 Furthermore, the reference to 'measures of commercial policy adopted by that State in conformity with the Treaty' is a reference to Article 115 with which *Donckerwolcke* was also concerned.[24] It is not entirely clear from the wording of the judgment whether, quite apart from the limitation explained in the preceding paragraph, declarations of origin may be required

   (i) only where the Commission has authorised the adoption of exceptional measures under Article 115 (in which case Article 30 is ousted in any case);

  (ii) also where the Member State is intending to apply to the Commission for authorisation to adopt exceptional measures under Article 115;

 (iii) under any circumstances.

From the general wording of the judgment it would appear that the first of these three interpretations is unduly restrictive.

In any case, where an obligation to make a declaration of origin constitutes a measure of equivalent effect, it is hard to envisage how it could ever be justified under Article 36.

Unreasonably limited customs facilities

7.15 It seems clear that Member States may not unduly restrict the operating hours of customs posts (e.g. open them only on Mondays). Nor may they unduly limit the points of entry (as would be the case, for instance, if Britain were to require all imported apples to be landed in Glasgow and nowhere else). In either case, the Member State would be infringing Article 30.[25]

On the other hand, it would probably be going too far to require that all points of entry into each Member State must remain open for all products 24 hours a day, since this would involve very considerable costs. What is more, certain categories of products require specialised personnel to carry out technical checks such as veterinary or sanitary controls. It is submitted, therefore, that in so far as restrictions on customs facilities are 'reasonable', they are compatible with Article 30—whether one considers either that they fall outside Article 30 altogether as being restrictions inherent in the customs clearance procedure,[26] or that they are justified under Article 36.[27] Whichever of these two theories is adopted, it will not be an easy task to determine what restrictions are 'reasonable', especially as this must vary from case to case.

---

[24] Para. 9.33 below.
[25] Para. 6.15 above; see also Ehlermann in Groeben, Boeckh, Thiesing, *Kommentar zum EWG-Vertrag* [1974] Vol. I, 257.
[26] Para. 7.61 below.
[27] Para. 8.11 below.

7.16 Only in one case, *United Foods and Van den Abeele* v. *Belgian State*,[28] has the Court been called upon to rule on a measure of this kind and even there the ruling on this particular point does not deal with this problem at any length. The national court asked the Court of Justice whether various aspects of a systematic and obligatory sanitary control on fish at the border were compatible with the Treaty. One of the questions posed was whether it was compatible with Article 30 that the national authorities limited the number of points and the hours at which such sanitary controls were carried out thus possibly limiting the customs posts and the hours for importing fish. The Court replied as follows:

> 'If, with regard to the determination by the customs authority of the premises where control is to be carried out as well as of days and times of their opening, it appears that the effect of these measures is to hinder imports they would be justified only on condition that they could be shown to satisfy objective requirements appertaining to the organisation of the public health service'.

Obligatory advance warning to customs

7.17 Also in the *United Foods* case[28] the Court was asked whether it was compatible with Article 30 that an importer of fish had to inform the customs authorities in writing at least 24 hours beforehand of the date and hour and point of importation and of the nature, quantity and provenance of the goods. In view of the extraordinarily onerous nature of these measures, the Court's ruling on this matter is perhaps rather cursory:

> 'The requirement that notice must be given in writing setting forth all the details prescribed under the legislation at issue at least 24 hours before importation appears to be incompatible with the speed of transactions and of transportation in this field, given the perishable nature of the goods in question'.

It is submitted that any obligation to give an advance warning of an importation to customs authorities is a measure of equivalent effect contrary to Article 30, even if the goods are not of a perishable nature. Only with respect to imports of a highly unusual nature or in other exceptional circumstances will such a requirement be justified.

Undue customs delays

7.18 The subjection of imports to unreasonable delays in customs clearance or other unreasonable delays in import formalities such as health controls will contravene Article 30. This proposition is borne out by the Court's order for interim measures in Case 42/82R *E.C.*

---

[28] Case 132/80; see note 18 above. In case 107/81 *E.C. Commission* v. *Italy*, the Commission claimed that Italy had infringed Art. 30 by unduly restricting the number of customs posts through which certain steel products could be imported. (The products in question fell under the EEC Treaty.) However, Italy has now withdrawn the measure complained of and the Commission's action has accordingly been struck out.

Commission v. *France*.[29] There, the Commission sought an order for interim measures against France for unreasonably delaying imports of Italian wine, notably by carrying out systematic analysis of all such imports and by paying undue regard to trivial irregularities in the accompanying documents. Since the Court considered that the Commission had made out a *prima facie* case that such practices infringed Article 30 and the Community wine Regulations, it granted the order requested. Nevertheless, this order is of necessity couched in procedural rather than substantive terms and thus provides little guidance as to the application of Article 30 to this type of measure.

The question of how long it is reasonable for the authorities to take to clear goods going through customs is obviously a vexed one. But is emerges from the *E.C. Commission* v. *France* case that, where delays have increased in the wake of pressure from domestic producers, regard must be had to the time taken by the authorities of the defendant Member State to clear the same goods through customs prior to such pressure.

Measures restricting the use of imported products or requiring the use of domestic products

7.19 Directive 66/683,[30] based on Article 33 (7), required Member States to abolish measures which

(a) partially or totally prohibited the use of an imported product;
(b) required the partial or total use of a domestic product;
(c) subjected the entitlement to a benefit, other than an aid within the meaning of Article 92 of the Treaty, to the total or partial use of a national product.[31]

A provision of this kind was at issue in *Peureux* v. *Directeur des Services Fiscaux*.[32] The plaintiffs wished to distil some oranges steeped in alcohol, which they had imported from Italy, where they were in free circulation. The defendant contested their right to do this, on the basis of a provision in the *Code Général des Impôts* stipulating that: 'distillation of all imported raw material with the exception of fresh fruit other than apples, pears or grapes shall be prohibited'. On a reference from a French court under Article 177, the Court found that such a measure constituted a measure of equivalent effect contrary to Article 30.

Discrimination in public supply contracts

7.20 Any measure by which public authorities discriminate against imported goods in the award of public supply contracts is a measure

---

[29] See note 18 above.
[30] [1966] J.O. 3748, para. 6.03 above.
[31] Dir. 66/683 itself exempted certain products from its operation, but those exemptions ceased to have effect at the end of the transitional period; para. 6.04 above.
[32] Case 119/78 [1979] E.C.R. 975, [1980] 3 C.M.L.R. 337.

of equivalent effect contrary to Article 30. Such measures were the subject of Commission Directive 70/32[33] based on Article 33 (7) of the Treaty. That Directive prohibited measures relating to the supply of goods to the State, regional or local authorities and other legal persons governed by public law, (a) which totally or partially prohibited the use of an imported product; or (b) which required the total or partial use of domestic products or granted domestic products a preference other than an aid under Article 92; or (c) made the supply of imported products more difficult or onerous. Foremost among such measures—though not specifically mentioned in the Directive—are those by which the public authorities of a Member State award a contract to a tenderer offering goods manufactured within that State, thus discriminating against another tenderer offering imported goods at more favourable terms.[34] Such infringements of Article 30 by the Member States are rife, but difficult to prove. An example of such a measure which has been the subject of infringement proceedings brought by the Commission under Article 169 is the case of preferential treatment accorded to Belgian manufactured products by the city of Liège.[35] At the time of writing, no case concerning public supply contracts has yet come to judgment before the Court.

7.21 It should also be pointed out that the Act of Accession of Greece contains a special provision on this type of measure. Article 35 of the Act requires measures of equivalent effect to be abolished as from the date of accession of Greece, namely as of 1 January 1981. By way of exception to this, Article 39 (1) requires Greece progressively to eliminate its 8 per cent. general preference in public contracts over a five-year period. Again, Article 39 (2) entitles Greece to 'postpone opening its lists of approved supplies to Community supplies' for two years from 1 January 1981.

Lastly, Community legislation has been passed so as to facilitate supervision of the prohibition of discrimination in the field of public supply contracts. That will be considered in Chapter 12.[36]

Incitement to purchase domestic products

7.22 Article 2 (3) (k) of Directive 70/50 defines as measures of equivalent effect, *inter alia*, those measures which '. . . encourage, require or give preference to the purchase of domestic products

---

[33] [1970] J.O. L13/1, para. 6.03 above; Turpin, 'Public Contracts in the EEC' [1972] C.M.L.Rev. 411.
[34] The concept of a 'measure' for the purposes of Art. 30 is a wide one: paras. 6.07 *et seq.* above.
[35] E.C. Bull. 1-1978 para. 3.3.1.
[36] Paras. 12.20 *et seq.* below.

only'.[37] A measure of this kind, which has been the subject of infringement proceedings, was the recommendation contained in public Departmental circulars addressed to civil servants in charge of public purchasing to 'Buy British'.[38] Those proceedings, which never reached the Court, have now been closed following the withdrawal of those circulars. Similar measures adopted by the French authorities are currently the subject of an action pending before the Court brought by the Commission under Article 169 EEC.[39] Another action brought by the Commission against a Member State and currently pending before the Court concerns the 'Buy Irish' advertising campaign which is financed and organised by the Irish Government and which seeks to encourage the Irish public to purchase Irish goods in preference to imported goods.[40]

The obligation to appoint a representative in the importing Member State

7.23 Article 2 (3) (g) of Directive 70/50 defines as measures of equivalent effect under Article 30 those measures which 'make access of imported products to the domestic market conditional upon having an agent or representative in the territory of the importing Member State'. Frequently, a measure of this kind will be couched in 'objective' terms, requiring any person selling goods of a particular type to be established on national territory or to appoint an agent established there. Such measures are discriminatory by their nature, since domestic products fulfil this requirement by definition. Perhaps the principal effect of such measures in practice is to deter parallel imports.

The Commission has commenced proceedings under Article 169 with respect to a number of such measures, for instance the obligation for manufacturers of motor vehicles and components in other Member States to have an accredited representative at the Ministry of Supply and Housing to handle formalities relating to type approved vehicles (France),[41] a similar obligation covering motor vehicles and motors for mopeds (Italy),[41] and the obligation for holders of authorisations to manufacture or sell pharmaceutical products to have a representative domiciled in Denmark.[42]

---

[37] On the other hand, measures by which a Member State promotes the sale or advertises its own products *outside* its own territory are in themselves entirely compatible with Article 30. Such measures in no way restrict trade between Member States. On the contrary, they promote exports. (This does not mean that all methods of promoting exports are open to the Member States: see, *e.g.* Arts. 92 *et seq*. EEC.)

[38] E.C. Bull. 1-1978 para. 3.31.

[39] Case 243/81 *E.C. Commission* v. *France*.

[40] Case 249/81 *E.C. Commission* v. *Ireland*.

[41] E.C. Bull. 7/8-1978, 129.

[42] E.C. Bull. 11-1979, 120. The Commission subsequently brought the case before the Court (Case 191/80) but withdrew it when Denmark repealed the measure complained of.

The Court has not yet had occasion fully to rule on any measure of this type.[43]

Conditions of payment and obligatory deposits and guarantees

7.24   Article 2 (3) of Directive 70/50 defines as measures of equivalent effect measures which

'(h) lay down conditions of payment in respect of imported products only
. . .;
(i) require, for imports only, the giving of guarantees or making of payments on account'.

The term 'guarantees' is clearly used to cover deposits.

Article 38 of the Act of Accession of Greece provides: 'Notwithstanding Article 35,[44] import deposits and cash payments in force in Greece on 31 December 1980 with regard to imports from the present Member States shall be progressively eliminated over a period of three years from 1 January 1981'. That provision goes on to state that the rate of those deposits and cash payments is to be reduced by 25 per cent. each year beginning on 1 January 1981 and ending on 1 January 1984.

At first sight these types of measure would appear to fall under Article 106[45] rather than Article 30. At all events, there is as yet no case law of the Court of Justice on them, although a number of cases are currently pending.[46]

Certain advertising restrictions

7.25   Article 2 (3) (m) of Directive 70/50 defines as measures of equivalent effect on imports measures which 'prohibit or limit publicity in respect of imported products only, or totally or partially confine publicity to domestic products only'.

In case 152/78 *E.C. Commission* v. *France*[47] the Commission brought infringement proceedings against a French measure setting out four different groups of alcoholic drinks and laying down different degrees of restriction for each group. For two of these groups there was no advertising restriction, for a third limited advertising was allowed and for the fourth no advertising was permitted at all. Although at first sight there was nothing discriminatory about these rules, the groups were so defined that drinks of a kind normally imported were subject to greater restrictions than drinks normally produced in France which had similar properties and therefore presented a similar health risk. For example, rum and products distilled from wine, cider or fruit were subject to no

---

[43] However, the Court did briefly touch on this matter in Case 159/78 *E.C. Commission* v. *Italy* [1979] E.C.R. 3247, [1980] 3 C.M.L.R. 446 on customs agents.

[44] On Art. 35 see para. 7.21 above.

[45] Para. 6.22 above.

[46] Cases 206, 207 and 209/80 *Orlandi* v. *Ministero del Commercio con l'Estero*, Case 95/81 *E.C. Commission* v. *Italy*.

[47] [1980] E.C.R. 2299, [1981] 2 C.M.L.R. 743; para 2.25 above.

restriction, whereas similar products with a cereal base such as whisky could not be advertised at all. The Court held that, even though some French products were subject to restrictions, this legislation put imported products at a disadvantage and thus fell under Article 30. Nor was it justified under Article 36, precisely because it constituted arbitrary discrimination.

Restrictions or requirements as to the stocking of goods

7.26 Article 2 (3) (n) of Commission Directive 70/50 defines as measures of equivalent effect under Article 30 measures which

'prohibit, limit or require stocking in respect of imported goods only; totally or partially confine the use of stocking facilities to domestic products only, or make the stocking of imported products subject to conditions which are different from those required for domestic products and more difficult to satisfy'.

There is as yet no other authority on *restrictions* on stocking goods.[48] On the other hand, *Eggers* v. *Freie Hansestadt Bremen*[49] concerned a measure *requiring* goods to be stocked. There the Court in effect held to be contrary to Article 30 a German measure providing that wine-based spirits could only bear certain designations of quality if they were stored for at least six months on German territory. This case will be discussed more fully below.[50]

The abusive reservation of designations of origin or quality or of generic terms

7.27 Article 2 (3) (s) of Directive 70/50 defines as measures of equivalent effect contrary to Article 30 measures which 'confine names which are not indicative of origin or source to domestic products only'. The French text reads: *qui ... réservent aux seuls produits nationaux des dénominations ne constituant pas des appellations d'origine ou des indications de provenance*. The terms *appellations d'origine* and *indications de provenance* are terms of art in French law,[51] but there is no equivalent term of art in English law.

Case 12/74 *E.C. Commission* v. *Germany*[52] concerned measures of this type. A German statute provided that in addition to other conditions the appellation *Sekt* could only be used to describe a

---

[48] However, see Case 75/81 *Blesgen* v. *Belgium*, judgment of 31 March 1982. See Annexe I below.

[49] Case 13/78 [1978] E.C.R. 1935, [1979] 1 C.M.L.R. 562.

[50] Para. 7.32 below.

[51] For a comparative study of the law of several western countries, see *Protection of Geographical Denominations of Goods and Services*, ed. Cohen Jehoram (1980).

[52] [1975] E.C.R. 181, [1975] 1 C.M.L.R. 340 noted by March Hunnings [1975] J.L. 171, Wyatt [1975] M.L.R. 679, Marenco [1975] *Dir. Int. Scamb.* 358; see Mattera 'L'indication d'origine sur les produits et les règles de la libre circulation des marchandises à l'intérieur de la Communauté' [1975] *Dir. Scamb. Int.* 208; Matthies 'Herkunftsangaben und Europäisches Gemeinschaftsrecht' in *Festschrift für Schiedermair* (1976); also Beier 'Das Schutzbedürfnis für Herkunftsangaben und Ursprungsbezeichnungen im Gemeinsamen Markt' [1977] G.R.U.R. Int. 1, and (in English) Cohen Jehoram, *op. cit.* note 51 above, at 183.

German sparkling wine or sparkling foreign wine if German was an official language throughout the whole of the country of production.[53] What is more, the appellation *Prädikatssekt* could only describe a *Sekt* containing at least 60 per cent. of German grapes. Again, the appellation *Weinbrand* was reserved to a certain type of German spirits and for similar foreign products if German was the official language throughout the whole of the country of production. On the other hand, sparkling wines and spirits produced in countries in which German is not such an official language were, in principle, compelled to use less prestigious appellations.

The Commission contended that the appellations *Sekt*, *Prädikatssekt* and *Weinbrand* were generic terms which the German authorities had attempted to transform into indirect indications of origin, at the same time requiring imported products to bear less attractive appellations. It therefore brought proceedings against the Federal Republic for infringement of Article 30 and, as regards sparkling wine, of the equivalent provision contained in Regulation 616/70 establishing the common market organisation in wine.[54] The Court found for the Commission. After citing Article 2 (3) (s) of the Directive[55] it held:

> 'To the extent to which [appellations of origin and indirect indications of origin] are protected by law they must satisfy the objectives of such protection, in particular the need to ensure not only that the interests of the producers concerned are safeguarded against unfair competition, but also that consumers are protected against information which may mislead them.
>
> These appellations only fulfil their specific purpose if the product which they describe does in fact possess qualities and characteristics which are due to the fact that it originated in a specific geographical area.
>
> As regards indications of origin in particular, the geographical area of origin of a product must confer on it a specific quality and specific characteristics of such a nature as to distinguish it from all other products'.

With reference to the appellations *Sekt* and *Weinbrand* the Court continued:

> 'An area of origin which is defined on the basis either of the extent of national territory or a linguistic criterion cannot constitute a geographical area within the meaning referred to above, capable of justifying an indication of origin,[56] particularly as the products in question may be produced from grapes of indetermined origin.
>
> In this instance, it is not disputed that the area of origin referred to by the legislation on wine products does not show homogeneous natural features which distinguish it in contrast to adjacent areas, as the natural characteristics of the basic products used in the manufacture of the product in question do not necessarily correspond to the line of the national frontier'.

---

[53] This 'language clause' was apparently designed to cover Austrian *Sekt* and *Weinbrand*: Advocate General Warner [1975] E.C.R. at 204, [1975] 1 C.M.L.R. 340 at 346.

[54] [1970] J.O. L99.

[55] See para. 6.04 above.

[56] See, however, the Advocate General at 207.

7.28   The Court went on to reject the argument to the effect that the products covered by the appellations *Sekt* and *Weinbrand* were different from all other products by virtue of their process of production:

> 'In the case of wine products, the natural features of the area of origin, such as the grape from which these products are obtained, play an important role in determining their quality and their characteristics.
>
> Although the method of production used for such products may play some part in determining these characteristics, it is not alone decisive, independently of the quality of the grape used, in determining its origin.
>
> Moreover, the method of production of a wine product constitutes a criterion which is all the less capable of being by itself sufficient [when] it is not linked with the use of a specific type of grape [so that] the method in question may be employed in other geographical areas'.

The wording of this part of the judgment implies that it applies only to 'wine products'.

7.29   Nor would the Court accept opinion polls put in evidence by the German Government, which data were intended to show that the German consumer took the terms *Sekt* and *Weinbrand* to refer to German products only. This was not only because such data were inherently unreliable, but also because:

> 'the protection accorded by the indication of origin is only justifiable if the product concerned actually possesses characteristics which are capable of distinguishing it from the point of view of its geographical origin [so that] in the absence of such a condition this protection cannot be justified on the basis of the opinion of consumers such as may result from polls carried out on the basis of statistical criteria.'

7.30   As regards the term *Prädikatssekt* the Court ruled that:

> 'as the legislation on wine products does not define the grapes which must be used in the production of *Prädikatssekt* with reference to their specific character but only on the basis of their national origin, the minimum percentage required does not necessarily imply that the product in question is actually of a special quality in comparison with *Sekt* and thus warrants the protection accorded to it'.

Lastly, the measures in question were not protected by Article 36 because they were caught by the second sentence of that provision. The Court therefore concluded that the measures in question were contrary to Article 30 and, as regards sparkling wine, to Regulation 816/70.

7.31   Beier has written a detailed critique[57] of this judgment. He agrees with the Court that the reservation of the national measures in question constituted measures of equivalent effect within the meaning of Article 30 without being justified under Article 36. Yet he would reach that conclusion by a different route: in his opinion the terms *Sekt* and *Weinbrand* are not designations of origin or indications of origin at all, but purely generic names (like 'potatoes' or 'gloves'); seen in this light, the reservation of these terms to

---

[57] *Op. cit.* note 52 above.

national products and the resulting use of less appealing terms for imported products could not possibly be justified under Article 36. On the other hand, the Court began by taking these terms as indirect appellations of origin and then, finding that they were not justified, held that they were not appellations of origin after all. Had the Court followed the approach which he suggests, this unduly complicated and circuitous reasoning would have been avoided. By this method, the Court would have avoided a number of pronouncements which Beier proceeds to criticise. He singles out for particular criticism the Court's statement that designations of origin and indications of origin 'only fulfil their specific purpose if the product which they describe does in fact possess specific qualities and characteristics which are due to the fact that it originated in a specific geographical area'. He asks whether such highly reputed appellations as 'Brussels lace' and 'Munich beer' can only be protected if it is shown that these products possess specific qualities or characteristics. In particular, he asks, to protect the term 'Munich beer' would it be necessary to show that the same product could not be produced outside Munich by reason of the special qualities of Munich water?[58]

7.32   Another case involving this kind of measure was *Eggers* v. *Freie Hansestadt Bremen*.[59] This concerned the compatibility with Article 30 of a German statutory provision according to which spirits from wine could be designated as *Qualitätsbranntwein aus Wein* (high quality spirits made from wine) or as *Weinbrand* (brandy) only if:

- at least 85 per cent. of the alcoholic content was derived from home-produced wine distillate; and
- the whole of the wine distillate used had been kept for at least six months in oaken casks in the factory where the distillate produced on national territory had been manufactured.

After citing Article 2 (3) (s) of Directive 70/50 the Court held:

> 'In order to be effective the prohibition on the reserving of certain designations (other than those indicative of origin or source), and in particular designations of quality, for domestic products only must extend to measures which distinguish between domestic products according to whether or not the raw materials or the semi-finished products from which they are manufactured have been produced or treated on national territory and which reserve for goods derived from semi-finished products, treated on national territory, special designations such as to give them an advantage in the opinion of the traders or consumers concerned.
>
> In fact in a market which, as far as possible, must present the features of a single market, entitlement to a designation of quality for a product can—except in the case of the rules applicable to registered designations of origin and indications of origin—only depend upon the intrinsic objective characteristics governing the quality of the product compared with a similar product of

---

[58] See also Marenco, *op. cit.* note 52.
[59] Note 49 above.

inferior quality, and not on the geographical locality where a particular production stage took place.

It follows from all the foregoing considerations that a national measure which makes the right to use a designation of quality for a domestic product subject to the condition that the semi-finished product from which it was manufactured was either produced or treated on national territory, and refuses to allow the use of that designation simply because the semi-finished product was imported from another Member State, is a measure having an effect equivalent to a quantitative restriction.

The fact that the use of that designation of quality is optional does not mean that it ceases to be an unjustified obstacle to trade if the use of that designation promotes or is likely to promote the marketing of the product concerned as compared with products which do not benefit from its use'.

7.33 The wording of these two judgments, and particularly that in *E.C. Commission* v. *Germany* does not readily accord with the theory that in deciding whether a measure is compatible with Articles 30 and 36 it is necessary to decide

(1) whether the measure constitutes a restriction on imports and if so,

(2) whether the measure is justified under Article 36.

The Court's approach in *E.C. Commission* v. *Germany* was to consider the question of justification before considering Article 36—which meant that consideration of Article 36 was superfluous. As Meij and Winter[60] put it, 'the *Sekt* case demonstrates that Article 36 is emptied of its substance and its meaning if no distinction is made between the problem of the qualification of State rules as measures of equivalent effect (Article 30) and the question under what circumstances Member States may continue to apply such measures (Article 36)'. However, in their *results* these judgments are compatible with the following analysis:

– the reservation to national products only of any designation which is attractive to the consumer constitutes a measure of equivalent effect;

– such reservation is only justified under Article 36 if on an objective view the designation can only be taken to describe national products.

7.34 It should also be pointed out that, while these two cases concern measures by which a Member State reserves a designation for its own products, an infringement of Article 30 could also occur in the following manner: Member State A reserves the right to use a particular designation within its territory to the products of Member State B, whereas in reality the products of other Member States should also be entitled to the use of that designation. Such a restriction would not be justified under Article 36, since it would constitute arbitrary discrimination.[61]

---

[60] 'Measures Having Equivalent Effect to Quantitative Restrictions' [1976] C.M.L.Rev. 79 at 103.

[61] Para. 8.05 below.

7.35   In Case 193/80 *E.C. Commission* v. *Italy*,[62] the Court was concerned *inter alia* with a national measure prohibiting the use of the term 'vinegar' (*aceto*) in Italy for vinegar other than wine vinegar.[63] The effect of this measure, which was clearly designed to protect Italian wine producers, was to make all vinegar other than wine vinegar virtually unsaleable in that country. Nevertheless, it is important to note that, unlike the measures at issue in the *E.C. Commission* v. *Italy* and *Eggers* cases, this particular measure applied in the same way to domestic products and to imports. The Italian Government sought to show that, for the Italian consumer, the term *aceto* had come to refer only to wine vinegar to the exclusion of all other vinegars. However, the Court found, by reference to the definition given in the relevant heading of the Common Customs Tariff, that the term was in fact a generic one, covering various different types of vinegar. The Court held that, where a generic term such as this refers to a number of different varieties of product, the reservation of that term to one of those varieties only constitutes a measure of equivalent effect contrary to Article 30.

On the other hand, the Court recognised that the Italian consumer might have become conditioned by the contested measure to think of *aceto* as covering only wine vinegar. The Italian Government could therefore adopt other, less restrictive measures to protect the consumer, such as a requirement that the precise nature of the product be set out on a label affixed to the product. But the Court stressed that such a requirement would have to apply in the same way to all varieties of vinegar, including wine vinegar.[64]

Obligatory origin marking

7.36   A measure requiring the origin of goods to be marked on them constitutes a measure of equivalent effect.[65] On the other hand, it is clear that it is perfectly lawful for traders to indicate the origin of their goods of their own accord, should they so wish.

Only very recently has the first case on this type of measure been decided by the Court of Justice: Case 113/80 *E.C. Commission* v. *Ireland*.[66] This case concerned two Irish statutory instruments prohibiting the importation into and sale in the Republic of Ireland of certain categories of metal articles bearing certain motifs unless they were marked with a word or words indicating that they were manufactured outside the Republic. The list of articles included not

---

[62] Judgment of 9 December 1981.
[63] As to the prohibition on the sale of vinegar other than wine vinegar, see para. 7.40 below.
[64] See para. 8.46 below.
[65] Written question 197/69 ([1969] J.O. C151/2), Written question 721/80 ([1980] O.J. C283/20), Written question 880/79 ([1980] O.J. C86/14), Written question 1116/79 ([1980] O.J. C82/21), Written question 1409/80 ([1981] O.J. C60/41), Written question 1634/80 ([1981] O.J. C78/12), Mattera, *op. cit.* note 52 above.
[66] [1982] 1 C.M.L.R. 706.

only jewellery but also such objects as buckles, dress-combs and key-rings. The motifs ranged from those with specifically Irish associations to thatched cottages and round towers. There was no corresponding origin marking requirement with respect to metal goods manufactured within the Republic of Ireland. Consequently, the measures in question were 'distinctly applicable'.[67]

The Commission brought infringement proceedings against Ireland with respect to these measures. It claimed that the obligation to mark the origin on goods was only justified if this is necessary to avoid the purchaser being misled as to the true origin of a product bearing a false or misleading indication. It pointed out that it will be more important for the purchaser to know whether a product is or is not of a particular origin where such origin implies a certain quality, basic materials or process of manufacture or a particular place in the folklore or tradition of the region in question.[68]

The Commission claimed that the metal articles covered by the Irish measures did not fall within these conditions and thus the measures were not justified on the grounds of consumer protection, the prevention of unfair competition or any other grounds. The Commission added that even if the statutory instruments had applied in the same way to Irish goods, they would still not have been justified.

7.37 While finding for the Commission in the case before it, the Court did not find it necessary to rule on all those points. Having noted that most of the products in question were souvenirs, it ruled that:

> 'The essential characteristic of the souvenirs in question is that they constitute a pictorial reminder of the place visited, which does not by itself mean that a souvenir, as defined in the [Irish] Orders, must necessarily be manufactured in the country of origin.
>   . . . it is important to note that the interests of consumers and fair trading would be adequately safeguarded if it were left to domestic manufacturers to take appropriate steps such as affixing, if they so wished, their mark of origin to their own products or packaging'.

Consequently, it held that the measures at issue infringed Article 30. In so doing, it expressly refrained from ruling on whether—as argued by the Commission—the same measures would still have been contrary to Article 30, if they had applied to domestic products in the same way. Yet the question whether 'indistinctly applicable' origin marking requirements can be contrary to Article 30 will fall to be decided in another case currently before the Court.[69]

---

[67] Para. 6.28 above.
[68] Certain types of alcoholic drinks fall within this head: Reg. 355/79 ([1979] O.J. L54/99) requires that certain categories of wine bear an indication of origin.
[69] Case 127/81 E.C. Commission v. France (motors).

Certain rules of procedure and evidence

7.38 It was established in *Procureur Général* v. *Arnaud*[70] that a rule of procedure can constitute an infringement of Article 30. The reference arose out of a series of prosecutions of French wine traders for illegal enrichment ('over-alcoholisation') of certain quantities of red wine. The French Code du vin creates a rebuttable presumption of over-alcoholisation of wine if the proportion of alcohol to reduced extract is in excess of a certain figure. The Cour d'Appel of Bordeaux asked, *inter alia*, whether this presumption was compatible with the Regulations setting up a common market organisation in wine, which included a provision prohibiting quantitative restrictions and measures of equivalent effect.

The Court replied that a rebuttable presumption of this kind was compatible with Article 30 'unless its application could put at a disadvantage wines from other Member States as where, for example, the presumption was harder to rebut in the case of wines from other Member States. There is every reason to suppose that the same ruling would apply to industrial products and to agricultural products not covered by a common market organisation. Presumably also this ruling would be applicable to any rule of judicial procedure.[71]

The prohibition on sale of goods

7.39 It has always been clear that a prohibition on sale applying to imported goods only was a measure of equivalent effect under Article 30. Thus Article 2(3) of Directive 70/50 defines as measures of equivalent effect measures which

'(j) . . . subject imported products to conditions which are different from those of domestic products and more difficult to satisfy;
(k) hinder the purchase by private individuals of imported products only . . .'

Thus a prohibition on selling imported goods owing to industrial property rights constitutes a measure of equivalent effect within the meaning of Article 30[72] although it might be justified under Article 36.[73]

However, the *Cassis de Dijon* judgment[74] showed, it is submitted, that all measures including 'indistinctly applicable measures' prohibiting the sale of a product containing particular ingredients are measures of equivalent effect under Article 30—though they will frequently be justified under Article 36. As the reader will be aware,

---

[70] Cases 89/74, 18-19/75 [1975] E.C.R. 1023, [1975] 2 C.M.L.R. 490; see also Cases 10-14/75 *Lahaille* [1975] E.C.R. 1053.

[71] See Case 22/80 *Boussac* v. *Gerstenmeier* [1980] E.C.R. 3427, [1982] 1 C.M.L.R. 202 on the compatibility of a rule of procedure with Art. 7 EEC.

[72] See, for instance, Case 58/80 *Dansk Supermarked* v. *Imerco* [1981] E.C.R. 181, [1981] 3 C.M.L.R. 590.

[73] See para. 8.57 *et seq*. below.

[74] Case 120/78 [1979] E.C.R. 649, [1979] 3 C.M.L.R. 494, para. 6.33 above.

the Court held in that case that the imposition of a minimum alcohol requirement with respect to drinks was contrary to Article 30. That judgment has been considered at length in the previous chapter and requires no further comment here.

7.40 The Court had occasion to build on that judgment in *Gilli and Andres*.[75] An Italian Decree prohibited the sale in Italy of all vinegar, be it Italian or imported, other than wine vinegar. Since such vinegar constitutes no health hazard, it was clear that the sole object of the Decree was to protect Italian wine growers. The defendants were charged before the Italian courts with contravening the Decree by selling quantities of cider vinegar imported from Germany, whereupon a reference for a preliminary ruling was made asking the Court whether this Decree was compatible with Article 30. The Court pointed out that it was undisputed that cider vinegar was harmless to health and that the vinegar at issue in the main proceeding was provided with a sufficiently clear label indicating that it was cider vinegar, thus avoiding any possibility of the consumer's confusing it with wine vinegar. It continued:

'Thus there is no factor justifying any restrictions on the importation of the product in question from the point of view either of the protection of public health or of the fairness of commercial transactions or of the defence of the consumer . . .

It appears therefore that a unilateral requirement, imposed by the rules of a Member State, prohibiting the putting on the market of vinegars not produced from the acetic fermentation of wine constitutes an obstacle to trade which is incompatible with the provisions of Article 30 of the Treaty'.

This judgment was confirmed, though in somewhat modified terms, in case 193/80 *E.C. Commission* v. *Italy*.[76]

7.41 Next, the case of *Officier van Justitie* v. *Koninklijke Kaas-fabriek Eyssen*[77] concerned a prohibition on the use of a preservative called nisin in processed cheese sold in the Netherlands. In criminal proceedings brought against a manufacturer for having in stock with a view to sale quantities of such cheese containing nisin, the national court asked the Court in effect whether the measure at issue was justified under Article 36. After pointing out that other Member States permitted the use of nisin either without limit or subject to certain maximum limits, the Court stated:

'In view of this disparity of rules it cannot be disputed that the prohibition by certain Member States of the marketing on their territory of processed cheese containing added nisin is of such a nature as to affect imports of that product from other Member States where, conversely, the addition of nisin is wholly

---

[75] Case 788/79 [1980] E.C.R. 2071, [1981] 1 C.M.L.R. 146, noted by Meier [1981] EuR. 43.
[76] See note 62 above. See also para. 6.37 above. In *Gilli and Andres*, the Court had said that the prohibition on the sale of all vinegar other than wine vinegar was contrary to Art. 30. But in Case 193/80, the Court limited its judgment to the prohibition on the sale of other *agricultural* vinegars. This was simply because, in its letter of formal notice opening the infringement proceedings, the Commission had expressly excluded *synthetic* vinegar from the scope of those proceedings.
[77] Case 53/80 [1981] E.C.R. 429.

or partially permitted and that it for that reason constitutes a measure having an effect equivalent to a quantitative restriction'.

The Court found, however, that the measure in question was justified on grounds of public health under Article 36.[78]

7.42 The reference in *Kelderman*[79] concerned the Dutch Broodbesluit, which stipulated that all bread sold in the Netherlands must contain a proportion of dry matter falling within fixed bands. The defendants were charged with selling in the Netherlands brioches from France containing a quantity of dry matter falling outside the permitted limits. Since the Court found that the measure of the kind in question was not necessary to fulfil any mandatory requirement such as the protection of public health or consumer protection, it held that it was contrary to Article 30.

7.43 In *Frans-Nederlandse Maatschappij voor Biologische Producten*,[80] the Court was asked whether a prohibition on the sale of plant protection products without prior Government approval was compatible with Article 30 in so far as it applied to a product imported from another Member State where it had received such approval. Once again, the national legislation applied in the same way to domestic products and to imports. However, it is significant that the justification advanced by the Member State for the measure, namely public health, is one of the grounds of justification set out in Article 36. Consequently, the Court framed its judgment in terms of Articles 30 and 36 taken together, even though the question put by the national court mentioned Article 30 alone.[81] At all events, it is clear from the judgment that a measure of this kind will be contrary to Article 30 in certain circumstances discussed more fully in paragraph 8.28 below.

7.44 Lastly, in *Industrie Diensten Groep* v. *Beele*,[82] the Court found that the prohibition on the sale of imported or domestically produced goods constituting a slavish imitation of other goods already on the national market of the Member State concerned was in principle a measure of equivalent effect under Article 30. The Court went on to find, however, that such a prohibition was, under certain circumstances set out in the next chapter,[83] justified on the grounds of consumer protection and the prevention of unfair competition.

Requirements as to the presentation of products

7.45 Article 2 (3) (j) of Directive 70/50 defines as measures of equivalent effect under Article 30 measures which 'subject imported

---

[78] Para. 8.29 below.
[79] Case 130/80 [1981] E.C.R. 527.
[80] Case 272/80, judgment of 17 December 1981.
[81] See note 104 to Chap. VI above.
[82] Case 6/81, judgment of 2 March 1982.
[83] See para. 8.53 below.

products only to conditions, in respect in particular of shape, size, weight, composition, presentation, identification or putting up . . . .

The *Cassis de Dijon* ruling[84] has now stated, it is submitted, that all obstacles to the sale of imported goods constitute measures of equivalent effect under Article 30, subject to the application of Article 36.

An 'indistinctly applicable' measure relating to the presentation of goods fell to be considered in *Fietje*.[85] The defendant was charged with marketing in the Netherlands an apple-based drink containing 25 per cent. alcohol which did not bear the legend 'liqueur' as required by the Dutch Likeurbesluit. The Court held that the measure was contrary to Article 30 in certain circumstances discussed more fully in the following chapter of this book.[86]

Restrictions on the delivery of goods

7.46 The case of *Oebel*[87] primarily concerned a German measure prohibiting the baking of bread during the night. This measure in itself had no bearing on imports. However, it was supplemented by an ancillary measure prohibiting the *delivery* of bread during the night. This prohibition on delivery, which applied in the same way to imports and to domestic products was considered by the German authorities to be necessary for the enforcement of the prohibition on night baking. On a reference from a German court, the Court of Justice was in effect asked to rule, *inter alia*, whether a prohibition on night delivery of this kind was compatible with Articles 30 and 34. The Advocate General took the view that such a measure did constitute a measure of equivalent effect although it might in certain circumstances be justified. The Court, taking a radically different view, ruled that such a measure was compatible with these provisions, on the following grounds:

It so happened that the German legislation at issue prohibited night deliveries to individual consumers and to points of retail sale, but did not apply to deliveries to depots or middle-men. The Court considered that in view of this there was no restriction on imports or exports between Member States, so that such legislation was compatible with Articles 30 and 34.

There would seem to be something of a *non sequitur* in this reasoning: surely a prohibition on delivering goods to individual consumers and to points of retail sale during the night *does* constitute an actual or potential, direct or indirect hindrance to interstate trade? Indeed it is hard to reconcile this ruling with the general principles laid down by the Court with respect to Articles 30 to 36.

---

[84] Note 74 above.
[85] Case 27/80 [1980] E.C.R. 3839, [1981] 3 C.M.L.R. 722.
[86] Para. 8.47 below.
[87] Case 155/80 [1981] E.C.R. 1993.

Certain price controls

7.47 The term 'price controls' is used here to cover the following types of measure: price freezes, minimum[88] and maximum prices, minimum and maximum profit margins. Countless variants and combinations of these types of measure are imposed by the different Member States with respect to various products.[89] All the Member States impose price controls of some kind on some products, most frequently highly sensitive products such as pharmaceuticals. It is thus of the greatest practical importance to determine to what extent State price controls are compatible with Article 30.[90]

Furthermore, price controls generally form an integral part of the economic policies of the Member States. The Treaty has in principle left intact the right of each Member State to take the economic policy measures it deems necessary; this emerges in particular from Articles 103 (1), 104 and 145.[91] This explains why the Court has trodden more warily with regard to price controls than with regard to other types of measure falling under Article 30. In particular, it would have been rash indeed to have held that all price controls automatically constituted measures of equivalent effect.

7.48 At all events the Commission in Article 2 (3) of Directive 70/50 defined as measures of equivalent effect measures which:

'(a) lay down, for imported products only, minimum or maximum prices below or above which imports are prohibited, reduced or made subject to conditions liable to hinder importation; or

(b) lay down less favourable prices for imported products than for domestic products; or

(c) fix profit margins or any other price components for imported products only or fix these differently for domestic products and for imported products, to the detriment of the latter; or

(d) preclude any increase in the price of the imported product corresponding to the supplementary costs and charges inherent in importation; or

(e) fix the prices of products solely on the basis of the cost price or the quality of domestic products at such a level as to create a hindrance to importation'.

7.49 This has now been supplemented by a body of case law of the Court. Of these cases only two—*GB-Inno* v. *ATAB* and *Openbaar*

---

[88] As regards minimum prices for agricultural products during the transitional period, see Art. 44 EEC.

[89] See Westphal and Jürgensen, 'The effects of national price controls in the European Economic Community' *Commission of the EC, Studies Collection,* Competition—Approximation of Legislation Series No. 9 (1970).

[90] Waelbroeck, *Les réglementations nationales de prix et le droit communautaire* (1975); Sabiani, 'L'incidence du droit de la Communauté Economique Européenne sur la réglementation française des prix' [1975] R.T.D.E. 470 and 633; Winkel, 'Die Vereinbarkeit staatlicher Preislenkungsmaßnahmen mit dem EWG-Vertrag' [1976] N.J.W. 2048; Matthies, 'Die Verantwortung der Mitgliedstaaten für den freien Warenverkehr im Gemeinsamen Markt' in *Festschrift für Ipsen* (1977); Mestmäcker, *Vereinbarkeit von Preisregelungen auf dem Arzneimittelmarkt mit dem Recht der Europäischen Wirtschaftsgemeinschaft* (1980) (summary in English); Capelli, *Controllo dei Prezzi e Normativa Communitaria* (1981).

[91] See also para. 7.64 below.

Ministerie v. *Van Tiggele*—concern products not subject to a common market organisation.[92]

The Court's case law[93] on the compatibility of national price controls with the common market organisations themselves—and in particular the provisions of those organisations relating to price formation—fall outside the scope of this book.

7.50 The first cases in which the Court ruled on the compatibility of price controls with Article 30 were the two parallel cases of *Tasca*[94] and *SADAM* v. *Comitato Interministeriale dei Prezzi*,[95] both involving *maximum prices* for sugar fixed by the Italian authorities. In each case the national court asked whether such maximum prices were compatible with Article 30 and with Regulation 1009/67.[96] As regards Article 30 the Court replied in each case:

> 'Article 30 of the Treaty prohibits in trade between Member States all measures having an effect equivalent to quantitative restrictions and this prohibition is repeated in Article 35 of Regulation No. 1009/67 as regards the market in sugar. For the purposes of this prohibition it is sufficient that the measures in question are likely to constitute an obstacle, directly or indirectly, actually or potentially, to imports between Member States. Although a maximum price applicable without distinction to domestic and imported products does not in itself constitute a measure having an effect equivalent to a quantitative restriction, it may have such an effect, however, when it is fixed at a level such that the sale of imported products becomes, if not impossible, more difficult than that of domestic products. A maximum price, in any event in so far as it applies to imported products, constitutes therefore a measure having an effect equivalent to a quantitative restriction, especially when it is fixed at such a low level that, having regard to the general situation of imported products compared to that of domestic products, dealers wishing to import the products in question into the Member State concerned can do so only at a loss'.

7.51 It would appear[97] that measures which the Court describes in this passage as applying in the same way to imports and to domestic products (and thus 'indistinctly applicable') in fact fall under Article 2 (3) (d) and (e) of Directive 70/50 since the objection to these measures is that they fail to take account of the special position of imports. Yet Article 2 (3) of Directive 70/50 covers 'distinctly applicable' measures only. This shows how precarious is the distinc-

---

[92] See paras. 10.08 *et seq.* below.
[93] Case 31/74 *Galli* [1975] E.C.R. 47, [1975] 1 C.M.L.R. 211, noted by VerLoren van Themaat [1973] C.M.L.Rev. 422; Case 154/77 *Dechmann* [1978] E.C.R. 1573, [1979] 2 C.M.L.R. 1; Case 223/78 *Grosoli* [1979] E.C.R. 2621; Case 10/79 *Toffoli* [1979] E.C.R. 3301; Cases 95–96/79 *Kefer* and *Delmelle* [1980] E.C.R. 103; Berardis, 'The common organisation of agricultural markets and national price regulations' [1980] C.M.L.Rev. 539; Colinet and Marsceau, 'Interprétation et application du droit communautaire dans le domaine des réglementation des prix des produits agricoles de l'arrêt Dechmann à l'arrêt Kefer—Delmelle' [1980] C.D.E. 507.
[94] Case 65/75 [1976] E.C.R. 291, [1977] 2 C.M.L.R. 183, noted by Waelbroeck [1977] C.M.L.Rev. 94.
[95] Cases 88-90/75 [1976] E.C.R. 323, [1977] 2 C.M.L.R. 183, noted by Waelbroeck, *op. cit.* note 94 above.
[96] [1967] O.J.Spec.Ed. 304.
[97] Winkel, *op. cit.* note 90 above, at 2051.

tion between 'distinctly applicable' and 'indistinctly applicable' measures.

More curious is the fact that the passage quoted from the *Tasca* and *SADAM* judgments appears to contradict itself. On the one hand the Court states that a maximum price applying to domestic products and to imports in the same way does not in itself constitute a measure of equivalent effect, but only does so when it makes the sale of imported products more difficult than that of domestic products. On the other hand, in the following sentence the Court holds that a maximum price does constitute a measure of equivalent effect 'especially when . . .'. There appears to be no way of reconciling these two statements. However, as will be seen below, subsequent judgments such as *GB-Inno* v. *ATAB*, *Buys*, and *Danis* follow the former line: maximum prices applying in the same way to domestic products and to imports do not in themselves constitute measures of equivalent effect.

7.52 The Court also held in *SADAM* that a Member State could not rely on Article 103[98] to justify a maximum consumer price contrary to Article 30. There is every reason to think that this ruling applies to all products, even those not covered by a common market organisation; and that it applies to all price controls. On this view Article 103 can never be relied on to justify a price control falling under Article 30.

7.53 This brings us to *GB-Inno* v. *ATAB*[99] itself. By Belgian law, excise duty on Belgian or imported manufactured tobacco was to be calculated on the basis of the price appearing on the tax label; furthermore this price, freely chosen by the manufacturer or the importer as the case may be, was the compulsory selling price to the consumer. This measure was therefore at once broadly equivalent to a *minimum* and a *maximum* price control. In an action in which it was accused of selling below this price, GB-Inno, a major Belgian supermarket chain, claimed that this system was contrary to a number of provisions of Community law, including Article 30. The national court asked four questions, the third of which concerned the compatibility of such a measure with Article 30.

Before the answers to those questions, the Court's judgment contains a section entitled 'general observations'. In this section the Court pointed out that the prohibition on selling cigarettes *above* the price used for calculating the tax was essential to make the tax workable.[100] This could not be said of the prohibition on selling below this price, which was designed rather to protect small retailers against destructive competition from supermarkets. It also noted

---

[98] See paras. 9.03 *et seq.* below.

[99] Case 13/77 [1977] E.C.R. 2115, [1978] 1 C.M.L.R. 283; see Koppensteiner, 'Vertikale Preisbindung durch Gesetz als Maßnahme gleicher Wirkung wie eine mengenmäßige Einfuhrbeschränkung' [1977] A.W.D./R.I.W. 518.

[100] See para. 8.42 below.

that while in theory there was nothing to prevent a retailer from determining his own price by obtaining tobacco products with appropriate labels, this required the co-operation of the manufacturer or importer and of the Belgian tax authorities and this co-operation might be difficult to obtain.

In answer to the third question the Court held:

> 'Although a maximum price applicable without distinction to domestic and imported products does not in itself constitute a measure having an effect equivalent to a quantitative restriction, it may have such an effect, however, when it is fixed at such a level that the sale of imported products becomes, if not impossible, more difficult than that of domestic products.
>
> On the other hand, a system whereby the prices are freely chosen by the manufacturer or the importer as the case may be and imposed on the consumer by a national legislative measure, and whereby no distinction is made between domestic products and imported products, generally has exclusively internal effects.
>
> However, the possibility cannot be excluded that in certain cases such a system may be capable of affecting intra-Community trade'.

The Court therefore concluded that, even taking into account the inherent barriers to trade due to differences in the tax systems of the Member States, it was possible that such a system might hinder, directly or indirectly, actually or potentially, imports between Member States. This was for the national court to assess.

7.54 The Court subsequently extended this case law to *price freezes* in *Openbaar Ministerie* v. *Danis*.[101] The defendants in the main case were traders in animal feedstuffs accused of increasing their prices without notifying the Belgian Minister of Economic Affairs as required by a Belgian Ministerial Order. That Order provided that all price increases were to be notified to the Minister at least two months before they took effect and that this Minister could extend this period. The Belgian court consequently asked the Court of Justice whether such a measure was compatible with Article 30.

After repeating the *Dassonville* formula the Court stated:

> 'National rules of this kind, even if they are confined to requiring the producer or importer to "notify" proposed price increases before they are applied, have the effect of a price freeze, since the prices quoted by the producer prior to his notification are, in fact, "frozen" for at least the duration of the waiting period.
>
> Whilst rules imposing a price freeze which are applicable equally to national products and to imported products do not amount in themselves to a measure having an effect equivalent to a quantitative restriction, they may in fact produce such an effect when prices are at such a level that the marketing of imported products becomes either impossible or more difficult than the marketing of national products. That is especially the case where national rules, while preventing the increased prices of imported products from being passed on in sale prices, freeze prices at a level so low that—taking into account the general situation of imported products in relation to that of national products —traders wishing to import the products in question into the Member State

---

[101] Cases 16–20/79 [1979] E.C.R. 3327, [1980] 3 C.M.L.R. 492, noted by Waelbroeck [1981] *Revue Critique de Jurisprudence Belge* 12.

concerned can do so only at a loss, or, having regard to the level at which prices for national products are frozen, are impelled to give preference to the latter products'.

Although the Court was only asked to rule on the compatibility of such measures with Article 30, it then went on to rule on their compatibility with the common market organisation in cereals.

7.55 Lastly, the Court has also had occasion to rule on the compatibility with Article 30 of *minimum prices* and *minimum profit margins*, in *van Tiggele*.[102] There the defendant was charged before a Dutch court with having sold spirits below minimum prices fixed by the Dutch authorities. Different rules applied to three different types of spirit:

(a) for 'new hollands gin' and *vieux* the retail price must be the manufacturer's catalogue price per unit (if any) plus 0.60 Fl. per unit and VAT, the total of which must in no case be lower than 11.25 Fl. per litre;

(b) for 'old hollands gin' the minimum retail price was fixed at 11.25 Fl. per litre;

(c) for other spirits, the minimum retail price was the actual purchase price plus VAT.

These are products not covered by a common organisation of the market.

The Court replied to the question put by the Dutch court as follows:

> 'Whilst national price-control rules applicable without distinction to domestic products and imported products cannot in general [hinder, directly or indirectly, actually or potentially imports between Member States], they may do so in specific cases.
>
> Thus imports may be impeded in particular when a national authority fixes prices or profit margins at such a level that imported products are placed at a disadvantage in relation to identical domestic products either because they cannot profitably be marketed in the conditions laid down or because the competitive advantage conferred by lower cost prices is cancelled out . . .'.

Applying this test, the Court found, firstly, that a prohibition on retail sales below the purchase price paid by the retailer 'cannot produce effects detrimental to the marketing of imported products alone' and therefore did not infringe Article 30. Secondly, the fixing of a minimum profit margin at a specific amount rather than as a percentage of the cost price, is 'likewise incapable of producing an adverse effect on imported products which may be cheaper, as in the present case where the amount of the profit margin constitutes a relatively insignificant part of the final retail price'. Thirdly, though, the Court took the view that:

> 'this is not so in the case of a minimum price fixed at a specific amount which, although applicable without distinction to domestic products and imported products, is capable of having an adverse effect on the marketing of the latter

---

[102] Case 82/77 [1978] E.C.R. 25, [1978] 2 C.M.L.R. 528.

in so far as it prevents their lower cost price from being reflected in the retail selling price'.

This last statement, it should be stressed, concerns minimum prices and not minimum profit margins.

7.56 It is submitted that the main principles laid down in this series of cases may be summarised as follows:

(a) A maximum price or price freeze applicable without distinction to domestic and imported products does not necessarily constitute a measure of equivalent effect.

(b) However, such measures do constitute measures of equivalent effect when prices are fixed or frozen at such a level that the marketing of imported products becomes either impossible or more difficult than the marketing of national products. This is particularly the case when prices are fixed at a level so low that—taking into account the general situation of imported products in relation to that of national products—traders wishing to import the products in question can only do so at a loss.

(c) A prohibition on retail sales at a loss does not constitute a measure of equivalent effect.

(d) The fixing of a minimum profit margin at a specific amount rather than as a percentage of the cost price does not constitute a measure of equivalent effect either.

(e) A minimum price fixed at a specific amount which, although applicable without distinction to domestic and imported products, can restrict imports by preventing their lower cost price from being reflected in the retail selling price, is a measure of equivalent effect.

7.57 The most important undecided questions are the following:

Firstly, what is meant by the 'general situation of imported products compared to that of domestic products' which, the Court has repeatedly said, must be considered in judging whether a maximum price is set too low? According to Mestmäcker[103] one must look at the market prices of the product in question in other Member States, add to them the costs of exporting and deduct the costs spared by exporting. This means that transport costs must be considered. The same applies to currency fluctuations. It follows that, since currencies can fluctuate considerably from day to day, a given price control can suddenly cease to be compatible with Article 30—or just as suddenly become compatible with Article 30.[104]

The same calculations must be made in deciding whether a particular minimum price restriction is such as to cancel out the competitive advantage of imports.

---

[103] *Op. cit.* note 90 above, at 53.

[104] It could perhaps be argued that the uncertainty created for potential importers would in itself make such a price control a measure of equivalent efect.

7.58   Secondly, are price controls contrary to Article 30 only if they discriminate against imports? This may be the case with regard to maximum prices, since the Court had repeatedly held that they only constitute measures of equivalent effect if they are fixed at a level such that the sale of imported products becomes, if not impossible, then more difficult than that of domestic products. Thus for price controls the criterion to be applied would seem to be whether the measures in question constitute discrimination in substance. If this is so, then maximum price controls constitute an exception to the principle formulated earlier in this book[105] according to which the concept of measures of equivalent effect under Article 30 extends to all restrictions on imports and does not merely cover discriminatory measures.

However, Mestmäcker[106] takes the view that maximum prices restricting imports do fall under Article 30 even if they do not discriminate against imports, at least in some cases. For example, he considers that a measure requiring both domestic products and imports to be sold at a loss would be caught by Article 30.

It is possible that a more stringent test is to be applied to minimum price controls, since by their very nature they are apt to prevent cheap imports.[107]

In any case, it is not yet clear whether the test to be applied to price controls is that of discrimination against imports or that of the restriction of imports.

7.59   Thirdly, can price controls ever be justified under Article 36? It is submitted that they can only very rarely, if ever, be justified under Article 36 even though the grounds of justification have been extended.[108] This is because Article 36 is 'directed to eventualities of a non-economic kind'.[109]

7.60   On the other hand, there can be no doubt that the Community has power to adopt legislation on prices, since in *Centrafarm* v. *Sterling Drug*[110] the Court held that 'it is part of the Community authorities' task to eliminate factors likely to distort competition between Member States, in particular by the harmonisation of national measures for the control of prices . . .'

What is the correct legal basis in the Treaty for such measures?[111] Waelbroeck[112] takes the view that Article 103 (2) EEC[113] relating to

---

[105] Para. 6.36 above.
[106] *Op. cit.* note 90 above, at 52–53.
[107] VerLoren van Themaat 'De artikelen 30-36 van het EEG-verdrag' [1980] R.M. Themis 4/5, 378 at 386.
[108] Paras. 6.34 *et seq.* above. On Art. 103, see para. 7.52 above.
[109] Para. 8.18 below.
[110] Case 15/74 [1974] E.C.R. 1147 at 1164; [1974] 2 C.M.L.R. 480 at 505.
[111] See generally Lambotte 'Le programme communautaire de lutte contre la hausse des prix' [1974] C.D.E. 515 and [1975] C.D.E. 371.
[112] *Op. cit.* note 90 above, 57 *et seq.*
[113] Paras. 9.03 and 12.04.

'conjunctural' policy provided the basis for Community price controls. On the other hand, he considers that Article 100[114] of the Treaty—the classic basis for harmonisation—would only permit the harmonisation of national price measures and not their substitution by Community price controls. Harmonisation under Article 100, he argues, would leave the national price structures substantially intact and thus serve no practical purpose.

More recently, the Commission has set out its position on this question in answer to Written Question No. 185/80.[115] As regards Article 100, the Commission said that this provision empowered the Community 'to bring national laws and regulations into line where they directly affect the establishment or functioning of the common market'. The Commission added that Article 103 (2) and (3) conferred on the Community the power to take action with respect to short-term economic policy in this regard and in particular with respect to inflation. However, it stated that 'so far . . . the Community has not considered it necessary to act under Articles 103 . . . or 100 with a view to influencing prices or approximating national pricing laws, either in individual sectors or in general'.

II. MEASURES FALLING OUTSIDE ARTICLE 30

7.61 In addition to the cases already mentioned, the following types of measure have been held to be compatible with Article 30 (without falling under any other provision of the Treaty):

> (i) Article 2 (3) (r) of Directive 70/50 in effect excludes from the definition of measures of equivalent effect such import controls as are 'inherent in the customs clearance procedure'. This raises the fundamental question of what controls are 'inherent' in the customs clearance procedure.

At all events, in Case 159/78 *E.C. Commission* v. *Italy*[116] the Court embroidered on that provision, in the following terms:

> 'As regards intra-Community trade, since all customs duties on imports and exports and all charges having equivalent effect and all quantitative restrictions on imports and exports and measures having equivalent effect had to be abolished, pursuant to Title I of the Treaty, by the end of the transitional period at the latest, it should be emphasised that customs controls properly so-called have lost their *raison d'être* as regards such trade. Frontier controls remained justified only in so far as they are necessary either for the implementation of the exceptions to free movement referred to in Article 36 of the Treaty; as for the levying of internal taxation, within the meaning of Article 95 of the Treaty when the crossing of the frontier may legitimately be assimilated to the situation which, in the case of domestic goods, gives rise to the levying of the tax, as for transit controls; as finally where they are essential in order to obtain reasonably complete and accurate information on movement of goods

---

[114] Para. 12.02 below.
[115] [1980] O.J. C316/1.
[116] [1979] E.C.R. 3247, [1980] 3 C.M.L.R. 446.

119

within the Community. These residuary controls must nevertheless be reduced as far as possible so that trade between Member States can take place in conditions as close as possible to those prevalent on a domestic market'.

The express mention of Article 36 at the beginning of the list may indicate that the rest of the list is an interpretation of Article 30 and not of Article 36. In other words, it appears to confirm the implication in Article 2 (3) (r) of the Directive that formalities and restrictions inherent in the customs clearance procedure fall outside Article 30 altogether rather than being justified under Article 36. The reference to the compilation of 'reasonably complete and adequate information on movement of goods within the Community' perhaps covers the ruling in *Donckerwolcke*[117] to the effect that an importer may be required to state the origin of goods on the customs documents when he knows such origin or can reasonably be expected to know it.

7.62 Applying that general statement to the facts, the Court dismissed the Commission's claim that certain provisions of the Italian Customs Code infringed Articles 30 and 34 because they required the owner of goods either to clear them through customs himself or to appoint a professional customs agent, so that clearance by a non-professional agent was almost impossible. The Italian Government stated that by a legal fiction any person was deemed to be the owner for this purpose if he had possession of the goods when they entered or left the customs territory and acted in his own name and bore liability jointly with the owner. Accepting this assertion, the Court found that there was no infringement of Article 30 or 34.

7.63   (ii) In *Kramer*[118] the Court was asked by a national court to rule on the compatibility of fishing conservation quotas with Articles 30 and 34 and the common market organisation for fish.[119] The Court replied as follows:

> 'National regulations such as those forming the subject-matter of the present proceedings on the one hand and the prohibition laid down in Article 30 *et seq.* of the Treaty on the other hand relate to different stages of the economic process, that is to say, to production and to marketing respectively.
>
> The answer to the question whether a measure limiting agricultural production impedes trade between Member States depends on the global system established by the basic Community rules in the sector concerned and on the objectives of those rules. In this connection, the nature and the circumstances of "production" of the product in question, fish in the present case, should also be taken into consideration. Measures for the conservation of the resources of the sea through fixing catch quotas and limiting the fishing effort, whilst restricting "production" in the short term, are aimed precisely at preventing such "production" from being marked by a fall which would seriously jeopardise supplies to customers. Therefore, the

---

[117] Paras. 7.13 *et seq.* above.
[118] Cases 3, 4 and 6/76 [1976] E.C.R. 1279, [1976] 2 C.M.L.R. 440.
[119] See paras. 10.07 *et seq.* below.

> fact that such measures have the effect, for a short time, of reducing the quantities that the States concerned are able to exchange between themselves, cannot lead to these measures being classified among those prohibited by the Treaty, the decisive factor being that in the long term these measures are necessary to ensure a steady, optimum yield for fishing'.

While this ruling is obviously of the utmost importance to the fisheries sector, it may well not apply to any other product.

7.64   (iii) A deflationary economic policy consisting of keeping interest rates and the national currency high and/or an incomes policy is designed to slow down the economy as a whole and thus one of its effects will be to reduce imports. Yet it is submitted that such measures probably do not fall under Article 30.[120] This is probably because under the Treaty the primary responsibility for economic policy rests with the Member States.[121] This emerges particularly from Article 104: 'Each Member State shall pursue the economic policy needed to ensure the equilibrium of its overall balance of payments and to maintain confidence in its currency, while taking care to ensure a high level of employment and a stable level of prices.' Nevertheless, Member States are to regard 'conjunctural policy' and exchange rates as a matter of common concern (Articles 103 (1) and 107 (1)[122] respectively); and indeed they are required to co-ordinate their economic policies (Articles 6 (1) and 145).

In spite of this, Member States must conduct their economic policies within the bounds permitted by Community law. Thus in Case 6/69 *E.C. Commission* v. *France*[123] the defendant State was held to have infringed Article 92 by granting a preferential rediscount rate for exports. Again the Court has held that a Member State could not rely on Article 103 to justify a measure falling under Article 30.[124] On the other hand, the measures being discussed here are an inherent part of economic policy and it is hard to see how they could fall outside the bounds permitted by Community law. Perhaps the Court had this type of measure in mind when it ruled in *GB-Inno* v. *ATAB*[125] that the concept of measures of equivalent effect did not cover measures which 'are *per se* permitted as being the visible or hidden expression of powers retained by the Member States'.

7.65   (iv) Clearly any measure not restricting imports is compatible with Article 30. It is perhaps on these grounds that one

---

[120] See also para. 6.31 above.
[121] See generally Mégret in *Le droit de la Communauté Economique Européenne* (1976)Vol. 6.
[122] On Art. 107 see paras. 9.12 *et seq.*
[123] [1969] E.C.R. 523, [1970] C.M.L.R. 43.
[124] Para. 7.52 above.
[125] Note 99 above, at 2147.

might say that legislation limiting shop opening hours is compatible with that provision. This perhaps depends on whether there is any reliable evidence to show whether or not people buy less because shop opening hours are limited.

III. MEASURES OF EQUIVALENT EFFECT UNDER ARTICLE 34

7.66   As we saw in the previous chapter,[126] many of the principles applying to measures of equivalent effect on imports under Article 30 apply *mutatis mutandis* to measures of equivalent effect on exports under Article 34. In so far as discrimination is relevant under Article 34 it is discrimination in favour of goods intended for the national market against goods intended for export.

Some of the cases on Article 34 have been dealt with earlier in this chapter[127] and there is consequently no need to repeat them. Furthermore, the cases on export restrictions which are interpretations of common market organisations rather than Article 34 are dealt with in chapter X.[128]

Export licences and certificates

7.67   This type of measure arose for consideration in Case 68/76 *E.C. Commission* v. *France*.[129] As a result of the sharp drop in potato production in Europe in 1975, the French Government subjected exports of potatoes to the production of an export certificate endorsed by a Government body bearing the acronym FORMA. Citing its ruling in the *International Fruit Company*[130] case the Court held that

> 'even if in connection with intra-Community trade the FORMA granted its endorsement without delay and for all quantities requested and even if the object of the measures was merely to ascertain the intentions of the exporters, it must be held to be a measure having an effect equivalent to a quantitative restriction on exports'.

7.68   The measure at issue in *Procureur de la République* v. *Bouhelier*[131] was somewhat more complex. Exporters of particular categories of watches were required either to obtain an export licence or to obtain a certificate attesting that the watches were of a given quality. Such certificates were issued by a technical body recognised by the French Government, known as Cetehor. Should the watches fail to reach the quality standard requested, Cetehor would refuse to

---

[126] Paras. 6.52 *et seq.* above.
[127] Paras. 7.46 and 7.63 above.
[128] Paras. 10.10 *et seq.* below.
[129] Note 6 above.
[130] Note 4 above.
[131] Case 53/76 [1977] E.C.R. 197, [1977] 1 C.M.L.R. 436.

grant a certificate. In criminal proceedings the accused admitted to having forged certificates of quality, but claimed that the French measure was contrary to Article 34. Accordingly, the national court made a reference under Article 177 asking in effect if this was so. The Court replied that the obligation to obtain an export licence was contrary to Article 34, as was the obligation to obtain a certificate of quality. What is more, the latter obligation could not be justified since it constituted arbitrary discrimination.[132]

Restrictions on production

7.69 The first case to come before the Court concerning the compatibility with Article 34 of a restriction on the production of goods not covered by a common market organisation[133] was *Groenveld* v. *Produktschap voor Vee en Vlees*.[134] On a reference under Article 177 the Court was asked to rule on the compatibility with Article 34 of a Dutch measure prohibiting a manufacturer of processed meat products from having in stock and processing horsemeat. The plaintiffs wished to begin the manufacture of horsemeat sausages and consequently sought a determination by the courts as to the validity of this measure. The unusual aspects of the Dutch regulation were that:

- butchers dealing in horsemeat were entitled to manufacture horsemeat sausages provided they sold them directly to consumers and not to middlemen;
- the import and export of horsemeat sausages were not in themselves prohibited so that traders could import them, either from Member States or third countries, and re-export them either to Member States or third countries.

The defendant body stated that it had adopted these rules in view of the strong aversion felt in the United Kingdom, the United States and the Federal Republic of Germany to the consumption of horsemeat by human beings. The mere fact that British consumers might think that Dutch exports of processed meat might contain horsemeat would seriously harm Dutch exports. Furthermore, the defendant claimed that it was practically impossible to detect the presence of horsemeat in processed meat products, and this is why it found it necessary to prohibit manufacturers of such products from having in stock or processing horsemeat.

The Court was swayed by these arguments. It held that Article 34

'concerns national measures which have as their specific object or effect the restriction of patterns of exports and thereby the establishment of a difference in treatment between the domestic trade of a Member State and its export trade in such a way as to provide a particular advantage for national production or

---

[132] Para. 8.05 below.
[133] For cases on products covered by such organisations see paras. 7.63 above and 10.10 *et seq.* below.
[134] Case 15/79 [1979] E.C.R. 3409, [1981] 1 C.M.L.R. 207. para. 6.55 above.

for the domestic market of the State in question at the expense of the production or of the trade of other Member States. This is not so in the case of a prohibition like that in question which is applied objectively to the production of goods of a certain kind without drawing a distinction depending on whether such goods are intended for the national market or for export.

The foregoing appreciation is not affected by the circumstance that the regulation in question has as its objective *inter alia* the safeguarding of the reputation of the national production of meat products in certain export markets within the Community and in non-member countries where there are obstacles of a psychological or legislative nature to the consumption of horsemeat where the same prohibition is applied identically to the product in the domestic market of the State in question. The objective nature of that prohibition is not modified by the fact that the regulation in force in the Netherlands permits the retail sale of horsemeat by butchers. In fact that concession at the level of local trade does not have the effect of bringing about a prohibition at the level of industrial manufacture of the same product regardless of its destination'.

The Court concluded that a prohibition of the kind in question was compatible with Article 34.

Yet it is submitted that there are two inconsistencies in this argument: first, the Dutch rules with respect to the domestic market allowed butchers to manufacture processed horsemeat and sell it to consumers, so that the rules did in fact discriminate against exports; secondly, the Court overlooked the fact that the effect desired by the Produktschap could have been achieved by adequate labelling requirements, and that the prohibition was excessive for this reason. It is submitted therefore that the Court should have followed the Advocate General, who found that a measure of the kind in question was contrary to Article 34.

Consequently it is submitted that the result arrived at in the judgment, which was delivered by a Chamber of the Court, should be treated with the greatest caution.

7.70 Nevertheless, the test laid down in the first paragraph quoted above from the *Groenveld* judgment was expressly confirmed by the full Court in *Oebel*.[135] Applying this criterion, the Court found that a prohibition on night baking applying in the same way to goods intended for the domestic market and to goods intended for export was not a measure of equivalent effect within the meaning of Article 34.

It remains to be seen what restrictions on production will be held contrary to Article 34.

IV. CONCLUSION

7.71 This is clearly a remarkable body of case law. The Court has plotted a bold course ever since its ruling in *International Fruit* that

---

[135] See note 87 above.

an import licensing system constituted a measure of equivalent effect even if licences were granted automatically on demand.[136]

Nevertheless, in view of the large numbers of cases relating to Article 30, there are inevitably certain differences of approach. In particular, some judgments[137] tend to blur the distinction between the *existence* of a restriction and the *justification* for it, while most do not. Yet, apart from a few difficult cases,[138] all the judgments can in their result be reconciled with the view that, except as regards certain types of price control[139] the concept of measures of equivalent effect under Article 30 embraces all restrictions on imports not covered by any other provision in the Treaty and regardless of whether such restrictions discriminate against imports. On the other hand, as regards measures of equivalent effect under Article 34 the Court is only beginning to lay down the basic principles.

It is to be hoped that despite any political pressures arising out of the current recession the Court will not be tempted to go back on the principles it has established[140].

---

[136] See para. 7.03 above.
[137] See, *e.g.* para. 7.33 above.
[138] See in particular paras. 7.07 and 7.46 above.
[139] See para. 7.56 above.
[140] There are, however, grounds for fearing that it may now have done so in its very recent judgment in Case 75/81 *Blesgen* v. *Belgian State* (see Annexe I to this book).

CHAPTER VIII

The main exception: Article 36 EEC

8.01   Article 36[1] of the EEC Treaty reads:

'The provisions of Articles 30 to 34 shall not preclude prohibitions or restrictions on imports, exports or goods in transit justified on grounds of public morality, public policy or public security; the protection of health and life of humans, animals or plants; the protection of national treasures possessing artistic, historic or archaeological value; or the protection of industrial and commercial property. Such prohibitions or restrictions shall not, however, constitute a means of arbitrary discrimination or a disguised restriction on trade between Member States'.[2]

The wording of this provision shows that it applies both to quantitative restrictions and to measures of equivalent effect. It is submitted, moreover, that it covers the latter whether they are 'distinctly' or 'indistinctly applicable'.[3] Moreover, it is also clear from the wording of Article 36 that it merely entitles the Member States to exercise certain powers subject to certain limits: it does not oblige them to exercise those powers.

8.02   As the Court held in *Bauhuis* v. *Netherlands*,[4] Article 36 'constitutes a derogation from the basic rule that all obstacles to the free movement of goods between Member States shall be eliminated and must be interpreted strictly'. Rulings of like effect are to be found in several other judgments.[5] However, as suggested earlier in this book,[6] in its *Cassis de Dijon* judgment the Court in effect added to the list of grounds of justification set out in the first sentence of Article 36. Accordingly, these will also be considered in this chapter.

---

[1] See generally Ehlermann 'Die Bedeutung des Artikels 36 EWGV für die Freiheit des Warenverkehrs' [1973] EuR. 1 and materials cited in notes 61 and 83 to Chap. VI.

[2] This provision is clearly modelled on the considerably lengthier Art. XX of GATT which begins: 'Subject to the requirement that such measures are not applied in a manner which would constitute a means of arbitrary or unjustifiable discrimination between countries where the same conditions prevail, or a disguised restriction on international trade, nothing in this Agreement shall be construed to prevent the adoption or enforcement by any contracting party of measures: (a) necessary to protect public morals; (b) necessary to protect human, animal or plant life or health . . . etc.' However, the exceptions allowed by the two Articles are not all identical: in particular, Art. XX includes a number of specific exceptions such as restrictions on the import or export of gold or silver and restrictions on the products of prison labour, which are not to be found in Art. 36 EEC.

[3] For this terminology, see para. 6.28 above.

[4] Case 46/76 [1977] E.C.R. 1.

[5] e.g. Case 7/68 *E.C. Commission* v. *Italy* [1968] E.C.R. 423, [1969] C.M.L.R. 1; Case 13/68 *Salgoil* v. *Italian Ministry for Foreign Trade* [1968] E.C.R. 453, [1969] C.M.L.R. 181; Case 13/78 *Eggers* v. *Freie Hansestadt Bremen* [1978] E.C.R. 1935, [1979] 1 C.M.L.R. 562.

[6] Paras. 6.39 *et seq.*

8.03   It should also be pointed out at this stage that the Court has held that a national authority relying on Article 36 bears the burden of proving that contentious measures are justified under that provision: *Denkavit Futtermittel* v. *Minister of Agriculture*.[7] It is submitted that this ruling cannot be limited to national authorities, so that any party seeking to rely on Article 36 bears the burden of proof. Indeed, it is submitted that the Court made the same point in different terms in *Gilli and Andres*[8] when it held:

> 'It is only where national rules . . . may be justified as being necessary in order to satisfy imperative requirements relating in particular to the protection of public health, the fairness of commercial transactions and the defence of the consumer that they may constitute an exception to the requirements arising under Article 30'.

8.04   Having made these preliminary points we can now turn to the essence of Article 36. This is that to be justified under that exception a national provision:

- must fall within one of the grounds of justification set out in the first sentence or within one of the other 'mandatory requirements'; and
- must not constitute arbitrary discrimination nor a disguised restriction on trade between Member States and must be justified.

Although it is rather artificial to separate the two conditions, it is necessary to do so here. It is appropriate to deal with the second condition before the first.

I. PROPORTIONALITY AND NON-DISCRIMINATION

'Arbitrary discrimination'

8.05   It is generally considered that the word 'arbitrary' is superfluous in Article 36.[9] Its use is no doubt due to the fact that the term 'arbitrary discrimination' appears in Article XX of GATT, on which Article 36 is modelled. Such discrimination can take the following forms:

- the most obvious is discrimination against imports in favour of domestic products, either by applying a restriction to imported products only or by applying a greater restriction with respect to imported products. An example in Case 152/78 *E.C. Commission* v. *France*[10] where advertising restrictions on alcoholic drinks were framed in such a way as to fall more heavily on imports. The Court held that, even though in principle adver-

---

[7] Case 251/78 [1979] E.C.R. 3369, [1980] 3 C.M.L.R. 513.
[8] Case 788/79 [1980] E.C.R. 2071, [1981] 1 C.M.L.R. 146; para. 6.32 above.
[9] Ehlermann in Groeben, Boeckh, Thiesing, *Kommentar zum EWG-Vertrag* (1974) 293–294—see, however, Graf, *Der Begriff 'Massnahmen gleicher Wirkung wie mengenmässige Einfuhrbeschränkungen' in dem EWG-Vertrag* (1972) 106 *et seq.*
[10] [1980] E.C.R. 2299, [1981] 2 C.M.L.R. 743; see para. 7.25 above.

tising restrictions on alcoholic drinks would be justified under Article 36 on public health grounds, the particular measures in question were not so justified because they constituted arbitrary discrimination—even though some domestically produced drinks were caught by the heavier restrictions;

- conversely, a restriction falling solely or more heavily on exports to the exclusion of products intended for the domestic market also constitutes arbitrary discrimination. Thus in *Bouhelier*[11] the requirement to obtain certificates of quality for exports of watches was held to constitute arbitrary discrimination, since no corresponding obligation existed as regards watches intended for the domestic market;[12]

- *Dassonville*[13] shows that discrimination between imports coming directly from the State of production and indirect imports will constitute arbitrary discrimination.[14] The *Dassonville* case itself shows that this holds good even where the goods were produced outside the Community: at the material time the United Kingdom had not yet acceded to the Community;

- it can be deduced from the *De Peijper*[15] case discussed below that discrimination against parallel imports will also constitute arbitrary discrimination;

- finally, where Member State A discriminates in favour of goods coming from or originating in Member State B as against those coming from or originating in Member State C, that is also arbitrary discrimination.

8.06   However, there will be no arbitrary discrimination in any of these cases if the difference of treatment is objectively justified. Thus in a quite different context in *Italy* v. *E.C. Commission*[16] the Court defined the principle of non-discrimination under the Treaty as follows: 'The different treatment of non-comparable situations does not lead automatically to the conclusion that there is discrimination. An appearance of discrimination in form may therefore correspond in fact to an absence of discrimination in substance. Discrimination in substance would consist in treating either similar situations differently or different situations identically'.

Also, in *Rewe-Zentralfinanz* v. *Landwirtschafskammer*[17] the Court was asked, *inter alia*, whether the obligation to submit imports of apples to phytosanitary controls constituted arbitrary discrimination

---

[11] Case 53/76 [1977] E.C.R. 197, [1977] 1 C.M.L.R. 436.
[12] It is true that Art. 36 was not expressly mentioned, but the mere use of the words 'arbitrary discrimination' in the judgment can be taken as an implied reference to that provision.
[13] Case 8/74 [1974] E.C.R. 837, [1974] 2 C.M.L.R. 436.
[14] [1980] E.C.R. 2299, [1981] 2 C.M.L.R. 743; see para. 7.25 above.
[15] Case 104/75 [1976] E.C.R. 613, [1976] 2 C.M.L.R. 271.
[16] Case 13/63 [1963] E.C.R. 165, [1963] C.M.L.R. 289; the case concerned Art. 226 (see Chap. IX, note 4).
[17] Case 4/75 [1975] E.C.R. 843, [1977] 1 C.M.L.R. 599.

under Article 36, when no corresponding requirement existed with respect to domestically produced apples. The Court replied that:

'The different treatment of imported and domestic products, based on the need to prevent the spread of the harmful organism could not, however, be regarded as arbitrary discrimination if effective measures are taken in order to prevent the distribution of contaminated domestic products and if there is reason to believe, in particular on the basis of previous experience, that there is a risk of the harmful organism's spreading if no inspection is held on importation'.

8.07   On a different but related point the Court held in *Procureur du Roi* v. *Debauve*[18] that 'differences, which are due to natural phenomena, cannot be described as "discrimination" within the meaning of the Treaty; the latter regards only differences in treatment arising from human activity'. Although this case concerned services rather than goods, it is submitted that this particular part of the judgment is of general application. The case involved the prosecution of a number of individuals and undertakings engaged in the diffusion in Belgium of cable television from other Member States for infringing the prohibition on television advertising in Belgium. One of the questions referred by the Belgian court under Article 177 was whether a prohibition of this kind constituted 'discrimination based on the geographical locality of the foreign broadcasting station which would be able to transmit advertisements only within its natural receiving zone [inside Belgian territory], as these zones may, because of the differences in density of population, be of very different interest from the advertising point of view'. The point of this question was that even if the prohibition of television advertising in Belgium covered re-transmission by cable television of broadcasts of other Member States, nevertheless broadcasting networks in neighbouring countries could not avoid reaching certain frontier districts of Belgium. The Court, however, reached the conclusion that this would not constitute discrimination.

8.08   What if the laws of some of the constituent parts of a Member State are less restrictive than the measures applying to imports into the entire territory of that Member State? This was essentially one of the issues in *R* v. *Henn and Darby*,[19] which concerned the offence of importing 'indecent or obscene articles' into the United Kingdom. That offence covered certain categories of article which might be lawfully sold in some, but not all, constituent parts of the United Kingdom. On this point the Court held that:

'the fact that certain differences exist between the laws enforced in the different constituent parts of a Member State does not thereby prevent that State from

---

[18] Case 52/79, [1980] E.C.R. 881, [1981] 2 C.M.L.R. 362; see para. 2.05 above.
[19] Case 34/79 [1979] E.C.R. 3795, [1980] 1 C.M.L.R. 246, noted by Faull [1980] C.D.E. 446; Weiler [1981] M.L.R. 91, Catchpole and Barav [1980] *Leg. Issues Eur.Int.* 1. The Court's judgment was applied by the House of Lords at [1980] 2 W.L.R. 633.

applying a unitary concept in regard to prohibitions on imports imposed on grounds of public morality, on trade with other Member States'.

Later passages of the judgment could perhaps be taken as implied acceptance by the Court of the Advocate General's view[20] that 'where the Member State concerned is so constituted that there are variations in the laws of different parts of it, that in my opinion is a factor—it may be an important factor—to be taken into account in applying the test' of whether more restrictive treatment of imports is reasonable. This judgment will be more closely examined under the heading 'public morality' below.

'Disguised restriction'

8.09 It has been suggested[21] that Article 36 would have much the same meaning even if this expression were not there. In *Henn and Darby*[22] the Court stated that the second sentence of Article 36 'is designed to prevent restrictions on trade based on the grounds mentioned in the first sentence of Article 36 from being diverted from their proper purpose'.[23] This may presumably be taken as an interpretation of the words 'disguised restriction'.

'Justified'

8.10 According to the rule of proportionality a measure may not restrict trade between Member States more than is necessary to achieve its legitimate object. This was clearly set out by the Court in *De Peijper*[24] as follows:

> 'It emerges from Article 36 that national rules or practices which do restrict imports of pharmaceutical products or are capable of doing so are only compatible with the Treaty to the extent to which they are necessary for the effective protection of health and life of humans.
>
> National rules or practices do not fall within the exception specified in Article 36 if the health and life of humans can [be] as effectively protected by measures which do not restrict intra-Community trade so much'.

The Court made the same point in a different way in *Eggers* v. *Freie Hansestadt Bremen*[25] when it held:

> 'Article 36 is an exception to the fundamental principle of the free movement of goods and must, therefore, be interpreted in such a way that its scope is not extended any further than is *necessary*[26] for the protection of those interests which it is intended to secure'.

It is submitted that the Court was making the same point once again in *Cassis de Dijon*[27] when it held: 'Obstacles to movement within

[20] At 3831 (E.C.R.), 265 (C.M.L.R.).
[21] Ehlermann, *op. cit.* 294.
[22] Note 19 above.
[23] With respect to trade marks, see para. 8.70 *et seq.*
[24] See note 15 above.
[25] Case 13/78 [1978] E.C.R. 1935, [1979] 1 C.M.L.R. 562; para. 7.32 above.
[26] The italics are those of the author.
[27] See note 49 below.

the Community . . . must be accepted in so far as those provisions may be recognised as being necessary in order to satisfy mandatory requirements.' The view was put forward in Chapter VI[28] that this statement is to be taken as an interpretation of Article 36, even though that provision was not mentioned in the judgment. On this view, the principle of equivalence discussed in Chapter VI[29] is an interpretation of the word 'justified' in Article 36.

8.11 Moreover, the Court also held in the *De Peijper* case that:

> 'Article 36 cannot be relied on to justify rules or practices which, even though they are beneficial, contain restrictions which are explained primarily by concern to lighten the administration's burden or reduce public expenditure, unless, in the absence of the said rules or practices, this burden or expenditure clearly would exceed the limits of what can reasonably be required.'[30]

8.12 A further principle of Article 36 is that it cannot be used by a Member State to impose its own standards or morals on other Member States. This point was made—perhaps even overstated—by the Advocate General in *Dassonville*[31] when he said that on the basis of this provision Member States may derogate from the prohibition on quantitative restrictions and measures of equivalent effect 'only for the purpose of the protection of their own interests and not for the protection of the interests of other States'.

However, this principle is clearly subject to limitations as is shown by the *Bauhuis* case.[32] One of the questions which arose there was whether, even in the absence of Community legislation, exporting Member States could carry out veterinary and public health controls on animals for the benefit of the importing Member State. The Court held that such a practice was compatible with Article 36. This was subsequently confirmed in Case 89/76 *E.C. Commission* v. *Netherlands*[33] concerning phytosanitary inspections on plants. Moreover, it is submitted that a Member State may be entitled to prohibit trade in animals or plants threatened with extinction even if they are not indigenous to that Member State.

8.13 Next, what if imports are subject to restrictions justified under Article 36 but the public authorities are empowered to relax the restrictions in individual cases?

In *Denkavit Futtermittel*[34] the Court ruled as follows:

---

[28] Paras. 6.39 *et seq.* above.

[29] Para. 6.44 *et seq.* above.

[30] See also para. 8.26 below. At first sight this statement would appear to mean that the avoidance of undue expenditure is itself a ground of justification under Art. 36. On closer examination, however, it would seem that it is an interpretation of 'justified'. This means the avoidance of undue expenditure can only justify a restriction on trade when it is linked to a ground of justification, in this case public health. For this view see Ehlermann 'Das Verbot der Massnahmen gleicher Wirkung in der Rechtsprechung des Gerichtshofes' in *Festschrift für Ipsen* (1977), 579 at 590–591.

[31] See note 13 above at 860.

[32] See note 4 above.

[33] [1977] E.C.R. 1355, [1978] 3 C.M.L.R. 630.

[34] See note 7 above.

'Article 36 of the Treaty cannot be interpreted as meaning that it forbids in principle a national authority, which has imposed by a general rule veterinary and public health restrictions on imports . . ., from providing that it will be possible to derogate therefrom by individual measures left to the discretion of the administration if such derogations assist the simplification of the restrictions imposed by the general rules and if this power of derogation does not[35] give rise to arbitrary discrimination between traders of different Member States.

Nevertheless it does not automatically follow that each of the conditions to which the national authority subjects the grant of authorisation itself complies with what is permitted by Article 36. It is in each case for the national courts . . . to determine whether these conditions are necessary to attain the objective which Article 36 allows to be sought . . .'

This approach was later confirmed by the Court in *Fietje*.[36] There it held:

'in the case of a measure justified on grounds recognised by the Treaty, the Treaty does not forbid in principle provision being made for the possibility of granting derogations therefrom by individual decisions left to the discretion of the administration. However, exceptions must not lead to the favouring of domestic products because this would constitute arbitrary discrimination against or a disguised restriction on products imported from other Member States'.

On the other hand, said the Court in *Denkavit Futtermittel*, if the individual dispensation 'only made possible a relaxation of a general supervisory system which went beyond what Article 36 permits it would be necessary to consider it on its own merits in the light of the exceptions permitted by Article 36 . . .'[37]

8.14 Lastly, as regards the relationship between Article 36 and Community legislation, the Court held in *Simmenthal* v. *Italian Minister of Finance*[38] that:

'Article 36 is not designed to reserve certain matters to the exclusive jurisdiction of Member States but permits national laws to derogate from the principle of the free movement of goods to the extent to which such derogation is and continues to be justified for the attainment of the objectives referred to in that Article'.

The question referred by the national court was whether systematic veterinary and public health checks on meat imports to Italy from another Member State were compatible with Articles 30 and 36. The Court found that certain Community Directives harmonising health checks in the exporting Member State rendered systematic import checks unnecessary so that they were no longer justified under Article 36.

---

[35] The word 'not' is missing from the English text but it is clear from the sense and from other language texts that it should be there.

[36] Case 27/80, [1980] E.C.R. 3839, [1981] 3 C.M.L.R. 722.

[37] See also Case 82/77 *Van Tiggele* [1978] E.C.R. 25, [1978] 2 C.M.L.R. 528; para. 7.55 above.

[38] Case 35/76 [1976] E.C.R. 1871, [1977] 2 C.M.L.R. 1.

In the subsequent cases of *Tedeschi* v. *Denkavit*,[39] *Ratti*,[40] and *Denkavit Futtermittel* v. *Minister of Agriculture*[41] the Court repeated the passage quoted above, adding:

> 'Where, in application of Article 100 of the Treaty, Community directives provide for the harmonisation of the measures necessary to ensure the protection of animal and human health and establish Community procedures to check that they are observed, recourse to Article 36 is no longer justified and the appropriate checks must be carried out and the measures of protection adopted within the framework outlined by the harmonising directive'.[42]

8.15 This is not to say that every Directive provides exhaustive guarantees such as to oust the application of Article 36.[43] It is a question of the wording of each Directive whether the guarantees it provides are exhaustive. Thus in the *Rewe-Zentralfinanz*[44] case concerning phytosanitary controls on apple imports to check for San José Scale insects, the Court found that recourse could still be had by Member States to Article 36 in spite of the existence of a Directive[45] on the control of that very insect; this was because that Directive expressly authorised the Member States to adopt such stricter provisions as might be necessary.

8.16 On the other hand, directives cannot extend the powers enjoyed by the Member States under Article 36. This was held in *De Peijper*,[46] which was concerned with the formalities laid down by the Dutch authorities for giving approval to pharmaceutical products imported from other Member States. Having ruled that formalities of this kind might constitute measures of equivalent effect, the Court went on to consider the contention of the British, Danish and Dutch Governments that such measures were necessary to comply with the Council Directives on the approximation of national provisions relating to proprietary medicinal products.[47] The Court rejected this contention on the grounds that 'the sole aim of these directives is to harmonise national provisions in this field; they do not and cannot aim at extending the very considerable powers left to Member States in the field of public health by Article 36'. This is merely a particular manifestation of the general rule discussed earlier in this book to the effect that Community legislation may not create undue barriers to trade between Member States.[48]

---

[39] Case 5/77 [1977] E.C.R. 1555, [1978] 1 C.M.L.R. 1.
[40] Case 148/78 [1979] E.C.R. 1629, [1980] 1 C.M.L.R. 96.
[41] See note 7 above.
[42] This passage is in fact taken from the *Tedeschi* case; there are insignificant textual differences between the three judgments.
[43] Even a Regulation setting up a common organisation of the market may fail to oust Art. 36 in the absence of express wording: written question 468/80 ([1980] O.J. C302/3) concerning a ban on growing hemp. However, this will only occur in highly exceptional circumstances.
[44] See note 17 above.
[45] Dir. 69/466 ([1969] O.J. L323/5).
[46] See note 15 above.
[47] Dir. 65/65 ([1965] O.J. Spec. Ed. 20); Dirs. 75/318 and 75/319 ([1975] O.J. L147/13).
[48] Paras. 4.07 *et seq*.

II. THE GROUNDS OF JUSTIFICATION

8.17 As explained at the beginning of this chapter, it is intended to cover here the 'mandatory requirements' set out in the *Cassis de Dijon* case[49]: the 'effectiveness of fiscal supervision' (*i.e* the prevention of tax evasion), the 'fairness of commercial transactions' (*i.e.* the prevention of unfair competition) and consumer protection. The protection of the environment and the improvement of working conditions will also be discussed.

It is submitted that these requirements are to be assimilated to the grounds of justification expressly set out in Article 36.[50] For reasons of convenience these points will be considered before industrial and commercial property.

8.18 It must be borne in mind, however, that in Case 7/61 *E.C. Commission* v. *Italy*,[51] the first case on Article 36, the Court held that Article 36 is directed to eventualities of a non-economic kind'. Thus such objects as the promotion of employment or investment, curbing inflation and controlling the balance of payments fall outside Article 36. This crucial ruling has not been altered in any way by the Court's recent case law extending the grounds of justification under Article 36.[52]

8.19 Lastly, the first four grounds of justification are similar to the exceptions to the free movement of workers, the freedom of establishment and the free provision of services as regards public policy, public security and public health (Articles 48 (3), 56 (1) and 66 respectively).[53] It is probable that the same meaning should be given to those terms in Article 36 as in the equivalent articles, yet this is not necessarily so. Certain disparities will be due to the inherent differences between movements of goods on the one hand and persons and services on the other. Other differences may be due to the fact that the list of grounds in Article 36 is more detailed so that the term 'public policy' can be interpreted more narrowly.

Public morality

8.20 The only judgment[54] of the Court of Justice on public morality

---

[49] Case 120/78 *Rewe* v. *Bundesmonopolverwaltung für Branntwein* [1979] E.C.R. 649, [1979] 3 C.M.L.R. 494, see paras. 6.33 *et seq.* above.

[50] Paras. 6.39 *et seq.* above.

[51] [1961] E.C.R. 317, [1962] C.M.L.R. 39.

[52] See para. 8.23 below.

[53] On workers see in particular Dir. 64/221 ([1964] J.O. 850) Case 41/74 *Van Duyn* v. *Home Office* [1974] E.C.R. 1337, [1975] 1 C.M.L.R. 1; Case 30/77 *R.* v. *Bouchereau* [1977] E.C.R. 1999, [1977] 2 C.M.L.R. 800; Wooldridge, 'Free Movement of EEC Nationals: "The limitation based on public policy and public security"' [1977] E.L. Rev 190, Evans, 'Ordre Public, Public Policy and the United Kingdom Immigration Law' [1978] E.L. Rev. 370; Hartley, *EEC Immigration Law* (1978), Chap. 5; on services see in particular Dir. 64/221 already referred to and Case 52/79 *Procureur du Roi* v. *Debauve* [1980] E.C.R. 881, [1981] 2 C.M.L.R. 362; Case 62/79 *Coditel* v. *Ciné Vog Films* [1980] E.C.R. 883 [1981] 2 C.M.L.R. 362, especially the Advocate General at 877.

[54] See however written question 375/77 ([1977] O.J. C265/8): the Commission took the view that a Member State, which bans cruelty in the rearing and slaughtering of poultry (*e.g.*

under Article 36 is *R.* v. *Henn and Darby*[55] which is also the only case yet to be referred to the Court by the House of Lords. At its simplest the Court's decision in this case means that a Member State may rely on this provision to prohibit imports of pornographic material when there is no lawful trade in such goods within its territory. Yet on closer examination it proves more complex.

The facts were that the defendants were convicted of importing into the United Kingdom a lorry-load of pornographic films and magazines originating in Denmark, contrary to section 42 of the Customs Consolidation Act 1876. The object of the reference was to ascertain primarily whether this provision was compatible with Articles 30 and 36.[56]

As to whether such a measure was justified on the grounds of public morality within the meaning of Article 36, the Court ruled:

> 'In principle, it is for each Member State to determine in accordance with its own scale of values and in the form selected by the requirements of public morality in its territory. In any event, it cannot be disputed that the statutory provisions applied by the United Kingdom in regard to the importation of articles having an indecent or obscene character come within the powers reserved to the Member States by the first sentence of Article 36'.

The use of the words 'in principle' indicates that the Member States may only exercise their discretion within the boundaries of a Community-wide concept of public morality. This is much the same as the Court's rulings on the concept of public policy in Article 48 (3) in *Van Duyn* v. *Home Office* and *R.* v. *Bouchereau:*[57]

> 'the concept of public policy in the context of the Community and where, in particular, it is used as a justification for derogating from the fundamental principle of freedom of movement for workers, must be interpreted strictly, so that its scope cannot be determined unilaterally by each Member State without being subject to control by the institutions of the Community. Nevertheless the particular circumstances justifying recourse to the concept of public policy may vary from one country to another, and it is therefore necessary in this matter to allow the competent national authorities an area of discretion within the limits imposed by the Treaty'.[58]

As will be clear from the passage quoted above, in *Henn and Darby* the Court did not seek to define the boundaries of the concept of public morality.

---

a ban on battery rearing), may *not* ban imports from other Member States applying less stringent rules. In particular, such an import ban would not be justified on the grounds of public morality, since 'any affront to public morals . . . would occur solely in the country where the cruel treatment takes place and can be witnessed by the local population, and not in the importing country'. This view may perhaps be regarded as unduly restrictive, if it is indeed correct that a Member State is entitled to prohibit trade in animals or plants threatened with extinction even if they are not indigenous to that Member State. (See para. 8.12 above.)

[55] See note 19 above.
[56] See also paras. 5.06 above and 9.55 below.
[57] See note 53 above.
[58] The parallel with the *Van Duyn* and *Bouchereau* cases was made by the Advocate General in *Henn and Darby* at 3828 (E.C.R.).

8.21 So much for the general principle. However, the picture in *Henn and Darby* itself was complicated by the fact that section 42 of the Customs Consolidation Act 1876 was more restrictive than the laws applying within the United Kingdom in three respects:

- in no part of the United Kingdom is it a criminal offence merely to possess pornographic material otherwise than with a view to sale, yet such possession at a point of entry into the United Kingdom contravenes section 42;

- whereas section 42 prohibits 'indecent and obscene' articles (standard A), within certain parts of the United Kingdom, at least in England and Wales, only the sale of 'obscene' material is prohibited, while 'indecent' material may be sold (standard B); thus articles which are merely 'indecent' without being so offensive as to be considered 'obscene' may be sold within England and Wales but may not be imported into any part of the United Kingdom;

- again as far as articles sold within England and Wales are concerned, the Obscene Publications Acts 1959 and 1964 except from the provisions of those Acts obscene articles of which the publication is, despite their obscenity, 'justified as being for the public good on the ground that it is in the interests of science, literature, art or learning, or of other objects of general concern'. No equivalent defence exists under the Customs Consolidation Act.

The object of the fifth and sixth questions posed by the House of Lords was in effect to ascertain whether the import prohibition could be justified under Article 36. The Court held that such a prohibition was so justified, in the following terms:

> '[The second sentence of Article 36] is designed to prevent restrictions on trade based on the grounds mentioned in the first sentence of Article 36 from being diverted from their proper purpose and used in such a way as either to create discrimination in respect of goods originating in other Member States or indirectly to protect certain national products. That is not the purport of a prohibition such as that in force in the United Kingdom, on the importation of articles which are of an indecent or obscene character. Whatever may be the differences between the laws on this subject in force in the different constituent parts of the United Kingdom, and notwithstanding the fact that they contain certain exceptions of limited scope, these laws, taken as a whole, have as their purpose the prohibition, or at least , the restraining, of the manufacture and marketing of publications or articles of an indecent or obscene character. In these circumstances it is permissible to conclude, on a comprehensive view, that there is no lawful trade in such goods in the United Kingdom. A prohibition on imports which may in certain respects be more strict than some of the laws applied within the United Kingdom cannot therefore be regarded as amounting to a measure designed to give indirect protection to some national product or aimed at creating arbitrary discrimination between goods of this type depending on whether they are produced within the national territory or another Member State'.

8.22 The statement that there was no lawful trade in indecent or obscene articles within the United Kingdom lies at the core of this argument, but is factually incorrect: in most parts of the United

Kingdom there is in fact lawful trade in articles which are indecent but not obscene and in obscene articles justified 'for the public good'. Furthermore, the Court has side-stepped the important issue of whether Articles 30 to 36 apply to movements of goods between Member States involving no commercial transactions.[59]

The approach followed by the Advocate General appears to be more in keeping both with the facts and with the previous case law of the Court. In his view the test must in each case be whether any element of discrimination inherent in the prohibition or restriction on imports under consideration is in all the circumstances proportionate to its legitimate purpose. To prevent, to guard against or to reduce the likelihood of breaches of the domestic laws of the Member State concerned was a legitimate purpose. The Advocate General pointed out that in the present case there was probably no discrimination since (1) the articles appeared so obscene and unmeritorious that it was probably a criminal offence to sell them in any part of the United Kingdom, and (2) it is clear that a man who imports in bulk does so with a view to sale. Yet in so far as there was discrimination there might well be arbitrary discrimination under Article 36:

> 'I doubt if the application of that test [of proportionality] would justify the prohibition of the importation into the United Kingdom of a book that was lawfully on sale in English bookshops. Clearly it would be unreasonable and disproportionate to forbid the importation of such a book just because of the risk that it might be . . . put on sale in Scotland or the Isle of Man. Those very same risks flow from the publication of the book in England'.

Public policy

8.23 With respect to the public policy exception to the free movement of workers the Court held in *Bouchereau*[60] that 'recourse by a national authority to the concept of public policy presupposes . . . the existence . . . of a genuine and sufficiently serious threat to the requirements of public policy affecting one of the fundamental interests of society'.[61]

An echo of that ruling is to be found in *R v. Thompson, Johnson and Woodiwiss*,[62] the only judgment to date to consider the public policy exception in Article 36. As we saw in an earlier chapter,[63] that case concerned a prohibition on the import and export of certain coins into and out of the United Kingdom. We also saw how the Court found that only one of the three categories of coin in issue was to be regarded as goods under Community law: the British silver alloy half-crowns minted before 1947 which, although no longer legal tender,

---

[59] See para. 2.30 above.
[60] See note 53 above.
[61] 'Public policy' does not necessarily have the same meaning under Art. 36: see para. 8.19 above.
[62] Case 7/78 [1978] E.C.R. 2247, [1979] 1 C.M.L.R. 47.
[63] See paras. 2.06 and 2.07.

could be exchanged at the Bank of England and were protected from destruction other than by the State. In its fourth and final question the Court of Appeal (Criminal Division) asked, *inter alia*, whether the prohibition on the export of such coins was justified on the grounds of public policy under Article 36. In its submissions to the Court the United Kingdom Government put forward three reasons for the prohibition on the export of these coins:

(i) to ensure that there was no shortage of current coins for use by the public;

(ii) to ensure that any profit resulting from any increase in the value of the silver content of the coins would accrue to the United Kingdom, since it had minted them;

(iii) to prevent the destruction of United Kingdom coins occurring outside its jurisdiction, it being a criminal offence to destroy coins of the realm within the United Kingdom.

The Court was clearly swayed by these arguments, since it ruled:

> 'It is for the Member States to mint their own coinage and to protect it from destruction.
>
> A ban on exporting such coins with a view to preventing their being melted down or destroyed in another Member State is justified on grounds of public policy within the meaning of Article 36 of the Treaty, because it stems from the need to protect the right to mint coinage which is traditionally regarded as involving the fundamental interests of the State'.

It has been objected[64] that this is a retreat from the Court's earlier ruling that Article 36 does not justify measures of economic protection.[65] Yet it is submitted that that objection is ill-founded, since the judgment is in fact based on the assertion that the State enjoyed a right akin to a property right in the coins. The protection of a property right is a very different thing from the protection of the economy as a whole.

Public security

8.24 This limb of Article 36 covers in particular security matters normally associated with the police, such as crime detection and prevention and the regulation of traffic. In so far as trade in arms, munitions and war material is concerned, the more general provisions of Article 223 apply.[66] Again, in the event of sedition, war or threat of war, Member States are granted sweeping powers to disregard the Treaty by Article 224.[67] That would presumably be the appropriate provision to apply in the event of civil disturbances caused by economic difficulties (*e.g.* unrest of consumers in the case of price increases, of producers in the case of falling prices, or workers in the case of redundancies).[68]

---

[64] Wyatt [1981] E.L.Rev. 483.
[65] See para. 8.18 above.
[66] See para. 9.46 below.
[67] See para. 9.49 below.
[68] Ehlermann, *op. cit.* note 9 above, at 291.

The protection of human health and life

8.25 In the *De Peijper*[69] case the Court ruled that the 'health and the life of humans rank first among the property or interests protected by Article 36 and it is for the Member States, within the limits imposed by the Treaty, to decide what degree of protection they intend to assure, and in particular how strict the checks to be carried out are to be. Consequently, a Member State may take steps to guard against a risk of this kind, however slight, so long as that risk is genuine. For instance, if a disease is liable to claim one life in the entire population of a Member State over a 20-year period, then that Member State is entitled to adopt stringent controls against it—provided always that those controls are not more restrictive of trade between the Member States than is necessary to prevent anyone catching the disease.

8.26 The *De Peijper* case itself arose out of criminal proceedings brought before the Dutch courts against a parallel importer accused of contravening Dutch public health legislation by supplying pharmacies in the Netherlands with pharmaceutical products imported from the United Kingdom without the consent of the Dutch authorities, and with failing to have in his possession certain documents connected with these products. Having ruled in effect that measures restricting parallel imports were measures of equivalent effect within the meaning of Article 30, the Court went on to consider the compatibility of rules of the kind in question with Article 36. In this connection, the Court held in the operative part of its judgment that:

> 'Given a factual situation such as that described in the first question national rules or practices which make possible for a manufacturer of the pharmaceutical product in question and his duly appointed representatives, simply by refusing to produce the documents relating to the medicinal preparation in general or to a specific batch of that preparation, to enjoy a monopoly of the importing and marketing of the product, must be regarded as being unnecessarily restrictive and cannot therefore come within the exceptions specified in Article 36 of the Treaty, unless it is clearly proved that any other rules or practices would obviously be beyond the means which can reasonably be expected of an administration operating in a normal manner'.

In the grounds of its judgment the Court did in fact suggest two methods by which such restrictions might be lessened: Member States might compel the manufacturer or his duly appointed representative to deliver up the necessary information, and 'simple co-operation between the authorities of the Member States would enable them to obtain on a reciprocal basis the documents necessary for checking certain largely standardised and widely distributed products'. The Court continued:

> 'Taking into account all these possible ways of obtaining information the national public health authorities must consider whether the effective protection

---

[69] See note 15 above.

of health and life of humans justifies a presumption of the non-conformity of an imported batch with the description of the medicinal preparation, or whether on the contrary it would not be sufficient to lay down a presumption of conformity with the result that, in appropriate cases, it would be for the administration to rebut this presumption'.

What if there are minor differences in composition between the 'official' and the parallel imports? This was in effect the second question put by the national court, which indicated that the differences might be so minor that it was likely that they were deliberately created by the manufacturer with a view to preventing parallel imports. The Court replied in the following terms:

'It is only if the information or documents to be produced by the manufacturer or his duly appointed importer show that there are several variants of the medicinal preparation and that the differences between these variants have a therapeutic effect that there would be any justification for treating the variants as different medicinal preparations, for the purpose of authorising the relevant documents, it being understood that the answer to the first question remains valid as regards each of the authorisation procedures which have become necessary'.[70]

8.27 The Court had occasion to extend these principles in the *Denkavit Futtermittel* case.[71] On a reference for a preliminary ruling, the Court was called upon to rule, *inter alia*, whether a double veterinary check on imports of animal feed was permitted by Article 36. This double check took the form of, first, the requirement of a veterinary certificate from the authorities of the exporting Member State and, secondly, a systematic veterinary inspection at the frontier. After citing its judgment in *De Peijper* the Court stated:

'That judgment shows that if co-operation between the authorities of the Member States makes it possible to facilitate and simplify frontier checks, which continue to be permissible by virtue of the exception provided for by Article 36 of the EEC Treaty, the authorities responsible for veterinary and public health inspections must ascertain whether the substantiating documents issued as part of such co-operation do not raise a presumption that the imported goods comply with the requirements of national veterinary and public health legislation intended to simplify the checks carried out when the goods pass from one Member State to another.

It is in each case for the national courts to apply these criteria in the light of all the circumstances relating to the actions brought before them taking into account the fact that it must always be the duty of a national authority relying on Article 36 to prove that the measures which it enforces satisfy these criteria'.

8.28 In *Frans-Nederlandse Maatschappij voor Biologische Producten*,[72] the Court was able to build on the principles laid down in *De Peijper* and *Denkavit*. This case concerned a Dutch law prohibiting the sale of plant protection products without prior government approval, which could only be granted after lengthy scientific tests. The particular product in question had not been so approved in the

---

[70] See also Case 32/80 *Kortmann* [1981] E.C.R. 251.
[71] See note 7 above.
[72] Case 272/80, judgment of 17 December 1981.

Netherlands but it was imported from France, where it had been approved after tests similar to those which the Dutch authorities would have carried out. The defendant company was charged with having contravened the Dutch law by selling quantities of this product in the Netherlands. The Dutch court hearing the case referred a question to the Court of Justice asking whether the law was contrary to Article 30 or whether it was justified on public health grounds.

The problem as to what extent considerations of public health will justify restrictions on sale was thus posed in a most acute form. Not only was the product in question a relatively novel chemical substance, but it was also designed for such purposes as the disinfecting of sugar vats and thus came into immediate contact with foodstuffs intended for human consumption. On the other hand, it is clear that national rules on the approval of such products could be misused by the Member States for protectionist ends. Advocate General Madame Rozès implied that such abuse had perhaps occurred in the present case, mentioning that the defendant had abandoned its attempts to obtain approval in the Netherlands for this product after seven years of unsuccessful negotiations with the Dutch authorities.

In the light of these considerations, the Court answered the question as follows:

> 'It follows from Article 30 in conjunction with Article 36 of the Treaty that a Member State is not prohibited from requiring plant protection products to be subject to prior approval, even if those products have already been approved in another Member State. The authorities of the importing State are however not entitled unnecessarily to require technical or chemical analyses or laboratory tests when the same analyses or tests have already been carried out in another Member State and the results are available to those authorities or may at their request be placed at their disposal'.

There can be no doubt that discussion of this ruling will focus on what is meant by 'unnecessarily'.

8.29 Another case in which the Court was, of necessity, cautious about public health was *Officier van Justitie* v. *Koninklijke Kaasfabriek Eyssen*.[73] The case arose out of a prosecution before the Dutch courts of a Dutch company manufacturing processed cheese both for the home market and for export. The defendant was charged with having in stock with a view to sale quantities of cheese containing a preservative known as nisin. Dutch Regulations forbade the use of nisin in processed cheese sold on the home market, although they laid down an exemption with respect to exports. Reliable studies showed that nisin was not necessarily harmful in itself, but only became harmful when consumed in excessive quantities. However, it had not yet been established what the acceptable daily intake was. In view of this, a number of Member States permitted the use of nisin up to certain specified limits, and the

---

[73] Case 53/80 [1981] E.C.R. 429.

United Kingdom and France even permitted its use without limit. It was in the light of these data that the Dutch court asked in effect whether a national prohibition on the use of nisin in processed cheese was justified under Article 36.

The Court of Justice held that it was so justified. In reaching this conclusion the Court cited the fact that the acceptable daily intake had not yet been established, that such intake depended not only on one particular product but on the entire dietary habits of an individual, and that such habits varied from one Member State to another. Given such varying dietary habits, the specific exemption with respect to exports did not render the measure in issue arbitrarily discriminatory.

However, the Court avoided ruling on whether the system of 'positive lists' is justified under Article 36. This is the system applied throughout the Western world, whereby additives are presumed to be harmful until the contrary is proved; unless an additive figures on the list of permitted additives established by legislation, its use is unlawful. Nisin did not figure on the positive list laid down by Dutch legislation. At first sight, the system of positive lists runs counter to the presumption that a restriction is not justified under Article 36 until the contrary is proved.[74] The German Government therefore seized this opportunity to invite the Court to rule that the system of positive lists was justified under Article 36, since there was no other scientific method of determining whether additives were harmless. As the Advocate General pointed out, however, it was not necessary to decide this point in the case.

8.30   The Court is clearly better equipped to rule on less technical restrictions on inter-State trade. Accordingly, in some cases it has been able to state categorically that a measure is not justified on grounds of public health. Examples[75] are:

- a minimum alcohol requirement: *Cassis de Dijon;*[76]
- a prohibition on the importation of meat-based products manu-factured in one Member State from animals slaughtered in another Member State: *E.C. Commission* v. *Germany;*[77]
- a prohibition on the importation and sale of vinegar other than wine vinegar: *Gilli and Andres;*[78]
- a prohibition on the sale of bread containing more than a certain quantity of dry matter: *Kelderman.*[79]

---

[74] See para. 8.03 above.
[75] See also Case 35/76 *Simmenthal,* note 38 above; Case 46/76 *Bauhuis,* note 4 above; Case 152/78 *E.C. Commission* v. *France,* note 10 above.
[76] Case 120/78 *Rewe,* note 49 above.
[77] Case 153/78 [1979] E.C.R. 2555, [1980] 1 C.M.L.R. 198, para. 5.08 above.
[78] See note 8 above.
[79] Case 130/80, [1981] E.C.R. 527.

8.31 Lastly, it should be borne in mind that there is a large body of Community legislation relating to public health[80]; when it provides exhaustive guarantees, such legislation ousts Article 36 in accordance with the rule discussed earlier in this chapter.[81]

Flora and fauna

8.32 The principles relating to the health and life of animals[82] and plants[83] are the same as those relating to human life and health— with the obvious and fundamental difference that the human health and life is more important. The term 'plants' must be taken to cover plants and trees and their produce generally. The question of whether a Member State may protect animals or plants not indigenous to its territory has been adverted to earlier in this chapter.[84] It should be pointed out, lastly, that there is a body of Community legislation relating to animal[85] and plant health.[86]

The protection of national treasures possessing artistic, historic or archaeological value

8.33 Normally this head of justification[87] will be relied on to justify restrictions on exports; indeed, it will rarely, if ever, be invoked to prevent imports. So it is that the only case concerning this ground of justification to come before the Court of Justice, Case 7/68 *E.C. Commission* v. *Italy*[88] involved an export restriction on art treasures. However, as already explained,[89] that restriction took the form of an export tax and the Court held that Article 36 could not be relied on to justify a tax. In view of this neither the Court nor the Advocate General found it necessary to interpret this limb of Article 36.

8.34 The following questions arise in this connection:

---

[80] *e.g.* Directive of 23 October 1962 on colouring matters for use in foodstuffs intended for human consumption ([1962] J.O. 2645); Dir. 64/54 on preservatives for use in such foodstuffs ([1964] J.O. 161); Dir. 76/893 on articles intended to come into contact with foodstuffs ([1976] O.J. L340/19); there is also a large body of veterinary legislation beginning with Dir. 64/432 on intra-Community trade in animals and swine ([1964] J.O. 1977) and Dir. 64/433 on trade in fresh meat ([1964] O.J. 2012).

[81] See para. 8.15 above.

[82] See, *e.g.* Case 38/76 *Simmenthal*, note 38 above; Case 46/76 *Bauhuis*, note 4 above; Case 251/78 *Denkavit Futtermittel*, note 7 above.

[83] See Case 4/75 *Rewe-Zentralfinanz*, note 17 above; Case 89/76 *E.C. Commission* v. *Netherlands*, note 33 above.

[84] See para. 8.12 above.

[85] See, *e.g.* the veterinary legislation in note 80 above.

[86] *e.g.* Dir. 69/464 on potato disease ([1969] J.O. L323/1), Dir. 69/466, note 45 above.

[87] See generally Mattera Ricigliano, 'Cultura e libera scambio dei beni artistici all'interno della Communità' [1976] Dir. Scambi Int. 12; 'Community action in the cultural sector' Suppl. 6/77 to Bulletin.

[88] See note 5 above.

[89] Para. 2.03 above.

(a) What is meant by a 'treasure'? Clearly the use of this term indicates that the work must be of special importance.[90] If an item satisfies this standard on historical or archaeological grounds then it need have no artistic merit.

If not, then it must be decided whether it is of sufficient artistic merit to be described as an artistic treasure. This is a type of decision which a court is not well equipped to make, so that it must inevitably rely to a considerable extent on expert evidence. When the expert witnesses agree, this matter will be relatively straightforward[91] but it will be an almost intractable problem in the face of contradictory evidence.

As Mattera points out,[92] it is only in exceptional circumstances that works by contemporary artists will satisfy this test.

8.35   (b) Does the use of the term 'national treasures' exclude objects of artistic, historical or archaeological value only to a *region* of a Member State? At a time of growing interest in regional culture, it does not seem plausible to exclude such objects from the protection of Article 36. It seems fitting to apply the maxim that the greater includes the lesser: the reference to national treasures must be taken to include regional treasures.

8.36   (c) Does this limb of Article 36 only cover objects which are products of the civilisation or culture of the Member State concerned? Where an item is a historical or archaeological treasure without being an artistic treasure, then it would seem that a Member State can only retain it if it has such value to that Member State. On this view, the Netherlands could not prevent the exportation of an item of historical or archaeological importance only to Italy (a Member State) or Peru (a third country).

8.37   However, the situation may possibly be different where artistic treasures are concerned; if so, the United Kingdom may prevent the export to another Member State of a Titian or a Ming vase. On this reading 'national treasures' is taken to refer to art treasures belonging to the nation and not to treasures of national art. In favour of this view one might rely on the practical consideration that once Member States are required to let such works of art out of their clutches, then they may often disappear from the Community altogether; the cultural loss would then be borne by the

---

[90] It is true that there is some difference between the French, German and English language versions on the one hand and Italian on the other. The latter does not speak of 'treasures' but only of 'artistic heritage'.

[91] In the English case of *Re Pinion* [1965] 2 W.L.R. 919 the Court of Appeal was in the rather unusual position of having to rule on the artistic merit of certain objects, but was spared the difficulty of contradictory evidence as to merit. There a testator had directed that his studio and its contents be endowed as a museum. On the basis of undivided expert evidence the Court of Appeal found that the material in question was merely a 'mass of junk' so that the bequest did not constitute a valid charitable trust. (One of the experts expressed his surprise that 'so voracious a collector should not by hazard have picked up even one meritorious object'.)

[92] See note 87 above.

entire Community. Ranged against this practical view is the formidable argument that Article 36, as an exception to a fundamental rule of the Treaty, must be interpreted restrictively.

8.38 Clearly the question whether Member States may prevent the export of artistic treasures produced by other cultures is of considerable practical importance. Suffice it to mention a recent article in *The Times*[93] concerning a difference of opinion between the British authorities and the Rijksmuseum of Amsterdam over a silver plaque of the 'Adoration of the Shepherds' dated 1617 by Paul van Vianen, considered one of the greatest Dutch silversmiths. The Rijksmuseum had agreed to buy the plaque and when the British authorities witheld an art export licence, it apparently claimed that this was contrary to Article 36 on the grounds that the work of art was Dutch and not British. This case posed the problem in a most poignant way because the work was a product of the culture of the very country to which it would have been exported.

8.39 Be that as it may, whether we are concerned with artistic, historical or archaeological treasures, it is submitted that the test must be whether the treasures have a place in the history, civilisation or culture of the Member State concerned: the Community rules for determining the origin of goods, which have been discussed earlier in this book,[94] can be of little assistance here. For instance, a treaty or other document may have a central place in Belgian history even though it was signed outside Belgium (on non-Belgian paper). Likewise, a work by Turner is a part of British culture, even if it was painted in Italy.

8.40 Applying this test, it can happen that more than one Member State has a claim to a particular work. This may occur in particular where an artist settled outside his home country or where territory has changed hands.

8.41 In the light of these considerations it is tentatively suggested that the following approach should be adopted in deciding whether a particular Member State may retain a given object on the grounds of its artistic, historical or archeological value:

- first, is the object of such historical or archaeological value to *this* Member State or any of its regions as to qualify as a 'treasure'? If so, then the Member State is entitled to retain it without more, regardless of whether it has any artistic value. If not, then:
- can the object be described as an *artistic* treasure? If not, then it falls outside this limb of Article 36. If it is an artistic treasure, then:
- is it a product of the civilisation or culture of *this* Member State? If so, then it may be retained under this part of Article

---

[93] *The Times*, 8 October 1980.
[94] Para. 2.10.

36. If not, then one has to decide the point of principle whether the Member State concerned may retain the object nevertheless.

The effectiveness of fiscal supervision

8.42 This is the first of the three 'mandatory requirements' added by the Court in the *Cassis de Dijon*[95] case. It would appear that this term, which is something of a newcomer to the English language, is intended to cover the prevention and detection of tax evasion.

It is probable that the mention of the effectiveness of fiscal supervision is a reference to the earlier case of *GB-Inno* v. *ATAB*.[96] That case arose out of the prosecution of a Belgian supermarket chain, GB-Inno, for selling cigarettes below the price appearing on the tax label, contrary to Belgian law. The Belgian Cour de Cassation asked the Court of Justice whether this provision was compatible with, *inter alia*, Article 30. In what amounted to an *obiter dictum* the Court stated:

> 'In a system in which, as in Belgium, the basis of assessment to excise duty and to VAT is the retail selling price, a prohibition on selling tobacco products at a price higher than the retail selling price appearing on the tax label constitutes an essential fiscal guarantee, designed to prevent producers and importers from undervaluing their products at the time of paying the taxes'.

8.43 The Court had occasion to consider this ground of justification once again in *Carciati*.[97] The facts were that one Mr. Fink, a German national, had entrusted a car registered in Germany to the defendant for him to use in Italy on his frequent business visits. Since the defendant was resident in Italy, he was charged with having in his possession and using within the Italian customs territory a car registered abroad in infringement of the provisions governing temporary importation. The Italian court therefore referred to the Court of Justice the question whether the Italian provisions governing the matter were compatible with 'the Community rules in relation to the free movements of goods'. The Italian provisions were essentially dictated by the New York Customs Convention of 1954, to which all Member States are party, and by Community VAT directives. In the light of this, the Court held that:

> 'Member States retain broad powers to take action in respect of temporary importation, specifically for the purpose of preventing tax frauds. It follows that if the measures adopted to that end are not excessive, they are compatible with the principle of the free movement of goods.
>
> As regards the prohibition imposed by a Member State on persons resident in its territory on the use of vehicles imported temporarily tax-free, it is an effective way of preventing tax frauds and ensuring that taxes are paid in the country of destination of the goods'.

---

[95] Note 49 above.
[96] Case 13/77 [1977] E.C.R. 2115, [1978] 1 C.M.L.R. 283. Para. 7.53 above.
[97] Case 823/79 [1980] E.C.R. 2773, [1981] 2 C.M.L.R. 193; see also Case 159/78 *E.C. Commission* v. *Italy* 'customs agents' [1979] E.C.R. 3247, [1980] 3 C.M.L.R. 446, discussed at para. 7.61 above.

Although neither the reference nor the judgment refers to Articles 30 to 36, they refer generally to the Treaty provisions on the free movement of goods so that they are of relevance here.

Consumer protection

8.44 In Case 12/74 *E.C. Commission* v. *Germany*[98] the Court held that:

> 'To the extent to which [registered designations of origin and indirect indications of origin] are protected by law they must satisfy the objectives of such protection, in particular the need to ensure not only that the interests of the producers concerned are safeguarded, but also that consumers are protected against information which may mislead them'.[99]

This appears to mean that a measure may be justified on the ground both of consumer protection and of the prevention of unfair competition, but not on one of these grounds alone. As Beier[100] has pointed out, this view is open to the most severe doubt. At all events, it seems clear from the subsequent case-law generally and in particular *Cassis de Dijon*,[101] which appears to treat consumer protection and the prevention of unfair competition as two wholly separate mandatory requirements, that the Court has gone back on this statement in *E.C. Commission* v. *Germany*. Having said that, we can now turn to the case law on consumer protection itself.

8.45 What might be termed the 'golden rule' in this respect is the principle that the sale of a product should never be prohibited when the consumer will be sufficiently protected by adequate labelling requirements.[102] Thus in *Cassis de Dijon*[103] itself the Court ruled that one cannot 'regard the mandatory fixing of minimum alcohol contents as being an essential guarantee of the fairness of commercial transactions, since it is a simple matter to ensure that suitable information is conveyed to the purchaser by requiring the display of an indication . . . of the alcohol content on the packaging of products'. Similarly in *Gilli and Andres*,[104] where the defendants had been prosecuted for importing apple vinegar contrary to Italian law, the Court held that the national prohibition in question was not justified on the grounds of consumer protection because 'the recep-

---

[98] [1975] E.C.R. 181, [1975] 1 C.M.L.R. 340, para. 7.27 above. See the caveat about this case at para. 7.33 above.

[99] It is true that that part of the judgment purports to be an interpretation of Art. 30 rather than Art. 36.

[100] 'Das Schutzbedürfnis für Herkunftsangaben und Ursprungsbezeichnungen im Gemeinsamen Markt' [1977] G.R.U.R. Int. 1., which appeared in English as 'The Need for Protection of Indications of Source and Appellations of Origin in the Common Market' in *Protection of Geographic Denominations of Goods and Services* ed. Cohen Jehoram, (1980), 183 *et seq*.

[101] See note 49 above.

[102] On labelling, see generally Dir. 79/112 on the approximation of the laws of the Member States relating to the labelling, presentation and advertising of foodstuffs for sale to the ultimate consumer ([1979] O.J. L33/1).

[103] See note 49 above.

[104] See note 8 above, see also Case 130/80, note 79 above.

tacles containing [the] vinegar are provided with a sufficiently clear label indicating that it is in fact apple vinegar, thus avoiding any possibility of the consumers confusing it with wine vinegar'.

8.46   In the same way, in Case 193/80 *E.C. Commission* v. *Italy*[105] the Court held that, while it was contrary to Article 30 to reserve the use of the term 'vinegar' (*aceto*) to wine vinegar, it would be justified to require the exact nature of the product to be set out on a label affixed to that product. But the Court stated that such a labelling requirement would only be justified if it applied to wine vinegar in the same way as to other types of vinegar. It is significant that on this point the Court did not follow the Advocate General's approach: he took the view that Italy was justified in prohibiting the use of the word *aceto* used alone as a description of vinegar not derived from wine, but that it was unjustified in prohibiting the use of that word coupled with another word or words indicating that the product is derived from a substance other than wine, such a cider or malt. The Court was clearly at pains to ensure that the same treatment should be accorded to wine vinegar (the 'typically Italian' product) and other types of vinegar.[106]

8.47   Another case on labelling requirements is *Fietje*.[107] The defendant in the main case was a trader, who had sold in the Netherlands an alcoholic drink imported from West Germany bearing the label in German *Berentzen Appel—Aus Apfel mit Weizenkorn 25 vol.%*. He was prosecuted for not indicating the word *likeur* or *liqueur* on the bottles as required by Dutch law: drinks with an alcohol content of 22 per cent. or more and a certain sugar content were required to bear this indication. In reply to a reference by the Dutch court as to the compatibility of such a measure with Article 30, the Court ruled:

> 'If national rules relating to a given product include the obligation to use a description that is sufficiently precise to inform the purchaser of the nature of the product and to enable it to be distinguished from products with which it might be confused, it may well be necessary, in order to give consumers effective protection, to extend this obligation to imported products also, even in such a way as to make necessary the alteration of the original labels of some of these products . . .
>
> However, there is no longer any need for such protection if the details given on the original label of the imported product have as their content information on the nature of the product and that content includes at least the same information, and is just as capable of being understood by consumers in the importing State, as the description prescribed by the rules of that State. In the context of Article 177 of the EEC Treaty, the making of the findings of fact necessary in order to establish whether there is such equivalence is a matter for the national court'.

---

[105] Judgment of 9 December 1981.
[106] Synthetic vinegars, however, fell outside the scope of this ruling; see Chap. VII, note 76.
[107] See note 36 above.

This passage shows clearly that what matters in the field of consumer protection is the understanding of the consumer in the importing Member State, not of some hypothetical Community consumer. It also emerges from this passage that a Member State will not always be justified in requiring all labelling to be in its own language: if the particular words appearing in the label are just as comprehensible to the consumer of that Member State as the equivalent words in his own language, then the requirement is not justified.

8.48 It would appear that the heading of consumer protection may justify measures designed to ensure the authenticity[108] or quality[109] of a product, provided that such measures are proportionate to their purpose and do not constitute arbitrary discrimination. Thus the reservation of appellations of origin[110] or designations of quality[111] to products deserving their use is justified, but the abusive reservations of such appellations[112] and designations[113] to national products or partly national products is not justified under Article 36—even when their use is optional.[114] Again, under certain circumstances the obligation to indicate the origin of goods will be justified.[115] Lastly, in *Industrie Diensten Groep* v. *Beele*,[116] the Court in effect held that the prohibition on passing off was justified on consumer protection grounds; but, since that case is primarily concerned with the prevention of unfair competition it is discussed more fully below.

8.49 In conclusion, it should not be overlooked that the charge has been levelled against the judgments in *Cassis de Dijon* and the subsequent cases that they have resulted in a lowering of quality standards. However, this is not necessarily so.[117] The Court has held that certain particular restrictions (a minimum alcohol requirement, a prohibition on the sale of cider vinegar and a prohibition on the sale of bread containing a certain proportion of dry matter)[118] were not justified on consumer protection grounds or any other grounds. Moreover, in each case the products concerned were traditional products of another Member State. But the Court has not ruled that a Member State may *never* prohibit the sale of a product on quality grounds, as distinct from health grounds. Nevertheless, it is arguable

---

[108] Case 2/78 E.C. Commission v. Belgium [1979] E.C.R. 1761, [1980] 1 C.M.L.R. 216, para. 7.07 above. See also generally the Council Resolution of 19 May 1981 on a second programme for consumer protection and information policy ([1981] O.J. C133/1); Rambow 'Möglichkeiten und Grenzen der Verbraucherpolitik in Gemeinsamen Markt' [1981] EuR. 240.
[109] Case 53/76 Procureur de la République v. Bouhelier [1977] E.C.R. 197, [1977] 1 C.M.L.R. 436, para. 7.68 above; Case 13/78, note 25 above.
[110] Case 12/74, note 98 above.
[111] Case 13/78, note 25 above.
[112] Case 12/74, note 98 above.
[113] Case 13/78, note 25 above.
[114] Case 13/78, note 25 above.
[115] Paras. 7.36 and 7.37 above.
[116] Case 6/81, judgment of 2 March 1982.
[117] Para. 6.51 above.
[118] See paras. 7.39 et seq. above.

that it will always be sufficient guarantee for the consumer to ban the sale of low quality products under a given designation rather than to ban them altogether. For example, on this view there is no necessity to prohibit the sale of 'orange juice' containing only 2 per cent. orange, since it is enough to ban its sale under that name.

The prevention of unfair competition

8.50   The term 'prevention of unfair competition' is used here as being more appropriate than the expression 'the fairness of commercial transactions' used in the *Cassis de Dijon*[119] case. Indeed the term 'unfair competition' was used in *E.C. Commission* v. *Germany*.[120]

Since this concept is unfamiliar to English lawyers, it requires a brief explanation here. Perhaps the best guidance on this matter can be drawn from Article 10 *bis* inserted into the Paris Convention for the Protection of Industrial Property of 1883[121]. This provision reads as follows:

> '(1) The countries of the Union are bound to assure the nationals of such countries effective protection against unfair competition;
>
> (2) Any act of competition contrary to honest practices in industrial or commercial matters constitutes an act of unfair competition;
>
> (3) The following in particular shall be prohibited:
>   1. all acts of such a nature as to create confusion by any means whatever with the establishment, the goods, or the industrial or commercial activities, of a competitor;
>   2. false allegations in the course of trade of such a nature as to discredit the establishment, the goods, or the industrial or commercial activities, of a competitor;
>   3. indications or allegations the use of which in the course of trade is liable to mislead the public as to the nature, the manufacturing process, the characteristics, the suitability for their purpose, or the quantity, of the goods'.[122]

The concept of unfair competition therefore broadly corresponds to practices actionable in English law for passing off or slander of title.[123]

8.51   As already pointed out,[124] the Court stated in effect in *E.C. Commission* v. *Germany*[125] that a measure might only be justified on the grounds of unfair competition if it was simultaneously justified on the grounds of consumer protection; the Court appears to have retreated from that unduly restrictive position. Yet the fact remains

---

[119] Note 49 above.

[120] Note 98 above.

[121] In principle the Treaty of Rome prevails over the Convention as between Member States: see paras. 9.53 *et seq*. below. Consequently, the Paris Convention only gives guidance on this matter, rather than being binding.

[122] See Bodenhausen's *Guide to the Paris Convention* (1968). All the Member States are parties to the Convention, but not all of them are parties to each amendment thereto.

[123] For a comparative study, see Ulmer's series of volumes entitled *La répression de la concurrence déloyale dans les Etats membres de la Communauté économique européenne* (1967).

[124] Para. 8.44 above.

[125] Note 98 above.

that the ground of the prevention of unfair competition is so often closely linked to that of consumer protection as to stand or fall with it: if there is no danger of the consumer being misled, then frequently other producers will not be subject to unfair competition.[126]

8.52 However, in the recent case of *Dansk Supermarked* v. *Imerco*[127] the question of unfair competition did arise quite independently of consumer protection. The facts were that Imerco, a syndicate of Danish ironmongers, had a dinner service made in the United Kingdom to celebrate its 50th anniversary. Each item of the service was decorated with pictures of Danish royal castles and bore Imerco's name and a legend referring to its 50th anniversary. The exclusive right to sell this service was reserved to the members of the syndicate. It was agreed between Imerco and the British manufacturer that 'seconds'—which amounted to about 20 per cent. of production because of the criteria chosen—could be sold on the British market, but should on no account be exported to Denmark or to other Scandinavian countries. However, Dansk Supermarked acquired some such 'seconds' on the British market and proceeded to sell them in Denmark, whereupon Imerco brought an action against it before the Danish courts. The action reached the Supreme Court of Denmark which put a question to the Court for a preliminary ruling asking in effect whether it was compatible with Article 36 to prevent such imports on the grounds of copyright protection, trade mark protection or the prevention of unfair competition.

The Court replied with respect to unfair competition as follows:[128]

> 'In order to reply to that question it must first of all be remarked that Community law does not in principle have the effect of preventing the application in a Member State to goods imported from other Member States of the provisions on marketing in force in the State of importation. It follows that the marketing of imported goods may be prohibited if the conditions on which they are sold constitute an infringement of the marketing usages considered proper and fair in the Member State of importation.
>
> It must nevertheless be emphasised, as the Court of Justice has stressed in another context in its judgment of 25 November 1971 (Case 22/71 *Béguelin* [1971] E.C.R. 949, [1972] C.M.L.R. 81), that the actual fact of the importation of goods which have been lawfully marketed in another Member State cannot be considered as an improper or unfair act since that description may be attached only to offer or exposure for sale on the basis of circumstances distinct from the importation itself . . .
>
> The second part of the reply to the question submitted must thus be that Article 30 of the Treaty must be interpreted as meaning:
>
> > That the importation into a Member State of goods lawfully marketed in another Member State cannot as such be classified as an improper or unfair commercial practice, without prejudice however to the possible

---

[126] e.g. Case 12/74, note 98 above; Case 120/78, note 49 above.

[127] Case 58/80 [1981] E.C.R. 181, [1981] 3 C.M.L.R. 590 noted by Dyckjaes-Hansen [1982] 3 E.I.P.R. 85.

[128] See also notes 169 and 172 below.

> application of legislation of the State of importation against such practices
> on the ground of the circumstances or methods of offering such goods for
> sale as distinct from the actual fact of importation . . .'

This last proviso appears to relate to a point made by the Advocate General: he took the view that, although in principle sales of 'seconds' could not be prevented on the grounds of unfair competition, it would be otherwise if they held themselves out to the consumers as being of first quality.

8.53 The prevention of unfair competition was also in point in *Industrie Diensten Groep* v. *Beele*.[129] There, the appellants in the main case had imported certain cable conduits into the Netherlands for a number of years. The Dutch patent had now expired and the respondents had begun to market in the Netherlands other cable conduits imported from Germany, which bore a striking resemblance to those imported by the appellants. The appellants alleged before the Dutch courts that the respondents' goods constituted slavish imitation of their own, and thus sought an injunction preventing the respondents from marketing their products in the Netherlands. In English law, this would have amounted to an action for passing off. In its reference for a preliminary ruling, the Dutch court asked the Court of Justice in essence whether it would be contrary to Articles 30 to 36 to grant such an injunction, stating that the similarity between the two products was greater than necessary.

Citing Article 10 *bis* of the Paris Convention, the Court replied that it was justified on the grounds of the prevention of unfair competition and on consumer protection grounds to prohibit the sale of imported goods which were virtually identical to other goods marketed in the same Member State over a long period of time and thus gave rise to unnecessary confusion with those other goods.

The protection of the environment

8.54 It appears that the protection of the environment is also a ground of justification under Article 36. The Commission took this view in its answer to Written Question 1285/77[130] on a Danish measure prohibiting the use of one way (non-reusable) bottles. In its answer the Commission stated that 'there is no doubt that environmental protection can be regarded as a matter of general concern which may justifiably be accorded priority over the free movement of goods'.[131] It repeated this view in its Communication on the *Cassis de Dijon* case.[132]

Frequently, measures justified on environmental grounds will be justified on the ground of the protection of the health and life of human beings, animals or plants. However, this will not always be so.

---

[129] See note 116 above.
[130] [1979] O.J. C214/5.
[131] See also the Advocate General in Cases 3, 4 and 6/76 *Kramer* [1976] E.C.R. 1279 at 1325, [1976] 2 C.M.L.R. 440.
[132] [1980] O.J. C256/2, see para. 6.35 above.

The improvement of working conditions

8.55 Health and safety at work fall under the heading of public health in Article 36. It would appear, though, that the improvement of working conditions constitutes a 'mandatory requirement' even in the absence of any health considerations. This emerges from *Oebel*,[133] which concerned national legislation prohibiting the baking of bread at night. The Advocate General found that such a measure was justified on the grounds that it served to improve working conditions. In so doing he referred to Article 117 of the Treaty, which begins: 'Member States agree upon the need to promote improved working conditions and an improved standard of living for workers . . .'

Although the Court found that a measure of this kind fell outside Articles 30 and 34 altogether, it indirectly confirmed the Advocate General's finding on this point, by stating that the prohibition on night baking was a legitimate economic and social policy decision aimed at improving working conditions in a manifestly sensitive sector and thus compatible with the objects of general interest recognised by the Treaty.

Article 117 was not referred to by the Court. What is more, the Court's observations on this point were confined to the promotion of improved working conditions. The promotion of an improved standard of living for workers, also mentioned in Article 117, is not mentioned in the judgment. It is submitted that this is simply because the promotion of an improved standard of living is a goal of a purely economic nature and therefore cannot justify restrictions on imports and exports.[134]

Other possible grounds

8.56 As has already been pointed out earlier in this book,[135] the 'mandatory requirements' set out in *Cassis de Dijon* do not purport to be exhaustive. It follows that further grounds could be added to the list of grounds of justification contained in Article 36. It should be borne in mind, however, that Article 36 is 'directed to eventualities of a non-economic kind'.[136]

Industrial and commercial property

8.57 The most important types of industrial and commercial property are patents,[137] trade marks[138] and copyright[139] with plant

---

[133] Case 155/80 [1981] E.C.R. 1993.
[134] Para. 8.18 above.
[135] Para. 6.31 above.
[136] Para. 8.18 above.
[137] As with trade marks and copyright, the literature is vast; see, *e.g.* Johannes, *Gewerblicher Rechtsschutz und Urheberrecht im Europäischen Gemeinschaftsrecht* (1973); *Industrial property and copyright in European Community law* (1976); Demaret, *Patents, Territorial Restrictions and EEC Law* (1978); Guy and Leigh, *The EEC and Intellectual Property* (1981).

* Footnotes 138 and 139 are on p. 154.

breeder's rights[140] being of lesser importance. In the terminology of the legal systems of some Member States copyright is not regarded as 'industrial and commercial property' but rather as 'intellectual or artistic property' so that there was some doubt as to whether copyright fell under this heading of Article 36. However, this doubt has been finally dispelled by the recent judgment of the Court in *Membran* v. *GEMA*[141] in ruling that this expression in Article 36 'includes the protection conferred by copyright, especially when exploited commercially in the form of licences capable of affecting distribution in the various Member States of goods incorporating the protected literary or artistic work'.

In addition, other types of rights are perhaps to be included within the concept of industrial and commercial property under Article 36.[142] For instance, it is not clear whether appellations and indications of origin fall within this ground of justification or are rather to be subsumed under the joint headings of consumer protection and unfair competition.[143] At all events, there would seem no objection to these rights falling under all three headings. It would seem wrong that any consequences should turn on whether or not particular rights or interests fall under the heading of industrial and commercial property rather than any other heading. What matters rather is how far such rights or interests may be permitted, on their proper construction, to restrict trade between Member States.

8.58 The Community law relating to industrial and commercial property can be divided into three aspects:

(i) Articles 30 to 36;

(ii) Articles 85 and 86; and

(iii) harmonisation and co-ordination.

Clearly, only the first of these three aspects falls squarely within the scope of this book. However, since these three aspects are to a considerable extent interdependent, one cannot avoid a brief mention of the second and third aspects.

---

[138] See *e.g.* Ullrich, 'Libre circulation des marchandises et droit des marques' [1975] R.T.D.E. 395; von Bar, *Territorialität des Warenzeichens und Erschöpfung des Verbreitungsrechts im Gemeinsamen Markt* (1977); Hefermehl, Ipsen, Schluep, Sieben, *Nationaler Markenschütz und freier Warenverkehr in der Europäischen Gemeinschaft* (1979); Johannes, *op. cit.* note 137 above; Guy and Leigh, *op. cit.* note 137 above.

[139] See, *e.g.* Dietz, *Das Urheberrecht in der Europäischen Gemeinschaft* (1978); *Copyright Law in the European Community* (1978); Johannes, *op. cit.* note 137 above; Guy and Leigh, *op. cit.* note 137 above; Hoffmann, 'Copyright and the Treaty of Rome, Recent Developments: an overview' (1981) 9 E.I.P.R. 254.

[140] See Case 258/78 *Nungesser and Eiseler* v. *E.C. Commission* (pending), an action for the annulment of Competition Dec. 78/823. In Britain plant breeders' rights are governed by the Plant Varieties and Seeds Act 1964: see Cornish, *Intellectual Property: Patents, Copyright, Trade Marks and Allied Rights* (1981), 613.

[141] Cases 55 and 57/80 [1981] E.C.R. 147, [1981] 2 C.M.L.R. 44, noted by Alexander [1981] C.M.L.Rev. 422.

[142] See Harris, 'The Application of Article 36 to Intellectual Property' [1976] 1 E.L. Rev. 515.

[143] See paras. 7.27 *et seq.* and 8.44 *et seq.* above.

8.59   It is appropriate to begin with the measures adopted by the Community and under Community auspices to harmonise and co-ordinate industrial and commercial property law.

As regards patents, the Community Patent Convention[144] was signed by the Member States in Luxembourg in 1975. The C.P.C. interlocks with the international patent system created by the European Patent Convention, signed at Munich in 1973, which covers a wider range of West European States and which entered into force in 1977. Nevertheless the C.P.C. is expressed to be subject to the Treaty of Rome: Article 93. By virtue of Article 5 of the Convention, the Court of Justice has jurisdiction in respect of it. Its essential object is to enable an applicant to obtain a single patent applying throughout the Community without prejudice to the right of the Member States to grant national patents. In addition, it contains a small number of provisions harmonising aspects of national patent laws. In the present context Articles 32 and 81 of the C.P.C. are of particular importance and will be mentioned again below. It should be noted, however that the C.P.C. has not been ratified by all the Member States and has consequently not entered into force.

With respect to trade marks the Commission has now formally proposed two draft instruments[145] to be adopted by the Council. These consist respectively of a proposal for a first Council Directive to approximate the laws of the Member States relating to trade marks, which proposal is based on Article 100 of the Treaty[146]; and a proposal for a Council Regulation based on Article 235 of the Treaty[147] setting up a Community trade mark system operating alongside those of the Member States.

Work has also begun in the Commission on harmonising copyright laws.[148]

8.60   It is now appropriate to return briefly to Articles 85 and 86. The Court has held repeatedly[149] that the exercise of an industrial

---

[144] [1976] O.J. L17; see Cornish, 'The European Patent Conventions' [1976] J.B.L. 112; McClellan, 'La Convention sur le brevet communautaire' [1978] C.D.E. 202; Singer, *Das Neue Europäische Patentsystem* (1979).

[145] [1980] O.J. C351/1 (the draft Directive) and 5 (the draft Regulation). Supplement 5180 to the Bulletin contains an article by article commentary on these draft provisions. See also Morcom, 'The legitimacy of a European Trade Mark System' [1980] E.I.P.R. 359, Armitage, 'The CTM: Comments on the Latest Drafts of the Proposed EEC Regulation and Directive' [1981] E.I.P.R. 72; Schwartz, 'Das Markenrecht in der Europäischen Gemeinschaft–Eine Zwischenbilanz' [1981] G.R.U.R. Int. 1; Gormley, 'The Commission's proposals on trade marks' [1981] E.L. Rev. 385 and 463; Morcon, 'The Future of Trade Marks in the E.E.C.' [1982] J.B.L. 70.

[146] Para. 12.01 below.

[147] Para. 12.05 below.

[148] Written question 792/80 ([1980] O.J. C269/28); see Report of a meeting held by the Commission on the duration of copyright protection [1980] E.I.P.R. D310; Davies, 'Harmonisation of copyright legislations in the European Communities' [1981] E.I.P.R. 67.

[149] *e.g.* Case 40/70 *Sirena* v. *Eda* [1971] E.C.R. 69, [1971] C.M.L.R. 260; Case 51/75 *EMI Records* v. *CBS United Kingdom* [1976] E.C.R. 811, [1976] 2 C.M.L.R. 235.

property right[150] may fall foul of Article 85 when it constitutes 'the subject, the means or the result of a restrictive practice.' Moreover, it has held[151] that the exercise of an industrial property right will not in itself constitute an abuse of a dominant position under Article 86. For that provision to be infringed three elements must be present: the undertaking must have a dominant position within the common market or a substantial part of it; the exercise of the industrial property right must be an improper exploitation thereof; and that improper exploitation must be liable to affect trade between Member States.

A considerable body of Commission Decisions and other instruments has been established on the compatibility of the exercise of industrial property rights with Articles 85 and 86.[152] Moreover, the first cases[153] on industrial and commercial property to come before the Court related to Articles 85 and 86, not least because the prohibitions in Article 30 on quantitative restrictions on imports and measures of equivalent effect did not come into effect until 1968 and 1970 respectively.[154] Although Article 36 had come to be relied on by the Court as an aid to the interpretation of Articles 85 and 86,[155] it was not until the Court's landmark decision in *Deutsche Grammophon* v. *Metro*[156] that the Court applied Articles 30 to 36 to industrial property rights quite independently of the Treaty provisions on competition. Accordingly, since Articles 85 and 86 fall outside the scope of this book, we can begin with the *Deutsche Grammophon* case.

8.61 The case law on the compatibility with Articles 30 to 36 of the exercise of industrial property rights can be summarised in the following rules:

Rule 1: Although the Treaty does not affect the existence of industrial and commercial property rights recognised by the legislation of a Member State, the *exercise* of those rights may nevertheless fall foul of Article 30.

Rule 2: Subject to certain exceptions, the exclusive right guaranteed by national legislation on industrial and commercial property is exhausted when a product has been lawfully distributed on the market of a Member State by the owner of the right or with his consent. Thereafter the owner of the right may not oppose the importation of the product into any other Member State, nor may

---

[150] The term 'industrial property' is used here for convenience instead of industrial and commercial property.
[151] *e.g.* Case 40/70, note 149 above.
[152] See, *e.g.* Bellamy and Child, *Common Market Law of Competition* (1978).
[153] Cases 56 and 58/64 *Consten and Grundig* v. *E.C. Commission* [1966] E.C.R. 299, [1966] C.M.L.R. 418; Case 24/67 *Parke, Davis* v. *Centrafarm* [1968] E.C.R. 55, [1968] C.M.L.R. 47; Case 40/70, note 149 above.
[154] Paras. 5.01 *et seq.* and 6.02 *et seq.* above.
[155] Case 40/70, note 149 above.
[156] Case 78/70 [1971] E.C.R. 487, [1971] C.M.L.R. 631.

he oppose its re-importation into the Member State where it was first marketed.

Rule 3: A trade mark right may not be relied on with a view to prohibiting the marketing in a Member State of goods lawfully produced in another Member State under an identical trade mark having the same origin.

Rule 4: Where the same person holds a particular industrial property right in all the Member States, another person holding that right with respect to a third country may not manufacture or market his goods within the Community in reliance on that right—even when there is a common origin.

Rule 5: Subject to Rules 2 and 3 above (and to the application of Articles 85 and 86), the holder of an industrial property right may rely on that right to prohibit the importation or sale of goods from other Member States. However, such rights may not be exercised in such a way as to constitute arbitrary discrimination or a disguised restriction on trade between Member States.

Each of these rules will now be examined in turn.

Rule 1

8.62 This rule, which appears in nearly all the cases on industrial and commercial property, appears to be derived from Article 222 which stipulates that: 'This Treaty shall in no way prejudice the rules in Member States governing the system of property owner-ship'.[157] The effect of this rule is simply that industrial property rights remain unaffected by the Treaty except in so far as they may not be used to prohibit or restrict imports in the circumstances set out in the following rules and may not be used in such a way as to fall foul of Articles 85 and 86.

Rule 2: The exhaustion of rights principle

8.63 This rule was first laid down in *Deutsche Grammophon* v. *Metro*. The facts were that Deutsche Grammophon had manufac-tured certain records in Germany, which it had sold to its subsidiary Polydor in Paris and which then came into the hands of Metro. Deutsche Grammophon sought an injunction against Metro to prevent it from selling these records in Germany in breach of the protection granted by German law to manufacturers of sound recordings, which protection is akin to copyright. The Hamburg Court requested the Court of Justice to rule, *inter alia*, on whether the application of such a national law to exclude goods in these circumstances was contrary to Articles 5 and 85 (1) of the Treaty. Article 5 (2) imposes on the Member States a general obligation to

---

[157] This provision was in issue in the first cases on industrial property, see note 153 above; see also para. 9.45 below.

'abstain from any measure which could jeopardise the attainment of the objectives of this Treaty.'

The Court held that if the exercise of an industrial property right was not the subject, the means or the result of an agreement so as to fall under Article 85, its compatibility with the provisions of the Treaty on the free movement of goods must be examined and in particular Article 36. It continued:

> 'On the assumption that those provisions may be relevant to a right related to copyright, it is nevertheless clear from that article that, although the Treaty does not affect the existence of rights recognised by the legislation of a Member State with regard to industrial and commercial property, the exercise of such rights may nevertheless fall within the prohibitions laid down by the Treaty. Although it permits prohibitions or restrictions on the free movement of products, which are justified for the purpose of protecting industrial and commercial property, Article 36 only admits derogations from that freedom to the extent to which they are justified for the purpose of safeguarding rights which constitute the specific subject-matter of such property.
>
> If a right related to copyright is relied upon to prevent the marketing in a Member State of products distributed by the holder of the right or with his consent on the territory of another Member State on the sole ground that such distribution did not take place on the national territory, such a prohibition which would legitimise [sic] the isolation of national markets, would be repugnant to the essential purpose of the Treaty, which is to unite national markets into a single market'.

8.64   It has recently been made clear that an industrial property right will be exhausted in this way even if the products were not covered by any such industrial property right under the law of the Member State where the goods were distributed by the holder of the right in the importing Member State or with his consent. This was laid down in *Merck* v. *Stephar*.[158] There Merck held the patent in the Netherlands for a certain pharmaceutical product, which it also put on the market in Italy. That product was not covered by any patent in Italy, because at the time when it was first sold there pharmaceutical products could not be patented under Italian law. Although that particular provision of Italian law was held unconstitutional in 1978, the product in question no longer fulfilled the requirement of novelty under Italian law so that it still could not be patented. At all events, Stephar acquired quantities of this product on the market and resold them in the Netherlands. The question that arose for decision was whether Merck could use its Dutch patent to prevent such imports.

On a reference from a Dutch court, the Court of Justice held in effect that a patent could not be used in this way since it had been exhausted when the goods were put on the Italian market. If the holder of a patent in a product chose to market it in a Member State where it was not patentable, then he must bear the consequences.

---

[158] Case 187/80 [1981] E.C.R. 2063, [1981] 3 C.M.L.R. 463, noted by Handoll [1982] 1 E.I.P.R. 26; compare Case 24/67, note 153 above.

8.65 There can be little doubt that Merck could have prevented the imports if the goods had been put on the Italian market by a third party without Merck's consent, at least if that third party had no economic connections of any kind with Merck.[159]

On a different point it would appear that, since the Court reached this solution in a case where patent protection never was available in the Member State of first distribution, then *a fortiori* the same solution must apply when the patent has lapsed in that Member State for whatever reason (*e.g.* expiry of maximum protection period, failure to pay a renewal fee, etc.). In addition the ruling in Merck would appear to be applicable not only to patents but to other forms of industrial property as well.

At this stage, it is appropriate to consider the application of the exhaustion of rights principle to patents, trade marks and copyright in turn.

A. PATENTS

8.66 The first case in which the exhaustion of rights principle was applied to patents was *Centrafarm* v. *Sterling Drug*.[160] This case arose against the background of widely divergent prices for pharmaceuticals on the Dutch and British markets: these were some 50 per cent. higher in the Netherlands than in Britain. Centrafarm therefore bought in Britain and resold in the Netherlands quantities of a certain drug bearing the trade-mark 'Negram'. The patents for this product in both these countries were held by an American company, Sterling Drug Inc., which had granted a licence to its respective subsidiary in each country. The goods had been put on the British market in the normal way by subsidiaries of Sterling Drug Inc.. A reference was made by the Dutch court hearing an action by Sterling Drug to prevent the parallel import. In that reference the Court of Justice was asked in particular to rule on whether it was compatible with Articles 30 to 36 to exercise the patent to prevent such imports.

In its reply the Court first reiterated its established distinction between the existence and the exercise of industrial property rights, and then continued:

> 'Inasmuch as it provides an exception to one of the fundamental principles of the common market, Article 36 in fact only admits of derogations from the free movement of goods where such derogations are justified for the purpose of safeguarding rights which constitute the specific subject-matter of this property.
> In relation to patents, the specific subject-matter of the industrial property is the guarantee that the patentee, to reward the creative effort of the inventor,

---

[159] Indeed, in Case 15/74 the Court implied this: see the passage quoted at para. 8.66 below. As to "economic connections" see para. 8.68 below.
[160] Case 15/74 [1974] E.C.R. 1147, [1974] 2 C.M.L.R. 480, noted by van Nieuwenhoven Helbach [1976] C.M.L.Rev. 37. For a national measure which apparently flaunts the principles laid down in that case, see written question 1257/81 ([1982] O.J. C53/5).

has the exclusive right to use an invention with a view to manufacturing industrial products and putting them into circulation for the first time, either directly or by the grant of licences to third parties, as well as to oppose infringements . . .

Whereas an obstacle to the free movement of goods . . . may be justified on the grounds of protection of industrial property where such protection is invoked against a product coming from a Member State where it is not patentable and has been manufactured by third parties without the consent of the patentee and in cases where there exist patents, the original proprietors of which are legally and economically independent, a derogation from the principle of the free movement of goods is not, however, justified where the product has been put on to the market in a legal manner, by the patentee himself or with his consent, in the Member State from which it has been imported, in particular in the case of a proprietor of parallel patents'.

Thus the Court held in effect that Articles 30 to 36 did not permit the use of patents to prevent the sale of an imported product in a case such as that before the Dutch court.[161]

In addition, in answer to a specific question on the point, the Court ruled that it was irrelevant whether or not the patentee and the licensees belonged to the same concern:

'the factor which above all else characterises a restriction of trade between Member States is the territorial protection granted to a patentee in one Member State against importation of the product which has been marketed in another Member State by the patentee himself or with his consent'.

8.67 This case law has now been given legislative form in the Community Patent Convention (which, as already mentioned, has not yet come into force). Article 32 governs the exhaustion of rights under Community patents. More relevant in the present context is Article 81, which closely mirrors Article 32 but which governs the exhaustion of rights conferred by national patents. Article 81 (1) provides:

'The rights conferred by a national patent in a Contracting State shall not extend to acts concerning a product covered by that patent which are done within the territory of that Contracting State after that product has been put on the market in any Contracting State by the proprietor of the patent or with his express consent, unless there are grounds which, under Community law, would justify the extension to such acts of the rights conferred by the patent'.

It is not entirely clear what is meant by 'express' consent. At all events, the requirement that the consent be 'express' is apparently designed to avoid any claim that a patent holder had tacitly consented to a product being put on the market by a third party in a Member State where no patent protection existed.[162]

---

[161] The Court also held that the existence of price differences or health considerations did not justify the use of a patent to prevent imports in this way. As regards public health measures, the Court said these 'must be such as may properly be adopted in the field of health control; and must not constitute a misuse of the rules concerning industrial and commercial property'.

[162] McClellan, *op. cit.* note 144 above, at 215.

Nor is the scope of the last half-sentence ('unless there are grounds') clear.[163]

8.68 Article 81 (2) stipulates that:

'Paragraph 1 shall also apply with regard to a product put on the market by the proprietor of a national patent, granted for the same invention in another Contracting State, who has economic connections with the proprietor of the patent referred to in paragraph 1. For the purpose of this paragraph, two persons shall be deemed to have economic connections where one of them is in a position to exert a decisive influence on the other, directly or indirectly, with regard to the exploitation of a patent, or where a third party is in a position to exercise such an influence on both persons'.

This means that the principle of exhaustion set out in Article 81 (1) shall apply to prevent a patent holder in one Member State from exercising his patent rights to prevent imports of patented goods put on the market in another Member State by another patent holder, provided that 'economic connections' exist between the two patent owners.[164]

8.69 Lastly, Article 81 (3) states that:

'The preceding paragraphs shall not apply in the case of a product put on the market under a compulsory licence'.

It is common in national patent laws to find provisions according to which, where a patent is not being sufficiently worked within the territory of the State concerned, compulsory licences can be granted to other parties. In some Member States compulsory licences can be granted on other grounds. There is as yet no case law on whether the exhaustion of rights principle applies so as to prohibit a patent holder from preventing imports marketed in another Member State, where they have been produced under a compulsory licence.[165]

The effect of Article 81 (3) is simply that the exhaustion principle does not apply with respect to compulsory licences *under the conditions set out in Article 81 (1) and (2)*. It does not prevent the exhaustion principle from applying altogether with respect to compulsory licences, since by virtue of Article 93 the Treaty of Rome takes precedence over the Community Patent Convention.[166]

B. TRADE MARKS

8.70 *Centrafarm* v. *Winthrop*[167] arose out of the same facts as the *Sterling Drug* case. The only difference was that while *Sterling Drug* concerned the patent, *Winthrop* concerned the trade mark 'Negram'.

---

[163] See generally the Advocate General in Case 187/80, note 158 above.

[164] This provision does not contemplate the application to patents of the doctrine of common origin; see paras. 8.77 *et seq.* below.

[165] This question was raised in the reference made in Case 271/80 *Pharmon* v. *Hoechst* but the reference was subsequently withdrawn.

[166] Arts. 47, 82 and 89 of the Convention also relate to compulsory licences but are not strictly relevant here.

[167] Case 16/74 [1974] E.C.R. 1183, [1974] 2 C.M.L.R. 480, noted by van Nieuwenhoven Helbach, *op. cit.* note 160 above.

These trade marks were owned outright by the subsidiaries of the Sterling Drug group in Britain and the Netherlands respectively, rather than being owned by the American patent company and licensed to the local subsidiary as in the case of the patents. The question referred by the national court was analogous to that in *Sterling Drug*.

The Court's ruling was also along the same lines as in *Sterling Drug*. It defined the specific subject-matter of trade marks as 'the guarantee that the owner of the trade mark has the exclusive right to use that trade mark, for the purpose of putting products protected by the trade mark into circulation for the first time, and is therefore intended to protect him against competitors wishing to take advantage of the status and reputation of the trade mark by selling products illegally bearing that trade mark'. The Court's conclusion was on the same lines as in the patent case: it was incompatible with the Treaty provisions on the free movement of goods to exercise a trade mark in one Member State to prohibit the sale there of a product which one has marketed oneself under that trade mark in another Member State or which has been so marketed with one's consent.[168]

8.71 The judgment in *Winthrop* has been developed by that in *Hoffmann-La Roche* v. *Centrafarm*.[169] There *Centrafarm* had acquired Valium tablets on the British market, where they had been marketed by Hoffmann-La Roche. It then repackaged them for the German market, affixed the plaintiffs' trade mark to the new packages, and put them on the German market. The Hoffmann-La Roche group owned this particular mark both in Britain and in Germany. The question posed by the German court was in essence whether it was compatible with the Treaty for the plaintiffs to rely on their German trade mark to prevent Centrafarm effecting parallel imports under these conditions.

The Court first repeated its definition of the specific subject-matter of trade marks already laid down in *Winthrop*. It continued:

> 'In order to answer the question whether that exclusive right involves the right to prevent the trade mark being affixed by a third person after the product has been repackaged, regard must be had to the essential function of the trade mark, which is to guarantee the identity of the origin of the trade marked product to the consumer or ultimate user, by enabling him without any possibility of confusion to distinguish that product from products which have another origin. This guarantee of origin means that the consumer or ultimate

---

[168] The Court also made the points already discussed with respect to patents in note 161 above. However, it did not allude to the fact that the goods had not been put on the market by Winthrop B.V., but by another subsidiary of the Sterling Drug group. Nor did Winthrop B.V. give its express consent. However, in view of the fact that Winthrop B.V. was part of the same group as the company that put the goods on the market, tacit assent can be deemed to have been given.

[169] Case 102/77 [1978] E.C.R. 1139, [1978] 3 C.M.L.R. 217; noted van Empel [1979] C.M.L. Rev. 251, Alexander [1979] C.D.E. 75, Röttger [1980] E.I.P.R. 322; the exhaustion principle was also reaffirmed with respect to trade marks in Case 58/80, note 127 above.

user can be certain that a trade marked product which is sold to him has not been subject at a previous stage of marketing to interference by a third person, without the authorisation of the proprietor of the trade mark, such as to affect the original condition of the product. The right attributed to the proprietor of preventing any use of the trade mark which is likely to impair the guarantee of origin so understood is therefore part of the specific subject-matter of the trade mark right.

It is accordingly justified under the first sentence of Article 36 to recognise that the proprietor of a trade mark is entitled to prevent an importer of a trade marked product, following repackaging of that product, from affixing the trade mark to the new packaging without the authorisation of the proprietor.'

The Court added, however, that the prevention of marketing repackaged products constitutes a disguised restriction on trade between Member States within the meaning of the second sentence of Article 36 where:

It is established that the use of the trade mark right by the proprietor, having regard to the marketing system which he has adopted, will contribute to the artificial partitioning of the markets between Member States; and

- it is shown that the repacking cannot adversely affect the original condition of the product; and
- the proprietor of the mark receives prior notice of the marketing of the repackaged product; and
- it is stated on the new packaging by whom the product has been repackaged.

In this connection, the Court expressly stated that 'it is irrelevant in answering the legal question raised . . . that the question referred by the national court is exclusively concerned with medical products'.

8.72   Analogous problems were raised in *Centrafarm* v. *American Home Products Corporation*.[170] American Home Products (AHPC) owned the trade mark 'Serenid D' for the United Kingdom, which mark covered a particular pharmaceutical product. It also owned the trade mark 'Seresta' in the Benelux countries for a product which had the same therapeutic properties as 'Serenid D' but presented certain minor differences such as a difference of taste. Centrafarm acquired quantities of this product on the British market, where it had been marketed by the AHPC group. It then removed the 'Serenid D' mark, affixed the 'Seresta' mark instead and placed this product on the Dutch market. The question referred by the Dutch court was once again whether under the Treaty the trade mark holder could prevent such parallel imports.

The Court once again repeated its definition of the specific subject-matter of a trade mark and added that the essential function of the trade mark is to guarantee the identity of the origin of the

---

[170] Case 3/78 [1978] E.C.R. 1823, [1979] 1 C.M.L.R. 326, noted by van Empel, Alexander, Röttiger, *op. cit.* note 169.

trade marked product to the consumer or ultimate user. It concluded that:

> 'This guarantee of origin means that only the proprietor may confer an identity upon the product by affixing the mark. The guarantee of origin would in fact be jeopardised if it were permissible for a third party to affix the mark to the product, even to an original product . . . The right granted to the proprietor to prohibit any unauthorised affixing of his mark to his product accordingly comes within the specific subject-matter of the trade mark'.

The Court then considered whether the exercise of this right may constitute a disguised restriction on trade between Member States within the meaning of Article 36:

> 'In this connection it should be observed that it may be lawful for the manufacturer of a product to use in different Member States different marks for the same product.
>
> Nevertheless it is possible for such a practice to be followed by the proprietor of the marks as part of a system of marketing intended to partition the markets artificially.
>
> In such a case the prohibition by the proprietor of the unauthorised affixing of the mark by a third party constitutes a disguised restriction on trade for the purposes of the above-mentioned provision.
>
> It is for the national court to settle in each particular case whether the proprietor has followed the practice of using different marks for the same product for the purpose of partitioning the markets'.

8.73   Further refinements were added by *Pfizer* v. *Eurim-Pharm.*[171] Eurim-Pharm was a parallel importer, which had imported into Germany quantities of an antibiotic called Vibramycin, which had been produced and marketed in Britain by the British subsidiary of Pfizer. The trade marks 'Vibramycin' and 'Pfizer' for Germany were owned by Pfizer. It is the practice in Germany for doctors to prescribe packets of 8, 16 or 40 tablets, whereas in Britain they were sold in packets of 10 and 50. Consequently, to take account of German usage it was necessary for Eurim-Pharm to repack the tablets. However, it was possible for them to do this without tampering with or touching the tablets, because they were contained in blister-packs of five. So Eurim-Pharm simply removed the blister-packs from their original packets and put them inside new packets. These new packets contained a window through which could be seen a label bearing the words 'Vibramycin' and 'Pfizer'. The outer packing also stated that the tablets had been produced by Pfizer Ltd. of Great Britain and that they had been repacked and imported by Eurim-Pharm. Also, Eurim-Pharm had obviously done its homework on the case law of the Court, because it took the trouble to inform Pfizer of what it was doing.

In the resulting action for trade mark infringement, the German court in its first question asked the Court of Justice whether a trade mark could be relied on to prevent such imports. The Court replied as follows:

---

[171] Case 1/81 [1982] 1 C.M.L.R. 406 noted by Handoll [1982] 3 E.I.P.R. 83.

'Article 36 of the Treaty must be interpreted as meaning that the proprietor of a trade mark right may not rely on that right in order to prevent an importer from marketing a pharmaceutical product manufactured in another Member State by the subsidiary of the proprietor and bearing the latter's trade mark with his consent, where the importer, in repackaging the product, confined himself to replacing the external wrapping without touching the internal packaging and made the trade mark, affixed by the manufacturer to the internal packaging, visible through the new external wrapping, at the same time clearly indicating on the external wrapping that the product was manufactured by the subsidiary of the proprietor and repackaged by the importer'.

In its second question, the national court asked whether, for the purpose of establishing that there is a disguised restriction on trade between Member States within the meaning of Article 36, it was necessary to prove an intention on the part of the trade mark owner to partition the common market or whether it was sufficient to prove that he exercised his trade mark rights in such a way that the common market was in fact partitioned. In other words, was the test a subjective or an objective one?

This question was obviously posed in the light of the *American Home Products* judgment, where the Court had concentrated on the subjective element, namely the trade mark owner's intention. Following the Commission, the Advocate General took the view that it was only in the special circumstances of the *American Home Products* case, where one person owned a different trade mark in each Member State concerned for the same product, that the test was a subjective one. If it were otherwise, 'on the basis of the objective criterion adopted in the judgment in *Hoffmann-La Roche* v. *Centrafarm*, the proprietor of the parallel trade marks would ultimately find himself, in the light of Community law, in a position where he could never lawfully exercise his right. To avoid this excessively restrictive result, the Court took the view that in such circumstances it is not appropriate to speak of a disguised restriction on intra-Community trade except where the practice, adopted by or under the direction of the same proprietor, of using different trade marks for the same product in the various Member States is indicative of a plan to partition the markets'. However, in other cases the correct test was, according to the Advocate General, an objective one.

The Court ruled that, in view of its answer to the first question, it need not reply to the second question.

C. COPYRIGHT

8.74 The first judgment relating to the exhaustion of copyright was the *Deutsche Grammophon* case already discussed. That judgment was developed in *Musik-Vertrieb* v. *GEMA*.[172] That case concerned

---

[172] See note 141 above. This judgment in effect confirms the judgment of the Brussels Court of Appeal in *Time Limit* v. *SABAM* [1979] 2 C.M.L.R. 578; see also Case 58/80 note 127 above.

sound recordings put on the British market and imported into Germany. GEMA, the German copyright protection society, acting on behalf of the copyright owners, brought two actions before the German courts against importers of these sound recordings. It sought the difference between the royalty fees of 6.25 per cent already paid in Britain in accordance with the Copyright Act 1956, and the 8 per cent. due under German law. The question which arose was whether the principle of exhaustion operated to prevent GEMA recovering that difference.

The Court held that in view of the principle of exhaustion a party was indeed barred from recovering the difference between the two rates of copyright. It pointed out that a copyright owner was free to decide in which Member State to put his work on the market, and in so doing must be aware of the different rates of royalties. It also took the view that GEMA's demand for additional royalties was to be regarded as a demand for damages for infringement of the copyright in Germany.[173]

8.75 *GEMA* is the first case in which the Court expressly ruled that copyright falls under the concept of industrial and commercial property in Article 36.[174] In *Deutsche Grammophon* the Court avoided a decision on the point and consequently avoided defining the specific subject-matter of copyright. In *GEMA* the Court did not in terms rule on the specific subject-matter of copyright either. However, it is interesting to note what the Court said in rejecting an argument put forward by the French Government. That argument was to the effect that the exhaustion principle did not apply to copyright because the purpose of copyright was to enable an author to claim authorship of the work and to object to any distortion, mutilation or other alteration thereof, or any other action in relation to that work which would be prejudicial to his honour or reputation. The Court refuted this argument in the following terms:

> 'It is true that copyright comprises moral rights of the kind indicated by the French Government. However, it also comprises other rights, notably the right to exploit commercially the marketing of the protected work, particularly in the form of licences granted in return for payment of royalties'.

It was on this basis that the Court concluded that the principle of exhaustion applied to copyright.

8.76 It is difficult to know what general conclusions to draw from *Coditel* v. *Ciné Vog*,[175] which concerned not the free movement of goods but the free provision of services under Article 59 of the Treaty. That case concerned the film rights for the film *Le Boucher*. In 1969 the owners of the film rights assigned those rights with respect to Belgium to Ciné Vog, stipulating that the film was not to

---

[173] See para. 6.18 above.
[174] Para. 8.57 above.
[175] Case 62/79 [1980] E.C.R. 833, [1981] 2 C.M.L.R. 362, noted by Harris [1980] E.I.P.R. 163.

be shown on television in Belgium until 40 months after the first performance in that country. The owners then assigned the rights to broadcast the film in the Federal Republic of Germany to the German television broadcasting station. The Belgian cable television companies, Coditel, picked up directly on their aerial the film *Le Boucher* broadcast on German television in January 1971 and retransmitted it directly in Belgium. Ciné Vog then brought an action for infringements before the Belgian courts.

On a reference under Article 177 the Court found in effect that Ciné Vog's copyright had been infringed.

> 'A cinematographic film belongs to the category of literary and artistic works made available to the public by performances which may be infinitely repeated. In this respect the problems involved in the observance of copyright in relation to the requirements of the Treaty are not the same as those which arise in connection with literary and artistic works, the placing of which at the disposal of the public is inseparable from the circulation of the material form of the works, as in the case of books or records'.

Consequently, it held that 'the right of the copyright owner and his assigns to require fees for any showing of a film is part of the essential function of copyright in this type of literary and artistic work'. It would appear that the term 'essential function' is equivalent to that of 'specific subject-matter'.

The Court continued:

> 'Whilst Article 59 of the Treaty prohibits restrictions upon freedom to provide services, it does not thereby encompass limits upon the exercise of certain economic activities which have their origin in the application of national legislation for the protection of intellectual property, save where such application constitutes a means of arbitrary discrimination or a disguised restriction on trade between Member States. Such would be the case if that application enabled parties to an assignment of copyright to create artificial barriers to trade between Member States'.

There can be no doubt that, although this case concerned Article 59, the terminology used has been borrowed from Article 36. At all events, the Court found that the mere fact that the geographical limit of a particular assignment of performing rights coincided with national frontiers did not constitute either arbitrary discrimination or a disguised restriction on trade between Member States.

The Court concluded that:

> 'The exclusive assignee of the performing right in a film for the whole of a Member State may therefore rely upon his right against cable television diffusion companies which have transmitted that film on their diffusion network having received it from a television broadcasting station established in another Member State, without thereby infringing Community law'.

In the light of the subsequent ruling in *Musik-Vertrieb* v. *GEMA* it may be that the ratio of *Coditel* is that the specific subject-matter of performing rights is different from that of other types of copyright.

Rule 3: The common origin principle

8.77   This rule was spelt out in *Van Zuylen Frères* v. *Hag*.[176] The facts were that at the beginning of this century Hag AG, a German company, acquired trade marks in the name 'Hag' for coffee in a number of countries. As regards Belgium and Luxembourg it became the holder of these rights in 1908. Between the two World Wars Hag created a Belgian subsidiary and transferred to it its trade mark rights for Belgium and Luxembourg. In 1944 the Belgian authorities sequestered the shares of Hag Belgium as enemy property and subsequently sold them to the Van Oevelen family. Later, Hag Belgium assigned its trade marks for Belgium and Luxembourg to Van Zuylen Frères, the distributors of their coffee. The result was that the German 'Hag' trade mark on the one hand and the Belgian and Luxembourg 'Hag' trade mark on the other, although of common origin, were now held by two totally unconnected parties, Hag AG and Van Zuylen. When the German company began marketing its products under the name 'Hag' in Luxembourg, Van Zuylen commenced infringement proceedings before the Tribunal d'Arrondissement of Luxembourg. In a reference under Article 177 that court asked in effect whether the exclusion of goods from a Member State in such circumstances was contrary *inter alia* to Articles 30 and 36. In its reference the referring court stated that 'no legal, financial, technical or economic link' existed between the parties.

The Court's answer was as follows:

> 'The exercise of a trade mark tends to contribute to the partitioning of the markets and thus to affect the free movement of goods between Member States, all the more so since—unlike other rights of industrial and commercial property—it is not subject to limitations in point of time.
>
> Accordingly, one cannot allow the holder of a trade mark to rely upon the exclusiveness of a trade mark right, which may be a consequence of the territorial limitation of national legislations—with a view to prohibiting the marketing in a Member State of goods legally produced in another Member State under an identical trade mark having the same origin . . . .
>
> Whilst in such a market the indication of origin of a product covered by a trade mark is useful, information to consumers on this point may be ensured by means other than such as would affect the free movement of goods'.

In its subsequent judgment in *Terrapin* v. *Terranova*[177] the Court sought to provide further justification for this ruling in stating that in a case such as this 'the basic function of the trade mark to guarantee to consumers that the product has the same origin is already undermined by the sub-division of the original right.'

8.78   In its second question the national court asked whether the same would be the case if the marketing of the product covered by

---

[176] Case 192/73 [1974] E.C.R. 731, [1974] 2 C.M.L.R. 127, noted by Alexander [1974] C.M.L. Rev. 387, Jacobs [1975] I.C.L.Q. 643.
[177] Case 119/75 [1976] E.C.R. 1039, [1976] 2 C.M.L.R. 482.

the trade mark were effected not by the holder of the trade mark in that Member State but by a third party, who has duly acquired the goods in that Member State. The Court replied that 'if the holder of a trade mark in one Member State may himself market the product covered by the trade mark in another Member State, then this also applies to a third party who has duly acquired this product in the first State'.

8.79   It is clear from the Court's answer to the first question that a person acquiring a trade mark in one Member State may sell goods under that mark throughout the Community. Moreover, it will be remembered that the Belgian and Luxembourg marks had been confiscated from the German company by the public authorities. It follows that the common origin principle applies not only where a trade mark has been split up by voluntary assignment, but also where it has been split up by an act of the public authorities contrary to the will of the trade mark holders.[178]

8.80   It is the latter aspect of the Hag case that has attracted very considerable criticism. Indeed, Leigh and Guy go as far as to say that 'one is hard pressed to think of any objective justification for the Court's decision in the *Hag* case, at least as regards its answer to the first question referred to it'.[179] The most important criticisms are:

Firstly, that the *Hag* ruling seems inconsistent with the ruling in *Centrafarm* v. *Winthrop* to the effect that the specific subject-matter of a trade mark is 'the guarantee that the owner of the trade mark has the exclusive right to use that trade mark, for the purpose of putting products protected by the trade mark into circulation for the first time.' Under *Hag*, that 'exclusive' right must now be shared between Van Zuylen and Hag.

Secondly, it is not clear why the historical fact that two trade marks have a common origin should affect their exercise today, when there are no continuing links between the parties. It is hard to see why the result should be any different from that in *Terrapin* v. *Terranova* discussed below.

8.81   In any case, although the Court had not had the opportunity to hear a second case raising the question of common origin, it did expressly confirm that principle in the *Terrapin* case in what amounts to an *obiter dictum*. Consequently, unless and until the Court overturns *Hag*, it must be regarded as a true statement of the law.

On the other hand, in the passage quoted above from *Hag* the Court appeared to consider that for these purposes trade marks are different from other forms of industrial and commercial property. Accordingly, it may be that the common origin principle applies to trade marks alone.

---

[178] In *Terrapin* the Court expressly affirmed that the Common origin rule applied when a trade mark had been divided 'as a result of public constraint'.
[179] *Op. cit.* note 137 above, at 222.

Rule 4

8.82 At this stage it will come as no surprise to the reader to learn that Articles 30 to 36 only apply to restrictions on trade between Member States. This simple principle is the basis of the Court's ruling in the *EMI Records* v. *CBS* cases.[180] Those cases concerned the Columbia trade mark which until 1917 had belonged to the same undertaking both in Europe and the United States. However, by a series of transactions that trade mark had become vested in CBS as regards the United States and in the EMI group as regards every single Member State of the EEC. When CBS sought to import records into the EEC bearing the Columbia trade mark, EMI commenced infringement proceedings before the British, German and Danish courts. Each of the three courts in question proceeded to make a reference under Article 177 asking in particular whether the sale of such goods could lawfully be prevented.

After pointing out that Article 30 only prohibited quantitative restrictions and measures of equivalent effect between Member States, the Court found that 'the exercise of a trade mark right in order to prevent the marketing of products coming from a third country under an identical mark . . . does not affect the free movement of goods between Member States and thus does not come under the prohibitions set out in Article 30 *et seq.* of the Treaty'. The Court added that it was not necessary to examine whether there was a common origin between the two Columbia trade marks, 'since that question is relevant only in relation to considering whether within the Community there are opportunities for partitioning the market'.[181]

The Court also held that Articles 30 to 36 did not entitle the holder of the trade mark in a third country to manufacture and market his products within the Community either himself or through his subsidiaries established in the Community. As the Court pointed out, if it were otherwise a coach and horses would be driven through the protection of industrial and commercial property established by Article 36.

8.83 The essential point in these cases was that EMI held the Columbia trade mark with respect to all the Member States. Had there been one Member State in which CBS had held the mark, then the common origin principle laid down in *Van Zuylen Frères* v. *Hag*

---

[180] Case 51/75, note 149 above; Case 86/75 [1976] E.C.R. 871, [1976] 2 C.M.L.R. 235; Case 96/75 [1976] E.C.R. 913, [1976] 2 C.M.L.R. 235. The ruling in each of the three cases is virtually identical. See casenotes by Laddie [1976] E.L.Rev. 499, Alexander [1976] C.D.E. 431.

[181] See also para. 2.13 above. The Court also held that there was no trade agreement on which CBS could rely; However, this question is raised in Case 270/80 *Polydor* v. *Harlequin Records* [1982] 1 C.M.L.R. 677, where the point at issue is whether the exhaustion principle applies to the EEC-Portugal agreement.

would have applied. Consequently, CBS could have distributed its Columbia records from that Member State to all the others.

Rule 5

8.84 This rule emerges from *Terrapin* v. *Terranova*. Terranova was a German company manufacturing dry plaster and other building materials in the Federal Republic under the 'Terranova' trade mark. Terrapin was a British company manufacturing prefabricated houses in Britain under the trade mark 'Terrapin' and exporting them to Germany under that mark. The trade marks were duly registered in Germany and the United Kingdom respectively and could be lawfully used there. There was no connection between the two companies or the two trade marks. An action was brought before the German courts in which the German company objected to the use of the 'Terrapin' mark in Germany. The case reached the Bundesgerichtshof which took the view that a risk of confusion existed so that the sale of the imported goods under the 'Terrapin' mark constituted an infringement under German law. It duly made a reference under Article 177 asking whether Articles 30 to 36 prohibited an import ban on such goods in these circumstances.

After rehearsing the general principles already discussed here, the Court ruled as follows:

> 'On the other hand in the present state of Community law an industrial or commercial property right legally acquired in a Member State may legally be used to prevent under the first sentence of Article 36 of the Treaty the import of products marketed under a name giving rise to confusion where the rights in question have been acquired by different and independent proprietors under different national laws. If in such a case the principle of the free movement of goods were to prevail over the protection given by the respective national laws, the specific objective of industrial and commercial property rights would be undermined. In the particular situation the requirements of the free movement of goods and the safeguarding of industrial and commercial property rights must be so reconciled that protection is ensured for the legitimate use of the rights conferred by national laws, coming within the prohibitions on imports "justified" within the meaning of Article 36 of the Treaty, but denied on the other hand in respect of any improper exercise of the same rights of such a nature as to maintain or effect artificial partitions within the common market'.

This last sentence is perhaps a reference back to an earlier passage in the judgment where the Court said that industrial property rights may not be exercised in such a way as to constitute arbitrary discrimination or a disguised restriction on trade between Member States. In particular, it held that a trade mark owner must exercise his rights with the same strictness whatever the national origin of the infringer.

8.85 *Terrapin* v. *Terranova* concerned trade marks and trade names, but there is every reason to think that the principles laid

171

down in that judgment apply by analogy to other forms of industrial property.[182] As the Court pointed out in the passage quoted here, if industrial property rights could not be relied on to prevent imports even in the absence of any exhaustion, common origin, restrictive agreement between the parties or discriminatory exercise, then such rights would in general be undermined.

---

[182] See Leigh and Guy, *op. cit.* note 137 above, at 158.

CHAPTER IX

Other exception clauses[1]

9.01 No small degree of academic effort, and, one suspects, intellectual excitement, has been expended in the search for a satisfactory definition of the closely related concepts of 'exception clauses' and 'escape clauses' in the Treaty of Rome. No attempt will be made here to join this search. The term 'exception clause' is merely used in this chapter as a convenient overall concept to cover provisions in the Treaty which permit measures to be taken which would otherwise fall foul of Articles 30 to 34. Such Treaty provisions are of various kinds: some vest the powers in question in the Member States as of right, while others require the adoption of a Decision or other binding act by the Commission or, in some cases, the Council. This act will normally take the form of an authorisation to the Member State in question to take a particular measure. Again, some exception clauses such as Articles 36 and 223 may only be invoked on non-economic grounds, while others such as Articles 108 and 109 may be relied on only in cases of economic difficulty. However, all these provisions share one common trait: since they constitute an exception to a fundamental principle of the Treaty, namely the free movement of goods, measures taken pursuant to them may be no more restrictive than is necessary to realise the legitimate object in view.[2]

9.02 Article 36, which is by far the most important exception clause in relation to Articles 30 to 34, has already been discussed at length in the previous chapter. It therefore requires no further examination here.

Nor is it intended to consider here the exceptions (other than Article 115) to the rule that on being put into free circulation goods from third countries are assimilated to goods of Community origin; these exceptions have already been discussed at length in Chapter II

---

[1] See generally Gori, *Les clauses de sauvegarde des traités CECA et CEE* (1967); Oppermann, 'Schutzklauseln in der Endphase des gemeinsamen Marktes' [1969] EuR. 231; Müller-Heidelberg, *Schutzklauseln im Europäischen Gemeinschaftsrecht* (1970); Lejeune, *Un droit des temps de crise: les clauses de sauvegarde de la CEE* (1975); Groeben, Boeckh, Thiesing, *Kommentar zum EWG Vertrag* (1974); Mégret, *Le droit de la Communauté économique européenne* (1976), Vol. 6.

[2] This rule of proportionality is expressly laid down in Arts. 109 (1), 115 (3) and 226 (3) but applies to all exception clauses; see in particular Müller-Heidelberg, *op. cit.* at 114; Lejeune, *op. cit.* at 305 and paras. 9.31 *et seq.* below; with respect to Art. 36 see Case 104/75 *de Peijper* [1976] E.C.R. 613, [1976] 2 C.M.L.R. 271, para 8.10 above; with respect to Art. 226 (note 4 below), see Cases 73–74/63 *Handelsvereniging Rotterdam* v. *Minister van Landbouw* [1974] E.C.R. 1, [1964] C.M.L.R. 198.

of this book.[3] Lastly, it is not proposed to examine here the exception clauses which only apply during the various transitional periods.[4]

This leaves the following Articles of the Treaty to be considered in turn in this chapter: Articles 103, 107–109, 115, 222–225, 233 and 234. Although it is doubtful whether Article 222 can ever be an exception to Articles 30 to 34, an analysis of this provision is included here for completeness.

ARTICLE 103

9.03 Article 103 provides:

'1. Member States shall regard their conjunctural policies as a matter of common concern. They shall consult each other and the Commission on the measures to be taken in the light of the prevailing circumstances.

2. Without prejudice to any other procedures provided for in this Treaty, the Council may, acting unanimously on a proposal from the Commission, decide upon the measures appropriate to the situation.

3. Acting by a qualified majority on a proposal from the Commission, the Council shall, where required, issue any directives needed to give effect to the measures decided upon under paragraph 2.

4. The procedures provided for in this Article shall also apply if any difficulty should arise in the supply of certain products'.

The authors of the English version of the Treaty appear to have donated a new word to the language: the English reader who does not recall meeting the word 'conjunctural' will be gratified to learn that this predicament is shared by the *Shorter Oxford English Dictionary.* Yet it is clear from the meaning of the term in other Community languages that it is intended to mean 'relating to short-term economic policy'. No definition of 'conjunctural policy' is to be found in the Treaty, however. For such a definition one must turn to the following statement in the Advocate General's conclusions in *Balkan* v. *HZA Berlin-Packhof*[5]: 'one is able to think in terms of conjunctural policy when the whole course of the economic process is guided by reference to short-term goals (in which connection one also has to consider goals of general economic policy—*e.g.* stable price levels, a high rate of employment, controlling the balance of payments, optimum economic growth)'.

---

[3] Paras. 2.15 *et seq.*

[4] Art. 226 EEC empowered the Commission to authorise a Member State in serious economic difficulties to take exceptional measures *during the transitional period*. Equivalent provisions are to be found in Arts. 135 and 130 respectively of the two Acts of Accession, though these only contemplate exceptional measures being taken by or against the acceding Member State(s). In addition, Arts. 136 and 131 of the respective Acts of Accession provide for exceptional measures to be taken against dumping during the respective transitional periods by a Member State with the Commission's authorisation. On Art. 226 see Case 13/63 *Italy* v. *E.C. Commission* [1963] E.C.R. 165, [1963] C.M.L.R. 289, Cases 73–74/63 *Puttershoek* v. *Minister van Landbouw* [1964] E.C.R. 1, [1964] C.M.L.R. 198; Case 37/70 *Rewe-Zentrale* v. *Hauptzollamt Emmerich* [1971] E.C.R. 23, [1971] C.M.L.R. 238.

[5] Case 5/73 [1973] E.C.R. 1091 at 1122. This case is based on the same facts as Case 10/73 *REWE-Zentral* v. *Hauptzollamt Kehl* [1973] E.C.R. 1175. See para 4.10 above.

9.04 Is Article 103 (4) to be read in the light of the preceding paragraphs and therefore limited to conjunctural policy? In Ehlermann's view[6] it is not so limited. This means that it allows for measures intended to combat difficulties of supply, which only affect the products in question and not the economy as a whole. Another —quite separate—question is whether in addition to shortages of supply Article 103 (4) also covers cases of excess supply. Opinions are divided on this point.[7]

9.05 In *SADAM* v. *Comitato Interministeriale dei Prezzi*[8] the Court held that a Member State could not rely on Article 103 to justify a measure falling under Article 30. Although that case concerned an agricultural product subject to a common organisation of the market, there is every reason to think that this ruling is of general application. It follows that Article 103 does not create an exception to Article 30 on which Member States can rely.

9.06 On the other hand, it has now become clear that Article 103 grants the Council considerable freedom to adopt exceptional measures. The leading case here is the *Balkan* case already referred to, which concerned the validity of the system of monetary compensatory amounts.[9] At the time of the events giving rise to the litigation Regulation 974/71,[10] which established this system, was based on Article 103. One of the questions referred by the German court hearing the case was whether the Regulation was invalid by virtue of its basis. In fact, shortly before the reference was made, Articles 28, 43 and 235 of the Treaty were substituted as its legal bases by Regulation 2746/72,[11] but that did not deprive the question of its purpose. The Court held that the agricultural provisions of the Treaty conferred power on the Community institutions to take short-term economic policy measures in the agricultural sector. On the other hand, Article 103 did not 'relate to those areas already subject to common rules, as is the organisation of agricultural markets'. In spite of this, the Court went on to rule that owing to the time needed to give effect to the procedures laid down in Articles 40 and 43, the Council was justified in making interim use of the powers conferred on it by Article 103 of the Treaty. In support of this conclusion the Court cited 'the suddenness of the events with which the Council was faced, the urgency of the measures to be adopted, the seriousness of the situation and the fact that these measures were adopted in an area intimately connected with the monetary policies of Member States'.

---

[6] In Groeben, Boeckh, Thiesing, *op. cit.* note 1 above, Vol. 1, 1354.

[7] For the view that Art. 103 (4) applies to gluts Gori, *op. cit.* 179, Müller-Heidelberg, *op. cit.* 292–293; *contra* Ehlermann, *op. cit.* 1354.

[8] Cases 88-90/75 [1976] E.C.R. 323, [1977] 2 C.M.L.R. 183, see paras. 7.50 *et seq.* above.

[9] This is the mechanism informally known as the 'green currencies'. See Gilsdorf, 'The System of Monetary Compensation from a Legal Standpoint' [1980] E.L.Rev. 341 and 433.

[10] [1971] J.O. L106/1.

[11] [1972] J.O. L291/148.

The Court also rejected the plaintiff's submission that only directives and decisions could be passed on the basis of Article 103, not regulations. It held, on the contrary, that the second paragraph of that Article confers on the Council 'the powers necessary to adopt, in principle, any conjunctural measures which may appear to be needed in order to safeguard the objectives of the Treaty'. From this it is clear that this provision is not to be interpreted narrowly. What is more, the phrase 'measures appropriate to the situation' in Article 103 (2) meant that the Council could choose the type of act most suitable to the circumstances.

9.07 It is clear, then, that the powers conferred on the Community institutions by Article 103 are extensive. Thus:

(a) the *Balkan* ruling seems to imply that Article 103 may be used as the basis for measures of a general and permanent nature;[12]

(b) by holding that Article 103 was inappropriate merely because it does not relate to 'areas already subject to common rules', this judgment implies that a similar measure could be adopted under Article 103 if it fell within an area not yet subject to common rules;

(c) it is clear that even within those wide boundaries the Council enjoys a considerable margin of discretion; this was stated by the Court in two judgments which are of no further concern in the present context, *Compagnie d'Approvisionnement* v. *E.C. Commission*[13] and *Merkur* v. *E.C. Commission*.[14]

9.08 Article 103 does not constitute an express exception to the general rules of the Treaty. Nevertheless, it is generally agreed that in certain circumstances measures of conjunctural policy or supply policy based on Article 103 may create restrictions on inter-State trade.[15] This is clearly subject to the general requirement already discussed to the effect that such measures may not be more restrictive than is necessary to attain the legitimate object in view. It has also been suggested that exceptional measures based on Article 103 may only be of a temporary nature.[16] On the other hand, it would appear to follow from the broad wording of Article 103 ('measures appropriate to the situation') that the exceptional measures may be taken under it not only when a crisis actually occurs but also when there is an imminent threat of a crisis. At all events, the Commission and the Council appear to have arrived at an early stage at the conclusion that measures based on Article 103 could restrict inter-State trade in a way which would otherwise be contrary to Articles 30 to 34: by

---

[12] Mégret, *op. cit.* 4.

[13] Cases 9 and 4/71 [1972] E.C.R. 391, [1973] C.M.L.R. 529.

[14] Case 43/72 [1973] E.C.R. 1055.

[15] Gori, *op. cit.* 178–179; Müller-Heidelberg, *op. cit.* 295; Mégret, *op. cit.* Vol. 6, 5; Ehlermann, *op. cit.* 1351–1352.

[16] Lejeune, *op. cit.* 247; Mégret, *op. cit.* Vol. 6, 5.

Decision 63/689[17] the Council on the proposal of the Commission authorised Belgium to restrict exports of pork and live pigs for a fixed period, in view of the serious shortage of these products; such a restriction would normally have fallen foul of Article 34, if imposed by a Member State.

9.09 Still in force today is the elaborate system set up by the Council on the basis of Article 103 with respect to exports between Member States of crude oil and petroleum products.[18] Decision 77/186,[19] as amended by Decision 79/879,[20] provides that where difficulties arise in the supply of these products in one or more Member States, the Commission may make intra-Community trade in some of them subject to a system of licences to be granted automatically by the exporting Member State. These licences are to be granted without delay and free of administrative charges in respect of any quantity requested and for a minimum period of 15 working days and a maximum period of one month. By virtue of Article 2 of the Decision, whenever a shortfall in the supply of crude oil and/or petroleum products, whether actual or imminent, creates an abnormal increase in trade in petroleum products between Member States, the Commission may, at the request of a Member State, authorise that Member State to suspend the issue of export licences or cut short the period of validity of existing licences or, if necessary, to revoke them. By virtue of Article 3, the same applies where the supply of the products in a Member State is endangered or may reasonably be expected to be so. In either case, the Council may meet within 48 hours to amend or repeal the Commission's authorisation. Article 4 empowers a Member State, in the event of a sudden crisis in that Member State, when any delay would be gravely prejudicial to its economy, to suspend the issue of export licences for 10 days, after consulting the Commission and informing the other Member States. Article 4 (a) also empowers a Member State faced with such a crisis to suspend for 10 days the validity of licences already granted. In either case the Council may decide on further appropriate measures. Lastly, Article 5 provides for the early amendment or repeal of exceptional measures, should they prove no longer necessary.

9.10 It is also worth noting a dictum of the Court in *BP* v. *E.C. Commission*,[21] an action for annulment of a Commission Decision to the effect that the companies concerned had abused a dominant position contrary to Article 86 by various practices during the acute

---

[17] [1963] J.O. 3108.
[18] On the Community's oil policy generally see Evans, 'The Development of a Community Policy on Oil' [1980] C.M.L.Rev. 371, Forster and Syngellakis, 'Developments in EEC energy policy from 1977' [1980] E.L.Rev. 402; see also Case 77/77 *BP* v. *E.C. Commission* [1978] E.C.R. 1513, [1978] 3 C.M.L.R. 174.
[19] [1980] O.J. L61/23 supplemented by Commission Dec. 78/890 [1978] O.J. L311/13.
[20] [1979] O.J. L270/58.
[21] Note 18 above.

oil shortage in the Netherlands of 1973–74. In this dictum the Court in effect stated that Article 103 was a legal basis for Community legislation imposing rationing in times of crisis. Indeed, it expressed its regret at the absence of any such rules; this in its view amounted to a serious failure to act which revealed 'a neglect of the principle of Community solidarity which is one of the foundations of the Community'.

9.11 It is clear, then, that various measures already adopted under Article 103 have created restrictions to intra-Community trade. Yet it should be pointed out that such measures only constitute a minority of the measures based on Article 103, some of which concern such matters as the temporary suspension of customs duties on certain goods[22] or the co-ordination of the conjunctural policies of Member States.[23] What is more, it would seem that as regards matters falling within its purview, Article 103 can be used as a legal basis for Community harmonising legislation—at least of a short-term nature—which in no way restricts the free movement of goods between Member States.[24]

Be that as it may, there seems little room for doubt that Article 103 is the appropriate basis for Community measures restricting exports between Member States of goods in short supply, at least if they are of brief duration. In this respect it goes beyond the bounds within which the Community legislator must normally keep.[25] It is not clear what other types of measure derogating from the free movement of goods Article 103 permits. Yet, unlike some of the other provisions discussed in this chapter, it will only permit absolute import bans in extreme cases, if at all.[26]

ARTICLE 107

9.12 Article 107 provides:

'1. Each Member State shall treat its policy with regard to rates of exchange as a matter of common concern.

2. If a Member State makes an alteration in its rate of exchange which is inconsistent with the objectives set out in Article 104 and which seriously distorts conditions of competition, the Commission may, after consulting the Monetary Committee, authorise other Member States to take for a strictly limited period the necessary measures, the conditions and details

---

[22] e.g. Dec. 64/530 ([1964] J.O. 2389), Dec. 65/266 ([1965] J.O. 1462), Reg. 2101/76 ([1976] O.J. L235/17).

[23] e.g. Dec. of 9 March 1960 ([1960] J.O. 764), Dec. 75/785 ([1975] O.J. L330/50).

[24] See para. 12.04 below.

[25] See paras. 4.10 et seq. above.

[26] In particular, even if Art. 103 (4) does cover gluts (para. 9.04 above), it could presumably not be used to create import bans between Member States: while this would divide up the Community market, it is hard to envisage any resulting gain to the Community as a whole; such measures would thus fail to meet the requirement of proportionality (note 2 above). On the other hand, it is submitted that Art. 103 might well be an appropriate basis for the imposition of production quotas or similar measures.

of which it shall determine, in order to counter the consequences of such alteration'.

Article 104 in turn provides:

'Each Member State shall pursue the economic policy needed to ensure the equilibrium of its overall balance of payments and to maintain confidence in its currency, while taking care to ensure a high level of employment and a stable level of prices'.

9.13 Three conditions must be satisfied before an authorisation under Article 107 (2) can be granted by the Commission:

- The Member State must alter its exchange rate. In certain circumstances the maintenance of a particular rate of exchange may run counter to Article 104, but such a state of affairs cannot fall under Article 107 (2). On the other hand, the condition is satisfied if the Member State allows its currency to float or introduces a multiple exchange rate.[27]
- The alteration must be inconsistent with the objectives set out in Article 104.
- The alteration must seriously distort conditions of competition; an alteration in an exchange rate can be incompatible with Article 104 by being excessively high or excessively low, but it would appear that only a devaluation can fall under Article 107 (2) because only this can seriously distort conditions of competition.[28]

9.14 On no account may a Member State rely on this exception without prior authorisation from the Commission. This the Commission may grant either on its own initiative or at the request of a Member State. In the latter case, the Commission may not simply act as a rubber stamp but must actively exercise its discretion, since it is the guardian of the Treaty.[29] By whatever method the procedure has been initiated, the Commission cannot grant an authorisation without first consulting the Monetary Committee provided for in Article 105 (2); this consists of two members appointed by each Member State and two members appointed by the Commission. Should the Commission decide to authorise exceptional action by a Member State, no provision is made for the Council to overturn or alter the Commission's decision.

The exceptional measures which may be taken under this Article include quantitative restrictions and measures of equivalent effect[30]—provided always that less restrictive measures would be inadequate.[31] Whatever the nature of the measures, Article 107 expressly states that they must be strictly limited in time.

---

[27] Carreau, 'La Communauté économique européenne face aux problèmes monétaires' [1971] R.T.D.E. 589; Ehlermann, *op. cit.* 1397.

[28] Ehlermann, *op. cit.* 1397.

[29] See paras. 9.31 *et seq.* below.

[30] Ehlermann, *op. cit.* 1398.

[31] See note 2 above.

It would appear that the exemption clause contained in Article 107 (2) has never been applied.

ARTICLE 108

9.15   By virtue of Article 108 (3) the Commission may authorise a Member State to 'take protective measures, the conditions and details of which the Commission shall determine'. However, this is only the culmination of an elaborate procedure set in train

> 'where a Member State is in difficulties or is seriously threatened with difficulties as regards its balance of payments either as a result of an overall disequilibrium in its balance of payments, or as a result of the type of currency at its disposal, and where such difficulties are liable in particular to jeopardise the functioning of the common market or the progressive implementation of the common commercial policy'.

It is widely accepted that the term 'balance of payments difficulties' may cover difficulties arising out of a balance of payments surplus, and is not confined to cases of deficit.[32] As is clear from its express words, Article 108 may be applied before such difficulties arise; it is enough that there is a serious threat of them arising.

9.16   The procedure is divided into three stages. At the first stage the Commission examines the monetary position of the Member State in question and then makes recommendations as to the action which that State should take. Should this prove to be insufficient the procedure moves on to the second stage, that of 'mutual assistance' consisting of directives or decisions adopted by the Council by a qualified majority on a proposal put forward by the Commission after consulting the Monetary Committee.[33] The Article sets out a non-exhaustive list of forms which the mutual assistance may take, including in particular the granting of credits by other Member States. Only if 'the mutual assistance recommended by the Commission is not granted by the Council or if the mutual assistance granted and the measures taken are insufficient' may the Commission authorise the Member State in difficulty to take exceptional measures. Indeed, according to Ehlermann[34], if these conditions are fulfilled, the Commission is bound to grant such an authorisation, since Article 108 (3) states that the Commission 'shall authorise . . .' However, the Commission is required actively to exercise its discretion in this matter and not act merely as a rubber stamp[35]. Such an authorisation, which, it would seem, must be granted by a decision

---

[32] Ehlermann, *op. cit.* 1404–1405; Mégret, *op. cit.* 33; as to exceptional measures taken by Germany to counteract its balance of payments surplus, though without any authorisation under Art. 108 (3), see Case 27/74 *Demag* v. *Finanzamt Duisburg* [1974] E.C.R. 1037 and particularly Advocate General Reischl at 1057.
[33] See para. 9.14 above as to the composition of the Monetary Committee.
[34] Ehlermann, *op. cit.*1412.
[35] See para. 9.31 below.

within the meaning of Article 189[36], may be revoked or altered by the Council acting by a qualified majority: Article 108 (3), second paragraph.

9.17 The exceptional measures which the Commission may authorise under Article 108 (3) include quantitative restrictions and measures of equivalent effect[37], provided always that such draconian measures are necessary to counteract the balance of payments difficulties in question.[38] Accordingly, by Decision 68/301[39] adopted under Article 108 (3) the Commission authorised France to restrict imports of cars and certain other products, in order to overcome the economic difficulties encountered by France in the wake of the political unrest of May 1968. Another example is Decision 74/287[40], by which the Commission authorised Italy to subject imports to the lodging with the Bank of Italy of a six-month interest-free loan amounting to not more than 50 per cent. of the value of the goods.

The Commission has also granted authorisations under Article 108 (3) in favour of the United Kingdom,[41] Ireland[42] and Denmark,[43] though these concerned only the free movement of capital and the purchase of investments and securities and had no bearing on the free movement of goods.

ARTICLE 109

9.18 Where a Member State suffers a sudden crisis in its balance of payments and mutual assistance is not granted immediately by the Council under Article 108 (2), then Article 109 empowers it to take the necessary protective measures itself. As the two Articles are part of one and the same procedure, they must be construed analogously. This means that protective measures adopted under Article 109 may include quantitative restrictions and measures of equivalent effect.[44] Article 109 (1) states that 'such measures must cause the least possible disturbance in the functioning of the common market and must not be wider in scope than is strictly necessary to remedy the sudden difficulties which have arisen.' However, this is merely the expression of a general principle common to all exception clauses in the Treaty.[45]

9.19 It is clear, then, that Article 109 empowers Member States unilaterally to take exceptional measures striking at the very core of

---

[36] Advocate General Reischl in *Demag*, note 32 above, at 1057.
[37] Ehlermann, *op. cit.* 1412.
[38] See note 2 above.
[39] [1968] J.O. L178/15.
[40] [1974] O.J. L152/18.
[41] In particular Dec. 75/487 ([1975] O.J. L211/21).
[42] Dec. 78/152 ([1978] O.J. L45/28).
[43] Dec 78/153 ([1978] O.J. L45/29).
[44] Ehlermann, *op. cit.* 1417.
[45] See note 2 above.

the Community on purely economic grounds. For this reason it is subject to important guarantees:

(i) Although the balance of payments difficulties must be of the same kind as those in Article 108, they must fulfil three additional conditions:

1. They must be in the nature of a crisis;
2. This crisis must actually have occurred; and
3. It must be sudden.

Furthermore, Article 109 cannot be applied if mutual assistance under Article 108 (2) is forthcoming.

(ii) The unilateral measures are merely to act as a stop-gap until the crisis is dealt with by the Community. This is why Article 109 (2) provides that 'the Commission and the other Member States shall be informed of such protective measures not later than when they enter into force.' This was the provision which the court had occasion to interpret in Cases 6 and 11/69 *E.C. Commission* v. *France.*[46] The background to this case is the economic crisis which arose in France in 1968. By Decision 68/301 of 23 July 1968 based on Article 108 (3)[47] the Commission authorised France to take various protective measures, including the fixing of a rediscount rate for exports more favourable than the general rate. However, that Decision stipulated that as from 1 November 1968 the difference between the two rates was not to exceed 1·5 points. When France exceeded that limit, the Commission brought infringement proceedings against it. In ruling that France had in fact committed an infringement, the Court rejected, *inter alia*, France's defence that the failure to respect the conditions attached to the Commission's Decision was covered by Article 109 in view of a fresh monetary crisis which had arisen in the autumn of 1968.[48] The Court held that to rely on this provision a Member State must inform the Commission and the other Member States of its protective measures in accordance with Article 109 (2) and in so doing must make express reference to Article 109. Since France had not done this, it could not rely on Article 109.

9.20   The second sentence of Article 109 (2) provides:

'The Commission may recommend to the Council the granting of mutual assistance under Article 108.'

Article 109 (3) provides:

'After the Commission has delivered an opinion and the Monetary Committee has been consulted, the Council may, acting by a qualified majority, decide

---

[46] [1969] E.C.R. 523, [1970] C.M.L.R. 43.
[47] See note 39 above.
[48] France had in fact relied on Art. 109 in June and July 1968 before Dec. 68/301 was taken, but that was not in question before the Court.

that the State concerned shall amend, suspend or abolish the protective measures referred to above.'

At first sight it might appear from these provisions that the Commission and the Council may stand back and refrain from all intervention, but the Court has held in effect that it is incumbent on them to intervene at the earliest possible moment.[49] This is natural in view of the sweeping powers which Member States enjoy by virtue of Article 109.

It is not necessary in this context to explore all the procedural permutations which may occur.[50] Suffice it to point out the following possible trains of events:

- the Council may consider that there are no balance of payments difficulties such as to render Article 108 or 109 applicable, in which case it must require the Member State concerned to abolish its unilateral measures or at least amend them so that they no longer constitute exceptional measures;
- the Commission may recommend mutual assistance under Article 108 (2) to the Council; if the Council proceeds to adopt that recommendation, then Article 109 ceases to be applicable and Article 108 takes over;
- if the Commission recommends mutual assistance but the Council does not grant it or the mutual assistance granted proves insufficient, then the Commission may authorise exceptional measures under Article 108 (3); once again, Article 109 ceases to have effect.

ARTICLE 115[51]

9.21 Article 115 provides as follows:

'In order to ensure that the execution of measures of commercial policy taken in accordance with this Treaty by any Member State is not obstructed by deflection of trade, or where differences between such measures lead to economic difficulties in one or more of the Member States, the Commission shall recommend the methods for the requisite co-operation between Member States. Failing this, the Commission shall authorise Member States to take the necessary protective measures, the conditions and details of which it shall determine.

In case of urgency during the transitional period, Member States may themselves take the necessary measures and shall notify them to the other

---

[49] Cases 6 and 11/69, see note 46 above.
[50] For these, see in particular Ehlermann, *op. cit.* 1418, Lejeune, *op. cit.* 155.
[51] Opperman, 'La Clause de sauvegarde de l'Article 115 du Traité de la CEE' [1965] R.M.C. 376; Ernst and Beseler in Groeben, Boeckh, Thiesing, *op. cit.*, note 1 above, Vol. I, 1458; Lejeune, *op. cit.* 189; Mégret, *op. cit.* note 1 above, 384; Börner in *Schutzmassnahmen im Gemeinsamen Markt'* (1976), 67; Weber, 'Die Bedeutung des Art. 115 EWGV für die Freiheit des Warenverkehrs' [1979] EuR. 29; Lux, 'Ausschluss von der Gemeinschaftshandlung bei Umwegeinfuhren (Art. 115 EWGV)' [1979] EuR. 359; Kretschmer, 'Beschränkungen des innergemeinschaftlichen Warenverkehrs nach der Kommissionsentscheidung 80/47 EWG' [1981] EuR. 63; Vogelzang, 'Two Aspects of Article 115 EEC Treaty' [1981] C.M.L.Rev. 169.

183

Member States and to the Commission, which may decide that the States concerned shall amend or abolish such measures.

In the selection of such measures, priority shall be given to those which cause the least disturbance to the functioning of the Common Market and which take into account the need to expedite, as far as possible, the introduction of the common customs tariff.'

After Article 36, this is in practice the most important exception to Articles 30 and 34. It can only be applied with respect to goods originating in third countries in free circulation in the Community.[52] This can be deduced from the case law on Article 115 discussed below according to which it constitutes a major exception to the rule laid down in Article 9 of the Treaty that such goods are assimilated to goods originating in the Community.[53] In particular, in *Donckerwolke* v. *Procureur de la République*[54] the Court stated that:

'Article 115 allows difficulties [due to differences in commercial policy capable of bringing about deflections of trade or of causing economic difficulties in certain Member States] to be avoided by giving to the Commission the power to authorise Member States to take protective measures particularly in the form of derogation from the principle of free circulation within the Community of products which originated in third countries and which were put into free circulation in one of the Member States.'

Indeed it can be described as the major exception to this rule.

9.22 From its wording it is quite clear that Article 115 continues to apply after the end of the transitional period. However, it can only apply where national measures of commercial policy have not been supplanted by Community measures. Nevertheless, the establishment of the common commercial policy is not yet complete, and in view of the grave economic situation the use of Article 115, far from receding, has increased dramatically in recent years, particularly with regard to textiles. This is clearly shown by the following table[55]:

	Number of requests to the Commission by Member States (figures in brackets concern textiles)	Number of requests granted by the Commission
1976	110 (60)	74
1977	121 (60)	79
1978	317 (258)	197
1979	347 (269)	260

9.23 Community measures supplanting national commercial policy measures will most often be based on Article 113 governing the

---

[52] Nor does Art. 115 apply to goods from third countries not yet in free circulation in the Community—even if such goods have already transited through one or more Member States. In any case, such goods fall outside the scope of this book.

[53] Para. 2.11 *et seq.* above.

[54] Case 41/76 [1976] E.C.R. 1921 at 1937, [1977] 2 C.M.L.R. 535 at 551.

[55] Source: Agence Europe 25 January 1980.

common commercial policy on trade with third countries,[56] though they may be based on other provisions of the Treaty such as Article 43 concerning the common agricultural policy. In either case such measures may take the form of autonomous Community legislation or of agreements with third States. These measures relate only to direct trade with third countries and do not cover goods in free circulation in the Community, whether they originate in the Community or in third countries. Thus they fall outside the scope of this book.[57]

Suffice it to say therefore that the systems provided for by these measures and the roles of Member States under them are varied and complex.[58] At which point the threshold is crossed beyond which Article 115 cannot be applied, is unclear. Yet it is submitted that Lux and Vogelzang[59] go too far in suggesting that Article 115 can be applied to bolster quotas divided out between Member States by the Community.

At all events, the test to be applied in each case is whether *this* product originating in *this* third country is subject to Community measures of commercial policy such as to oust Article 115.

9.24 Before examining the relevant case law and legislation, an overall description of the nature of Article 115 is required. The following will be discussed in turn: the circumstances in which the provision may be applied, the procedure to be followed, the exceptional measures which may be taken and the application of Article 115 to exports.

9.25 The circumstances in which Article 115 may be applied appear to be twofold:

(a) Where exceptional measures are necessary to 'ensure that the execution of measures of commercial policy taken in accordance with this Treaty by any Member State is not obstructed by deflection of trade'. The typical situation envisaged here is this: there are as yet no Community rules creating or banning quantitative restrictions on the import of wooden toys from Ruritania (a third country). Italy has imposed a quota or other commercial policy measure on wooden toys coming from Ruritania. However, this measure is being undermined because such toys are being put into free circulation in France and then

---

[56] On the common commercial policy see in particular Ernst and Beseler, *op. cit.* 1421; Mégret, *op. cit.* 365; Pescatore, 'External Relations in the Case Law of the Court of Justice of the European Communities' [1979] C.M.L.Rev. 615.

[57] On quantitative restrictions and measures of equivalent effect in direct trade with third countries, see note 121 to Chap. VI above.

[58] See in particular Reg. 925/79 on common rules for imports from State-trading countries ([1979] O.J. L131/1) which prohibits Member States from imposing quantitative restrictions on particular goods originating in particular East-block countries, subject, however, to various safeguard clauses. Reg. 288/82 ([1982] O.J. L35) lays down a similar prohibition with respect to particular goods originating in virtually all other countries, again subject to the application of various safeguard clauses. Neither instrument concern measures of equivalent effect.

[59] *Op. cit.* note 51 above. See generally Kretschmer, *op. cit.* note 51 above.

imported into Italy from France. Once the toys are put into free circulation in the Community they are assimilated to Community goods, so that the Italian Government cannot prevent its quota from being undermined in this way without resorting to Article 115.

According to various authors,[60] deflection of trade may also occur by the phenomenon of substitution. Here the Ruritanian toys are absorbed in the French markets (or the market of another Member State), thereby enabling French wooden toys to come on to the Italian market in their stead. Yet, even if these authors are correct in their view that this constitutes a deflection of trade, how can Article 115 be applied? It has already been explained that this provision can only be used against goods originating in third countries, and not against goods originating in the Community.

No deflection of trade will occur where the toys have acquired Community origin in France. They will have done this if they have undergone there a 'substantial process or operation that is economically justified . . ., having been carried out in an undertaking equipped for the purpose, and resulting in the manufacture of a new product or representing an important stage of manufacture' by virtue of Article 5 of Regulation 802/68 on the concept of origin of goods.[61] As already explained, Article 115 can have no application to goods originating in the Community.

It has also been suggested[62] that even under this limb of Article 115 disparities must exist between the relevant commercial policy measures of the Member States. It is true that in its answer to Written Question 772/78[63] the Commission stated that the existence of such disparities was a necessary condition for the application of Article 115. Yet it may be that Article 115 could be applied in the following hypothetical situation: France and Italy have an identical quota for toys originating in Ruritania (to return to the first example above); both quotas have been exhausted, but most of the toys put into free circulation make their way to Italy. Indeed the toys may have been imported through France with the very intention of evading the Italian quota. There is no disparity between the national measures, but it is submitted that a deflection of trade may have occurred nevertheless.

It appears that a mere danger of deflection of trade would suffice to bring Article 115 into play.[64] Naturally this would have to be a real danger, not merely a fanciful one.

---

[60] Opperman, *op. cit.* 381; Lejeune, *op. cit.* 194; Börner, *op. cit.* 73.
[61] [1968] J.O. L148/1; see para. 2.10 above.
[62] Lux, *op. cit.* 362.
[63] [1979] O.J. C45/21.
[64] Mégret, *op. cit.* 386; the Advocate General in Case 62/70 *Bock* v. *E.C.Commission* [1971] E.C.R. 897 at 916, [1972] C.M.L.R. 160.

Lastly, the national measure of commercial policy to be protected must have been taken 'in accordance with this Treaty'. This, it is submitted, merely means that the measure must be compatible with Community law.

9.26 (b) Where 'differences between such measures [of national commercial policy] lead to economic difficulties in one or more of the Member States.' It is hard to give any precise definition of 'economic difficulties' in this context, but it must be borne in mind that Article 115 constitutes an exception to one of the fundamental rules of the Treaty, so that it cannot be invoked lightly. There must also be a causal connection between the economic difficulties and the disparities between national commercial policy measures[65] which once again must be compatible with the Treaty. The view has been advanced that a serious threat of economic difficulties will suffice.[66]

9.27 Frequently situations (a) and (b) will occur at one and the same time. Yet it is widely considered that they are alternative.[67] This would appear to mean that Article 115 can be used to protect a national measure of commercial policy even in the absence of any economic difficulties or danger of such difficulties in the Member State concerned.

9.28 The procedure for applying Article 115 has been more stringent since the end of the transitional period. During the transitional period, Article 115 (2) empowered the Member States to take measures themselves in urgent cases and then to notify them to the Commission, which could confirm them or direct that the measures be abolished. In *Amministrazione delle Finanze dello Stato* v. *Rasham*[68] the Court in effect held that during the transitional period failure by the Member State to notify such measures to the Commission did not render them invalid. The Court also ruled in that case that Decision 66/532,[69] which accelerated the abolition of most customs duties and quantitative restrictions, had no bearing on Article 115 (2), which therefore continued to have effect until the end of the transitional period, namely 1 January 1970.

Since the end of the transitional period, Member States may only take measures under Article 115 on the prior authorisation of the Commission. This is shown unequivocally by the Court's case law which is discussed below. Although under Article 115 the Commission could grant such an authorisation without the Member State making a request, it is not the Commission's practice to do so.

---

[65] As to when such disparity exists, see Lux, *op, cit.* 362.
[66] Ernst and Beseler, *op, cit.*1460; Mégret, *op. cit.* 386.
[67] Oppermann, *op, cit.,* 378, Ernst and Beseler, *op. cit.* 1459, Lejeune, *op, cit.* 193, Mégret, *op. cit.* 386, Börner, *op. cit.* 72, Lux, *op. cit.* 361.
[68] Case 27/78 [1978] E.C.R. 1761, [1979] 1 C.M.L.R. 1.
[69] [1966] J.O. 165; see para. 5.01 above.

Another feature of this provision is that before granting an authorisation for exceptional measures, the Commission is called upon to 'recommend the methods for the requisite co-operation between Member States'. Some recommendations of this kind have been issued,[70] but it has long been obvious that in practice they are little more than pious hopes. This is why it has become the practice of the Commission to take decisions under Article 115 without first sending recommendations.[71] In *Bock* v. *E.C. Commission*[72] Advocate General Dutheillet de Lamotte held that this practice did not constitute a defect in form such as to vitiate a decision, notably on the grounds that 'the omission of a formality which was known to be futile would not constitute . . . a defect sufficiently substantial to vitiate the contested provision'.

9.29 As regard the measures which may be taken under Article 115, paragraph 3 states that 'in the selection of such measures, priority shall be given to those which cause the least disturbance to the functioning of the common market . . .'. This is merely an expression of the general principle that measures taken under exception clauses must be no more restricted than is necessary.[73] Accordingly, an import ban may not be authorised where a less restrictive measure would suffice. Again, the Commission may only grant authorisations for a limited period.[74]

9.30 Can Article 115 be used to restrict exports? The classic situation envisaged is where a product is in short supply; if supplies of this product are being exported from Member State A to Member State B and then on to Ruritania (a third country); if there are no Community measures governing the exportation of these particular goods to Ruritania, then may Article 115 be relied on to restrict re-exports to Ruritania? The Commission has been known to issue recommendations[75] under Article 115 in such cases to the effect that the Member States should prohibit re-exports to third countries, but it appears never to have applied binding measures to exports. In any case, Article 103 (4) is a more appropriate basis for exceptional measures designed to cope with shortages of supply. The normal case in which Article 115 is applied concerns imports and the case law and legislation discussed below concern imports only.

9.31 Having made these general remarks, we can now turn to consider the Court's case law on Article 115 before discussing the main legislation adopted by the Commission under this provision.

---

[70] *e.g.* Recom. 64/100 ([1964] J.O. 374); Recom. 67/80 ([1967] J.O. 272).

[71] In many decisions of this kind the Commission has explained why no prior recommendation had been made; see, *e.g.* Dec. of 5 March 1962 ([1962] J.O. 1099); Dec. of 31 July 1963 ([1963] J.O. 2338); Dec. 79/229 ([1979] O.J. L47/18).

[72] See note 64 above, at 916.

[73] See note 2 above.

[74] Lejeune, *op. cit.* 213.

[75] *e.g.* Recom. 71/108 ([1971] J.O. L50/7).

The case law consists of six cases, including the *Rasham* case which has already been discussed and which requires no further comment.

The first two cases, *Bock* v. *E.C. Commission*[76] and *Kaufhof* v. *E.C. Commission*[77] were based on remarkably similar facts, arising in each case after the end of the transitional period. The plaintiffs in *Bock* sought to import into the Federal Republic of Germany a consignment of preserved mushrooms originating in the People's Republic of China and in free circulation in the Netherlands. They therefore lodged an application for an import licence with the German authorities, as did one other prospective importer.

However, in the absence of common rules[78] the German authorities proceeded to apply to the Commission for permission to 'exclude from Community treatment' the import of preserved mushrooms falling under tariff heading 20.02 originating in the People's Republic of China and in free circulation in any Member State. This authorisation was duly granted by the Commission under Article 115 with respect to such mushrooms in free circulation in the Benelux countries. The plaintiffs were therefore unable to import the mushrooms into Germany.

Consequently, they brought an action under Article 173 of the Treaty to have the Commission's Decision annulled. The Commission first argued that the Decision was not of direct and individual concern to the plaintiffs within the meaning of Article 173 so that the action was inadmissible. The Court rejected the Commission's argument in the following terms:

'The applicant has challenged the decision only to the extent to which it also covers imports for which applications for import licences were already pending at the date of its entry into force. The number and identity of importers concerned in this way was already fixed and ascertainable before that date. The defendant was in a position to know that the contested provision in its decision would affect the interests and situation of those importers alone. The factual situation thus created differentiates the latter from all other persons and distinguishes them individually just as in the case of the person addressed'.

The action was therefore ruled to be admissible—a ruling of considerable significance to any person who finds himself in the same situation.

As to the substance, the Court began by stating that Article 115 constitutes an exception to Article 30 as well as to Article 113 on the common commercial policy so that derogations allowed under Article 115 must be strictly interpreted and applied. It continued:

'It appears from the file that at the date of the contested decision the German authorities were considering only two applications, amounting to a total import

---

[76] See note 64 above.
[77] Case 29/75 [1976] E.C.R. 431.
[78] Reg. 865/68 on the common organisation of the market for products processed from fruit and vegetables ([1968] O.J.Spec.Ed. 228) did not lay down common rules on quantitative restrictions with respect to third countries. Such rules did not exist until the adoption of Reg. 1927/75 ([1975] O.J. L198/7), after the material facts in the *Kaufhof* case had occurred.

of some 120 metric tons, that is to say, about 0·26 per cent., according to the defendant's own statements, of the total of 46,122 metric tons of preserved mushrooms imported into Germany in 1969. In these circumstances the Commission, by extending the authorisation at issue to an application relating to a transaction which was insignificant in terms of the effectiveness of the measure of commercial policy proposed by the Member State concerned and which in addition had been submitted at a time when the principle of the free circulation of goods applied unrestrictedly to the goods in question, has exceeded the limits of what is "necessary" within the meaning of Article 115—interpreted within the general framework of the Treaty, following the expiry of the transitional period'.

Accordingly, the contested Decision was annulled.

9.32 The *Kaufhof* case was based on virtually identical facts, with the immaterial difference that the goods in issue were preserves of beans in pod rather than preserved mushrooms. In view of the *Bock* case the Commission did not contest the admissibility of the action. Again, the Court repeated its earlier statement that since Article 115 constitutes an exception to Articles 30 and 113, derogations allowed under it are to be strictly construed and applied (a statement which also appears in the subsequent cases on Article 115). However, the Court set out rather different reasons for annulling the Commission's Decision from those given in *Bock*:

'It appears from the statements made by the defendant's Agent during the oral proceedings that it considers that the authorisation requested should be granted if the measure of commercial policy adopted by the Member State concerned is compatible with the Treaty, without having to take account of the reasons on which that measure is based, and when it involves an absolute prohibition on imports, without having to take account of the quantity, whether large or negligible, concerned in the applications already received.

By failing to review the reasons put forward by the Member State concerned in order to justify the measures of commercial policy which it wishes to introduce, the Commission was in breach of its duty under Article 115 to examine whether the measures have been "taken in accordance with this Treaty" and whether the protective measures sought are necessary within the meaning of the same provision.

By extending the authorisation to applications already received, without taking account of the size or insignificance of the quantity in question in these applications, the Commission has also exceeded the limits of its discretion'.

In *Bock* the Court had annulled the Commission's Decision because of the insignificant amount of imports involved. On the other hand, in *Kaufhof* the Court pointed to the Commission's failure to review the reasons put forward by the Member State to justify its request,[79] and to the retroactive nature of the Decision.

9.33 The other three judgments of the Court on Article 115 are rather different from *Bock* and *Kaufhof* in that they were all delivered in reply to questions put under Article 177 as to the powers which Member States may exercise under Article 115 before making an

---

[79] Reich, 'La politique commerciale commune de la C.E.E. et le contrôle de l'utilisation de la clause de sauvegarde de l'article 115 du traité CEE' [1978] R.T.D.E. 33.

application to the Commission. Therefore the powers and duties of the Commission were not directly in issue.

The first of this batch of cases is *Donckerwolcke* v. *Procureur de la République*.[80] There a reference arose out of criminal proceedings brought against a number of persons who had imported various consignments of cloth sacks from Belgium into France in 1969 (before the end of the transitional period) and in 1970 (after the end of the transitional period). In the customs documents the importers gave the Belgo-Luxembourg Economic Union as the place of origin of the goods. Subsequent inquiries revealed, however, that the goods in fact originated in Lebanon and Syria and were in free circulation in Belgium; the importers were therefore charged before the French courts with making false customs declarations. The object of the questions was essentially to ascertain whether, during and after the transitional period, it was compatible with Article 30 for a Member State to require declarations of origin to be made with respect to imports and to subject imports to a system of import licences so as to monitor them with a view to applying Article 115.

The Court began by considering the situation obtaining after the expiry of the transitional period. As explained earlier in this book, the Court held that goods in free circulation in the Community though originating in a third country were totally assimilated to goods originating in the Community[81]; that the requirement of import licences even as a pure formality was contrary to Article 30[82]; that it was compatible with Article 30 for a Member State to require an importer to make a declaration of origin of goods in so far as he knew or could reasonably be expected to know that origin[83] (probably a Member State may impose this requirement even without obtaining an authorisation under Article 115, though the Court does not spell this out); but that it was contrary to Article 30 for a Member State to impose penalties for making a false declaration, which were excessive in regard to the purely administrative nature of the contravention.[84] For the present purposes the most important passage of the judgment is the ruling to the effect that the requirement of an import licence is contrary to the Treaty unless the goods are the subject of a derogation properly authorised by the Commission under Article 115. Implied in this is the assertion that after the end of the transitional period a Member State requires authorisation from the Commission before it can take exceptional measures under Article 115. A Member State can no longer take such measures on its own and submit them to the Commission for subsequent approval.

---

[80] See note 54 above; case notes by Schmidt [1977] EuR. 263; Usher [1977] E.L.Rev. 304.
[81] Para. 2.12 above.
[82] Para. 7.03 above.
[83] Para. 7.13 above.
[84] Para. 7.11 above.

However, the Court went on to hold that during the transitional period the Member States could do precisely this, as indeed the second paragraph of Article 115 makes clear: at that time a Member State could take exceptional measures in case of urgency on condition that it notified them to the other Member States and the Commission subsequently; the Commission then had the power to require the Member State concerned to amend or abolish its unilateral measures. Without considering the requirement of urgency at all, the Court concluded that 'the obligations imposed on the importer of goods put into free circulation in another Member State to obtain an import licence was, so far as its principle is concerned, compatible with Community law in its state of development at that time'. The Court did add one rider, however: by virtue of Articles 31 and 32[85] the exceptional measures could not be more restrictive then than they were on 1 January 1958.

9.34　In *Cayrol* v. *Rivoira*[86] many of the points already decided in *Donckerwolcke* reared their heads again. In December 1970 and December 1971 Cayrol imported into France various consignments of table grapes dispatched from Italy by Rivoira. The grapes bore the Italian export mark and were accompanied by the certificate of the *Istituto Nazionale per il Commercio Estero* certifying that the goods were in conformity with the quality standards and stating that they were of Italian origin. This proved to be false: the grapes were in fact of Spanish origin and had been put into free circulation in Italy. Since the French import quota for grapes from Spain had been exhausted, both Cayrol and Rivoira were charged with and convicted of having imported prohibited goods by means of a false declaration of origin and on the basis of false or inaccurate documents. Cayrol, having reached a settlement with the French authorities as to the amount of the fine, now brought an action before the Italian courts to recover from Rivoira part of this sum on the grounds that Rivoira had deceived the customs authorities as to the origin of the grapes. The Italian court then put a series of questions to the Court of Justice as to the application of Article 115. In broad terms, the object of these questions was to establish whether Article 115 could be applied in the circumstances and whether the French measures complied with Community law.

The Court first found that it followed from a combination of Regulation 2513/69[87] on the co-ordination of treatment accorded by Member States to fruit and vegetable imports from third countries and of the Agreement concluded between the EEC and Spain on 29 June 1970[88] that table grapes from Spain were not covered by a Community import system between 1 July and 31 December.

---

[85] Paras. 5.01 and 6.02 above.
[86] Case 52/77 [1977] E.C.R. 2261, [1978] 2 C.M.L.R. 253.
[87] [1969] J.O. L318/6.
[88] See Reg. 1524/70 ([1970] J.O. L182/1).

Therefore Article 115 was not ousted during that period. Thus it is clear beyond doubt that Community rules on imports may apply for part of the year only so that Article 115 may be applied during the rest of the year.

In so far as it concerns us in the present context, the rest of the judgment adds nothing to the *Donckerwolcke* decision.

9.35 The sequel to *Cayrol* was *Procureur de la République* v. *Rivoira*,[89] involving a reference from the French Court seised of the criminal proceedings. Unfortunately, in *Cayrol* the Court had not stated in express terms that France was not entitled to prohibit the importation of the grapes without prior authorisation from the Commission under Article 115—though this is undoubtedly the effect of the judgment. This was the object of the French court's first question.

The Court began by stating that Regulation 2513/69 only restricted direct imports from third countries of the products concerned: it did not and could not restrict or prohibit inter-State trade of products in free circulation, because this would constitute a derogation from the fundamental rules of the Treaty on the free movement of goods. Only Article 115 gave the Commission power to authorise a Member State to take protective measures against products originating in third countries and in free circulation in Member States. Article 115 can only be applied if the substantive and procedural conditions set out in that provision are fulfilled. It followed that in 1970 and 1971 a Member State could not prohibit the importation of grapes in free circulation without the prior authorisation of the Commission under Article 115.

The second and final question was whether criminal penalties could be imposed on persons making false declarations of the kind in question. The Court replied that

'although the fact that Spanish grapes imported into France from Italy have been declared as being of Italian origin may in appropriate cases give grounds for the application of the criminal penalties provided against false declarations, it would be disproportionate to apply without distinction the criminal penalties provided in respect of false declarations made in order to effect prohibited imports'.

This adds nothing to *Donckerwolcke* and *Cayrol*, but it clarifies those judgments: it shows that once a Member State has been authorised to prohibit imports under Article 115, it may impose higher penalties for false declarations than it could previously.

9.36 This case law has answered a number of important questions about Article 115, but the accidents of litigation have left untouched the questions discussed at paragraph 9.27 above: can Article 115 be used to protect a national measure of commercial policy even in the absence of any economic difficulties or danger of such difficulties in

---

[89] Case 179/78 [1979] E.C.R. 1147, [1979] 3 C.M.L.R. 456.

the Member State concerned? As will be seen, the Commission has taken the view that Article 115 can be applied in such circumstances.
9.37   As regards the measures adopted by the Commission under Article 115, a glance at the table of figures set out earlier in this section will suffice to show that these are legion. We can only consider here the legislation of general application and certain more specific Decisions which are indicative of present trends.

The first Decision laying down general procedures and criteria for the application of Article 155 was Decision 71/202.[90] This was subsequently modified by Decision 73/55.[91] These Decisions provided for Member States to take exceptional measures without prior authorisation from the Commission. Although the *Donkerwolcke*, *Cayrol* and *Rivoira* judgments did not concern those Decisions, they stated that prior authorisation from the Commission is necessary for the taking of exceptional measures since the end of the transitional period. It was clear therefore that these Decisions were incompatible with the Treaty. Indeed, Advocates General Capotorti and Warner stated this expressly in the *Donckerwolcke* and *Cayrol* cases respectively.[92].

9.38   Accordingly, the Commission adopted Decision 80/47[93] which effects a fundamental reform in the application of Article 115. In view of its importance, it is necessary to reproduce in full various provisions of that Decision.

The scope of the Decision is laid down by Article 1 as follows:

'This Decision shall apply to imports into a Member State of products originating in a third country which have been put into free circulation in the Community, in cases where they are subject either to quantitative import restrictions in that Member State or to voluntary export restraint measures applied by the third country concerned by virtue of a trade agreement and are likely to be the subject of protective measures under Article 115 of the Treaty'.

The Decision then goes on to make provision for two types of exceptional measure: intra-Community surveillance (Article 2) and protective measures (Article 3).

9.39   Article 2 begins:

'1. Where there is a danger that imports into a Member State of a product referred to in Article 1 will give rise to economic difficulties, imports of that product may, following an authorisation given by the Commission for a specific period, be made subject to the issue of an import document.

2. Without prejudice to the provisions of Article 3, this document shall be issued by the Member State concerned, for any quantity requested and free of charge, within a maximum period of five working days from the date on which the application by the importer was received irrespective of where he has his place of business in the Community'.

---

[90] [1971] O.J. L121/26.
[91] [1973] O.J. L80/22.
[92] [1976] E.C.R. at 1948, [1977] E.C.R. at 2290 respectively.
[93] [1980] O.J. L16/14, amended by corrigendum [1980] O.J. L89/22, see Kretschmer, *op. cit.* note 51 above.

Article 2 (2) makes it clear that a Member State may not withhold an import document. Article 2 (3) lays down precisely which particulars a Member State shall supply for the purpose of obtaining authorisation to apply this system of intra-Community surveillance. Article 2 (4) provides that a Member State which has obtained such authorisation may only require the following information from an applicant for an import document:

(a) the name of the importer and of the consignor in the exporting Member State;
(b) the country of origin and the exporting Member State;
(c) a description of the product with details of:
- its trade designation,
- its heading number in the Common Customs Tariff and the NIMEXE code;[94]
(d) the value and the quantity of the product in the units customarily in use in trade;
(e) the scheduled date or dates for delivery;
(f) supporting evidence that the product is in free circulation. Failing such supporting evidence, the validity of the import document shall be limited to a period of one month following the issue of the document.

9.40 As to protective measures Article 3 (1) provides:

'Where imports into a Member State of a product referred to in Article 1 give rise to economic difficulties, the Member State in question may take protective measures after obtaining the prior authorisation of the Commission, which shall determine the conditions and details of such measures'.

Article 3 (2) stipulates what information a Member State must provide to the Commission to obtain such authorisation, including details for the two preceding years and the current year of the volume and quantity of imports of the product in question and of the economic difficulties in the sector. Article 3 (3) and (4) provides:

'(3) The introduction of the request by the Member States may not prevent the issue under the conditions and within the period laid down in Article 2 of import documents for which application was made prior to the Commission's decision.

(4) However, where the Member State finds that the volume or total quantity covered by applications pending in respect of the product in question originating in the third country concerned is more than either 5 per cent. of possible direct imports from the third country concerned or 1 per cent. of the total extra-EEC imports during the latest 12 months period for which statistical information is available:
(i) the maximum period for the issue of import documents shall be increased to 10 working days from the date on which the application by the importer was received;
(ii) the Member State may reject the application for import documents if the Commission's decision authorises it to do so.'

---

[94] See Reg. 3062/79 ([1979] O.J. L346).

Article 3 (5) requires the Member State to inform applicants for import documents of the introduction of a request for protective measures and to send a copy of this request to the other Member States.

Article 3 (6) requires the Commission to decide on the request of the Member State within five working days of its receipt.

The crux of this system is that a Member State may no longer take exceptional measures without prior authorisation from the Commission, which principle is in keeping with the Court's case law. The only action which a Member State may take under Articles 2 and 3 without such prior authorisation is to wait an additional five working days before granting an import licence, where the conditions set out in Article 3 (4) are fulfilled; but this can only be relied on where the Commission has already authorised the Member State to take intra-Community surveillance measures under Article 2.

A further important feature of this system is that it only provides for exceptional measures where economic difficulties exist actually (Article 3) or potentially (Article 2). Thus it does not allow for the protection of national measures of commercial policy where the applicant Member State is not suffering economic difficulties by virtue of the imports in question and is not in danger of doing so. As will be seen below, however, the Commission has subsequently allowed the United Kingdom to apply intra-Community protective measures to bananas originating in certain countries, although there is of course no British production of bananas.

It is not entirely clear from the wording of Decision 80/47 whether intra-Community surveillance measures must be taken under Article 2 before protective measures may be taken under Article 3. This requirement is not expressly stated, but it appears from the terms of Article 3 that it will normally be applied once intra-Community measures are in force.[95]

9.41   Article 4 of the Decision relates to proof of origin. It will be recalled that according to the case law of the Court a Member State may require an importer of goods from another Member State to state their origin on the import document. However, so long as no authorisation has been granted by the Commission under Article 115 this information may only be required of the importer in so far as he knows or can reasonably be expected to know it. Since Article 4 applies where such authorisation has already been granted by the Commission, it is wider:

'1. As part of the completion of formalities in connection with the importation of products of a type which are subject to intra-Community surveillance

---

[95] Kretschmer, *op. cit.* note 51 above, states in his note 49 that the wording of the Decision does not require Art. 2 measures to have been taken before protective measures are authorised under Art. 3. However, he points out that in practice a Member State will normally need to take surveillance measures under Art. 2 so as to obtain the statistical evidence necessary for an application under Art. 3.

measures or protective measures, the relevant authorities of the importing Member State may ask the importer to state the origin of the products on the customs declaration or on the application for an import document.

2. Additional proof may be requested only in cases where serious and well-founded doubts make such proof essential in order to establish the true origin of the products in question. However, a request for such additional proof may not in itself prevent the import of the goods'.

9.42 The transitional and final provisions are laid down in Article 5 which provides:

'1. This Decision shall apply from 1 April 1980.

2. Commission Decision 71/202/EEC of 12 May 1971, as amended by Decision 73/55/EEC of 9 March 1973, shall be repealed as from that date.

3. Measures taken by the Member States in accordance with Article 1 of Decision 71/202/EEC shall remain valid until the grant of an authorisation by the Commission pursuant to Article 2 of this Decision, or until 30 June 1980, whichever is the earlier.

4. Requests for such authorisations must be lodged with the Commission not later than 30 April 1980.

5. The Commission's decision on the requests will be taken not later than 30 June 1980'.

In accordance with Article 5 the Commission adopted Decision 80/605 [96] on 27 June 1980. This authorised each Member State to introduce until 31 December 1981 and in accordance with Decision 80/47, intra-Community surveillance of the products listed in the Annexes to Decision 80/605. As one would expect, textile products and footwear account for the majority of the items listed. For other products it extends the time limit laid down in Article 5 (3) of Decision 80/47 to 31 July 1980. [97]

9.43 Shortly after this, the Commission adopted Decision 80/776 [98] which shows that the procedures and conditions laid down in Decision 80/47 are not exclusive: the Commission is prepared to grant authorisations under Article 115 in cases where the conditions

---

[96] [1980] O.J. L164/20. Dec. 80/605 has now been replaced by Dec. 82/205 ([1982] O.J. L97/1) authorising each Member State to introduce until 30 June 1983 intra-Community surveillance of the products set out in the Annexes to the later Dec.

[97] In the recitals to Decision 80/605 the Commission has set out its criteria in deciding whether to grant an authorisation. It begins by stating that:

'Whereas the information received [from the Member States] was then examined as regards the economic difficulties alleged, that is in relation to the development of such factors as national production, imports, consumption, the market share held by national production, by imports from third countries and the third country concerned in the application, prices charged by national producers and by importers on the domestic markets, and employment in the sector concerned.'

It goes on to state that

– no surveillance would be agreed to where, for the reference years set out in Dec. 80/47, there had been no deflection of trade and no intra-Community licence applications had been submitted;

– an exception would be made to this rule for Group I textiles as defined by Reg. 3059/78 ([1978] O.J. L365/1) as last amended by Reg. 3063/79 ([1979] O.J. L347/1) in view of the sensitivity of these products;

– actual or potential economic difficulties may generally be regarded as negligible as regards those third countries from which the total possible imports to the Community taken together are less than 1 per cent. of the quantitative limit at Community level.

[98] [1980] O.J. L224/15.

set out in Decision 80/47 are not satisfied. Decision 80/776 permits the United Kingdom to take intra-Community surveillance measures under Article 2 (4) of Decision 80/47 and to require proof of origin under Article 4 of Decision 80/47 with respect to bananas originating in certain third countries. As explained earlier, no such authoriation could be granted under Decision 80/47 because, in the absence of any national production, no economic difficulties were caused to the United Kingdom by banana imports. The reasoning behind the Decision is explained by the following recitals:

> 'Whereas the first Article of Protocol 4 to the Lomé Convention signed on 31 October 1979 and put into effect unilaterally by the Community from 1 March 1980 provides that "as regards its exports of bananas to the markets of the Community, no ACP State will be placed, as regards access to its traditional markets and its advantages on those markets, in a less favourable situation than in the past or at present";
>
> Whereas to fulfil that requirement the United Kingdom, which constitutes a major traditional market for certain ACP States, still makes imports of bananas originating in other non-member countries subject to quantitative restrictions;
>
> Whereas, in order to control imports of such products via the other Member States, the United Kingdom has applied to the Commission for authorisation to introduce intra-Community surveillance of such imports;
>
> Whereas, although under Commission Decision 80/47/EEC, adopted by virtue of the powers conferred on the Commission by Article 115 of the Treaty, such surveillance measures can only be taken where there is a danger that the imports will give rise to economic difficulties in the Member States concerned. It does not appear necessary in these very specific circumstances to require compliance with that condition, since the surveillance measures which the United Kingdom wishes to introduce are sufficiently justified by the need to ensure the effectiveness of the commercial policy measures it has to implement to fulfil the requirements of Protocol 4 to the Lomé Convention'.

This Decision was followed first by measures authorising the United Kingdom temporarily to suspend the grant of import licences for bananas originating in certain third countries[99] and finally by a Decision[100] authorising it to impose import quotas.

9.44   This same tendency to create exceptions to the principles laid down in Decision 80/47 can be observed in the Commission's Statement concerning Article 115 made in response to the Council's Resolution of 22 July 1980 concerning access to Community public supply contracts for products originating in third countries.[101] As part of the Multilateral Agreements concluded under the auspices of the GATT and generally known as the Tokyo Round, the Com-

---

[99] Dec. 80/949 ([1980] O.J. L267/35), extended by Dec. 80/1088 ([1980] O.J. L320/35); see also Dec. 81/85 ([1981] O.J. L58/31) authorising Italy to take intra-Community surveillance measures with respect to bananas originating in certain third countries.

[100] Dec. 80/1158 ([1980] O.J. L343/41). That Dec. has now been extended in time ([1981] O.J. C334/13) and is the subject of an action for annulment in Case 91/82 *Chris International* v. *E.C. Commission*.

[101] Both the statement and the resolution are to be found at [1980] O.J. C211. Neither has a binding effect in law: Case 59/75 *Pubblico Ministero* v. *Manghera* [1976] E.C.R. 91, [1976] 1 C.M.L.R. 557; Case 43/75 *Defrenne* v. *Sabena* [1976] E.C.R. 455, [1976] 2 C.M.L.R. 98.

munity had concluded an Agreement on government procurement.[102] By its Resolution of 22 July 1980 the Council declared that 'Member States may continue to apply, in accordance with the Treaty, existing commercial policy measures in respect of public supply contracts' falling outside the Agreement on government procurement. The Resolution further 'note[d] the possibility referred to by the Commission of taking any necessary protective measures, under Article 115 of the Treaty, to ensure that the implementation of such provisions is not obstructed by deflection of trade'.

The Commission's Statement is in the same vein:

'The Commission notes the concern expressed by the Council in its Resolution.

The Commission is aware that in awarding public supply contracts Member States may still, in accordance with the Treaty, apply certain measures of national commercial policy with regard to the eligibility of products originating in third countries for such contracts. The Commission recognises that, until these national measures are harmonised within the framework of the contractual or unilateral common commercial policy and in the light of the outcome of current or future international negotiations, their application may give rise to difficulty in cases where tenders include products originating in third countries in free circulation in another Member State.

The Commission would recall that Article 115 of the Treaty enables the efficacy of such national measures to be safeguarded against deflection of trade resulting from the free movement within the Community of products originating in third countries.

In accordance with Article 115 of the Treaty, the Commission intends to authorise those Member States concerned which have applied for such authorisation to provide, in respect of all entities not covered by the Agreement, in respect of entities covered by the Agreement, vis-à-vis non-signatory countries and in respect of entities covered by the Agreement, but as regards products or contracts not covered by it, for the exclusion from their public contracts of certain products or categories of products originating in third countries which are in free circulation in another Member State, in all cases where similar arrangements are made as regards directly imported products originating in third countries . . .'

There is no mention here of any economic difficulties, nor is Decision 80/47 referred to.[103]

ARTICLE 222

9.45 Article 222 provides:

'This Treaty shall in no way prejudice the rules in Member States governing the system of property ownership'.

Article 222 is not one of the most straightforward provisions in the Treaty. It appears to have been conceived primarily to show that

---

[102] See Dec. 80/271 ([1980] O.J. L71/1). See para. 12.23 below.
[103] It is true that the Resolution and the Statement closely mirror a Resolution and a Statement on the same subject made on 21 December 1976, when the Tokyo Round negotiations were still under way: [1977] O.J. C11/1.

nationalisation was compatible with the Treaty.[104] However, the position of nationalised industries under Community law cannot be explored here.[105] At all events it is suggested that Article 222 does not permit discrimination by a nationalised industry against imported goods.[106]

This provision has been considered by the Court in *Consten and Grundig* v. *E.C. Commission*,[107] *Parke, Davis* v. *Centrafarm*[108] and *Italy* v. *E.C. Commission*.[109] In each of these cases it held that Article 222 could not be relied on. In particular, in the first two cases[110] it held that it was compatible with Article 222 for the general rules of the Treaty to affect the exercise of industrial property rights, so long as their existence was not affected.

Indeed, it is doubtful if Article 222 can ever constitute an exception to Articles 30 to 34.

ARTICLE 223

9.46   Article 223 provides:

'1. The provisions of this Treaty shall not preclude the application of the following rules:

(a) . . .

(b) Any Member State may take such measures as it considers necessary for the protection of the essential interests of its security which are connected with the production of or trade in arms, munitions and war material; such measures shall not adversely affect the conditions of competition in the common market regarding products which are not intended for specifically military purposes.

2. During the first year after the entry into force of this Treaty, the Council shall, acting unanimously, draw up a list of products to which the provisions of paragraph 1 (b) shall apply.

3. The Council may, acting unanimously on a proposal from the Commission, make changes in this list'.

This must be read in conjunction with Article 225, which provides:

'If measures taken in the circumstances referred to in Articles 223 and 224 have the effect of distorting the conditions of competition in the common market, the Commission shall, together with the State concerned, examine how these measures can be adjusted to the rules laid down in this Treaty.

By way of derogation from the procedure laid down in Articles 169 and 170, the Commission or any Member State may bring the matter directly before the Court of Justice if it considers that another Member State is making improper use of the powers provided for in Articles 223 and 224. The Court of Justice shall give its ruling in camera'.

---

[104] Neri and Sperl *Répertoire du Traité CEE* (1960), 410; see also Written Question 346/80 ([1980] O.J. C213/6)..
[105] See para. 4.05 and Chap. XI of this book.
[106] Hochbaum in Groeben, Boeckh, Thiesing, *op. cit.* note 1 above, Vol. I, 657.
[107] Cases 56 and 58/64 [1966] E.C.R. 299, [1966] C.M.L.R. 418.
[108] Case 24/67 [1968] E.C.R. 55, [1968] C.M.L.R. 47.
[109] Case 32/65 [1966] E.C.R. 389, [1969] C.M.L.R. 39.
[110] Para. 8.60 above.

9.47 'Security' in Article 223 (1) (*b*) refers both to internal and external threats to the State. However, the use of the terms 'war material' and 'specifically military purposes' indicates that the provision does not cover security matters normally dealt with by the police, such as crime detection and prevention and traffic regulation.[111]

The term 'arms, munitions and war material' is contrasted with 'products which are not intended for specifically military purposes'. Thus supplies such as petrol, which can be used for military purposes but are not specifically intended for them, are not arms, munitions or war material within the meaning of Article 223. Daig suggests[112] that 'war material' extends to items which are neither arms nor munitions, such as military uniforms, and that it covers goods required by the military even in peacetime. The exception clause in Article 223 (1) (*b*) only operates with respect to goods figuring at the material time on the list provided for in Article 223 (2). In answer to Written Question 336/79[113] the Council has stated that such a list was drawn up on 15 April 1958 and has not been published or amended up to the date of that answer (November 1979).

It would seem clear that the measures which Member States may take under Article 223 (1) (*b*) include quantitative restrictions and measures of equivalent effect with respect to goods figuring on the list[114] where such measures are necessary. The wording of the provision ('any Member State may take such measures as it considers necessary') shows that the appreciation of the necessity lies with the Member State, though it may be subject to the judicial control of the Court. Article 223 does not permit any exceptional measures at all with respect to goods not appearing on the list.

9.48 Should the Commission or a Member State consider that another Member State is making improper use of these powers, then by virtue of Article 225 it can bring the matter to the Court without sending the reasoned opinion required by Articles 169 and 170 respectively. This exception was presumably created in view of the likely urgency of such an action. The stipulation in Article 225 (2) that proceedings are to be held in camera is an exception to the rule in Article 28 of the Protocol on the Statute of the Court of Justice of the EEC, which states that the hearings shall be in open court unless the Court 'decides otherwise for serious reasons'.[115]

---

[111] Daig in Groeben, Boeck, Thiesing, *op. cit.* note 1 above, Vol. I, 663.

[112] Daig *Op. cit.* 664.

[113] [1979] O.J. C310/5.

[114] Daig, *op. cit.* 662; on measures adopted under Art. 223 see generally the Advocate General in Case 15/69 *Württembergische Milchverwerkung- Südmilch* v. *Ugliola* [1969] E.C.R. at 373, [1970] C.M.L.R. 194.

[115] On Art. 225 (2) proceedings generally see Gori, *op. cit.* 309.

ARTICLE 224

9.49 Article 224 provides:

> 'Member States shall consult each other with a view to taking together the steps needed to prevent the functioning of the common market being affected by measures which a Member State may be called upon to take in the event of serious internal disturbances affecting the maintenance of law and order, in the event of war, serious international tension constituting a threat of war, or in order to carry out obligations it has accepted for the purpose of maintaining peace and international security'.

At first sight this provision appears merely to impose an obligation on Member States—to consult each other on the occurrence of one of the serious events enumerated there—but not to vest any powers in the Member States. However, that Article 224 does give rise to powers on the part of the Member States is shown by the reference in Article 225 to 'the powers provided for in Articles 223 and 224'.[116]

9.50 Unlike Article 224, the exceptional measures envisaged by this provision are not limited to arms, munitions and war material. It empowers Member States to impose quantitative restrictions and measures of equivalent effect with respect to any category of goods, including the sequestration of or import bans on goods of nationals of a particular third country or territory, which is a protagonist to international tension. This is possibly the only instance in the Treaty where goods can be discriminated against by reason of the nationality of their owner, rather than their origin.[117] Indeed, if the circumstances set out in Article 224 arise, virtually any provision of the Treaty may be disregarded.[118]

What are these circumstances? Broadly speaking, they are the existence or serious threat of war, civil war or sedition or the existence of obligations which a Member State has 'accepted for the purpose of maintaining peace and international security', by which is meant primarily UN resolutions.[119] Thus a gamut of very different situations is covered. For instance, all the Member States may be affected in the same way, or only one may be affected. Again, the measures will normally be very urgent, but they need not be, as where measures are taken against a distant territory that constitutes no real security threat to the Member States.

9.51 In view of this, it is perhaps too sweeping to suggest that in applying Article 224 Member States are never required to ensure that the functioning of the common market be disturbed as little as possible.[120] Frequently measures taken under Article 224 will be so urgent that the Member State will have no time to take this factor

---

[116] Müller-Heidelberg, *op. cit.* 315-6; Daig, *op. cit.* 660. For the text of Art. 225 see para. 9.46 above.

[117] Para. 2.19 above.

[118] See generally *Ugliola*, note 114 above.

[119] Neri and Sperl, *op. cit.* note 104 above, at 412.

[120] See Daig, *op. cit.* 661.

into account, but this will not always be so. It is suggested that the question whether the Member States must consult each other before taking any measures,[121] should be answered in the same light.

At all events, measures taken under Article 224 may be subjected to the procedures set out in Article 225, which has already been discussed above.[122]

Article 224 has in particular been applied by the Member States in adopting sanctions against Rhodesia[123] pursuant to a United Nations Security Council Resolution adopted after that Country's Unilateral Declaration of Independence and against Iran[124] after the taking of the American hostages in Teheran. The latter case was somewhat unusual in that no resolution on sanctions was passed by the Security Council so that there was technically no obligation in international law on the Member States to impose the sanctions: the requirement that there be an 'obligation . . . accepted' was thus somewhat liberally interpreted. The sanctions adopted against Argentina following that country's invasion of the Falkland Islands are enshrined in a Council Regulation[124a] based on Article 113 of the Treaty relating to the common commercial policy. However, the preamble to that Regulation states that the Member States have consulted each other pursuant to Article 244.

ARTICLE 233

9.52   Article 233 provides as follows:

'The provisions of this Treaty shall not preclude the existence or completion of regional unions between Belgium and Luxembourg, or between Belgium, Luxembourg and the Netherlands, to the extent that the objectives of these regional unions are not attained by the application of this Treaty'.

The regional unions in question are, first, the Belgo-Luxembourg Economic Union created by a Convention of 1921; and the Benelux, set up in London during the Second World War by a Convention between the Governments in exile of Belgium, the Netherlands and Luxembourg.[125]

By virtue of Article 233, the Member States concerned may integrate more rapidly than the Community as a whole. On the other hand, this provision does not apply where the objectives of these regional unions are attained by application of the Treaty of

---

[121] Daig, *op. cit.* 667; Kuyper, 'Sanctions against Rhodesia. The EEC and the Implementation of General International Rules' [1975] C.M.L. Rev. 231; *The Implementation of International Sanctions* (1978).

[122] Para. 9.46 above.

[123] See Kuyper, note 121 above; Written Questions 526/75 ([1976] O.J. C89/6) and 527/75 ([1976] O.J. C89/8).

[124] E.C. Bull 5 [1980] 26.

[124a] Reg. 877/82 ([1982] O.J. L102/1).

[125] See Van Damme, 'Benelux and its Relationship with the EEC' in *Legal Problems of an Enlarged European Community*, ed. Bathurst, (1972).

Rome. Both Reuter[126] and Petersmann[127] agree that within these limits Article 233 constitutes an exception to the rule against non-discrimination—a fact which is obviously of some significance for the interpretation of Articles 30 to 36. It would appear to follow that the Member States concerned, acting within these limits, may grant preferential treatment to one another pursuant to the BLEU or Benelux Conventions; the resulting less favourable treatment of other Member States would not constitute arbitrary discrimination contrary to Article 36.[128]

ARTICLE 234

9.53 The first paragraph of Article 234 provides:

> 'The rights and obligations arising from agreements concluded before the entry into force of this Treaty between one or more Member States on the one hand, and one or more third countries on the other, shall not be affected by the provisions of this Treaty'.

This is qualified by the second paragraph, which reads:

> 'To the extent that such agreements are not compatible with this Treaty, the Member State or States concerned shall take all appropriate steps to eliminate the incompatibilities established. Member States shall, where necessary, assist each other to this end and shall, where appropriate, adopt a common attitude'.

The third and final paragraph of Article 234 is not relevant for present purposes.

By virtue of Article 5 of the first Act of Accession, Article 234 applies for the new Member States to agreements or conventions concluded before accession.[129] Article 5 of the Act of Accession of Greece contains a stipulation of like effect.

It should also be pointed out that paragraph 5 of Article 37, which governs State monopolies, provides that 'the obligations on Member States shall be binding only in so far as they are compatible with existing international agreements'. This provision, which only applies to State monopolies, is generally taken to go beyond the first paragraph of Article 234. It is discussed in a later chapter of this book.[130]

9.54 The exception clause contained in the first paragraph is limited in four ways:

   (i) It only applies to agreements concluded before the Treaty came into force or, for the new Member States, before Accession.

   (ii) It only applies to agreements concluded between one or more Member States on the one hand and one or more third

---

[126] In *Les Novelles, Droit des Communautés Européennes* (1969), para. 2.13.
[127] In Groeben, Boeckh, Thiesing, *op. cit.* Vol. II, 734.
[128] Para. 8.05 above.
[129] See generally Puissochet, *The Enlargement of the European Communities* (1975).
[130] See para. 11.17 below.

countries on the other. It therefore does not apply to agreements between Member States.

This principle was forcefully laid down by the Court in one of its earliest judgments concerning the EEC Treaty, in Case 10/61 *E.C. Commission* v. *Italy*.[131] The Commission claimed that Italy was infringing the Treaty by failing to reduce its customs duties on certain goods from other Member States in accordance with Articles 12 and 14 of the Treaty requiring the gradual abolition of customs duties between Member States. In its defence Italy claimed that it was obliged to charge the higher level of duty by virtue of the 1956 Geneva Agreements concluded under the auspices of GATT. To this end Italy invoked Article 234. However, this defence was rejected by the Court, which ruled that 'in matters governed by the EEC Treaty, that Treaty takes precedence over agreements concluded between Member States before its entry into force, including agreements made within the framework of GATT'.

9.55 Yet it is submitted that there are exceptions to this rule. If a Member State was required to carry out certain border controls under a prior treaty with a third State, that obligation would fall within Article 234—even as regards controls at frontiers with other Member States. Now there is no reason why the result should be different where more than one Member State is bound by a prior treaty obligation.

This question was considered by the Advocate General in *Henn and Darby*.[132] This glamorous case has already received considerable prominence in earlier chapters of this book, so that it is not necessary to rehearse all the facts once again. Suffice it to say that the Court of Justice had been asked a series of questions by the House of Lords as to the compatibility with Community law of a prohibition on imports of indecent and obscene articles. In its seventh and final question the House of Lords asked, *inter alia*, whether this prohibition was lawful in view of the Geneva Convention of 1923 for the suppression of the traffic in obscene publications and of Article 234.

The Advocate General found that the 1923 Convention lent itself to two possible interpretations:

– either the Convention only created, at all events as regards imports and exports, a series of bilateral obligations between the parties; if so, the Convention had been superseded as between Member States by the EEC Treaty in line with the Court's ruling in *E.C. Commission* v. *Italy*;
– alternatively, the Convention created multilateral obligations between all the parties to it, so that States which are parties to the Convention but are not Members of the Community have

---

[131] [1962] E.C.R. 1, [1962] C.M.L.R. 187.
[132] Case 34/79 [1979] E.C.R. 3795, [1980] 1 C.M.L.R. 246; see paras. 5.06, 8.08 and 8.20 above.

a right to the enforcement of the Convention even as respects imports and exports between Member States on the footing that a 'flourishing trade in obscene material' within the Community could prejudice other States' efforts to suppress the traffic in it. (Although the Advocate General did not refer to illicit trafficking in drugs, the same reasoning could clearly apply to a prior multilateral convention aimed at combatting that problem.)

Since the Court of Justice had no jurisdiction to interpret the 1923 Convention, the Advocate General concluded that it was for the national court to decide which of these two interpretations was correct.

The Court, however, saw no need to enter into these finer points: it merely replied that 'in so far as a Member State avails itself of the reservation relating to the protection of public morality provided for in Article 36 of the Treaty, the provisions of Article 234 do not preclude that State from fulfilling the obligations arising from the Geneva Convention of 1923 . . .'

9.56   (iii) the exception clause in Article 234 (1) is also subject to the limitation contained in Article 234 (2): Member States are required to do all in their power to eliminate any inconsistencies between the Treaty and prior agreements. At the very least, this means that if an agreement with one or more third countries comes up for renewal after the Treaty entered into force (or, for new Member States, since accession), then no Member State may renew it unless elements incompatible with the Treaty are removed from that agreement.

(iv) the exception laid down by Article 234 (1) only applies to obligations of Member States and to rights of third States, and not the other way round; thus a Member State cannot, it appears, rely on Article 234 for the continued enjoyment of rights derived from a prior treaty with a third State and which conflict with Community law: Case 10/61 *E.C. Commission* v. *Italy*, already referred to.

9.57   Further light on the meaning of this exception clause has been shed by the recent ruling in *Attorney General* v. *Burgoa*.[133] The defendant, the skipper of a Spanish vessel, was charged with various offences under Irish fisheries legislation alleged to have been committed within the exclusive fishery limits of the Irish State. During the hearing before the Irish Circuit Court the defendant relied on the London Fisheries Convention of 1964, to which both Spain and Ireland were party. Thereupon the Irish court referred to the Court of Justice a series of questions, the bulk of which concerned Article 234. Only the first two questions are of relevance here:

(i) First, the Irish court asked whether Article 234 created rights

---

[133] Case 812/79 [1980] E.C.R. 2787, [1981] 2 C.M.L.R. 193.

and obligations for the Community institutions as well as for
the Member States.

After confirming its ruling in *E.C. Commission* v. *Italy* to the effect
that the rights at issue were those of third countries only, the Court
continued:

> 'Although the first paragraph of Article 234 makes mention only of the
> obligations of Member States, it would not achieve its purpose if it did not
> imply a duty on the part of the institutions of the Community not to impede
> the performance of the obligations of Member States which stem from a prior
> agreement. However, that duty of the Member States is directed only to
> permitting the Member State concerned to perform its obligations under the
> prior agreement and does not bind the Community as regards the non-member
> country in question'.

(ii) Secondly, the Irish court asked whether Article 234 or any
     other rule of Community law maintained or upheld rights of
     the beneficiaries of Treaties to which Article 234 applied,
     which national courts must apply.

The Court replied that

> 'since the purpose of the first paragraph of Article 234 is to remove any
> obstacle to the performance of agreements previously concluded with non-
> member countries which the accession of a Member State to the Community
> may present, it cannot have the effect of altering the nature of the rights which
> may flow from such agreements'.

9.58   What then is the effect of Article 234 as an exception to
Articles 30 to 34? Often a prior agreement to which Article 234
applies will cover the same ground as Article 36, as the Court found
to be the case with the particular convention at issue in *Henn and
Darby*. Sometimes, however, a prior agreement covered by Article
234 may require a Member State to impose quantitative restrictions
or measures of equivalent effect not justified under Article 36.

CHAPTER X

Agriculture

10.01   Central to the common agricultural policy is the concept of the common organisation of the market. Although Article 40 (2) of the Treaty provides that

'this organisation shall take one of the following forms, depending on the product concerned:

(a) common rules on competition;

(b) compulsory coordination of the various national market organisations;

(c) a European market organisation',

it has always been option (c) that has been chosen. A common market organisation will normally include rules on price formation (under which supplies will usually be bought up when prices fall below a certain level) and measures relating to imports from outside the Community coupled with export refunds for goods exported to third countries.[1] In addition, all regulations establishing common market organisations during the transitional period—and some since—have included a provision prohibiting customs duties and taxes of equivalent effect and quantitative restrictions and measures of equivalent effect between Member States. However, for reasons explained in this chapter it has become clear that such a clause is now superfluous.

In view of the fundamental importance of common market organisations this chapter is divided into two sections: the first covers the application of the prohibition on quantitative restrictions and measures of equivalent effect in the absence of such an organisation, the second deals with its application to products covered by such an organisation. It should be borne in mind that nearly all agricultural products[2] are now covered by common organisations: the only agricultural products still not subject to a common organisation are potatoes and ethyl alcohol. Until quite recently 'sheepmeat' and 'goatmeat' were not covered by a common organisation of the market either.[3]

---

[1] See generally Waelbroeck in *Le droit de la Communauté économique européenne* (1970), Vol. 2, 59 *et seq.*; Ries, *L'ABC du Marché commun agricole* (1978); Fennell, *The Common Agricultural Policy of the European Community* (1979).

[2] Agricultural products are those listed in Annex II to the Treaty: Art. 38 (3).

[3] See now Reg. 1837/80 ([1980] O.J. L183).

I. WHERE NO COMMON MARKET ORGANISATION EXISTS

10.02 In the absence of a common market organisation for a product can a Member State maintain import or export quotas for that product even after the end of the transitional period, providing those quotas form part of a national market organisation? Until the Court's judgment in *Charmasson* v. *Minister of Economic Affairs*[4] it was widely thought that a Member State could maintain such quotas and indeed this was the view taken both by the Commission and by the Advocate General in that case. The Court was to reject that view in favour of a more integrationist approach.

In fact, the case concerned imports from outside the Community. The plaintiff imported bananas from a number of countries including Zaire and Somalia. Both those States were associated with the Community by the Yaoundé Convention of 1963,[5] Article 5 of which provided, *inter alia,* that 'as regards the elimination of quantitative restrictions, the Member States shall apply to goods originating in the Associated States the corresponding provisions of the Treaty'. Nevertheless, while the French authorities granted free access to bananas from certain former French colonies, banana imports from other countries such as Zaire and Somalia were subject to a system of quotas.

The plaintiff sought the annulment by the Conseil d'Etat of an official notice published in the French *Journal Officiel* opening a quota for bananas from countries other than those enjoying the privileged treatment referred to. He claimed that the system of quotas infringed the Yaoundé Convention and Article 33 EEC providing for the progressive abolition of quotas during the transitional period. The latter provision was involved because the notice appeared in October 1969 and thus before the end of the transitional period. Yet the crux of the case concerned the legality of such quotas after the end of this period.

The principal question referred to the Court of Justice was whether the existence of a national market organisation for a product not yet subject to a common organisation impeded the application of Article 33. Like the French Government, the Commission took the view that it did. It deduced this in particular from Article 45 which provides for the conclusion of long-term agreements or contracts between importing and exporting Member States 'until national market organisations have been replaced by one of the forms of common organisation referred to in Article 40 (2)'; and from Article 43 (3) which provides that a common organisation may replace national organisations provided the common organisation

---

[4] Case 48/74 [1974] E.C.R. 1383, [1975] 2 C.M.L.R. 208; noted by Paulin and Forman [1975] C.M.L. Rev 399, and Wyatt [1976] E.L. Rev. 310.
[5] Now replaced by the Second Lomé Convention [1980] O.J. L347.

offers 'equivalent safeguards for the employment and standard of living of the producers concerned'—it considered that such safeguards would not be offered by the mere abolition of restrictions to inter-State trade. However, it added a rider to the effect that this exception only applied to organisations which already existed when the Treaty came into force. The Advocate General reached the same conclusion, which was shared by the authors of the Acts of Accession: 'see Article 60 (2) of that Act, which indeed would make nonsense on any other view'. As we shall see,[6] the Court has recently held that Article 60 (2) does in fact have a different meaning.

The Court swept away all these objections. Its starting-point was Article 38 (2) EEC which reads: 'Save as otherwise provided in Articles 39 to 46, the rules laid down for the establishment of the common market shall apply to agricultural products'. An examination of Articles 39 to 46 led the Court to conclude that

> 'whilst a national organisation of the market existing at the date of coming into force of the Treaty could, during the transitional period, preclude the application of Article 33 thereof, to the extent that such application would have impaired its functioning, this cannot, however, be the case after the expiration of that period, when the provisions of Article 33 must be fully effective'.

10.03 To say that Article 33 is fully effective after the end of the transitional period is not quite accurate since Article 33 provides for the progressive abolition of quotas during the transitional period and is redundant thereafter. In any case, it is clear that the Court meant that import quotas were prohibited after the end of 1969. By necessary implication, this must be so for all quantitative restrictions on imports or exports and measures of equivalent effect.

In fact, the Court has since applied its ruling in *Charmasson* to measures of equivalent effect to quantitative restrictions on exports. During a potato shortage the French Government published a Notice to Exporters in the French *Journal Officiel* requiring potato exporters to make an export declaration to be endorsed by the French authorities. In an action brought under Article 169, the Court confirmed the Commission's view that the measure infringed Article 34: Case 68/76 *E.C. Commission* v. *France*.[7]

10.04 Since in the latter case the national measure was adopted only in 1975, it was not necessary to decide whether Article 34 took effect with respect to agricultural products as from January 1962, as with other products; or whether it did not take effect until the end of the transitional period. However, the Court held that 'following the end of the transitional period, the provisions of Articles 39 to 46 cannot be relied on in justification of a unilateral derogation from the requirements of Article 34 of the Treaty'. This appears to conflict with the Court's earlier ruling in *Cadsky* v. *Istituto Nazionale per*

---

[6] Para 10.05.
[7] [1977] E.C.R. 515, [1977] 2 C.M.L.R. 161. Wyatt [1977] E.L. Rev. 281.

il Commercio Estero[8] where it held that the prohibition in Article 16 on customs duties and taxes of equivalent effect on exports applied as from January 1962 to agricultural products as to other products. There appears to be no reason to make a distinction in this respect between Articles 16 and 34 and it is therefore submitted that the prohibition in Article 34 has applied to agricultural products since January 1962.

10.05 The Court recently had occasion to build on the *Charmasson* decision in two parallel cases raising the question whether, after the end of 1977, the United Kingdom could ban imports of potatoes. In the first case, *Meijer v. Department of Trade*,[9] the plaintiffs were seeking a declaration in the High Court that the United Kingdom was not entitled to impose this ban, a question being referred by the High Court under Article 177 of the Treaty. At the same time, the Commission brought proceedings against the United Kingdom under Article 169 EEC.[10]

Article 60 (2) of the first Act of Accession constitutes a clear exception to the basic rule in Article 42[11] of the same Act, since it provides:

'In respect of products not covered, on the date of accession, by a common organisation of the market, the provisions of Title I concerning the progressive abolition of charges having equivalent effect to customs duties and of quantitative restrictions and measures having equivalent effect shall not apply to those charges, restrictions and measures if they form part of a national market organisation on the date of accession. This provision shall apply only to the extent necessary to ensure the maintenance of the national organisation and until the common organisation of the market for these products is implemented'.

Does Article 60 (2) also constitute a special provision within the meaning of Article 9 (2) of the Act which reads:

'Subject to the dates, time limits and special provisions provided for in this act, the application of the transitional measures shall terminate at the end of 1977'?

This was in essence the question referred by the High Court and was also the only issue in the Article 169 proceedings: if Article 60 (2) was not a 'special provision' in this sense, it was clear that the ban would be contrary to Article 30 EEC.

The root of the problem was that Article 60 (2) does not expressly state that its provisions shall cease to have effect on 31 December

---

[8] Case 63/74 [1975] E.C.R. 281, [1975] 2 C.M.L.R. 246; noted by Wyatt [1976] E.L. Rev. 120.
[9] Case 118/78, [1979] E.C.R. 1387, [1979] 2 C.M.L.R. 398 noted by Wyatt (note 10 below).
[10] Case 231/78, *E.C. Commission* v. *United Kingdom* [1979] E.C.R. 1447, [1979] 2 C.M.L.R. 427 noted by Wyatt [1979] E.L. Rev. 359.
[11] Art. 42, which falls within Title I of the Act of Accession, provides:
'Quantitative restrictions on imports and exports shall, from the date of accession, be abolished between the Community as originally constituted and the new Member States and between the new Member States themselves.
Measures having equivalent effect to such restrictions shall be abolished by 1 January 1975 at the latest'.

1977. The simple reason for this was that when the Act of Accession was drafted the *Charmasson* case had not yet been decided, and it was generally thought then that quantitative restrictions forming part of a national market organisation could be maintained until the establishment of a common market organisation. Nevertheless, the Advocate General saw great significance in this lacuna and in the fact that in his view the Act of Accession did not provide for a 'transitional period' like Article 8 of the Treaty of Rome but merely a series of 'transitional measures'. He concluded that the United Kingdom was correct in alleging that Article 60 (2) was a 'special provision' within the meaning of Article 9.

Had the Court followed his conclusions, it would not only have dealt a severe blow to the principle of the free movement of goods, but it would also have removed much of the incentive for the Member States to strive for the establishment of common market organisations for products not yet subject to them. However, the Court took the opposite course.

Article 2 of the Act of Accession made it clear, the Court held, that the fundamental objective of the Act was the integration of the new Member States into the Community. This was why Article 9 of the Act stated that the special provisions were intended to 'facilitate the adjustment of the new Member States to the rules in force within the Communities'. It followed that 'the provisions of the Act of Accession must be interpreted having regard to the foundations and the system of the Community, as established by the Treaty'. After an analysis of the provisions of the Treaty concerning the abolition of quantitative restrictions and measures of equivalent effect as well as its agricultural provisions, the Court rejected the submission of the British Government.[12] The reservation contained in Article 9 (2) must be narrowly interpreted so as to include only special provisions 'which are clearly delimited and determined in time and not to a provision, such as Article 60 (2), which refers to an uncertain future event'.

The Court then reached the same conclusion by a different route: it would be contrary to the principle of the equality of the Member States before Community law to allow the effects of Article 60 (2) to continue for more than a provisional period, given that in its view this provision created an exception on which only the new Member States could rely. The Court gave no reasons for its view that the six original Member States could not rely on Article 60 (2), which was

---

[12] Contrast this with the Court's ruling on Art. 102 of the Act of Accession in Cases 185–204/78 *Van Dam en Zonen* [1979] E.C.R. 2345, [1980] 1 C.M.L.R. 350 noted by Churchill [1979] E.L. Rev. 391. Art. 102 states that from the sixth year after accession at the latest, the Council shall adopt fisheries conservation measures. When the Council had failed to take this action even after the expiry of the six-year period, the Court held in this judgment that the Member States had the right and the duty to take such measures pending this Community action.

not part of the Commission's case. Furthermore, this statement added nothing of value to its judgment.

In any event, the Court ruled that the import ban infringed Article 30.[13]

10.06 The Court subsequently confirmed these rulings in an action[14] concerning lamb, which was not yet subject to a common market organisation although such an organisation has been created since then.[15] It held that French restrictions on the importation of British lamb infringed Articles 12 and 30 EEC as from 1 January 1978.[16]

Following the ruling in the potato cases that the original Member States could not rely on Article 60 (2), the Commission sought to amend its submissions at the oral hearing so as to obtain a declaration that the French measures had infringed the Treaty as from January 1975 with respect to the measures of equivalent effect. Advocate General Reischl pointed out that Article 60 (2) referred back to provisions of Title I of Part Four of the Act of Accession—Articles 35, 36 and 42—which lay down reciprocal obligations as between the original Member States and the new Member States. Therefore it was wrong to hold that the old Member States were unable to rely on Article 60 (2) before 1978—and in his view the Court had probably not intended to convey this view in the potato cases. Accordingly he found that the infringement had only commenced in January 1978.

The Court was able to avoid ruling on the latter point by holding that the proposed amendment to the Commission's submissions was inadmissible under the Rules of Procedure of the Court. However, the Court might yet be faced with a preliminary ruling concerning this point.[17]

II. WHERE A COMMON MARKET ORGANISATION DOES EXIST

10.07 In view of the *Charmasson* judgment it has become clear that, since the end of the transitional period, the provisions of Articles 30 and 34 apply to all agricultural products so that it is

---

[13] Accordingly, Art. 65 (2) of the Act of Greek Accession ([1979] O.J. L291) which corresponds to Art. 60 (2) of the first Act of Accession, is expressed to apply only until 31 December 1985 at the latest.

[14] Case 232/78 *E.C. Commission* v. *France* [1979] E.C.R. 2729, [1980] 1 C.M.L.R. 418.

[15] See note 3 above.

[16] The Member State concerned consistently refused to comply with the Court's judgment until the common market organisation was set up. This failure to respect a judgment of the Court has caused a good deal of consternation in Community law circles; see, *e.g.* 'Editorial Comments' in [1980] C.M.L. Rev 311. It also led to a further action by the Commission against France, this time for failure to comply with a judgment of the Court: Case 24/80R and 97/80R [1980] E.C.R. 1319, [1981] 3 C.M.L.R. 25. The infringement in question was brought to an end on the adoption of the common market organisation for sheepmeat (note 3 above).

[17] On the other hand, this problem cannot arise in connection with the Act of Greek Accession: see note 13 above.

unnecessary to re-enact those provisions in regulations setting up a common market organisation.[18] Consequently, it has been the practice in recent years to forgo express provisions of this kind since they are superfluous. This practice was endorsed by the Court in *Kramer*:[19] it held that after the end of the transitional period the prohibition on measures of equivalent effect applied to products covered by a common market organisation, even where the regulation establishing that organisation did not expressly lay down the prohibition.[20]

10.08 When a national measure may be contrary to Article 30 or 34 and to a regulation setting up a common market organisation, should the Treaty provisions or the regulation be considered first?[21] The Court has had occasion to rule on a considerable number of cases of this kind.[22] However, the practice of the persons bringing these matters before the Court has not been consistent: the Court has been asked to rule on the compatibility of national measures now with the Treaty provisions, now with the common market organisation, and sometimes with both. It is not surprising, then, that the Court has tended to mingle the two, with the consequence that it is often unclear whether a particular judgment is limited to the common market organisation in question or whether it is an interpretation of Articles 30 and 34 applicable to all products.

Nevertheless, in *Pigs and Bacon Commission* v. *McCarren*[23] the Court affirmed that

'in the event of proceedings relating to an agricultural sector governed by a common organisation of the market the problem raised must first be examined from that point of view having regard to the precedence necessitated by Article 38 (2) of the EEC Treaty for the specific provisions adopted in the context of

---

[18] As to the situation during the transitional period, see paras. 5.01 *et seq.*, 6.02 *et seq.* above.

[19] Cases 3, 4 and 6/76 [1976] E.C.R. 1279, [1976] 2 C.M.L.R. 440.

[20] This was confirmed in Case 83/78 *Pigs Marketing Board* v. *Redmond* [1978] E.C.R. 2347, [1979] 1 C.M.L.R. 177 noted by Wyatt [1979] E.L. Rev. 115; Oliver [1980] C.M.L. Rev. 113.

[21] See generally Baumann, 'Common Organizations of the Market and National Law' [1977] C.M.L. Rev. 303; Usher, 'The Effects of Common Organisations and Policies on the Powers of a Member State' [1977] E.L. Rev. 428.

[22] In particular Case 190/73 *van Haaster* [1974] E.C.R. 1123, [1974] 2 C.M.L.R. 521, Case 4/75 *Rewe-Zentralfinanz* v. *Landwirtschaftskammer* [1975] E.C.R. 843, [1977] 1 C.M.L.R. 599; Cases 89/74, 18–19/75 *Arnaud* [1975] E.C.R. 1023, [1975] 2 C.M.L.R. 490; Cases 10–14/75 *Lahaille* [1975] E.C.R. 1053; Cases 3, 4 and 6/76 *Kramer* [1976] E.C.R. 1279, [1976] 2 C.M.L.R. 440; Case 35/76 *Simmenthal* v. *Minister for Finance* [1976] E.C.R. 1871, [1977] 2 C.M.L.R. 1; Case 111/76 *van den Hazel* [1977] E.C.R. 901; Case 154/77 *Dechmann* [1978] E.C.R. 1573, [1979] 2 C.M.L.R. 1; Case 83/78 *Pigs Marketing Board* v. *Redmond*, note 20 above; Case 153/78 *E.C. Commission* v. *Germany* [1979] E.C.R. 2555, [1980] 1 C.M.L.R. 198; Case 5/79 *Buys* [1979] E.C.R. 3203, [1980] 2 C.M.L.R. 493; Cases 16–20/79 *Danis* [1979] E.C.R. 3327, [1980] 3 C.M.L.R. 492; Case 251/78 *Denkavit Futtermittel* v. *Minister für Ernährung* [1979] E.C.R. 3369, [1980] 3 C.M.L.R. 513; Cases 95 and 96/79 *Kefer and Delmelle* [1980] E.C.R. 103; Case 94/79 *Vriend* [1980] E.C.R. 327, [1980] 3 C.M.L.R. 473.

[23] Case 177/78 [1979] E.C.R. 2161, [1979] 3 C.M.L.R. 389.

the common agricultural policy over the general provisions of the Treaty relating to the establishment of the Common Market'.

Having decided that a national measure of the kind at issue contravened the regulation establishing the common market organisation, there was no need for the Court to consider its compatibility with the Treaty provisions.[24]

On this approach a national measure, like a horse in a steeplechase, must clear the fence of the common market organisation before the fence of Articles 30 and 34. If it falls at the first fence, there is no need to consider Articles 30 and 34. It is submitted that this is the most appropriate approach, because common market organisations will often contain specific provisions which have a bearing on the national measure in question, for example with respect to price formation. In the absence of such provisions, one may fall back on Articles 30 and 34.

In other, quite unrelated matters the Court has followed a similar approach to the relationship between Community legislation and Articles 30 to 36. One instance of this is the form of words used in the *Cassis de Dijon* case[25]: 'in the absence of common rules relating to the production and marketing of alcohol . . . it is for the Member States to regulate [these] matters'. Another example is the Court's rulings to the effect that, once a Community Directive has harmonised measures necessary to protect public health, Member States can no longer adopt or maintain unilateral measures in reliance on Article 36.[26]

10.09 Consequently, it is generally considered[27] that judgments of the Court on measures of equivalent effect on imports and exports of products covered by common market organisations may be of limited significance as they may not be applicable to products not covered by such an organisation. Some of these judgments appear to be of general application; they have been discussed in Chapter VII. Other judgments appear to be interpretations of the common market organisation in question, even if they expressly refer to Articles 30 and 34. It is by no means a simple matter to decide which judgments are of general application and which are not.

The following cases appear not to be of general application but deserve mention in this book precisely because this point is uncertain:

---

[24] In *Kramer*, note 19 above, the Court adopted the same approach.

[25] Case 120/78 *Rewe-Zentral* v. *Bundesmonopolverwaltung für Branntwein* [1979] E.C.R. 649, [1979] 3 C.M.L.R. 494; a similar form of words appears in Case 8/74 *Dassonville* [1974] E.C.R. 837, [1974] 2 C.M.L.R. 436.

[26] Para 8.14 above.

[27] See, *e.g.* VerLoren van Themaat, 'De artikelen 30-36 van het EEG-Verdrag' [1980] R. M. Themis L4/5, 378 at 386; Barents, 'New Developments in Measures having Equivalent Effect' [1981] C.M.L. Rev. 271 at 299; *contra* the Advocate General in Case 155/80 *Oebel* [1981] E.C.R. 1993.

10.10 (i) *Pigs Marketing Board* v. *Redmond.*[28] The facts of that
case were that in January 1977 a police officer in Northern
Ireland stopped a lorry containing 75 'bacon pigs', pigs
weighing more than 77 kilogrammes. By the Movement
of Pigs Regulations (Northern Ireland) 1972 it was an
offence to transport bacon pigs otherwise than to one of
the Pigs Marketing Board's purchasing centres with a
document authorising transport, so that in effect the
Board had a purchasing monopoly of all bacon pigs
produced in Northern Ireland. Since the lorry driver was
unable to produce the requisite certificate, the owner of
the pigs was charged with an offence under the Regulations. The defendant having argued that the Regulations
and certain provisions relating to the establishment of the
Board were contrary to Community law, the Resident
Magistrate referred a number of questions to the Court.
These included the compatibility of the Northern Irish
provisions with Articles 30 and 34 and Regulation 2759/
75[29] setting up the common organisation of the market in
pigmeat.

On these points the Court held:

'A marketing system on a national or regional scale set up by the legislation of
a Member State and administered by a body which, by means of compulsory
powers vested in it, is empowered to control the sector of the market in
question or a part of it by measures such as subjecting the marketing of the
goods to a requirement that the producer shall be registered with the body in
question, the prohibition of any sale otherwise than to that body or through
its agency on the conditions determined by it, and the prohibition of all
transport of the goods in question otherwise than subject to the authorisation
of the body in question are to be considered as incompatible with the
requirements of Articles 30 and 34 of the EEC Treaty and of Regulation
2759/75 . . .'[30]

10.11 (ii) The ruling with respect to the first of these requirements,
the obligation to register with a particular body before
marketing goods, was subsequently confirmed by the
Court in *Vriend.*[31] There the defendant had been found
guilty of selling several lots of chrysanthemum cuttings
in the Netherlands without being affiliated to a body
which bore the acronym NAKS. By virtue of a Dutch
Royal Decree a person selling such products was required
to be affiliated to this body. The Dutch court hearing
the case referred two questions to the Court of Justice
asking whether a requirement of this kind was compatible

---

[28] See note 20 above.
[29] [1975] O.J. L282/1.
[30] One might have thought that these measures fell under Art. 37 rather than Arts. 30 and
34: see Chap. XI, note 1..
[31] Case 94/79 [1980] E.C.R. 327, [1980] 3 C.M.L.R. 473.

with Articles 30 to 47 of the Treaty and with Regulation 234/68[32] on the establishment of a common organisation of the market in trees and plants.

The Court replied that

'national rules of the kind referred to by the national court whereby a Member State, directly or through the intermediary of bodies established or approved by an official authority, reserves exclusively to persons affiliated to such bodies the right to market, resell, import, export and offer for export material for plant propagation such as chrysanthemum plants which are covered by the common organisation of the market in live trees and other plants . . . established by Regulation 234/68 . . . is incompatible with the said Regulation and also with Articles 30 and 34 of the EEC Treaty'.[33]

10.12   (iii) On the other hand, *van Haaster*[34] concerned restrictions on production.

By a Dutch decree it was forbidden to cultivate hyacinth bulbs without a cultivation licence for the year in question. This was in fact tantamount to a production quota. The defendant was prosecuted before the Dutch courts for contravening this decree, whereupon a reference was made under Article 177 of the Treaty asking whether this requirement was compatible with Article 10 of Regulation 234/68 already referred to.[35] That provision stipulated that: 'The following shall be prohibited in the internal trade of the Community: . . . any quantitative restriction or measure of equivalent effect; . . .' In finding that the requirement of a cultivation licence was contrary to this provision, the Court made it clear that it reached this conclusion 'in the light of the objects and the purposes of the Regulation'. Indeed Article 34 was not mentioned either in the question referred or in the judgment.

Advocate General Mayras, however, made the following statement:

'I consider that the prohibition in Article 10 of the Regulation has a scope wider than that of Article 34 . . . The common organisations of the market in the field of agriculture cover not only trade in agricultural products, but also their production.'

Thus in his view Article 34 did not cover restrictions on production.

10.13   (iv) The decision in *van den Hazel*[36] was along similar lines. The defendant had been prosecuted before the Dutch courts for exceeding quotas for the slaughter of poultry fixed by a national regulation. The national court made a reference under Article 177 asking whether this was

---

[32] [1968] J.O. L55/1.
[33] The observation made in note 30 applies equally to this case.
[34] Case 190/73 [1974] E.C.R. 1123, [1974] 2 C.M.L.R. 521.
[35] See note 32 above.
[36] Case 14/76 [1977] ECR 901.

compatible with Regulation 123/67[37] on the common market organisation in poultrymeat and with Articles 30 to 37 of the Treaty. The Court began by holding that quotas for slaughter constituted production quotas. These it considered to be contrary to the Regulation. Having reached that conclusion, it found it unnecessary to consider whether they were incompatible with Articles 30 to 36.

10.14   In conclusion, it should be pointed out that in one respect common organisations of the market may go beyond Articles 30 and 34: the regulations setting up these common organisations often prohibit restrictions on trade even within each Member State.[38] This is particularly the case with respect to price controls. On the other hand, it has been suggested earlier in this book[39] that Articles 30 and 34 only apply to restrictions on trade between one Member State and another.

---

[37] [1967] J.O. 2301.
[38] See, *e.g.* Art. 10 of Reg. 234/68, para. 10.12 above.
[39] See paras. 6.61 *et seq.* above.

CHAPTER XI

State monopolies of a commercial character

11.01 Article 37 of the Treaty provides as follows:

'1. Member States shall progressively adjust any State monopolies of a commercial character so as to ensure that when the transitional period has ended no discrimination regarding the conditions under which goods are procured and marketed exists between nationals of Member States.

   The provisions of this Article shall apply to any body through which a Member State, in law or in fact, either directly or indirectly supervises, determines or appreciably influences imports or exports between Member States. These provisions shall likewise apply to monopolies delegated by the State to others.

2. Member States shall refrain from introducing any new measure which is contrary to the principles laid down in paragraph 1 or which restricts the scope of the Articles dealing with the abolition of customs duties and quantitative restrictions between Member States.

3. The timetable for the measures referred to in paragraph 1 shall be harmonised with the abolition of quantitative restrictions on the same products provided for in Articles 30 to 34.

   If a product is subject to a State monopoly of a commercial character in only one or some Member States, the Commission may authorise the other Member States to apply protective measures until the adjustment provided for in paragraph 1 has been effected; the Commission shall determine the conditions and details of such measures.

4. If a State monopoly of a commercial character has rules which are designed to make it easier to dispose of agricultural products or obtain for them the best return, steps should be taken in applying the rules contained in this Article to ensure equivalent safeguards for the employment and standard of living of the producers concerned, account being taken of the adjustments that will be possible and the specialisation that will be needed with the passage of time.

5. The obligations on Member States shall be binding only in so far as they are compatible with existing international agreements.

6. With effect from the first stage the Commission shall make recommendations as to the manner in which and the timetable according to which the adjustment provided for in this Article shall be carried out'.

It should be noted that this provision applies only to trading monopolies and not to monopolies of production or the provision of services. This is why it appears in the same chapter of the Treaty as the provisions relating to quantitative restrictions and measures of equivalent effect.

By virtue of Article 44 of the first Act of Accession, Denmark, Ireland and the United Kingdom were required to adjust their State monopolies in accordance with Article 37 (1) EEC by 31 December

1977.[1] The six original Member States were correspondingly obliged to adjust their State monopolies with respect to goods from the new Member States by the same date. The Nine and Greece have equivalent obligations to make the necessary adjustments to their State monopolies by 31 December 1985 by virtue of Article 40 of the Act of Accession of Greece. However, the same provision requires Greece to abolish all exclusive export rights as from its accession, namely 1 January 1981; the same applies to exclusive import rights with respect to copper sulphate, saccharin and flimsy paper.

11.02 Paragraphs 1 and 2 of Article 37 have both been held to be sufficiently clear and precise to be directly applicable: in *Pubblico Ministero* v. *Manghera*[2] and *Rewe-Zentral* v. *HZA Landau*[3] the Court ruled that Article 37 (1) was directly applicable since the end of the transitional period, while in *Costa* v. *ENEL*[4] Article 37 (2) was held to have possessed this quality since the entry into force of the Treaty. Yet this is not an article which is notable for its clarity. Indeed, in 1964 Colliard wrote of the 'obscure clarity' of Article 37[5] and, though much water has flowed under the bridge since that time, that description still holds good today. So it is that various controversies have arisen over Article 37, which in turn have engendered an extensive literature on the subject.[6] However, in the present context it is not necessary to give a comprehensive analysis of this Article, but merely to answer the following questions: do the provisions of Article 37 oust those of Articles 30 to 34 since the end of the transitional period, and, if so, do they lead to different results?

---

[1] However, in so far as they concerned producers subject to a common market organisation on the date of accession and contained customs duties and charges of equivalent effect and quantitative restrictions and measures having equivalent effect, all these charges and measures were to be abolished by 1 February 1973, by virtue of Art. 60 (1) of the Act of Accession: Case 83/78 *Pigs Marketing Board* v. *Redmond* [1978] E.C.R. 2347, [1979] 1 C.M.L.R. 177; Wyatt [1979] E.L.Rev. 115; Oliver [1980] C.M.L.Rev. 113.

[2] Case 59/75 [1976] E.C.R. 91, [1976] 1 C.M.L.R. 557 noted by Wyatt [1975–76] I.E.L.Rev. 307.

[3] Case 45/75 [1976] E.C.R. 181, [1976] 2 C.M.L.R. 1 noted by Wyatt, *op. cit.*

[4] Case 6/64 [1964] E.C.R. 585, [1964] C.M.L.R. 425.

[5] 'L'obscure clarté de l'article 37 du traité de la Communauté économique européenne' [1964] Recueil Dalloz chronique 266. In this article the author criticises the Conseil d'Etat for refusing to refer a question of the interpretation of Art. 37 to the Court of Justice under Art. 177, because the Conseil d'Etat considered that the point was an *acte clair* so that a reference was unnecessary (*Société des pétroles Shell Berre*—Act.Jur. 1964 II 438). Hence the ironic expression 'obscure clarity'.

[6] In addition to the articles already cited at notes 1 and 5 above, see, *inter alia*, Van Hecke, 'Government Enterprises and National Monopolies under the EEC Treaty' [1965–66] C.M.L.Rev. 450; Waelbroeck in *Le droit de la Communauté économique européenne* (1970), Vol. 1; Hochbaum in Groeben, Boeckh, Thiesing, *Kommentar zum EWG-Vertrag* (1974); Béraud, 'L'aménagement des monopoles nationaux prévu à l'article 37 du traité CEE à la lumière des récents développements jurisprudentiels' (1979) 15 R.T.D.E. 573; Wooldridge, 'Some recent decisions concerning the ambit of Article 37 of the EEC Treaty', *Legal Issues of European Integration* (1979), 105; Wyatt and Dashwood, *The Substantive Law of the EEC* (1980), Chap. II.

11.03 It can be said at once that Article 37 shares two important characteristics with the articles preceding it:

- First, it only applies to 'goods', which concept has the same meaning as in Articles 30 to 34. The Court of Justice reached this conclusion in the *Sacchi*[7] case on the basis of the position of Article 37 in the Treaty (in the chapter on quantitative restrictions) and of its use of the terms 'imports', 'exports' and 'products'. It followed that a monopoly of television advertising, being a service under Article 59 *et seq.*, did not fall within Article 37.

- Secondly, it does not apply to trade with third countries. In *Hansen* v. *HZA Flensburg*[8] (Hansen II) the Court deduced this also from the position and the wording of Article 37. It concluded that 'the provisions of that article cannot be applied to products imported from third countries since the arrangements for the importation of such products are subject not to the provisions governing the internal market but to those relating to commercial policy'.[9]

11.04 Less straightforward, however, are the answers to the following questions:

- what is the precise meaning of the term 'State monopoly'?
- does the term 'discrimination regarding the conditions under which goods are procured and marketed' in Article 37 (1) embrace all quantitative restrictions and measures of equivalent effect?
- what is meant by the obligation to 'adjust' the monopoly?
- which aspects of a monopoly fall under Article 37 and which under other provisions of the Treaty?
- do Articles 37 (4), 37 (5) and 36 constitute exceptions to the prohibitions contained in Article 37?

11.05 Before examining such case law as there is on these matters, mention should first be made of a theory recently put forward by the Commission, which would answer the first four of these questions in one fell swoop. It is based on the Court's ruling in *Manghera*[10] to the effect that Article 37 could be relied on before national courts to set aside an exclusive right to import held by a monopoly, since such a right constituted discrimination prohibited

---

[7] Case 155/73 [1974] E.C.R. 409, [1974] 2 C.M.L.R. 177, see para. 2.05 above.

[8] Case 91/78 [1979] E.C.R. 935, [1980] 1 C.M.L.R. 162, noted by Wyatt [1980] E.L.Rev. 213.

[9] Even this point is not free from controversy: does Art. 37 apply, like Arts. 30 to 36, to goods originating in third countries but in free circulation in the Community within the meaning of Arts. 9 and 10 (see paras. 2.11 *et seq.*)? The passage here quoted from *Hansen II* might be read as implying that Art. 37 does apply to such goods. This would accord with the view already forcibly put forward by Waelbroeck, *op. cit.* note 6 above, at 132 and with Van Hecke, *op. cit.* note 6 above, at 460. The Commission refused to be drawn on this point in its answer to Written Question 51 ([1965] J.O. 391).

[10] See note 2 above.

by Article 37 (1). In the light of this the Commission has maintained in the more recent cases[11] on Article 37 discussed below that this provision also covers exclusive export rights and the exclusive right to market imported goods. The latter was included because the abolition of a monopoly's exclusive import rights would be hollow if that monopoly's exclusive right to market imported goods were maintained as, in the Court's words in the *Manghera* case, 'the free movement of goods from other Member States similar to those with which the national monopoly is concerned' would not be 'ensured'.

On the other hand, in the Commission's view, Article 37 constituting as it does an obligation on Member States to act during the transitional period, cannot be invoked for any other purpose since the end of that period. Indeed in its view, since these three exclusive rights constitute the essence of a State monopoly, a body enjoying no such rights is not a State monopoly within the meaning of Article 37 at all. Thus any other State measures or practices linked to a monopoly fall to be considered under other Articles of the Treaty, such as Articles 12, 16, 30, 34, 92 and 95. Likewise, any abuse by the monopoly of its dominant position might fall foul of Article 86. In particular, according to the Commission, a production monopoly is compatible with the Treaty by virtue of Article 222[12]; the same applies to a monopoly's exclusive right to market its own production.

The Commission's theory can thus be reduced to the following simple formula: since the end of the transitional period Article 37 can only be relied on to set aside exclusive import or export rights or the exclusive right to market imported goods and only bodies enjoying one or more of these exclusive rights are State monopolies within the meaning of Article 37. Thus all of the first four questions set out above are all answered at once.

However, the Court has never accepted this theory.

11.06 Turning, then, to the meaning of 'State monopoly', the second sub-paragraph of Article 37 (1) provides a wide definition of this term, which is not limited to public bodies but extends also to monopolies delegated by the State to a private enterprise or group of enterprises.[13]

Nor is it entirely free from doubt whether the monopoly must have some institutional structure as the term 'body' in the English text and similar terms in most of the other language texts would suggest.[14] The contrary view, based on the German *Einrichtung*, which means 'arrangement' as well as 'organisation' found favour

---

[11] For the Commission's earlier views see, *e.g.* Béraud, Waelbroeck and Wooldridge (all cited at note 6 above).

[12] See para. 9.45 above.

[13] See in particular Hochbaum, *op. cit.* note 6 above, at 306 and Waelbroeck, *op. cit.* note 6 above, at 125.

[14] See in particular Hochbaum, *op. cit.* note 6 above, at 306, Waelbroeck, *op. cit.* note 6 above, at 126, Wyatt and Dashwood, *op. cit.* note 6 above, at 116.

with the Commission in its Recommendation to the French Government requiring it to abolish its petroleum 'monopoly' based simply on the allocation of import licences to private undertakings.[15] It appears that it was generally thought, at the time when the Treaty was drafted, that Article 37 applied to such a system.[16]

In addition, a difference of opinion has arisen as to whether Article 37 covers monopolies limited to part of the territory of a Member State. In *SAIL*[17] Advocate General Roemer took the view that Article 37 did cover such a monopoly, while the Advocate General in *Pigs Marketing Board* v. *Redmond*[18] seems to have taken the opposite view. In neither case did the Court rule on the matter. It is submitted that the former view is to be preferred, since, as Advocate General Roemer pointed out, 'otherwise the rules contained in Article 37 would be easily evaded by the creation of a large number of local monopolies'.

11.07 It is not clear whether the concept of 'discrimination [between nationals of Member States] regarding the conditions under which goods are procured and marketed' in Article 37 (1) covers all quantitative restrictions and measures of equivalent effect. As the Advocate General pointed out in *Rewe* v. *Bundesmonopolverwaltung für Branntwein*[19] (*Cassis de Dijon*), some measures of equivalent effect are not discriminatory and so fail to come under Article 37 (1); indeed, that was the case with the minimum alcohol requirement at issue in those proceedings. Yet the Court held in *Manghera*[20] that the obligation laid down in Article 37 (1) 'aims at ensuring compliance with the fundamental rule of the free movement of goods throughout the common market, in particular by the abolition of quantitative restrictions and measures having equivalent effect in trade between Member States'.[21] This may not necessarily have any bearing on the point as issue here.

The point is made no easier by the wording of Article 37 (2) which applies to new measures introduced after the entry into force of the Treaty, whereas the preceding paragraph applies to pre-existing measures. Article 37 (2) prohibits any new measure 'which is contrary to the principles laid down in paragraph 1 or which restricts

---

[15] Recommendation of 24 July 1963 ([1963] J.O. 2271).
[16] Advocate General Gand in Case 20/64 *Albatros* v. *Sopéco* [1965] E.C.R. 29 at 44, [1965] C.M.L.R. 159. In this case a reference was made under Art. 177 asking in essence whether the French petroleum import licencing system was contrary to Arts. 30 to 37 as from 1959. The Court replied that there was no obligation at that time to abolish or adjust a system of this kind, which pre-dated the Treaty.
[17] Case 82/71 [1972] E.C.R. 119 at 143, [1972] C.M.L.R. 723.
[18] See note 1 above, at 2385.
[19] Case 120/78 [1979] E.C.R. 649 at 667, [1979] 3 C.M.L.R. 494 noted by Wyatt, *op. cit.* note 8 above; see paras. 6.33 *et seq.* above.
[20] See note 2 above.
[21] See also Case 86/78 *Peureux* v. *Directeur des Services Fiscaux* [1979] E.C.R. 897, [1980] 3 C.M.L.R. 337, para. 30 of judgment, noted by Wyatt, *op. cit.* note 8 above.

the scope of the Articles dealing with the abolition of customs duties and quantitative restrictions between Member States'.

11.08 As regards the third question, the meaning of the obligation to 'adjust', the Court has repeatedly held that it does not require the total abolition of the monopoly,[22] although, as already mentioned, it has held in the *Manghera* case that under Article 37 no State monopoly may have an exclusive import right after the end of the transitional period. For the rest, as shown below, the Court's case law on this point is far from clear.

11.09 The Court's answer to the fourth question—as to which aspects of a State monopoly fall under Article 37 and which under other provisions of the Treaty—has wavered considerably. For this reason it appears most appropriate to consider these cases in chronological order.

The first case on the matter concerning facts arising after the end of the transitional period was *Manghera*. There the national court making the reference only asked the Court of Justice to rule on the compatibility of the exclusive import rights with Article 37, and the Court limited its answer to Article 37 without mentioning Article 30.

However, in two cases decided shortly afterwards, *Hauptzollamt Göttingen* v. *Miritz*[23] and *Rewe* v. *Hauptzollamt Landau*,[24] the Court had to face the problem squarely. Although the two cases were decided on the same day and on similar facts, the approach adopted in each case was not quite the same. In the *Miritz* case the Court was asked by a German court to rule on the compatibility with Articles 12 and 37 (2) of a 'special equalisation' charge imposed by a German Law of 1970 on alcohol products imported into Germany with the aim of protecting national alcohol producers, all of which were subject to a State monopoly. The Court held that 'since the structure and character of the equalisation charge link it to the system of the German alcohol monopoly, the answer to the first question [on Article 12] must be ascertained from the text of Article 37, which deals specifically with the adjustment of State monopolies'. Later in the same judgment the Court added:

'Article 37 (1) is not concerned exclusively with quantitative restrictions but prohibits any discrimination, when the transitional period has ended, regarding the conditions under which goods are procured and marketed between nationals of Member States. It follows that its application is not limited to imports or exports which are directly subject to the monopoly but covers all measures

---

[22] *Manghera* (see note 2 above); Case 91/75 *HZA Göttingen* v. *Miritz* [1976] E.C.R. 217; Case 91/78 *Hansen* (see note 8 above); Case 119/78 *Peureux* v. *Directeur des Services Fiscaux* [1979] E.C.R. 975, [1980] 3 C.M.L.R. 337 noted by Wyatt, *op. cit.* note 8 above.
[23] See note 22 above.
[24] See note 3 above.

which are connected with its existence and affect trade between Member States in certain products, whether or not subject to the monopoly'.[25]

Thus, held the Court, a charge discriminating against imported products in favour of domestic products coming under a monopoly infringed Article 37 (2).

11.10   The *Rewe* case also concerned the German alcohol monopoly. There the national court asked the Court of Justice to rule on the compatibility with Articles 37 and 95 of a 'monopoly equalisation duty' imposed on alcohol imports. The Court first examined the problem from the point of view of Article 95. It found that Article 95 did not prohibit a tax such as that in question if it was imposed equally on the domestic product and on the similar imported product—even if the tax on the former were paid to the monopoly, while that on imported goods were imposed for the benefit of the general budget of the State. However, the Court found it necessary to consider Article 37 in addition, stating: 'The fact that a national measure complies with the requirements of Article 95 does not imply that it is valid in relation to other provisions of the Treaty, such as Article 37'. After making the statement already quoted from the *Miritz* case to the effect that Article 37 was not concerned exclusively with quantitative restrictions, the Court then reached the same conclusion with respect to Article 37 as it had in interpreting Article 95.

11.11   There then follows a gap in the case law on this subject, during which time the Commission developed its new theory already explained about the role of Article 37 since the end of the transitional period. The first case in which it expounded this theory was *Hansen* v. *Hauptzollamt Flensburg*[26] (Hansen I) in which the plaintiffs contested the validity of a tax on various types of alcohol from Guadeloupe and certain third countries imposed in connection with the German alcohol monopoly. In addition to a couple of questions on the territorial applicability of Article 95, the German court asked the Court of Justice whether a tax such as that in question infringed Article 37, 92 or 95.

The Court stated that it appeared from a comparative study carried out by the Commission that preferential tax arrangements of the type in question existed in several Member States, sometimes quite independently of a commercial monopoly.

'Accordingly' said the Court, 'it appears preferable to examine the problem raised by the national court primarily from the point of view of the rule on taxation laid down in Article 95, because it is of a general nature and not from the point of view of Article 37, which is specific to arrangements for State

---

[25] This follows the Court's judgment in Case 13/70 *Cinzano* v. *HZA Saarbrücken* [1970] E.C.R. 1089, [1971] C.M.L.R. 374, which, however, relates to facts arising during the transitional period.

[26] Case 148/77 [1978] E.C.R. 1787, [1979] 1 C.M.L.R. 604, noted by Wyatt, *op. cit.* note 8 above.

monopolies. This approach is further justified by the fact that Article 37 is based on the same principle as Article 95, that is the elimination of all discrimination in trade between Member States'.

The Court also considered that it was 'preferable' to examine the matter from the point of view of Article 95 rather than Article 92. The use of the word 'preferable' indicates that it was open to the Court to examine the matter under Article 37, and implies that it would have reached the same result.

11.12 Of all the cases the most straightforward in this respect is the *Rewe-Zentral, Cassis de Dijon*, case.[27] As already explained, the case concerned the compatibility with Articles 30 and 37 of a minimum alcohol requirement applying in the same way to domestic and imported drinks. It appears that the national court mentioned Article 37 in its reference merely because the basic rule fixing a minimum alcohol content for spirits is contained in the German Federal Law on the Monopoly in spirits. On this point the Court's answer was that:

> 'It should be noted . . . that Article 37 relates specifically to State monopolies of a commercial character. That provision is therefore irrelevant with regard to national provisions which do not concern the exercise by a public monopoly of its specific function—namely, its exclusive right—but apply in a general manner to the production and marketing of alcoholic beverages, whether or not the latter are covered by the monopoly in question. That being the case, the effect on intra-Community trade of the measure referred to by the national court must be examined solely in relation to the requirements under Article 30'.

The statement that the 'specific function' of the monopoly was its 'exclusive right' suggests a possible acceptance by the Court of the Commission's interpretation of Article 37. However, within a matter of weeks the Court was to veer away from that position once again. The change came in a batch of three cases decided on the same day, two cases entitled *Peureux* v. *Directeur des Services Fiscaux* on the French alcohol monopoly and *Hansen* v. *Hauptzollamt Flensburg* (Hansen II), which once again involved the German alcohol monopoly. What is more, the Court's approach in the two *Peureux* cases was different from that in *Hansen II*.

11.13 In the first *Peureux* case[28] the plaintiff company was claiming that the 'cash adjustment' which French producers of certain types of alcohol had to pay to release that produce from the national alcohol marketing monopoly was contrary to Community law. The action related to two separate periods:

- the period immediately before the entry into force of French Decree 77/842, during which the plaintiffs complained that they, as national producers, had to pay the 'cash adjustment',

---

[27] See note 19 above.
[28] See note 21 above.

whereas imported alcohol of the same kind was not subject to this charge; and
- the subsequent period, during which the plaintiffs' sole complaint was that they were obliged to pay this charge to which their counterparts in other Member States were not subject, so that the plaintiffs' produce was placed at a disadvantage when exported to other Member States.

The French court in effect asked the Court of Justice whether the 'cash adjustment' infringed Article 37 under these circumstances, not mentioning any other Treaty provision.

As to the earlier period the Court first held that Article 37 (1) no longer constitutes an exception to Article 95 since the end of the transitional period. Having found that Article 95 did not prohibit internal taxation involving reverse discrimination, the Court then ruled that the same applied in Article 37—whether or not that provision prohibited other types of reverse discrimination.[29] This was because

'the rules contained in Article 37 concern only activities intrinsically connected with the specific business of the monopoly and are irrelevant to national provisions which have no connection with such specific business. The fact that products are or are not subject to internal taxation according to whether they are subject or not to the monopoly is not a factor which determines how the specific business of the monopoly is conducted'.

Consequently, such a charge was prohibited neither by Article 37 nor by Article 95. *A fortiori* the same applied for the second of the two periods.

11.14 The Court adopted the same criteria in the second *Peureux*[30] case. As explained earlier in this book, the plaintiffs in the main action wished to distil some oranges steeped in alcohol, which they had imported from Italy. The defendant contested their right to do this, on the basis of an article in the French *Code Général des Impôts* prohibiting the distillation of all imported raw material with the exception of certain types of fresh fruit. The French court asked whether this provision was compatible with 'Articles 10 and 37 or any other provision of the Treaty of Rome on the free movement and circulation of products coming from third countries'.

After holding that the French provision in question was a measure of equivalent effect to a quantitative restriction under Article 30, the Court went on to consider Article 37. As in the first *Peureux* case it held that

'the rules contained in Article 37 (1) and (2) concern only activities intrinsically connected with the specific business of the monopoly and are irrelevant to national provisions which have no connection with such specific business'.

In view of the obligation on French producers to sell their alcohol to the monopoly the Court found that there was such an intrinsic

---

[29] On reverse discrimination see paras. 6.63 *et seq.* above.
[30] See note 22 above.

connection. It concluded that the French measure, in addition to infringing Article 30, also constituted a discrimination prohibited by Article 37 (1) because it treated the same kind of nationally produced alcohol differently according to whether it had been obtained from national or from imported raw material.

11.15 It is clear that the scope of Article 37 as laid down in the *Peureux* cases, though wider than that enunciated in the *Cassis de Dijon* judgment (*Rewe-Zentral*), does not constitute a major break from it. The same cannot be said of *Hansen II*.[31] In the light of the *Rewe*[32] and *Miritz* cases the Commission prevailed upon the German Government to deprive its alcohol monopoly of its exclusive rights over imports. However, the monopoly was still obliged to buy up national production at a price above that at which imported alcohol was now sold freely on the German market. The monopoly thus had to sell this national production at a loss. To raise money to pay for this loss a tax imposed on both imported and domestic alcohol was increased. The plaintiffs, obliged to pay this increased tax on various quantities of alcohol of both Community and non-Community origin, claimed that the increase was contrary to Community law. The national court therefore asked the Court of Justice whether Article 37 was a *lex specialis* in relation to Articles 92 and 93, and also whether a tax increase of the kind at issue infringed Article 37 (1) or (2). Although the plaintiffs also claimed that the increase was contrary to Article 95, no mention was made of that provision in the reference.

It is not without relevance that, although a measure of this kind would normally be defined as an aid, there were difficulties in the way of judging it under Articles 92 and 93. The alcohol in question is an agricultural product but no act has been adopted by the Council under Article 42[33] to apply Article 92 to it. Unlike the Commission, the Advocate General regarded this as irrelevant since the end of the transitional period and found that the tax increase infringed Article 93 (3) in that the German Government had not submitted it to the Commission in sufficient time.

A desire to avoid this particular point may well explain the Court's chosen course of deciding the case on Article 37 alone. The following statement of the Court is particularly noteworthy in this context.

> 'Article 37 remains applicable wherever, *even after the adjustment prescribed in the Treaty*,[34] the exercise by a State monopoly of its exclusive rights entails a discrimination or restriction prohibited by that Article.

---

[31] See note 8 above, with a critical note by Meier in [1979] EuR. 281.

[32] By thus is meant Case 45/75, see note 3 above.

[33] Art. 42 EEC reads:
'The provisions of the Chapter relating to rules on competition shall apply to production of and trade in agricultural products only to the extent determined by the Council within the framework of Article 43 (1) and (2) . . .'

[34] The italics are those of the author.

'In a case such as the present, which concerns an activity specifically connected with the exercise by a State monopoly of its exclusive right to purchase, process and sell spirits, the application of the provisions of Article 37 cannot be excluded'.

It followed, in the Court's view, that the applicability of Articles 92 and 93 need not be considered. An examination of Article 37 then led it to conclude that

'any practice by a State monopoly which consists in marketing a product such as spirits with the aid of public funds at an abnormally low resale price compared to the price, before tax, of comparable quality imported from another Member State is incompatible with Article 37 (1) of the EEC Treaty'.[35]

Precisely because the Court avoided deciding on the applicability of Articles 92 and 93—and was not asked about the applicability of Articles 12 and 95[36]—it is impossible to know whether the Court's conclusion could only have been reached on the basis of Article 37. That is a matter that will no doubt be clarified eventually.

After this review of the case law on the relationship between Article 37 and other Articles of the Treaty, it is clear that the Court's approach has not been consistent. However, the fact remains that—with the possible exception of Hansen II—the Court has always reached the same result whether or not it has applied Article 37.

11.16 As to the final question set out in paragraph 11.04 above, the Court held in *Miritz*[37] that Article 37 (4) did not derogate from the other provisions of Article 37: on the contrary it was expressed to have effect 'in applying the rules' contained in that Article. This ruling was the almost inevitable sequel to the Court judgment in *Charmasson* v. *Minister of Economic Affairs*.[38]

11.17 On the other hand, it is clear from the express wording of Article 37 (5) that that paragraph does constitute an exception to the other provisions of Article 37. This provision was added at the request of the German Government to take account of the agreement between itself and Svenska Tändsticks AB, the Swedish match concern. Accordingly, it would appear that the term 'international agreements' must be construed to cover agreements between a Member State and a private organisation of a non-Member State.[39]

---

[35] For reasons connected with Article 92 and thus beyond the scope of this book, this statement is much criticised by Meier, *op. cit.* note 31 above.

[36] The application of either of those Articles would have required an extension of the decisions in Case 77/76 *Cucchi* v. *Avez* [1977] E.C.R. 987 and Case 105/76 *Interzuccheri* v. *Rezzano* [1977] E.C.R. 1029. See the Commission and the Advocate General in *Hansen II*. In addition, the application of Art. 86 would have required the Court to decide whether this provision is applicable to State enterprises.

[37] See note 22 above.

[38] Case 48/74 [1974] E.C.R. 1383, [1975] 2 C.M.L.R. 208, discussed at para. 10.02 above. The imposition of the charge had in fact been suggested by the Commission in its Recommendation based on Art. 37 (6) to the German Government on the adjustment of its alcohol monopoly ([1970] J.O. L31/22). See Béraud, Wooldridge and Dashwood and Wyatt (all cited at note 6 above).

[39] Hochbaum, *op. cit.* note 6 above at 324.

In this respect it is wider than Article 234[40] which is expressed to apply only to agreements between States. Mention should also be made of the theory[41] that with respect to agreements falling under Article 37 (5) there is no obligation corresponding to that in Article 234 (2) to renegotiate agreements to eliminate inconsistencies with the Treaty.

11.18 A further undecided question is whether Article 36 can be applied to exempt measures falling under Article 37. Article 36 is expressed only to apply to restrictions covered by Articles 30 to 34, and, as already pointed out,[42] Article 36 must be restrictively interpreted. Yet in the *SAIL*[43] case the Commission claimed that Article 36 could constitute an exemption from the prohibitions contained in Article 37, in view of the parallelism between that provision and Articles 30 to 34. The Advocate General considered this argument to be at least plausible, though he found the measure in question unnecessarily restrictive and thus incapable of being justified by Article 36 in any case. Béraud[44] suggests that Article 36 should apply to measures falling within the scope of Article 37— provided such measures were introduced independently of the monopoly.

Thus, apart from the effect of Article 37 (4), no clear answer can be given to any of the five questions posed in paragraph 11.04.[45]

11.19 Indeed, one cannot avoid ending this chapter on a pessimistic note: despite no lack of case law on the point, it is impossible to give a clear answer to the question posed at the beginning, namely in what cases Article 37 ousts Articles 30 to 34 and whether it leads to a different result in those cases. The suspicion lingers that somewhere in the 'obscure clarity' of Article 37 the Court discerns obligations not found elsewhere in the Treaty and possibly even exemptions from other provisions in the Treaty, which it has one day to reveal—if it has not already begun to do so, in *Hansen II*. Otherwise, why not interpret Article 37 restrictively?

---

[40] See para. 9.53 above.
[41] See Waelbroeck, *op. cit.* at 134 and the sources there cited.
[42] Para. 8.02 above.
[43] See note 17 above.
[44] *Op. cit.* note 6.
[45] A further unsettled question is the relationship between Art. 37 and 90 and 222. On this relationship see, *e.g.* Van Hecke, *op. cit.* at 454 and Waelbroeck, *op. cit.* at 123; also the Advocates General in *SAIL* (note 17 above) and *Manghera* (note 2 above); see also paras. 4.05 and 9.45 above.

CHAPTER XII

Community legislation relating to the free movement of goods

12.01 A fully fledged discussion of harmonisation[1] in the Community in all aspects falls outside the scope of this book. Rather, the intention of this chapter is more limited: to show the reader how Community legislation can set aside the obstacles to the free movement of goods discussed in previous chapters and the relationship between such legislation and Articles 30 to 36.

After a general introductory section, we shall go on to consider the relationship between harmonisation and Articles 30 and 36, and finally look at the public purchasing Directives.

I. GENERAL

The legal basis for such legislation

12.02 The classic basis in the Treaty for this type of legislation is Article 100. This provides as follows:

> 'The Council shall, acting unanimously on a proposal from the Commission, issue Directives for the approximation of such provisions laid down by law, regulation or administrative action in Member States as directly affect the establishment or functioning of the common market . . .'.

The overwhelming majority of Directives are based wholly or partly on this provision. In view of its very considerable importance, many reams have been devoted to it. However, in the present context we can confine ourselves to the following remarks:

---

[1] See generally, Leleux, 'Le rapprochement des législations dans la CEE' [1968] C.D.E. 129; Beuve-Méry and Schaub, 'Die Beseitigung der Technischen Handelshindernisse zwischen den EWG-Mitgliedstaaten durch Richtlinien gemäß Art. 100 EWGV' [1970] EuR. 135; Vignes in *Le droit de la CEE* (1973), Vol. 3, 152 *et seq.*; Ficker in Groeben, Boeckh, Thiesing, *Kommentar zum EWG-Vertrag* (1974), Vol. I, 1270 *et seq.*; Marx, *Funktion und Grenzen der Rechtsangleichung nach Art. 100 EWG-Vertrag* (1975); *Les instruments du rapprochement des législations dans la CEE* ed. Waelbroeck, (1975); Vogelaar, 'The Approximation of the laws of the Member States under the Treaty of Rome' [1975] C.M.L.Rev. 24; Slot, *Technical and administrative obstacles to trade in the EEC* (1975); Lasnet, 'L'élimination des entraves techniques aux échanges dans la CEE' [1976] C.D.E. 4; Schneider, *Die Rechtsangleichung als Integrationsmittel der Europäischen Gemeinschaft* (1977); Editorial Comments [1978] C.M.L.Rev. 389; Close, 'Harmonisation of laws: use or abuse of the powers under the EEC Treaty' [1978] E.L.Rev. 461; Seidel, 'Ziele und Ausmaß der Rechtsangleichung in der EWG—zur britischen Auffassung' [1979] EuR. 171; 'Editorial Comments' [1980] C.M.L.Rev. 463; Leleux in 'Ecrits de Droit Européen' [1980] C.D.E. at 83; Case 148/78 *Publico Ministero v. Ratti* [1979] E.C.R. 1629, [1980] 1 C.M.L.R. 96; Case 815/79 *Cremonini and Vrankovitch* [1980] E.C.R. 3583, [1981] 3 C.M.L.R. 49.

- the only category of instrument which may be based on Article 100 is the Directive;
- while the concept of provisions which 'directly affect the establishment or functioning of the common market' is a vague one, there can be no doubt that it covers national provisions creating barriers to trade which are justified under Article 36.[2] Article 100 has also been used frequently as a basis for customs legislation;
- it is not necessary that all Member States possess measures covering the field to be harmonised. It is enough that one Member State has such a measure.[3]

12.03   The Treaty also contains other bases for legislation intended to remove obstacles to inter-state trade. Of these, Article 43 is an appropriate basis for harmonising legislation relating to agricultural products.[4] Unlike Article 100, it allows for legislation by means of Regulations and not only by means of Directives. The Community legislation harmonising veterinary controls on meat and livestock has been adopted on the basis, *inter alia*, of Article 43.

12.04   Article 103 would appear to be an appropriate basis for taking 'conjunctural policy' measures or measures designed to cope with a shortfall in supplies. Examples might be legislation imposing rationing or legislation relating to price controls.[5] Such legislation could take the form of Regulations or Directives. Article 103 requires no further comment here as it has already been considered at length in an earlier chapter.[6]

12.05   Lastly, Article 235[7] provides:

> 'If action by the Community should prove necessary to obtain, in the course of the operation of the common market, one of the objectives of the Community and this Treaty has not provided the necessary powers, the Council shall, acting unanimously on a proposal from the Commission and after consulting the Assembly, take the appropriate measures'.

It will be noted that this provision only applies if 'this Treaty has not provided the necessary powers'. Thus it will not normally be possible or necessary to rely on it with respect to the type of legislation we are concerned with here, since this is in general covered by Article 100. However, Article 100 only permits the adoption of Directives: if it is necessary to pass legislation in the

---

[2] See para. 12.15.
[3] Ficker, *op. cit.* 1288–1289.
[4] Agricultural products for this purpose are those listed in Annex II to the Treaty: Art. 38 (3).
[5] See para. 7.60 above.
[6] Paras. 9.03 *et seq.* above.
[7] See generally the special issue on Art. 235 in [1976] EuR. with articles by Everling (at 1), Schwartz (at 27) and Tomuschat (at 45).

form of a Regulation and neither Article 43 nor Article 103 is applicable, then it will be necessary to resort to Article 235.[8]

12.06 In addition to these legislative provisions, Article 101 provides for a special procedure for ironing out distortions caused by differences between national measures. If it finds the existence of such a distortion, the Commission is to consult the Member States concerned and, if necessary, it may propose to the Council a separate Directive which the Council may adopt by qualified majority after the end of the first stage of the transitional period. Article 102 further requires a Member State wishing to adopt a measure likely to cause such a distortion to consult the Commission, which is then required to recommend the appropriate measures to the Member States concerned. If the Member State in question adopts the measure contrary to the recommendation of the Commission, Article 102 states that other Member States cannot be required to amend their provisions under Article 101. In fact, Articles 101 and 102 have had very little impact: a handful of Commission recommendations have ensued[9] but no Directives.

Total and optional harmonisation

12.07 Having considered the various bases in the Treaty for harmonisation, it is now necessary to discuss the two basic types of harmonisation: total and optional. Total harmonisation imposes a two-fold obligation on the Member States:

- to permit goods complying with the Directive to be freely imported and marketed (the free movement clause); and
- to prohibit the sale of goods not complying with the Directive (the exclusivity clause).

On the other hand, optional harmonisation involves the first obligation only: the Member States are then free to allow the sale of goods not meeting the standards laid down in the Directive. This means that, should a Member State so wish, it can allow national norms to co-exist with the Community ones. It is then open to small producers to produce only according to national norms, although this reduces the possibility of exporting their goods.

This can best be illustrated by reference to examples. Directive 76/768[10] on the approximation of laws relating to cosmetic products provides for total harmonisation. Article 7 (1) of that Directive provides:

---

[8] Harmonisation of national laws has also been carried out by the Community Patent Convention, which is not based on any Treaty article but is expressed to be subject to the Treaty of Rome. However, the disadvantages of this method become obvious when it is realised that, although that Convention was signed in 1973, it has still not been ratified by all the Member States and is consequently not yet in force. See gen. para. 8.59 above.

[9] Recommendations are not binding: Art. 189 EEC.

[10] [1976] O.J. L262/169.

'Member States may not, for reasons related to the requirements laid down in this Directive and the annexes thereto, refuse, prohibit or restrict the marketing of any cosmetic products which comply with the requirements of this Directive and the Annexes thereto' (the free movement clause).

In addition, Article 3 provides:

'Member States shall take all necessary measures to ensure that only cosmetic products which conform to the provisions of this Directive and its Annexes may be put on the market' (the exclusivity clause).

On the other hand, Directive 71/316[11] on the approximation of laws relating to common provision for both measuring instruments and methods of methodological control provides for optional harmonisation. It contains a free movement clause (broadly similar to Article 7 (1) of Directive 76/768) but no exclusivity clause.

Precisely because optional harmonisation is more flexible, it tends to be more frequently used than total harmonisation.[12]

12.08 It is also quite common for a Directive to contain a safeguard clause. An example is Article 12 (1) of Directive 76/768 already referred to:

'If a Member State notes, on the basis of a substantiated justification, that a cosmetic product, although complying with the requirements of the Directive, represents a hazard to health, it may provisionally prohibit the marketing of that product in its territory or subject it to special conditions. It shall immediately inform the other Member States and the Commission thereof, stating the grounds for its decision'.

Subsequent provisions of the Directive require the Commission to deliver an opinion on whether the product constitutes a health hazard and, if necessary, to propose the technical adaptation of the Directive. Yet the effectiveness of optional harmonisation has recently been challenged by a written question discussed in paragraph 12.19 below.

Technical adaptation

12.09 In order to bring legislation into line with technical developments, it is obviously necessary to amend it from time to time. Clearly, it would be too cumbersome to follow through the same procedure as for the basic Directive on each occasion, culminating in the adoption of an amending Directive by the Council. To avoid this it is the practice for the Council to delegate to the Commission power to elaborate technical adaptations with the assistance of a special committee consisting of representatives of the Member States and chaired by a representative of the Commission. If the representatives of the Member States approve a draft amendment by a qualified majority according to Article 148 (2) of the Treaty, then it is adopted by the Commission. Should the draft not meet with this approval then it is put to the Council. If the Council fails to adopt

---

[11] [1971] J.O. L202/1.
[12] Lasnet, *op. cit.* note 1 above, at 12.

it by a qualified majority within three months, then the Commission shall adopt it. Such a procedure is provided for, for instance, by Articles 9 and 10 of Directive 76/768.

The legislative programmes

12.10 With a view to establishing timetables and priorities the Council has adopted a number of General Programmes laying down harmonisation plans for the future. The first of these, adopted on 28 May 1969,[13] consists of a bundle of resolutions notably on industrial products and on food products. This was later supplemented by the Council Resolution of 21 May 1973.[14] Also, by a Resolution of 14 April 1975[15] the Council adopted a preliminary programme laying down a consumer protection and information policy, replaced by a second programme adopted by a Council Resolution of 19 May 1981.[16]

The status quo agreements

12.11 In order to forestall national initiatives likely to undermine the General Programme of 28 May 1969, on the same day the Member States concluded a gentlemen's agreement[17] generally known as the status quo agreement. By this agreement the Member States undertook to notify any draft measure relating to products covered by the General Programme. The agreement then requires the Member States in question to refrain from adopting the measures for a period of five months,[18] to give the Council the opportunity to pass a Directive on the matter. By way of exception a Member State may adopt a measure at once if this is necessary for health or safety reasons; it must then inform the Commission afterwards.

As regards measures concerning goods not covered by the General Programme, the Member States undertook in the agreement to notify to the Commission any such measures which are likely to result in obstacles to trade. The Member State concerned is then required to refrain from bringing these measures into force for a period of two months after such notification.

A similar gentlemen's agreement was concluded by the Member States on 5 March 1973[19] in connection with measures concerning the protection of the environment. This provides for the Member States to notify the Commission of such draft measures in certain

---

[13] [1969] J.O. C76/1.
[14] [1973] O.J. C38/1.
[15] [1975] O.J. C92/1.
[16] [1981] O.J. C133/1.
[17] [1969] J.O. C76/9.
[18] Under the original agreement, a six-month period was laid down in certain cases, but that has now been reduced to five months': Agreement of 5 March 1973 [1973] O.J. C9/3.
[19] [1973] O.J. C9/1.

circumstances and in particular when they may 'directly affect the functioning of the common market'.

It can of course happen that the Commission becomes aware of a measure notified under one or other of these agreements, which, if adopted, would infringe Article 30 or Article 34.[20]

12.12 In August 1980 the Commission submitted to the Council a proposal[21] to replace the status quo agreements with a binding Decision laying down a procedure for the provision of information on technical standards and regulations, to be based on Article 213 of the Treaty. The Commission was moved[22] to take this step by the *Cassis de Dijon*[23] judgment.

In view of their very considerable importance, Articles 9 and 10 of the Draft Decision must be quoted in full:

> 'Article 9
> The Member States shall forward to the Commission:
> – a brief communication notifying their intention of drawing up technical regulations relating to certain industrial products;
> – add draft technical regulations relating to industrial products, stating the essential requirements which have led them to contemplate such measures.
> The Commission shall inform the other Member States of the notifications of intent and draft regulations which have been forwarded to it.
>
> Article 10
> 1. The Member States shall postpone the adoption of draft technical regulations for six months from the date of their communications as provided for in Article 9 if the Commission or another Member State delivers a reasoned opinion within two months of that date to the effect that the contemplated measure should be amended in order to remove or reduce any barriers which it might create to the free movement of goods.
> 2. This period shall be extended to 12 months if, within two months of the communication provided for in Article 9, the Commission notifies its intention to propose or adopt a Directive on the subject'.

The Tokyo Round

12.13 It should also be mentioned that as part of the Multilateral Agreements concluded under the auspices of the GATT and generally known as the Tokyo Round, the Community has concluded an Agreement on technical barriers to trade.[24] A detailed examination of that Agreement falls outside this book but, broadly speaking, its effect is that both the Community and the Member States must ensure that technical regulations and standards adopted by them do not constitute unnecessary obstacles to international trade with the other contracting parties. That principle is subject to a number of conditions, in particular the condition of reciprocity. In implemen-

---

[20] In certain circumstances even a draft measure may constitute a measure of equivalent effect within the meaning of Art. 30 : para. 6.08 above.

[21] [1980] O.J. C253/2.

[22] [1980] Bull. EC 7/8 points 1.3.1 to 1.3.4.

[23] Case 120/78 [1979] E.C.R. 649, [1979] 3 C.M.L.R. 494, paras. 6.33 et seq. above.

[24] [1980] O.J. L71/29, see also para. 9.44 above.

tation of these undertakings the Council adopted Decision 80/45,[25] which provides, *inter alia*, that 'the Commission shall examine the extent to which it is able to propose amendments to Directives already adopted in order to enable compliance with those Directives to be determined on the basis of test results, certificates or marks of conformity issued by the competent authorities of third countries' (Article 2 (2) (a)). Title III of the Decision sets out a 'procedure for applying the condition of reciprocity'. In further implementation of the Agreement, on 11 February 1980, the Commission submitted to the Council a proposal[26] for a draft Directive concerning a special procedure for the certification of products from third countries.

II. COMMUNITY LEGISLATION AND ARTICLES 30 to 36

12.14 First of all, it should be pointed out that any attempt[27] to define the scope of Articles 30 to 36 by reference to Article 100 (or other Articles providing for Community legislation) has always signally failed. The Court has always refused to find that the restriction on imports resulting from a particular measure could be set aside under Article 100 and that therefore such a measure fell outside Article 30. In Case 193/80 *E.C. Commission* v. *Italy*[28] the Court rejected this line of argument which the Government had put forward in the following terms:

> 'It is apparent that the purposes of Articles 30 and 100 are different. The purpose of Article 30 is, save for certain specific exceptions, to abolish in the immediate future all quantitative restrictions on the imports of goods and all measures having an equivalent effect, whereas the general purpose of Article 100 is, by approximating the laws, regulations and administrative provisions of the Member States, to enable obstacles of whatever kind arising from disparities between them to be reduced. The elimination of quantitative restrictions and measures having an equivalent effect, which is unreservedly affirmed in Article 3 (a) of the Treaty and carried into effect by Article 30, may not therefore be made dependent on measures which, although capable of promoting the free movement of goods, cannot be considered to be a necessary condition for the application of that fundamental principle.'

12.15 Frequently, Community legislation is designed to harmonise measures justified under Article 36. It will be recalled that where Community legislation provides extensive health or other guarantees, Member States may no longer rely on Article 36.[29]

Exceptionally, such Community legislation has the incidental effect of supplementing Articles 30 and 34 and ensuring their observance. This is the case with the public supply Directives discussed below.

---

[25] [1980] O.J. L14/36.
[26] [1980] O.J. C54/5.
[27] *e.g.* Marx, *op. cit.* note 1 above.
[28] Judgment of 9 December 1981, para. 17.
[29] See para. 8.14 above.

12.16 It will be remembered[30] at the same time that Community legislation may not create or permit unnecessary restrictions to inter-State trade—though whether in this respect the Community institutions are bound by Articles 9 to 17 and 30 to 36 as such, or by the principle of the free movement of goods, is an open question. At all events, it seems clear that, in the performance of the tasks with which they are entrusted, the Community institutions have greater freedom of action than do the Member States. Furthermore, while a norm enacted by some Member States only will restrict inter-State trade, it will cease to do so once it is introduced throughout the Community.[31]

12.17 In these circumstances, has the *Cassis de Dijon*[32] judgment, by construing Article 30 widely, undermined or restricted the Community's harmonisation programme?[33] Put more concretely, could this judgment result in the withdrawal of any draft Directives? At first sight, one might think that the judgment could have this effect. However, it is submitted that this judgment has actually acted as a catalyst to harmonisation. Evidence of this is provided by the Commission's recent proposal for a Council Decision laying down a procedure for the provision of information in the field of technical standards and regulations.[34]

It is suggested that the reasons for this are two-fold:

– in so far as national measures are not justified under *Cassis de Dijon*, then in some cases an analogous measure can be adopted by the Community;

– in so far as national measures are so justified, Member States still have to allow imports conforming to norms providing equivalent guarantees.[35] This means that a Member State may have to check the equivalence of other norms and, if need be, apply those other norms alongside its own. This could result in one and the same Member State applying a plethora of different norms. It is simpler to resort to harmonisation by a Community Directive.

12.18 Supposing, then, that certain barriers to inter-State trade have been removed by a harmonising Directive, it is submitted that

---

[30] See paras. 4.07 *et seq.* above.

[31] See para. 6.61 above.

[32] See note 23 above.

[33] See Mattera [1980] R.M.C. 505; Masclet 'Les articles 30, 36 et 100 du Traité EEC à la lumière de l'arrêt "Cassis de Dijon"', [1980] R.T.D.E. 611; editorial comments in [1980] C.M.L.Rev. 463.

[34] See para. 12.12 above. The first and second recitals to the draft Decision indirectly refer to *Cassis de Dijon* and suggest that that ruling has to some extent made the Decision necessary.

In his recent article entitled 'Les entraves techniques à la libre circulation des marchandises' [1982] Recueil Dalloz-Sirey, Chronique 37. Judge Touffait takes the Commission to task for implying in its Communication on *Cassis de Dijon* ([1980] O.J. C256/2—see paras. 6.35 and 6.46 above) that that judgment widened the scope of Art. 30 and correspondingly limited the scope of Art. 100.

[35] Para. 6.45 *et seq.* above.

the compatibility of a national measure with Community law should first be examined by reference to the Directive.[36] Only if the national measure is compatible with the Directive should it be examined in the light of Articles 30 to 36. This is because the Directive will contain more specific rules than Articles 30 to 36, which are, after all, generalities. Again, a Directive harmonising health or other guarantees covered by Article 36 may have exhausted the Member State's right to rely on that provision.[37] This approach is also suggested by the form of words used in the *Cassis de Dijon* case; 'in the absence of common rules relating to the production and marketing of alcohol . . . it is for the Member States to regulate [these] matters'.[38]

12.19   Lastly, a delicate question as to the usefulness of optional harmonisation after *Cassis de Dijon* was posed in Written Question 1176/81. The question referred to Directive 80/232[39] on the ranges of nominal quantities and capacities permited for certain prepackaged products, which provides for optional harmonisation. Belgium was apparently considering making the implementation of the provisions of the Directives mandatory so that only the ranges listed in the Directive may be marketed in Belgium. If another Member State, say France, were to proceed with optional harmonisation and allow other standards not set out in the Directive, the French goods conforming to those other standards could not then be sold in Belgium. In view of *Cassis de Dijon* the questioner asked whether Belgium would then be infringing Article 30. If so, why did the Directive provide for optional rather than total harmonisation? The whole of optional harmonisation was thus fundamentally put in question.

In its reply,[40] the Commission stated that:

'arguments based on the *Cassis de Dijon* judgment cannot be used in this instance to force a Member State which has made the provisions of the Directive mandatory to accept products which do not conform to it'.

III. THE PUBLIC SUPPLY DIRECTIVES

12.20   Harmonisation directives and regulations run into several hundreds. Consequently it would be quite impossible even to attempt to give an outline of them here. In the present context it is only possible to focus on the public supply Directives since they are linked particularly closely to Article 30.

---

[36] See also para. 10.08 above.
[37] Para. 8.14 above.
[38] A similar form of words was used in Case 8/74 *Dassonville* [1974] E.C.R. 837, [1974] 2 C.M.L.R. 436.
[39] [1980] O.J. L51/1.
[40] [1982] O.J. C92/2.

We saw in an earlier chapter[41] how discrimination in the award of public supply contracts was contrary to Article 30. Directive 77/62,[42] based on Article 100, is designed to supplement the prohibition in Article 30

'by the co-ordination of the procedures relating to public supply contracts in order, by introducing equal conditions of competition for such contracts in all the Member States, to ensure a degree of transparency allowing the observance of this prohibition to be better supervised.'[43]

It defines public contracts as contracts for the delivery of products, whether or not such delivery includes siting and installation operations (Article 1 (a)). It applies to the contracts entered into by the State, regional or local authorities and certain other public authorities (article 1 (b)). Certain types of contract are excluded from the Directive such as contracts awarded by bodies administering transport services (Article 2 (2) (a)) or producing, distributing and transmitting or transporting services for water or energy and telecommunications services (Article 2 (2) (b)). It applies in essence only to public supply contracts whose estimated value net of VAT is not less than 200,000 European units of account (Article 5 (1) (a)).

12.21   The Directive does not aim to create a Community procedure for the award of public supply contracts, but requires the Member States to adapt their national procedures in accordance with its provisions (Article 2 (1)). The first substantive part of the Directive is Title II entitled 'Common rules in the technical field'. Article 7 (1) provides in particular that the technical specifications defined in Annex II and the description of testing, checking and acceptance methods shall figure in the general or the contractual documents relating to each contract. Article 7 (2) provides in particular that

'Unless such specifications are justified by the subject of the contract, Member States shall prohibit the introduction into the contractual clauses relating to a given contract of technical specifications which mention goods of a specific make or source or of a particular process and which have the effect of favouring or eliminating certain undertakings or products.'

Title III relates to common advertising rules. It provides that where a public authority intends to award a contract covered by this Directive, it must advertise its intention by a notice in the Official Journal of the European Communities.

Title IV relates to the actual award of contracts. Article 20 states that a supplier may be excluded on a number of grounds such as that he is bankrupt or that he has failed to pay social security contributions or tax due in the country where he is established or

---

[41] See paras. 7.20 et seq.
[42] [1977] O.J. L13/1. This is only the second Directive on public contracts, the first being Directive 71/305 ([1971] O.J. L185/5). However, that Directive concerns only contracts to carry out works. It therefore relates to the provision of services rather than the movement of goods and thus falls outside the scope of this book. On Dir. 71/305 see Case 76/81 *Transporoute et Travaux* v. *Ministre des Travaux Publics*, judgment of 10.2.82.
[43] Second recital to the Directive.

the country of the contracting authority. The following articles relate to similar matters such as proof of the supplier's financial standing (Article 22) and of his technical ability (Article 23). Article 25 concerns the criteria for the award of public contracts, which shall be:

'(a) either the lowest price only;
(b) or, when the award is made to the most economically advantageous tender, various criteria according to the contract in question: *e.g.* price, delivery date, running costs, cost-effectiveness, quality, aesthetic and functional characteristics, technical merit, after-sales service and technical assistance'.

12.22 Although it is not expressly stated in this Directive, it does not cover third country suppliers.[44]

The Member States were required to implement this Directive within 18 months of its notification to them, that is to say by 23 June 1978.[45]

To ensure the effective operation of this Directive, an Advisory Committee for Public Contracts was set up by Directive 77/63.[46]

12.23 Annexed to the Multilateral GATT Agreements of 1979 already referred to[47] is an Agreement on government procurement.[48] In some respects that Agreement goes further than Directive 77/62. Since the Agreement does not apply as between the Member States, Directive 80/767[49] was passed to ensure that Community suppliers had at least the same rights as suppliers from third countries under the Agreement.[50]

Perhaps the most important respect in which this Directive goes beyond Directive 77/62 is that the threshold for the application of the procedures is brought down from 200,000 to 140,000 European units of account. However, this Directive does not apply to all the public authorities covered by Directive 77/62. It only applies to the entities listed in the Annex to the Directive which, in the case of the United Kingdom, range from the Royal Mint and the Imperial War Museum to Whitehall Departments. County and District Councils are not included in the list, however.

Member States were required to implement Directive 80/767 by 1 January 1981.

---

[44] See the Council Resolution and Commission Statements discussed at para. 9.44 above.

[45] Few Member States did in fact implement the Directive by that date: written question 872/78 ([1979] O.J. C172/2); written question 421/79 ([1980] O.J. C110/15); written question 721/79 ([1980] O.J. C74/11); in the case of Italy this resulted in successful proceedings being brought by the Commission under Art. 169 EEC: Case 133/80 *E.C. Commission v. Italy*, [1981] E.C.R. 457, [1981] 3 C.M.L.R. 456.

[46] [1977] O.J. L13/15.

[47] Para. 12.13 above.

[48] [1980] O.J. L71/44.

[49] [1980] O.J. L215.

[50] The recitals to this Directive are highly misleading in this respect.

CHAPTER XIII

Conclusion

It is not intended to rehearse here all the main points that have been discussed in this book. Rather it is proposed to take stock of the principal difficulties currently facing the Court, the Commission, the national courts and indeed the practitioner with respect to Articles 30 to 36. These problems are essentially of two kinds:

First, the problems of principle. The old chestnut of whether 'distinctly' and 'indistinctly applicable' measures are to be accorded the same treatment, has not yet been finally solved. Nor has the relationship between the *Cassis de Dijon*[1] judgment and Article 36. Furthermore, the list of 'mandatory requirements' under *Cassis de Dijon* is not closed and it remains to be seen what other grounds of justification will be added to the list.[2] Also, the case law on Article 34 is still in its infancy and much remains to be decided in respect of this provision, particularly as regards restrictions on production. What is more, the relationship between Articles 30 to 36 and Community legislation has yet to be fully worked out.

Perhaps more intractable, though, are the difficulties of the second phase, those of applying the principles. Is norm A on the toxicity of metal toys equivalent to norm B? Is the prohibition of a particular additive in a Member State justified, even though the same additive is allowed in other Member States? Is veterinary check A superfluous given that veterinary check B has already been carried out? These are hardly questions which many members of the legal profession are well qualified to decide. This is the type of question that the Court often refers back to the national court in proceedings under Article 177, since such proceedings are a matter of co-operation between the Court and the national courts. Yet this course of action is not free from danger, because on occasion the national judge—no better equipped for this task than the Court—may be guided by extraneous considerations. At all events, this task has been made somewhat easier by the Court's ruling[3] to the effect that the party seeking to show that a restriction is justified bears the burden of proof.

Hence the value of proceedings under Article 169 against Member States for failure to fulfil their Treaty obligations. Here the Court

---

[1] Case 120/78 [1979] E.C.R. 649, [1979] 3 C.M.L.R. 494, see para 6.33 above.
[2] Paras. 8.17 *et seq.* above.
[3] Para. 8.03 above.

must decide once and for all whether a given national measure is or is not compatible with Community law. That is not to say that the law will necessarily be observed, however, as certain cases of failure by a Member State to comply with a judgment of the Court have shown.[4] One can only deplore this practice which threatens the foundations on which Community law is built.

---

[4] See e.g. the case discussed at para. 10.06 and notes thereto.

ANNEXE I

Two Recent Cases

Case 75/81 Blesgen v. Belgian State; judgment of 31 March 1982

This case concerned a Belgian Statute of 1919 which prohibits the sale or offer for sale in a public place of spirits for consumption there. For these purposes, 'public place' includes bars, hotels and restaurants and 'spirits' means any drink with an alcohol content of over 22 degrees. As an ancillary measure, the same law also bans the storage of spirits in bars, hotels and restaurants and in adjoining places. It should be pointed out that Belgium has a small production of spirits, but most spirits consumed in Belgium are imported. On the other hand, Belgium's production and consumption of beer—which falls well below 22 degrees of alcohol—is considerable. But wine and vermouth, not typically Belgian products, also have an alcohol content below 22 degrees.

The defendant, who ran a hotel, was convicted of keeping quantities of spirits in premises adjoining his hotel. He appealed to the Belgian Cour de Cassation which asked the Court of Justice whether legislation of this kind constitutes a measure of equivalent effect under Article 30 and, if so, whether it was justified on public health grounds under Article 36.

Applying the theory put forward in this book, one would have little difficulty in reaching the conclusion that the legislation concerned constituted a measure of equivalent effect under Article 30, even though it applied to Belgian spirits and imported spirits in exactly the same way. This is because a restriction on the sale of a product for immediate consumption must be considered as an actual or potential, direct or indirect restriction on imports, in spite of the fact that spirits could be sold for consumption in private. Indeed, this was the conclusion reached by most of the parties which intervened before the Court.

On the other hand, the question whether the measures were justified was considerably more difficult. There was no doubt whatsoever that they were originally designed to reduce alcoholism and thus to protect public health (and indeed public morality). But were these measures appropriate to reduce the consumption of alcohol? There was evidence to suggest that they were not. Moreover, it was clear that the Belgian brewery industry benefited from this law.

Both the Advocate General and the Court simply side-stepped this difficult question of justification by holding that the legislation did not constitute a measure of equivalent effect in the first place. In a somewhat personal interpretation of the case law, the Advocate General claimed that that concept only covered *de jure* or *de facto* discrimination against imports. In support of this view, he cited *inter alia* the *Groenveld* formula,[1] which had hitherto been thought to apply only to export restrictions under Article 34. Throughout his opinion, the Advocate General was in effect attempting to put the clock back to before *Cassis de Dijon*,[2] while at the same time claiming to be consistent with that judgment.

The Court proceeded to follow him. Referring to Article 3 of Commission Directive 70/50,[3] it held that national measures affecting the marketing of products fell under Article 30 even if they applied to imports and domestic products in the same way, provided that their restrictive effect on the free movement of goods exceeded the effects intrinsic to trade rules. Since legislation of the kind in question did not fulfil the latter condition, it fell outside Article 30 altogether.

It is difficult to reconcile this ruling with the *Cassis de Dijon*, *Gilli*[4] and *Kelderman*[5] cases. Although that case law arguably needed to be qualified, the effect of the *Blesgen* judgment is simply to create uncertainty.

Cases 141-143/81 *Holdijk, Mulder and Alpuro; judgment of 1 April 1982*

The defendants were charged with contravening Dutch legislation providing that fatting calves must be kept in pens large enough for them to lie down unhindered on either side, stand easily on their legs and, in that position, freely move their heads. The Dutch court hearing these cases made a reference to the Court of Justice asking whether such legislation was 'contrary to or incompatible with the EEC Treaty', without referring to any particular provision of Community law.

Counsel for the defendants sought to show that measures of this kind infringe Article 34 in that they constitute a restriction on production. Both the Court and the Advocate General rejected this argument, since the *Groenveld* test[6] was not satisfied. They also

---

[1] See para. 6.55 above.
[2] See para. 6.33 above.
[3] See para. 6.28 above.
[4] See para. 7.40 above.
[5] See para. 7.42 above.
[6] See para. 6.55 above.

rejected the argument that such legislation infringed the common market organisation for beef and veal: the size of pens was a matter not covered by that organisation.

Lastly, it was claimed on behalf of the defendants that legislation of the kind in question related not to animal health, but only to animal welfare and thus could not be justified under Article 36. However, the Court and the Advocate General both implied that the concept of animal health under Article 36 was wide enough to cover a case such as this.[7]

---

[7] In any case, the prevention of cruelty to animals could probably be regarded as falling under public morality within the meaning of Article 36: para. 8.20 above.

ANNEXE II

Cases and materials

COMMISSION DIRECTIVE OF 22 DECEMBER 1969*

based on the provisions of Article 33 (7), on the abolition of measures which have an effect equivalent to quantitative restrictions on imports and are not covered by other provisions adopted in pursuance of the EEC Treaty

(70/50/EEC)

THE COMMISSION OF THE EUROPEAN COMMUNITIES,

Having regard to the provisions of the Treaty establishing the European Economic Community, and in particular Article 33 (7) thereof,

Whereas for the purpose of Article 30 *et seq.* 'measures' means laws, regulations, administrative provisions, administrative practices, and all instruments issuing from a public authority, including recommendations;

Whereas for the purposes of this Directive 'administrative practices' means any standard and regularly followed procedure of a public authority; whereas 'recommendations' means any instruments issuing from a public authority which, while not legally binding on the addressees thereof, cause them to pursue a certain conduct;

Whereas the formalities to which imports are subject do not as a general rule have an effect equivalent to that of quantitative restrictions and, consequently, are not covered by this Directive;

Whereas certain measures adopted by Member States, other than those applicable equally to domestic and imported products, which were operative at the date of entry into force of the Treaty and are not covered by other provisions adopted in pursuance of the Treaty, either preclude importation or make it more difficult or costly than the disposal of domestic production;

Whereas such measures must be considered to include those which make access of imported products to the domestic market, at any marketing stage, subject to a condition which is not laid down for domestic products or to a condition differing from that laid down for domestic products, and more difficult to satisfy, so that a burden is thus placed on imported products only;

Whereas such measures must also be considered to include those which, at any marketing stage, grant to domestic products a preference, other than an aid, to which conditions may or may not be attached, and where such measures totally or partially preclude the disposal of imported products;

Whereas such measures hinder imports which could otherwise take place, and thus have an effect equivalent to quantitative restrictions on imports;

Whereas effects on the free movement of goods of measures which relate to the marketing of products and which apply equally to domestic and imported products are not as a general rule equivalent to those of quantitative restrictions, since such effects are normally inherent in the disparities between rules applied by Member States in this respect;

---

* [1970] O.J. L13/29.

247

O—9

Whereas, however, such measures may have a restrictive effect on the free movement of goods over and above that which is intrinsic to such rules;

Whereas such is the case where imports are either precluded or made more difficult or costly than the disposal of domestic production and where such effect is not necessary for the attainment of an objective within the scope of the powers for the regulation of trade left to Member States by the Treaty; whereas such is in particular the case where the said objective can be attained just as effectively by other means which are less of a hindrance to trade; whereas such is also the case where the restrictive effect of these provisions on the free movement of goods is out of proportion to their purpose;

Whereas these measures accordingly have an effect equivalent to that of quantitative restrictions on imports;

Whereas the customs union cannot be achieved without the abolition of such measures having an equivalent effect to quantitative restrictions on imports;

Whereas Member States must abolish all measures having equivalent effect by the end of the transitional period at the latest, even if no Commission Directive expressly requires them to do so;

Whereas the provisions concerning the abolition of quantitative restrictions and measures having equivalent effect between Member States apply both to products originating in and exported by Member States and to products originating in third countries and put into free circulation in the other Member States;

Whereas Article 33 (7) does not apply to measures of the kind referred to which fall under other provisions of the Treaty, and in particular those which fall under Articles 37 (1) and 44 of the Treaty or form an integral part of a national organisation of an agricultural market;

Whereas Article 33 (7) does not apply to the charges and taxation referred to in Article 12 *et seq.* and Article 95 *et seq.* or to the aids mentioned in Article 92;

Whereas the provisions of Article 33 (7) do not prevent the application, in particular, of Articles 36 and 223;

HAS ADOPTED THIS DIRECTIVE:

Article 1

The purpose of this Directive is to abolish the measures referred to in Articles 2 and 3, which were operative at the date of entry into force of the EEC Treaty.

Article 2

1. This Directive covers measures, other than those applicable equally to domestic or imported products, which hinder imports which could otherwise take place, including measures which make importation more difficult or costly than the disposal of domestic production.

2. In particular, it covers measures which make imports or the disposal, at any marketing stage, of imported products subject to a condition—other than a formality—which is required in respect of imported products only, or a condition differing from that required for domestic products and more difficult to satisfy. Equally, it covers, in particular, measures which favour domestic products or grant them a preference, other than an aid, to which conditions may or may not be attached.

3. The measures referred to must be taken to include those measures which:
   (a) lay down, for imported products only, minimum or maximum prices below or above which imports are prohibited, reduced or made subject to conditions liable to hinder importation;
   (b) lay down less favourable prices for imported products than for domestic products;

(c) fix profit margins or any other price components for imported products only or fix these differently for domestic products and for imported products, to the detriment of the latter;

(d) preclude any increase in the price of the imported product corresponding to the supplementary costs and charges inherent in importation;

(e) fix the prices of products solely on the basis of the cost price or the quality of domestic products at such a level as to create a hindrance to importation;

(f) lower the value of an imported product, in particular by causing a reduction in its intrinsic value, or increase its costs;

(g) make access of imported products to the domestic market conditional upon having an agent or representative in the territory of the importing Member State;

(h) lay down conditions of payment in respect of imported products only, or subject imported products to conditions which are different from those laid down for domestic products and more difficult to satisfy;

(i) require, for imports only, the giving of guarantees or making of payments on account;

(j) subject imported products only to conditions, in respect, in particular of shape, size, weight, composition, presentation, identification or putting up, or subject imported products to conditions which are different from those for domestic products and more difficult to satisfy;

(k) hinder the purchase by private individuals of imported products only, or encourage, require or give preference to the purchase of domestic products only;

(l) totally or partially preclude the use of national facilities or equipment in respect of imported products only, or totally or partially confine the use of such facilities or equipment to domestic products only;

(m) prohibit or limit publicity in respect of imported products only, or totally or partially confine publicity to domestic products only;

(n) prohibit, limit or require stocking in respect of imported products only; totally or partially confine the use of stocking facilities to domestic products only, or make the stocking of imported products subject to conditions which are different from those required for domestic products and more difficult to satisfy;

(o) make importation subject to the granting of reciprocity by one or more Member States;

(p) prescribe that imported products are to conform, totally or partially, to rules other than those of the importing country;

(q) specify time limits for imported products which are insufficient or excessive in relation to the normal course of the various transactions to which these time limits apply;

(r) subject imported products to controls or, other than those inherent in the customs clearance procedure, to which domestic products are not subject or which are stricter in respect of imported products than they are in respect of domestic products, without this being necessary in order to ensure equivalent protection;

(s) confine names which are not indicative of origin or source to domestic products only.

Article 3

This Directive also covers measures governing the marketing of products which deal, in particular, with shape, size, weight, composition, presentation, identification or putting up and which are equally applicable to domestic and imported products, where the restrictive effect of such measures on the free movement of goods exceeds the effects intrinsic to trade rules.

This is the case, in particular, where:
- the restrictive effects on the free movement of goods are out of proportion to their purpose;
- the same objective can be attained by other means which are less of a hindrance to trade.

Article 4

1. Member States shall take all necessary steps in respect of products which must be allowed to enjoy free movement pursuant to Articles 9 and 10 of the Treaty to abolish measures having an effect equivalent to quantitative restrictions on imports and covered by this Directive.

2. Member States shall inform the Commission of measures taken pursuant to this Directive.

Article 5

1. This Directive does not apply to measures:
   (a) which fall under Article 37 (1) of the EEC Treaty;
   (b) which are referred to in Article 44 of the EEC Treaty or form an integral part of a national organisation of an agricultural market not yet replaced by a common organisation.

2. This Directive shall apply without prejudice to the application, in particular, of Articles 36 and 223 of the EEC Treaty.

Article 6

This Directive is addressed to the Member States.

Done at Brussels, 22 December 1969.

For the Commission
The President
Jean REY

Communication from the Commission concerning the consequences of the judgment given by the Court of Justice on 20 February 1979 in Case 120/78 ('Cassis de Dijon')**

The following is the text of a letter which has been sent to the Member States; the European Parliament and the Council have also been notifed of it.

In the Commission's Communication of 6 November 1978 on 'Safeguarding free trade within the Community', it was emphasized that the free movement of goods is being affected by a growing number of restrictive measures.

The judgment delivered by the Court of Justice on 20 February 1979 in Case 120/78 (the *Cassis de Dijon* case), and recently reaffirmed in the judgment of 26 June 1980 in Case 788/79, has given the Commission some interpretative guidance enabling it to monitor more strictly the application of the Treaty rules on the free movement of goods, particularly Articles 30 to 36 of the EEC Treaty.

The Court gives a very general definition of the barriers to free trade which are prohibited by the provisions of Article 30 *et seq.* of the EEC Treaty. These are taken to include 'any national measure capable of hindering, directly or indirectly, actually or potentially, intra-Community trade'.

In its judgment of 20 February 1979 the Court indicates the scope of this definition as it applies to technical and commercial rules.

Any product lawfully produced and marketed in one Member State must, in principle, be admitted to the market of any other Member State.

Technical and commercial rules, even those equally applicable to national and imported products, may create barriers to trade only where those rules are necessary to satisfy mandatory requirements and to serve a purpose which is in the general interest and for which they are an essential guarantee. This purpose must be such as to take precedence over the requirements of the free movement of goods, which constitutes one of the fundamental rules of the Community.

The conclusions in terms of policy which the Commission draws from this new guidance are set out below.

- Whereas Member States may, with respect to domestic products and in the absence of relevant Community provisions, regulate the terms on which such products are marketed, the case is different for products imported from other Member States.

  Any product imported from another Member State must in principle be admitted to the territory of the importing Member State if it has been lawfully produced, that is, conforms to rules and processes of manufacture that are customarily and traditionally accepted in the exporting country, and is marketed in the territory of the latter.

  This principle implies that Member States, when drawing up commercial or technical rules liable to affect the free movement of goods, may not take an exclusively national viewpoint and take account only of requirements confined to domestic products. The proper functioning of the common market demands that each Member State also give consideration to the legitimate requirements of the other Member States.

- Only under very strict conditions does the Court accept exceptions to this principle; barriers to trade resulting from differences between commercial and technical rules are only admissible:

  - if the rules are necessary, that is appropriate and not excessive, in order to satisfy mandatory requirements (public health, protection of consumers or the environment, the fairness of commercial transactions, etc.);
  - if the rules serve a purpose in the general interest which is compelling enough to justify an exception to a fundamental rule of the Treaty such as the free movement of goods;

** [1980] O.J. C256/2.

– if the rules are essential for such a purpose to be attained, *i.e.* are the means which are the most appropriate and at the same time least hinder trade.

The Court's interpretation has induced the Commission to set out a number of guidelines.

– The principles deduced by the Court imply that a Member State may not in principle prohibit the sale in its territory of a product lawfully produced and marketed in another Member State even if the product is produced according to technical or quality requirements which differ from those imposed on its domestic products. Where a product 'suitably and satisfactorily' fulfils the legitimate objective of a Member State's own rules (public safety, protection of the consumer or the environment, etc.), the importing country cannot justify prohibiting its sale in its territory by claiming that the way it fulfils the objective is different from that imposed on domestic products.

In such a case, an absolute prohibition of sale could not be considered 'necessary' to satisfy a 'mandatory requirement' because it would not be an 'essential guarantee' in the sense defined in the Court's judgment.

The Commission will therefore have to tackle a whole body of commercial rules which lay down that products manufactured and marketed in one Member State must fulfil technical or qualitative conditions in order to be admitted to the market of another and specifically in all cases where the trade barriers occasioned by such rules are inadmissible according to the very strict criteria set out by the Court.

The Commission is referring in particular to rules covering the composition, designation, presentation and packaging of products as well as rules requiring compliance with certain technical standards.

– The Commission's work of harmonization will henceforth have to be directed mainly at national laws having an impact on the functioning of the common market where barriers to trade to be removed arise from national provisions which are admissible under the criteria set by the Court.

The Commission will be concentrating on sectors deserving priority because of their economic relevance to the creation of a single internal market.

To forestall later difficulties, the Commission will be informing Member States of potential objections, under the terms of Community law, to provisions they may be considering introducing which come to the attention of the Commission.

It will be producing suggestions soon on the procedures to be followed in such cases.

The Commission is confident that this approach will secure greater freedom of trade for the Community's manufacturers, so strengthening the industrial base of the Community, while meeting the expectations of consumers.

Case 8/74 *Procureur du Roi* v. *Dassonville*
[1974] E.C.R. 837 at 852, [1974] 2 C.M.L.R. 436 at 453.
5. All trading rules enacted by Member States which are capable of hindering, directly or indirectly, actually or potentially, intra-Community trade are to be considered as measures having an effect equivalent to quantitative restrictions.

Case 104/75 *Officier van Justitie* v. *De Peijper*
[1976] E.C.R. 613 at 635–636, [1976] 2 C.M.L.R. 271 at 304.
4. National measures of the kind in question have an effect equivalent to a quantitative restriction and are prohibited under Article 30 of the Treaty if they are likely to constitute an obstacle, directly or indirectly, actually or potentially, to imports between Member States.

Rules of practices which result in imports being channelled in such a way that only certain traders can effect these imports, whereas others are prevented from doing so, constitute such an obstacle to imports. . . .
16. Nevertheless, it emerges from Article 36 that national rules or practices which do restrict imports of pharmaceutical products or are capable of doing so are only compatible with the Treaty to the extent to which they are necessary for the effective protection of health and life of humans.
17. National rules or practices do not fall within the exception specified in Article 36 if the health and life of humans can be as effectively protected by measures which do not restrict intra-Community trade so much.

Case 120/78 *Rewe-Zentral A G* v. *Bundesmonopolverwaltung für Branntwein*
(Cassis de Dijon)
[1979] E.C.R. 649 at 662–664, [1979] 3 C.M.L.R. 494 at 508.
8. In the absence of common rules relating to the production and marketing of alcohol—a proposal for a regulation submitted to the Council by the Commission on 7 December 1976 (Official Journal C309, p. 2) not yet having received the Council's approval—it is for the Member States to regulate all matters relating to the production and marketing of alcohol and alcoholic beverages on their own territory.

Obstacles to movement within the Community resulting from disparities between the national laws relating to the marketing of the products in question must be accepted in so far as those provisions may be recognised as being necessary in order to satisfy mandatory requirements relating in particular to the effectiveness of fiscal supervision, the protection of public health, the fairness of commercial transactions and the defence of the consumer. . . .

It is clear from the foregoing that the requirements relating to the minimum alcohol content of alcoholic beverages do not serve a purpose which is in the general interest and such as to take precedence over the requirements of the free movement of goods, which constitutes one of the fundamental rules of the Community.

In practice, the principle effect of requirements of this nature is to promote alcoholic beverages having a high alcohol content by excluding from the national market products of other Member States which do not answer that description.

It therefore appears that the unilateral requirement imposed by the rules of a Member State of a minimum alcohol content for the purposes of the sale of alcoholic beverages constitutes an obstacle to trade which is incompatible with the provisions of Article 30 of the Treaty.

There is therefore no valid reason why, provided that they have been lawfully produced and marketed in one of the Member States, alcoholic beverages should not be introduced into any other Member State; the sale of such products may not be subject to a legal prohibition on the marketing of beverages with an alcohol content lower than the limit set by the national rules.

Consequently, the first question should be answered to the effect that the concept of 'measures having an effect equivalent to quantitative restrictions on imports' contained in Article 30 of the Treaty is to be understood to mean that the fixing of a minimum alcohol content for alcoholic beverages intended for human consumption by the legislation of a Member State also falls within the prohibition laid down in that provision where the importation of alcoholic beverages lawfully produced and marketed in another Member State is concerned.

ANNEXE III

Table of Cases

I. NUMERICAL TABLE

15/69: Württembergische Milchverwertung-Südmilch AG v. Ugliola [1969] E.C.R. 363, [1970] C.M.L.R. 194
9.47fn114, 9.50fn118

26/69: E.C. Commission v. France (Tunisian olive oil) [1970] E.C.R. 565, [1970] C.M.L.R. 444
2.16fn47

77/69: E.C. Commission v. Belgium (wood) [1970] E.C.R. 237
4.04fn6

8/70 : E.C. Commission v. Italy (administrative levy) [1970] E.C.R. 961
4.04fn6

13/70: Francesco Cinzano & Cia GmbH v. Hauptzollamt Saarbrücken [1970] E.C.R. 1089, [1971] C.M.L.R. 374
11.09fn25

33/70: SACE v. Italian Ministry of Finance [1970] E.C.R. 1213, [1971] C.M.L.R. 123
6.04fn8

37/70: Rewe-Zentrale des Lebensmittel-Grosshandels GmbH v. Hauptzollamt Emmerich [1971] E.C.R. 23, [1971] C.M.L.R. 238
9.02fn4

40/70: Sirena Srl v. Eda Srl [1971] E.C.R. 69, [1971] C.M.L.R. 260
8.60fn149, 8.60fn150, 8.60fn155

62/70: Werner A. Bock KG v. E.C. Commission [1971] E.C.R. 897, [1972] C.M.L.R. 160
9.25fn64, 9.28, 9.31, 9.32, 9.33

78/70: Deutsche Grammophon Gesellschaft mbH v. Metro-SB-Grossmärkte GmbH & Co. KG [1971] E.C.R. 487, [1971] C.M.L.R. 631
2.21fn52, 4.18, 8.60, 8.63, 8.74, 8.75

9,11/71: Cie d'Approvisionnement de Transport & de Credit SA v. E.C. Commission [1972] E.C.R. 391, [1973] C.M.L.R. 529
9.07

22/71: Beguelin Import Co. v. G.L. Import-Export SA [1971] E.C.R. 949, [1972] C.M.L.R. 81
8.52

51–54/71: International Fruit Company NV v. Produktschap voor Groenten en Fruit [1971] E.C.R. 1107
6.10, 6.11, 6.50fn121, 7.03, 7.67, 7.71

82/71: Il Pubblico Ministero v. SpA Società Agricola Industria Latte (SAIL) [1972] E.C.R. 119, [1972] C.M.L.R. 723
11.06, 11.18

21–24/72: International Fruit Company NV v. Produktschap voor Groenten en Fruit (No. 3) [1972] E.C.R. 1219, [1975] 2 C.M.L.R. 1
1.00fn2, 1.00fn5

29/72: Marimex SpA v. Ministero delle Finanze [1972] E.C.R. 1309, [1973] C.M.L.R. 486
4.11fn26

43/72: Merkur-Aussenhandels-GmbH v. E.C. Commission [1973] E.C.R. 1055
9.07

2/73: Riseria Luigi Geddo v. Ente Nazionale Risi [1973] E.C.R. 865, [1974] 1 C.M.L.R. 13
5.06

5/73: Balkan-Import-Export GmbH v. Hauptzollamt Berlin-Packhof [1973] E.C.R. 1091
4.10fn21, 9.03, 9.06, 9.07

9/73: Carl Schlüter v. Hauptzollamt Lörrach [1973] E.C.R. 1135
1.00fn5, 4.10fn21

10–14/75: Procureur de la République at the Cour d'Appel Aix-en-Provence and Fédération Nationale des Producteurs de Vins de Table et Vins de Pays v. Paul Louis Lahaille and others [1975] E.C.R. 1053
   10.08fn22

29/75: Kaufhof AG v. E.C. Commission [1976] E.C.R. 431
   9.31, 9.32, 9.33

38/75: Douaneagent der NV Nederlandse Spoorwegen v. Inspecteur der Invoerrechten en Accijnzen [1975] E.C.R. 1439, [1976] 1 C.M.L.R. 167
   1.00fn4, 1.00fn5

43/75: Defrenne v. Sabena [1976] E.C.R. 455, [1976] 2 C.M.L.R. 98
   4.21, 9.44fn101

45/75: Rewe-Zentrale des Lebensmittel-Grosshandels eGmbH v. Hauptzollamt Landau/Pfalz [1976] E.C.R. 181, [1976] 2 C.M.L.R. 1
   11.02, 11.09, 11.10, 11.15

51/75: E.M.I. Records Ltd. v. CBS United Kingdom Ltd. [1976] E.C.R. 811, [1976] 2 C.M.L.R. 235
   2.13, 6.50fn121, 8.60fn149, 8.82

59/75: Pubblico Ministero v. Manghera [1976] E.C.R. 91, [1976] 1 C.M.L.R. 557
   9.44fn101, 11.02, 11.05, 11.07, 11.08, 11.09, 11.18fn45

65/75: Tasca [1976] E.C.R. 291, [1977] 2 C.M.L.R. 183
   7.50, 7.51

86/75: E.M.I. Records Ltd. v. CBS Grammofon A/S [1976] E.C.R. 871, [1976] 2 C.M.L.R. 235
   2.13, 6.50fn121, 8.82

88–90/75: SADAM v. Comitato Interministeriale dei Prezzi [1976] E.C.R. 323, [1977] 2 C.M.L.R. 183
   7.50, 7.51, 7.52, 9.05

91/75: Hauptzollamt Göttingen and Bundesfinanzminister v. Wolfgang Miritz GmbH & Co. [1976] E.C.R. 217
   11.08fn22; 11.09, 11.10, 11.15, 11.16

96/75: E.M.I. Records Ltd. v. CBS Schallplatten GmbH [1976] E.C.R. 913, [1976] 2 C.M.L.R. 235
   2.13, 8.82

104/75: Officier van Justitie v. De Peijper [1976] E.C.R. 613, [1976] 2 C.M.L.R. 271
   4.12fn31, 6.13fn29, 6.14, 6.15, 8.05, 8.10, 8.11, 8.16, 8.25, 8.26, 8.27, 8.28, 9.01fn2

118/75: The State v. Watson & Belman [1976] E.C.R. 1185, [1976] 2 C.M.L.R. 552
   2.29fn75

119/75: Terrapin (Overseas) Ltd. v. Terranova Industrie C.A. Kapferer & Co. [1976] E.C.R. 1039, [1976] 2 C.M.L.R. 482
   8.77, 8.80, 8.81, 8.84, 8.85

3–4, 6/76: Officier van Justitie v. Kramer [1976] E.C.R. 1279, [1976] 2 C.M.L.R. 440
   3.04, 7.63, 8.54fn131, 10.07, 10.08fn22, 10.08fn24

13/76: Donà v. Mantero [1976] E.C.R. 1333, [1976] 2 C.M.L.R. 578
   4.19

35/76: Simmenthal SpA v. Ministero delle Finanze [1976] E.C.R. 1871, [1977] 2 C.M.L.R. 1
   7.09, 8.14, 8.29fn74, 8.31fn81, 10.08fn22

41/76: Criel (Donckerwolcke) v. Procureur de la République Lille [1976] E.C.R. 1921, [1977] 2 C.M.L.R. 535
   2.12, 7.03, 7.11, 7.12, 7.13, 7.14, 9.21, 9.33, 9.34, 9.35, 9.37

46/76: W.J.G. Bauhuis v. The Netherlands State [1977] E.C.R. 1
   4.11, 4.12, 8.02; 8.12

1/78: Kenny *v*. Insurance Officer [1978] E.C.R. 1489, [1978] 3 C.M.L.R. 651
    6.63fn149
2/78: E.C. Commission *v*. Belgium (spirits imports) [1979] E.C.R. 1761, [1980] 1
    C.M.L.R. 216
    7.07, 7.08
3/78: Centrafarm BV *v*. American Home Products Corporation [1978] E.C.R.
    1823, [1979] 1 C.M.L.R. 326
    8.72, 8.73
7/78: Regina *v*. Thompson, Johnson & Woodiwiss [1978] E.C.R. 2247, [1979] 1
    C.M.L.R. 47
    2.06, 2.07fn24, 2.28, 8.02fn5, 8.23
13/78: Firma Joh. Eggers Sohn & Co. *v*. Freie Hansestadt Bremen [1978] E.C.R.
    1935, [1979] 1 C.M.L.R. 562
    6.14, 7.26, 7.32, 7.35, 8.02fn5, 8.10, 8.48fn109
27/78: Amministrazione delle Finanze dello Stato *v*. Ditta Rasham [1978] E.C.R.
    1761, [1979] 1 C.M.L.R. 1
    9.28, 9.31
34/78: Yoshida Nederland BV *v*. Kamer van Koophandel en Fabrieken voor
    Friesland [1979] E.C.R. 115, [1979] 2 C.M.L.R. 747
    2.10fn27, 2.11fn32, 4.09fn19
83/78: Pigs Marketing Board (Northern Ireland) *v*. Redmond [1978] E.C.R. 2347,
    [1979] 1 C.M.L.R. 177
    5.05, 10.07fn20, 10.08fn22, 10.10, 11.01fn1, 11.06
86/78: SA Des Grandes Distilleries Peureux *v*. Directeur des Services Fiscaux de la
    Haute-Sâone [1979] E.C.R. 897, [1980] 3 C.M.L.R. 337
    6.63fn149, 11.07fn21, 11.12, 11.13, 11.15
91/78: Hansen GmbH & Co. *v*. Hauptzollamt Flensburg [1979] E.C.R. 935, [1980]
    1 C.M.L.R. 162
    11.03, 11.08fn22, 11.12, 11.15, 11.19
114/78: Yoshida GmbH *v*. Industrie- und Handelskammer [1979] E.C.R. 151,
    [1979] 2 C.M.L.R. 747
    2.10fn27, 2.11fn32
115/78: Knoors *v*. Secretary of State for Economic Affairs [1979] E.C.R. 399,
    [1979] 2 C.M.L.R. 357
    6.63fn149
118/78: C.J. Meijer B.V. *v*. Department of Trade [1979] E.C.R. 1387, [1979] 2
    C.M.L.R. 398
    10.05
119/78: SA Des Grandes Distilleries Peureux *v*. Directeur des Services Fiscaux de
    la Haute Sâone [1979] E.C.R. 897, [1980] 3 C.M.L.R. 337.
    7.19, 11.08fn22, 11.12, 11.14, 11.15
120/78: Rewe-Zentrale AG *v*. Bundesmonopolverwaltung für Branntwein [1979]
    E.C.R. 649, [1979] 3 C.M.L.R. 494
    4.12, 6.33, 6.35, 6.36, 6.37, 6.38, 6.42, 6.45, 6.46, 6.50, 6.51, 6.59,
    6.60, 6.61, 7.01, 7.39, 7.45, 8.10, 8.15, 8.17, 8.30, 8.42, 8.44, 8.45,
    8.49, 8.50, 8.51fn126, 8.54, 8.56, 10.08, 11.07, 11.12, 11.15, 12.12,
    12.14, 12.17, 12.18, 12.19, 13.00
136/78: Ministère Public *v*. Auer [1979] E.C.R. 437, [1979] 2 C.M.L.R. 373
    6.61fn149
141/78: France *v*. United Kingdom (fishing net mesh sizes) [1979] E.C.R. 2923,
    [1980] 1 C.M.L.R. 6
    1.00fn12, 3.04fn22
148/78: Pubblico Ministero *v*. Ratti [1979] E.C.R. 1629, [1980] 1 C.M.L.R. 96
    8.14, 12.01fn1

34/79: The Queen *v.* Henn and Darby [1979] E.C.R. 3795, [1980] 1 C.M.L.R. 246
    2.21, 2.30, 5.06, 8.08, 8.09, 8.20, 8.21, 9.55, 9.58
52/79: Procureur du Roi *v.* Debauve [1980] E.C.R. 881, [1981] 1 C.M.L.R. 362
    2.05, 2.06, 2.25, 2.26, 8.07, 8.19fn53
55/79: E.C. Commission *v.* Ireland (duty on alcoholic drinks) [1980] E.C.R. 481,
    [1980] 1 C.M.L.R. 734
        6.21
62/79: Coditel SA *v.* Ciné Vog Films SA [1980] E.C.R. 833, [1981] 2 C.M.L.R.
    362
        2.26, 8.76
65/79: Procureur de la République *v.* Chatain, Laboratoires Sandoz [1980] E.C.R.
    1345, [1981] 3 C.M.L.R. 418
        2.28fn71, 6.50fn121, 7.11fn22
68/79: Hans Just I/S *v.* Danish Ministry for Fiscal Affairs [1980] E.C.R. 501,
    [1981] 2 C.M.L.R. 714
        6.63fn150
73/79: E.C. Commission *v.* (sugar charges) [1980] E.C.R. 1533, [1982] 1
    C.M.L.R. 1
        6.19fn45
94/79: *Re* Pieter Vriend [1980] E.C.R. 327, [1980] 3 C.M.L.R. 473
        10.08fn22, 10.11
95–96/79: Procureur du Roi *v.* Kefer and Delmelle [1980] E.C.R. 103, [1982] 2
    C.M.L.R. 77
        7.49fn93, 10.08fn22
788/79: Italian State *v.* Gilli and Andres [1980] E.C.R. 2071, [1981] 1 C.M.L.R.
    146
        6.38, 6.45fn113, 6.50, 6.51, 7.40, 8.03, 8.30, 8.45
812/79: Attorney-General *v.* Burgoa [1980] E.C.R. 2787, [1981] 2 C.M.L.R. 193
        9.57
815/79: Cremonini and Vrankovich [1980] E.C.R. 3583, [1981] 3 C.M.L.R. 49
        12.01fn1
823/79: Carciati [1980] E.C.R. 2773, [1981] 2 C.M.L.R. 193
        8.42
22/80: Boussac Saint-Frères SA *v.* Gerstenmeier [1980] E.C.R. 3427, [1982] 1
    C.M.L.R. 202
        7.37fn71
24, 97/80R: E.C. Commission *v.* France (lamb imports) [1980] E.C.R. 1319, [1981]
    3 C.M.L.R. 25
        10.06fn16
27/80: Fietje [1980] E.C.R. 3839, [1981] 3 C.M.L.R. 722
        6.10, 6.45, 6.49, 6.64, 7.45, 8.13, 8.47
32/80: Officier van Justitie *v.* Kortmann [1981] E.C.R. 251
        6.18, 8.26fn70
53/80: Officier van Justitie *v.* Koninklijke Kaasfabriek Eyssen BV [1981] E.C.R.
    429, [1982] 2 C.M.L.R. 20
        6.65, 7.41, 8.29
55, 57/80: Musik-Vertrieb Membran GmbH *v.* GEMA [1981] E.C.R. 147, [1981]
    2 C.M.L.R. 44
        6.18, 8.57, 8.74, 8.75, 8.76
58/80: Dansk Supermarked A/S *v.* Imerco A/S [1981] E.C.R. 181, [1981] 3
    C.M.L.R. 590
        4.04, 7.39fn 72, 8.52
113/80: E.C. Commission *v.* Ireland (jewellery) [1982] 1 C.M.L.R. 706
        6.43, 6.44, 7.36

National Courts
Time Limit *v.* SABAM (Brussels Cour d'Appel) [1979] 2 C.M.L.R. 578
Allgemeine Gold- und Silberscheideanstalt *v.* Customs and Excise Commissioners
   (English Court of Appeal) [1980] 2 W.L.R. 555, [1980] 1 C.M.L.R. 488
      2.07
Re Pinion (English Court of Appeal) [1965] 2 W.L.R. 919
      8.34fn90
Regina *v.* Henn and Darby (English Court of Appeal) [1978] 1 W.L.R. 1031
      5.06
Philadelphia *v.* New Jersey (U.S. Supreme Court) 437 U.S. 617, 98 S.Ct. 2531
   (1978)
      2.04

II. ALPHABETICAL TABLE

Albatros *v.* Sopeco—Case 20/64
American Home Products (Centrafarm *v.*)—Case 3/78
Amministrazione delle Finanze dello Stato *v.* Ditta Rasham—Case 27/78
Amministrazione delle Finanze dello Stato *v.* Simmenthal (No. 2)—Case 106/77
Arnaud—Case 89/74
Attorney-General *v.* Burgoa—Case 812/79
Auer—Case 136/78

B.P. *v.* Commission—Case 77/77
Balkan-Import-Export *v.* Hauptzollamt Berlin-Packhof—Case 5/73
Bauhuis *v.* The Netherlands—Case 46/76
Beele—Case 6/81
Beguelin Import *v.* G.L. Import-Export—Case 22/71
Belgium (United Foods and Van den Abeele *v.*)—Case 132/80
Benzine en Petroleum and others *v.* Commission—Case 77/77
Blesgen *v.* Belgium—Case 75/81
Bock *v.* Commission—Case 62/70
Bouchereau—Case 30/77
Bouhelier—Case 225/78
Boussac Saint-Frères *v.* Gerstenmeier—Case 22/80
Brachfeld (Diamantarbeiders *v.*)—Cases 2–3/69
Burgoa—Case 812/79
Buys—Case 5/79

CBS (E.M.I. *v.*)—Cases 51/75, 86/75 and 96/75
C. J. Meijer *v.* Department of Trade—Case 118/78
Cadsky *v.* Istituto Nazionale per il Commercio Estero—Case 63/74
Carapelli *v.* Ministry for Foreign Trade—Cases 206, 207, 209/80
Carciati—Case 823/79
Carl Schlüter *v.* Hauptzollamt Lörrach—Case 9/73
Carlheinz Lensing *v.* Hauptzollamt Berlin-Packhof—Case 147/73
Cassati—Case 203/80
Cassis de Dijon—Case 120/78
Cayrol *v.* Rivoira—Case 52/77
Centrafarm *v.* American Home Products—Case 3/78
Centrafarm (Hoffmann-La Roche *v.*)—Case 102/77
Centrafarm *v.* Sterling Drug—Case 15/74

Lahaille—Cases 10–14/75
Landwirtschaftskammer (Rewe-Zentral *v.*)—Case 4/75
Lensing-Kaffee-Tee-Import *v.* Hauptzollamt Berlin-Packhof—Case 147/73

Maize Seed—Case 258/78
Manghera—Case 59/75
Mantero (Donà *v.*)—Case 13/76
Marimex *v.* Ministero delle Finanze—Case 29/72
Meijer *v.* Department of Trade—Case 118/78
Merck *v.* Stephar—Case 187/80
Merkur-Aussenhandels *v.* Commission—Case 43/72
Meroni (Iannelli and Volpi *v.*)—Case 74/76
Metro-SB-Grossmärkte (D.G.G. *v.*)—Case 78/70
Minister for Fisheries *v.* Schonenberg—Case 88/77
Minister of Public Works (Transporoute et Travaux *v.*)—Case 76/81
Ministère Public *v.* Auer—Case 136/78
Miritz (Hauptzollamt Göttingen *v.*)—Case 91/75
Musik-Vertrieb Membran *v.* GEMA—Cases 55,57/80

Norddeutsches Vieh- und Fleischkontor *v.* Hauptzollamt Ausfuhrerstattung
    Hamburg-Jonas—Case 14/74
Nungesser and Eisele *v.* Commission—Case 258/78

Oebel—Case 155/80
Officier van Justitie *v.* De Peijper—Case 104/75
—— *v.* Koninklijke Kaasfabriek Eyssen—Case 53/80
—— *v.* Kortmann—Case 32/80
—— *v.* Kramer—Cases 3–4, 6/76
—— *v.* Van den Hazel—Case 111/76
—— *v.* Van Haaster—Case 190/73
Openbaar Ministerie *v.* Danis—Cases 16–20/79
—— *v.* Frans-Nederlandse Maatschappij voor Biologische Produkten—Case 272/
    80
—— *v.* Van Tiggele—Case 82/77
Orlandi Italo & Son, Carapelli SpA and Enrico and Luigi Saquella Snc *v.* Ministry
    for Foreign Trade—Cases 206, 207, 209/80

P.B. Groenveld *v.* Produktschap voor Vee en Vlees—Case 15/79
P.J. Van der Hulst's Zonen—Case 51/74
Parke, Davis & Co. *v.* Probel—Case 24/67
Peureux *v.* Directeur des Services Fiscaux de la Haute-Sâone—Cases 86, 119/78
Pfizer *v.* Eurim-Pharm—Case 1/81
Pharmon *v.* Hoechst—Case 271/80
Pigs Marketing Board *v.* Redmond—Case 83/78
Polydor *v.* Harlequin Record Shops—Case 270/80
Probel (Parke, Davis *v.*)—Case 24/67
Procureur de la Republique *v.* Bouhelier—Cases 53/76, 225/78
—— *v.* Chatain—Case 65/79
—— *v.* Lahaille—Cases 10–14/75
—— *v.* Rivoira—Case 179/78
Procureur du Roi *v.* Dassonville—Case 8/74
—— *v.* Debauve—Case 52/79
—— *v.* Dechmann—Case 154/77
—— *v.* Kefer and Delmelle—Cases 95–96/79

269

Stephar (Merck *v.*)—Case 187/80
Sterling Drug (Centrafarm *v.*)—Case 15/74

Tasca—Case 65/75
Tedeschi *v.* Denkavit Commerciale—Case 5/77
Terrapin (Overseas) Ltd. *v.* Terranova Industrie C.A. Kapferer & Co.—Case 119/75
Thompson—Case 7/78
Thompson, Johnson and Woodiwiss—Case 7/78
Toffoli *v.* Regione Veneto—Case 10/79
Transporoute et Travaux SA *v.* Minister of Public Works—Case 76/81

Ugliola—Case 15/69
Union Cycliste—Case 36/74
United Foods and Van den Abeele *v.* Belgium—Case 132/80

Van Dam en Zonen—Cases 185–204/78
Van den Abeele *v.* Belgium—Case 132/80
Van den Hazel—Case 111/76
Van der Hulst's Zonen *v.* Produktschap voor Siergewassen—Case 51/74
Van Duyn *v.* Home Office—Case 41/74
Van Haaster—Case 190/73
Van Tiggele (Openbaar Ministerie *v.*)—Case 82/77
Van Zuylen Frères *v.* Hag AG—Case 192/73
Vriend—Case 94/79

Walrave & Koch *v.* Association Union Cycliste Internationale—Case 36/74
Watson and Belman—Case 118/75
Werner A. Bock *v.* Commission—Case 62/70
Winthrop (Centrafarm *v.*)—Case 16/74
Württemburgische Milchverwertung-Südmilch *v.* Ugliola—Case 15/69

Yoshida GmbH *v.* Industrie- und Handelskammer—Case 114/78
Yoshida Nederland BV *v.* Kamer van Koophandel en Fabrieken voor Friesland—
    Case 34/78

ANNEXE IV

How a private party can obtain a judicial ruling that a particular measure is contrary to Articles 30 to 36

This can be done in two ways:

(1) An action can be brought before the appropriate national court. The appropriate defendant will normally be the relevant branch of the public authorities of the Member State in question. It is then open to the party to ask the national court to refer a question to the Court of Justice under Article 177 of the Treaty. Under that provision, only the court of final appeal in the case is bound to refer a question arising for decision. Lower courts have a discretion to refuse to refer the point and to decide it themselves.

and/or

(2) A complaint may be made to the Commission inviting it to commence proceedings under Article 169 of the Treaty. Such a complaint takes the form of a normal letter, since no official form is provided. The Commission cannot be compelled to bring such proceedings. Moreover, private parties may not intervene before the Court in Article 169 proceedings: Article 37 of the Statute of the Court of Justice of the EEC. On the other hand, in such proceedings the Court is obliged to rule whether or not a given national measure infringes the Treaty. Such proceedings therefore have a certain advantage over a reference under Article 177, which the Court may often answer in general terms leaving important aspects to the national court to decide (see Chapter XIII).

The most advisable course is therefore to bring proceedings before the national courts *and* to make a complaint to the Commission.

See generally notes 10 and 11 to Chapter I.

ANNEXE V

Selected Bibliography

Barents	'New Developments in Measures having Equivalent Effect' [1981] C.M.L.Rev. 271.
Beraud	'Les mesures d'effet équivalent au sens des articles 30 et suivants du Traité de Rome' [1968] R.T.D.E. 265.
Capelli	'Les malentendus provoqués par l'arrêt "Cassis de Dijon"' [1981] R.M.C. 421.
Dashwood	See Wyatt, below.
Dona	'Les mesures d'effet équivalent à des restrictions quantitatives' [1973] R.M.C. 224.
Ehlermann	(1) 'Die Bedeutung des Artikels 36 EWGV für die Freiheit des Warenverkehrs' [1973] EuR. 1. (2) Commentary on Articles 30 to 36 in Groeben, Boeckh, Thiessing, *Kommentar zum EWG-Vertrag* (Baden-Baden, 1974), Vol. I. (3) 'Das Verbot der Massnahmen gleicher Wirkung in der Rechtsprechung des Gerichtshofes' in *Festschrift für Ipsen* (Hamburg, 1977).
Grabitz	'Das Recht auf Zugang zum Markt nach dem EWG-Vertrag' in *Festschrift für Ipsen* (Hamburg, 1977).
Graf	'Der Begriff "Massnahmen gleicher Wirkung wie mengenmässige Einfuhrbeschränkungen" im EWG-Vertrag' (Munich, 1972).
Gulmann	'Handelshindringer i EF-Retten' (Denmark, 1980).
MacKenzie Stuart	'The Free Movement of Goods' (1979) 12 *Bracton Law Journal European Supplement* 17.
Masclet	'Les articles 30, 36 et 100 du traité CEE à la lumière de l'arrêt "Cassis de Dijon"' [1980] R.T.D.E. 611.
Mattera	(1) 'Libre circulation des marchandises et articles 30 à 36 du Traité CEE' [1976] R.M.C. 500. (2) 'L'arrêt "Cassis de Dijon": une nouvelle approche pour la réalisation et le bon fonctionnement du marché intérieur' [1980] R.M.C. 505.
Matthies	(1) 'Herkunftsangaben und Europäisches Gemeinschaftsrecht' in *Festschrift für Schiedermair* (Munich, 1976), 395. (2) 'Die Verantwortung der Mitgliedstaaten für den freien Warenverkehr im Gemeinsamen Markt' in *Festschrift für Ipsen* (Tübingen, 1977), 669. (3) 'Die Verfassung des Gemeinsamen Marktes' in 'Das Europa der zweiten Generation', *Gedächtnisschrift für Sasse* (Baden-Baden, 1981), Vol. I, 115.

Meier
(1) Commentary in Ehle and Meier 'EWG-Warenverkehr' (Cologne, 1971), 158 et seq.

(2) 'Zur Kombination von nationalen Lebensmittel-Begriffs-bestimmungen und Vorschriften zum Schutz des Verbrauchers gegen Irreführungen als Rechtsfertigungsgründe nach Art. 36 EWGV' [1980] W.R.P. 59.

(3) 'Kennzeichnung statt Verkehrsverbote – Die Rechtsprechung als Schrittmacher des Lebensmittelrechts' Schriftenreihe des Bundes für Lebensmittelrecht und Lebensmittelkunde, Heft 94, 47.

Meij and Winter
'Measures having an equivalent effect to quantitative restrictions' [1976] C.M.L.Rev. 79.

Mestmäcker
'Die Vereinbarkeit von Preisregelungen und dem Arzneimittelmarkt mit dem Recht der Europäischen Wirtschaftsgemeinschaft' (Baden-Baden, 1980).

Page
'The Concept of Measures having an Effect Equivalent to Quantitative Restrictions' [1977] E.L.Rev. 105.

Seidel
'Der EWG-rechtliche Begriff der "Massnahmen gleicher Wirkung wie eine mengemässige Beschränkung"' [1967] N.J.W. 2081.

Schiller
'Gewährt Art. 30 des EWG-Vertrages dem Gemeinschaftsbürger neben einem subjektiven Abwehrrecht auch ein subjektives Leistungsrecht?' [1980] R.I.W./A.W.D. 569.

Touffait
'Les entraves techniques à la libre circulation des marchandises' [1982] Recueil Dalloz-Sirey, Chronique 37.

Ulmer (Peter)
'Zum Verbot mittelbarer Einfuhrbeschränkungen im EWG-Vertrag' [1973] G.R.U.R.Int. 502.

Van Gerven
'The Recent Case Law of the Court of Justice concerning Articles 30 and 36 of the EEC Treaty' [1977] C.M.L.Rev. 5.

Veelken
'Massnahmen gleicher Wirkung wie mengenmässige Beschränkungen' [1977] EuR. 311.

VerLoren van Themaat
(1) 'Bevat art. 30 van het EEG-Verdrag slechts een non-discriminatie-beginsel ten anzien van invoerbeperkingen?' 15 S.E.W. 632.

(2) 'Zum Verhältnis zwischen Artikel 30 und Artikel 85 EWG-Vertrag' in Festschrift für Gunther (Baden-Baden, 1976), 373.

(3) 'De artikelen 30-36 van het EEG-Verdrag' [1980] R. M. Themis 4/5 at 378.

Waelbroeck
(1) Commentary on Articles 30 to 36 in 'Le droit de la Communauté économique européenne' (Brussels, 1970), Vol. I.

(2) 'Les réglementations nationales de prix et le droit communautaire' (Brussels, 1975).

Winkel
'Die Vereinbarkeit staatlicher Preislenkungsmassnahmen mit dem EWG-Vertrag' [1976] N.J.W. 2048.

Winter
See Meij, above.

Wyatt (with Dashwood)
'The Substantive Law of the EEC' (London, 1980).

Index

274